ENCYC
Brita

Encyclopædia Britannica, Inc. is a leader in reference and education publishing whose products can be found in many media, from the Internet to mobile phones to books. A pioneer in electronic publishing since the early 1980s, Britannica launched the first encyclopedia on the Internet in 1994. It also continues to publish and revise its famed print set, first released in Edinburgh, Scotland, in 1768. Encyclopædia Britannica's contributors include many of the greatest writers and scholars in the world, and more than 110 Nobel Prize winners have written for Britannica. A professional editorial staff ensures that Britannica's content is clear, current, and correct. This book is principally based on content from the encyclopedia and its contributors.

Introducer

Dr Maria Misra lectures in Modern History and is a Fellow of Keble College, Oxford. She is the author of *Vishnu's Crowded Temple: India since the Great Rebellion* (2007) and *Business, Race and Politics in British India* (1999). In 2001 she presented the Channel 4 documentary *An Indian Affair* and has contributed to the *Guardian*, the *New Statesman*, and *The Times*.

ENCYCLOPÆDIA
THE **Britannica** GUIDE TO

INDIA

A comprehensive introduction to the
world's fastest growing country

Introduction by Maria Misra

ROBINSON

RUNNING PRESS
PHILADELPHIA · LONDON

Constable & Robinson Ltd
3 The Lanchesters
162 Fulham Palace Road
London W6 9ER
www.constablerobinson.com

Encyclopædia Britannica, Inc.
www.britannica.com

First published in the UK by Robinson,
an imprint of Constable & Robinson, 2009

A copy of the British Library Cataloguing in Publication
Data is available from the British Library

UK ISBN 978-1-84529-820-3
1 3 5 7 9 10 8 6 4 2

US Library of Congress Number: 2007938547
US ISBN 978-0-7624-3372-8

Running Press Book Publishers
2300 Chestnut Street
Philadelphia, PA 19103-4371

www.runningpress.com

Printed and bound in the EU.

CONTENTS

Part 3   Religion, the Arts, and Philosophy

Part 4   India Today

Part 5   The Major Sites to Visit

LIST OF ILLUSTRATIONS AND MAPS

Illustrations

Maps

Maps © Encyclopædia Britannica Inc.

INTRODUCTION

MARIA MISRA

What's in a name? The subcontinent has so many; and all contentious. In ancient cosmography India was located in *Jambudvipa* – Rose-apple island – named after the Jambu tree at its centre. For the ancient Persians and Arabs it was, less romantically, simply the land beyond the river Sindu: Al-Hind or Hindustan. Later nationalists considered this too blandly physical an appellation, a name, moreover, humiliatingly coined by foreigners. Bipin Pal, one such critic, insisted instead on *Bharatavarsha*, after the ancient king Bharat, a name as richly evocative and as redolent of great power as Rome. For Gandhi, a less conventional nation-maker, it was another ancient monarch, the mythical Ram, who provided the preferred eponym – Ram's *Rajya* was the epitome of moral not geopolitical grandeur. Others – more preoccupied with race and ethnos than history and morality – preferred *Aryavarata*: the land of the Aryans. And for the British, downright dismissive of Indian national pretensions, both ancient and modern, India was merely a geographical expression. It is perhaps hardly surprising that a country so dazzling in its diversity, from its geology to its ethnicity, from its languages to its politics, should have so many names. But this very diversity, so obvious to all, has also spawned a diversity of clichés to capture its essence. To some it is "unity in diversity": an entity in which some immanent common spirit transcends apparent difference. But for others it is the very opposite: "diversity in unity", a centrifugal state reined in by only the very loosest and most fragile of bonds.

Perhaps geography and geomorphology are, as Persian and British commentators intuited, the place to look for unity. Certainly the elegant shapeliness cut by the subcontinent on modern maps – a diamond defined by mountain ranges and great oceans – suggests, at the very least, a sort of 'common-sense' integrity. And yet even the cartographical contours of India have been cause for contention. To many nationalist artists in the nineteenth and twentieth centuries, this diamond seemed to suggest nothing so much as a beautiful woman, her head at the apex of the Himalayas, her arms embracing the western tip of Gujarat and the eastern deltas of Bengal, her graceful legs the tapering peninsula – this was *Bharat Mata*, Mother India. And yet for India's sizeable Muslim population it was inconceivable that the nation should be imagined as a goddess. Meanwhile in the south, the knowledge of the continental drift that had brought a piece of Australasia crashing into Eurasia to form the Himalayas spawned a galaxy of fanciful theories concerning the distinctiveness and antiquity of a supposed southern Dravidian culture, not only separate from, but superior to the Sanskritic north.

Even beyond the realms of imagery and symbolism, the apparent geographical unity of the subcontinent belies complex profusion and a range of alternative "nations". Within the well-known contours of the country's physiography – the northern plains, the southern uplands, the peninsular and the southeastern coastal plain – lie a profusion of meso and micro cultures, climates, and histories. For many, India is the vast, dun-coloured Indo-Gangetic plain, the Hindu cow belt of Delhi-Agra land and the eastern territories from Bihar and Bengal – a region which was indeed from the second century BCE shaped by numerous warrior dynasties into the settled villages now thought of as typically Indian. But to the south lie the expansive hilly tracts encompassing the isolated enclaves of Chattisgarh, the deserts north of Gujarat, and old Rajput kingdoms now grouped into Rajasthan. Peninsular India is also divided into sub-regions, each with distinctive cultures: the lands of the Maratha farmer-warriors in the north-west, Hyderabad at the centre, and the old empires to the south and west of the Vijayanagara and Badami rulers, while the Mysore plateau hosted both Hindu kings and short-lived Muslim dynasties. Yet more ancient and distinctive kingdoms emerged on the south-east coast: in the hilly regions around Madras the Pallava dynasty presided between the fourth and the ninth centuries; further south, among the great temple complexes of Thanjavur (Tanjore), were the Cholas, and at the very tip, centred on Madurai, the Pandyas. It is not, then, in its diverse geography or in its profusion of antique dynasties that we will trace India's elusive unity.

Neither can bonds of race offer any potential homogeneity, for India is the home of an immense variety of ethnic types. Throughout its history the subcontinent has been the sphere of continuous interactions between the various peoples of central Asia, Afghanistan, Iran, and later Europe. From the ancient era to the twelfth century there has been a dynamic process of assimilation as "Aryans", Greeks, Scythians, Parthians, Shakas, Huns, Arabs, Persians, Turks, Afghans, and Mongols have galloped or wandered in. Unsurprisingly, therefore, there is also no unity of language. India hosts dozens of major languages and hundreds of dialects. Nor is there one overarching classical literature, but several: Sanskrit, Prakrit, Pali, and Dravidian. And also Persian, Arabic, and English, all blended into an awe inspiring linguistic matrix.

Confounded by the profusion of races, languages, and dynasties, some have suggested religion as a locus of unity, more particularly Hinduism, the religion with which India is most commonly associated. But the Hindu religion is very far from the only great religion to have originated here: Buddhism, Jain-ism, Sikhism, and a host of persistent animisms and magical cults all find their alma mater here. It is also the adoptive home of many more: Judaism and Zoroastrianism (the ancient Persian religion) have long been guests, while Christianity and Islam have been present in India for almost as long as they have been present anywhere. It would, moreover, be misconceived to regard Hin-duism as a sharply articulated and clear-cut set of beliefs and practices – a model more applicable to the more recent religions of the book. Hinduism, like India itself, encompasses various theologies, philosophies, rituals, rites, and sects.

Baffled by the country's apparent cohesion in the face of such diversity, the British proffered alternative sources of continuity. For some, caste – regarded as utterly unique to the subcontinent – was suggested. But caste seems neither unique enough nor suffi-ciently definable to bear the weight of this analysis. First men-tioned in ancient Vedic texts, it now seems not dissimilar to the divisions of men into orders found in all ancient Eurasian societies. And by the time the British arrived it was not, except perhaps in the northern plain, the four-fold hierarchy of priests, warriors, merchants/farmers, and workers of the Vedas, but a profusion of thousands of *jatis* (literally birth groups) reflecting local clans, kin groups, guilds, occupations and even petty mili-tias. Nor was caste always the rigidly fixed and birth-ordained ladder of western imagination, but an altogether more fluid and protean entity.

An alternative nexus of unity was, perhaps, the village. Ac-cording to the nineteenth-century administrator, Charles Metcalf, it was here, in "village India" that the essence of the country was to be located. For while "dynasty after dynasty tumbles down, revolution succeeds to revolution; Hindoo, Patan, Mogul, Mah-ratta, Sikh, English, are all masters in turn; but the village community remains the same". But it did not, and never had; India seems, indeed, to have become far more "village-ified" under British tutelage than it had been in the dynamic century preceding British paramountcy. India was not merely an arcadia of simple villages but, by the eighteenth century, a highly complex society. Its rich urban culture boasted flourishing artisans, courtly elites, well-equipped armies, and merchants with global reach. And though there were undoubtedly many villages of settled peasants, there were also large bands of wandering nomads, mendicant monks and forest-dwelling "tribal" peoples. Moreover the villages themselves took a variety of forms: some operating as republics of sorts, (though rather patriarchal ones), others dominated by a few powerful headmen or wealthy local landlords, where notions of egalitarian republicanism would have been given short shrift.

The search for the essence of Indian unity, and indeed for the "essence" of anything in this constantly churning subcontinent seems, therefore, fundamentally misconceived. Instead India is best seen as a crucible of cultures, peoples, and polities which have flourished, fought, fissured, and then re-configured. At certain times particular regions, communities, or groups have become dominant, and even, on occasion, one element in the great mêlée has succeeded in establishing the hub of an empire – though usually a somewhat fragile and loosely articulated one. It is flux, rivalry, and contestation that characterize India's past, as well as its present, far more than visions of timelessness or unchanging harmony. Nevertheless patterns do emerge, and two in particular: firstly cycles of centralization (or attempted centralization) have alternated with the assertion of local and regional power; and secondly potent tendencies towards rigid social hierarchy and cultural exclusivity have been persistently challenged by a robust egalitarianism and the logic of assimilation and synthesis.

India's two great epics – the *Mahabharata* and the *Ramayana* – both deal with the conflict between the unity of kingship (or empire) and looser more decentralized polities. And while both sagas depict the former as ideal and the latter as "demonic", the truth is rather more complex. India has known various periods of attempted centralization: the indigenous "classical" empires of the Mauryans (*c.*321–185 BCE) and the Guptas (320–*c.*540 CE); the early modern and modern empires of the foreign Mughals (1526–1707) and British (1757–1947); and, latterly, the most ambitious centralizing project yet – nationalism. All, to varying degrees, have aspired to impose a degree of political, economic, and cultural uniformity on the subcontinent, and all, again to varying degrees, have been forced to either compromise with or capitulate to the seemingly ineradicable forces of entropy. But, curiously, periods of entropy have often been just as, if not more, culturally and economically dynamic than those of empire. So, while the Mauryan empire may have fallen into sad decay, it was succeeded by an era of astonishing economic success as India became the hub of global commerce, with empires spanning the overland routes from eastern China to western Asia and the maritime trade of the Indian Ocean and the south-east Asian archipelago. Similarly, the great Moghul Leviathan's dismal demise throughout the eighteenth century was accompanied by the rise of highly creative new regional states such as the modernizing Marathas in the west, and the ambitious state-building regime of Hyder Ali and Tippu Sultan in Mysore; meanwhile its buoyant economy proved an irresistible magnet to hordes of wealthy French and British merchants. And India's more recent return to startling economic dynamism has been noticeably coincident with the loosening of its central political yoke and a renaissance of federalism.

One could also argue that cycles of centralization and devolution have tended to move congruently with the pendulum of hierarchy and egalitarianism – India's other great historical dialectic. The Gupta era was, for example, as notable for the sharpening of social hierarchy as for political prowess. Under the Guptas, Brahmanical Hinduism – with its rigid caste system, costly rituals, and priestly authorities – was most fully propounded. Eras of imperial decay, by contrast, have tended to favour the flowering of Shramanic Hinduism, a more egalitarian variety notable for the personal devotionalism of Bhakti and the blending of popular Hindu practices with those of Sufi Islam. Meanwhile the eighteenth century saw not only the decay of imperial authority but also, in much of India, of strict caste hierarchy. Under the British Raj however, caste, and indeed religious identity more generally, returned to centre stage – not only socially, but also politically. The Raj rested unashamedly on notions of order and hierarchy but, as an alien regime, sought to legitimize itself by rigidifying or even re-inventing the relationships between indigenous castes and religious communities. In effect the British, assisted by Brahmin officials, sought to restore the four-fold hierarchy of the ancient caste system among Hindus across the whole of India – something which caused especial resentment in the south and west of the country where caste hierarchies had never followed the rigid classical pattern. Muslims too, though a highly diverse community, were encouraged to stress their Muslim-ness above all other forms of identity.

By the mid-twentieth century, therefore, caste and religion had lost much of their fluidity, flexibility, and essentially local meaning, to become precisely defined all-Indian categories deeply imbricated with all manner of political and civil rights and privileges. Official posts, army recruitment, rights to land ownership, and even education were allocated by community; most damaging of all was the separation of communities into separate electorates – Hindus voting for Hindus and Muslims for Muslims. The consequence of this extraordinary project of ordering, defining, and balancing India's diverse communities was to unravel the delicately entwined skeins of Indo–Islamic culture that had flourished since the fourteenth century. By 1947 many assumed that despite 1,200 years of shared history and culture, India's Muslims and Hindus should become not one but two independent nations.

Indian nationalists have tried, with mixed success, to balance the competing demands of centre and region and of order and egalitarianism. But just as India has a profusion of names, races, languages, cultures, and empires it has also, of course, generated many nationalisms. Its advocates have espoused *inter alia* ideologies of modernity and tradition, of socialism and capitalism, of equality and difference – often within the same party. In Gandhi and Nehru the Indian National Congress, the leading nationalist movement, produced two leaders locked into one of the most paradoxical relationships in history. For while Gandhi loathed the British for foisting on India "modernity", industry, parliamentary politics, and administrative unity, Nehru hated them for not doing so. Both were, of course, united in their desire to see India freed from British rule, but they differed profoundly in their visions of what a non-British India should be. Gandhi is perhaps best seen as an arcadian anarchist: a votary of "village India", a low-tech, ascetic society of non-materialists, loosely bound together by skeins of morality emanating from India's various religious faiths. Nehru, by contrast, envisioned a more conventional nation state, fully equipped with the requisite panoply of high-tech industry, urbanized industry, and modernized citizenry – all organized into a single, benignly centralizing, democratic and secular republic.

It was Nehru's vision which shaped the first 50 years of India's independence. Though rhetorically Nehruvianism espoused socialism, centralization, and strict secularism, in reality all these aspirations were fudged. Supposedly socialist economic planning left plenty of room for the private sector; central projects of land reform, linguistic homogenization, and even mass education were trimmed or abandoned in the face of entrenched regional interests. Similarly, secularism – a constitutional commitment to strict state neutrality to all religions – was blurred by well-intentioned but ultimately divisive efforts to promote the interests of minorities and under-privileged castes. But in one respect, however, the Nehruvian vision has been amply fulfilled: India is a great democracy. It is, however, this very success that has forced another turn of the wheel in India's eternal centrifugal–centripetal cycle.

In the last 20 years India seems to have undergone a silent revolution: its millions of low-caste voters, long subordinated by deference to the higher castes who dominated Indian politics, have freed themselves. Since the mid-1980s, Congress, the party of nationalism which had dominated post-independence politics, has had to yield as more and more regional and low-caste parties have won parliamentary seats in the regional states and in Delhi. This revolution has driven Indian politics towards a new cycle of political decentralization on the one hand and social egalitarianism on the other. Like all revolutions, this one has fostered a reaction in the form of a radical right Hindu nationalism popular among high caste Hindus across north India. Hindu nationalism, unlike Gandhi's, is aggressively centralizing, and unlike Nehru's, deeply inegalitarian; in sharp contrast to both it is profoundly culturally exclusive, espousing a purely Hindu idea of the nation – hostile to Muslims and Christians. But though Hindu nationalism has been sufficiently popular to form all-India governments (between 1998 and 2004), it has, paradoxically, only been able to do so in partnership with its principal bêtes noire: regionalists and low caste parties. For the logic of India's democracy is such that no party can now achieve all-India majorities; coalitions and with them increased regional and low caste power seem to be here to stay.

But the upswing of regionalism and equality presents perplexing prospects for India's future. With the abandonment of the Nehruvian economic model and the dismantling of planning and the so-called "permit raj", India has embraced – partially at least – a much more market-orientated approach to its economy. Superficially this has been a great success. Growth rates, especially in sectors such as IT and business outsourcing, have been stratospheric and there has been talk of India attaining the sort of take-off now enjoyed by China. India now has a clutch of billionaire tycoons, who have been gleefully buying up the industrial jewels of their erstwhile colonial masters. In some respects India has advantages over China: it has a large population of English speakers (though only 3 per cent are truly fluent), it has pockets of excellent higher education (a legacy of the Raj) and produces world-class scientists, economists, and writers. But unlike China, its basic infrastructure – roads, power, and mass education – are poorly developed. Many have argued that this is the fault of the over-planned and closed economy of the Nehru years, while others argue that democracy itself is the culprit: successive politicians have frittered away resources on voter bribing (of various sorts) which should have been invested in education and communications.

However, in some ways it is the very diversity of India – so celebrated in the west – that accounts for its inability to match democracy to broader social and economic purposes. So long as voters see themselves principally as "castes" and "communities" it will be hard to forge the unity of purpose – and indeed sacrifice – necessary to achieve the deep structural modernizations that have underpinned China's remarkable success. Optimists argue that a more decentralized and federal system may resolve these issues, giving more power to politicians at the regional level, who are closer and more accountable to their constituents. Meanwhile competition with China itself, the culturally unifying effects of cinema, the success of a rich diaspora, and the spread of Hindi and English as link languages are all forces that may propel Indians away from their colourful if anarchic diversity in unity towards a genuinely creative unity in diversity.

PART ONE

OVERVIEW

INDIA – FACTS AND FIGURES

Official name: Bharat (Hindi); Republic of India (English).

Form of government: multiparty federal republic with two legislative houses (Council of States: 245[1]; House of the People: 545[2]).

Chief of state: President.

Head of government: Prime Minister.

Capital: New Delhi.

Official languages: Hindi; English.

Official religion: none.

Monetary unit: Indian rupee (Re, plural Rs).

Demography

Population (2007): 1,129,866,000.

Density (2007)[3]: persons per sq mile 924.2, persons per sq kilometre 356.8.

Urban-rural (2004): urban 28.5%; rural 71.5%.

Sex distribution (2005): male 51.57%; female 48.43%.

Age breakdown (2005): under 15, 32.1%; 15–29, 27.1%; 30–44, 20.2%; 45–59, 12.7%; 60–74, 6.2%; 75–84, 1.4%; 85 and over, 0.3%.

Population projection: (2010) 1,184,090,000; (2020) 1,362,053,000.

Doubling time: 50 years.

Major cities (2001; urban agglomerations, 2001): Greater Mumbai (Greater Bombay) 11,978,450 (16,434,386); Delhi 9,879,172 (12,877,470); Kolkata (Calcutta) 4,580,546 (13,205,697); Chennai (Madras) 4,343,645 (6,560,242); Bangalore 4,301,326 (5,701,446); Hyderabad 3,637,483 (5,742,036); Ahmadabad 3,520,085 (4,525,013); Kanpur 2,551,337 (2,715,555); Pune (Poona) 2,538,473 (3,760,636); Surat 2,433,835 (2,811,614); Jaipur 2,322,575 (2,322,575); New Delhi[4] 302,363.

Linguistic composition (1991)[5]: Hindi 27.58% (including associated languages and dialects, 38.58%); Bengali 8.22%; Telugu 7.80%; Marathi 7.38%; Tamil 6.26%; Urdu 5.13%; Gujarati 4.81%; Kannada 3.87%; Malayalam 3.59%; Oriya 3.32%; Punjabi 2.76%; Assamese 1.55%; Bhili/Bhilodi 0.66%; Santhali 0.62%; Kashmiri 0.47%[6]; Gondi 0.25%; Sindhi 0.25%; Nepali 0.25%; Konkani 0.21%; Tulu 0.18%; Kurukh 0.17%; Manipuri 0.15%; Bodo 0.14%; Khandeshi

0.12%; other 3.26%. Hindi (66.00%) and English (19.00%) are also spoken as lingua francas.

Castes/tribes (2001): number of Scheduled Castes (formerly referred to as "Untouchables") 166,635,700; number of Scheduled Tribes (aboriginal peoples) 84,326,240.

Religious affiliation (2005): Hindu 72.04%; Muslim 12.26%, of which Sunnī 8.06%, Shī'ī 4.20%; Christian 6.81%, of which Independent 3.23%, Protestant 1.74%, Roman Catholic 1.62%, Orthodox 0.22%; traditional beliefs 3.83%; Sikh 1.87%[7]; Buddhist 0.67%; Jain 0.51%; Bahā'ī 0.17%; Zoroastrian (Parsi) 0.02%[8]; non-religious 1.22%; atheist 0.17%; remainder 0.43%.

Households (2001). Total number of households 193,579,954. Average household size 5.3. Type of household: permanent 51.8%; semipermanent 30.0%; temporary 18.2%. Average number of rooms per household 2.2; 1 room 38.4%, 2 rooms 30.0%, 3 rooms 14.3%, 4 rooms 7.5%, 5 rooms 2.9%, 6 or more rooms 3.7%, unspecified number of rooms 3.2%.

Vital Statistics
Birth rate per 1,000 population (2005): 22.3 (world avg. 20.3). Death rate per 1,000 population (2005): 8.3 (world avg. 8.6). Natural increase rate per 1,000 population (2005): 14.0 (world avg. 11.7).

Total fertility rate (avg. births per childbearing woman; 2005): 2.78.
Marriage/divorce rates per 1,000 population: n.a./n.a.

Life expectancy at birth (2005): male 63.6 years; female 65.2 years.

Major causes of death per 100,000 population (2002): infectious and parasitic diseases 420, of which HIV/AIDS 34; diseases of the circulatory system 268, of which ischemic heart disease 146; accidents, homicide, and other violence 100; malignant neoplasms (cancers) 71; chronic respiratory diseases 58.

Adult population (ages 15–49) *living with HIV* (2005): 0.9% (world avg. 1.0%).

Social Indicators

Educational attainment (2001). Percentage of population age 25 and over having: no formal schooling 48.1%; incomplete primary education 9.0%; complete primary 22.1%; secondary 13.7%; higher 7.1%.

Quality of working life. Average workweek (2006): c.50 hours[9]. Rate of fatal injuries per 100,000 employees (2004) 28[9]. Agricultural workers in servitude to creditors (early 1990s) 10–20%. Children ages 5–14 working as child labourers (2003): 35,000,000 (14% of age group).

Access to services (2001). Percentage of total (urban, rural) households having access to: electricity for lighting purposes (2003) 61.5% (90.8%, 51.6%); kerosene for lighting purposes 36.9% (8.3%, 46.6%), water closets 18.0% (46.1%, 7.1%), pit latrines 11.5% (14.6%, 10.3%), no latrines 63.6% (26.3%, 78.1%), closed drainage for waste water 12.5% (34.5%, 3.9%), open drainage for waste water 33.9% (43.4%, 30.3%), no drainage for waste water 53.6% (22.1%, 65.8%). Type of fuel used for cooking in households (2003): firewood 61.1% (20.0%, 74.9%), LPG (liquefied petroleum gas) 20.8% (55.4%, 9.1%), cow dung 7.4% (1.8%, 9.3%), kerosene 4.7% (13.0%, 1.9%), coal 1.5% (3.3%, 0.9%), other 4.6% (6.6%, 3.9%). Source of drinking water: hand pump or tube well 41.3% (21.3%, 48.9%), piped water 36.7% (68.7%, 24.3%), well 18.2% (7.7%, 22.2%), river, canal, spring, public tank, pond, or lake 2.7% (0.7%, 3.5%).

Social participation. Eligible voters participating in April/May 2004 national election: 58.1%. Trade union membership (1998): c.16,000,000 (primarily in the public sector).

Social deviance (2003)[10]. Offence rate per 100,000 population for: murder 3.1; rape 1.5; dacoity (gang robbery) 0.5; theft 23.0; riots 5.4. Rate of suicide per 100,000 population (2002): 11.2, in Kerala 30.8.

Material well-being (2001). Total (urban, rural) households possessing: television receivers 31.6% (64.3%, 18.9%), telephones 9.1% (23.0%, 3.8%), scooters, motorcycles, or mopeds 11.7% (24.7%, 6.7%), cars, jeeps, or vans 2.5% (5.6%, 1.3%). Households availing banking services 35.5% (49.5%, 30.1%).

National Economy

Gross national income (at current market prices; 2006): US$887,483,000,000 (US$771 per capita).

Budget (2004). Revenue: Rs 3,941,400,000,000 (tax revenue 80.6%, of which taxes on income and profits 35.4%, excise taxes 27.7%; nontax revenue 18.1%; other 1.3%). Expenditures: Rs 5,104,800,000,000 (general public services 59.3%, of which *public debt* payments 24.6%; economic affairs 17.7%; defence 15.1%; housing 4.2%; education 2.2%; health 1.5%).

Public debt (external, outstanding; 2005): US$80,281,000,000.

Production in '000 short tons ('000 metric tons), except as noted:

Agriculture, forestry, fishing (2005): cereals 267,072 (242,284) − of which rice 150,547 (136,574), wheat 79,366 (72,000), corn (maize) 16,215 (14,710), millet 11,353 (10,300), sorghum 8,267 (7,500); sugarcane 256,067 (232,300); fruits 47,438 (43,035) − of which bananas 12,908 (11,710), mangoes 12,280 (11,140), oranges 3,824 (3,469), lemons and limes 1,784 (1,618), apples 1,491 (1,353), pineapples 1,438 (1,305); oilseeds 32,831 (29,784) − of which peanuts (groundnuts) 7,937 (7,200), rapeseed 7,496 (6,800), soybeans 6,945 (6,300), sunflower seeds 1,653 (1,500), castor beans 959 (870), sesame 750 (680); potatoes 26,049 (23,631); pulses 15,168 (13,760) − of which chickpeas 6,030 (5,470), dry beans 2,932 (2,660), pigeon peas 2,590 (2,350); eggplants 10,805 (9,802); coconuts 10,509 (9,534); seed cotton 8,267 (7,500); cauliflower 5,912 (5,363); okra 3,913 (3,550); jute 2,315 (2,100); allspice and pimiento 1,213 (1,100); tea 916 (831); natural rubber 860 (780); garlic 712 (646); tobacco 659 (598); betel 499 (453); ginger 385 (349); livestock (number of live animals) 185,000,000 cattle, 120,000,000 goats, 98,000,000 water buffalo, 62,500,000 sheep, 14,300,000 pigs, 635,000 camels; roundwood 429,893,285 cu yd (328,677,000 cu m) − of which fuelwood 93%; fisheries production 6,966 (6,319) (from aquaculture 41%). Mining and quarrying (2005): mica 1.8 (1.6, world rank: 1); iron ore 99,208 (90,000[11], world rank: 4); bauxite 13,200 (11,957); chromium 3,588 (3,255); barite 1,102 (1,000); manganese 705 (640[11]); zinc 220 (200[11]); lead 46.3 (42.0[11]); copper 29.6 (26.9[11]); gold 7,055 lb (3,200 kg); gem diamonds 16,000 carats. Manufacturing (value added in US$'000,000; 2003): refined petroleum 5,955; iron and steel 5,834; paints, soaps, varnishes, drugs, and medicines 4,891; industrial chemicals 4,105; food products 3,467; textiles 3,432; motor vehicles and parts 3,193; nonelectrical machinery and apparatus 2,333; cements, bricks, and tiles 2,029.

Energy production (consumption): electricity in 2005–06 697,300,000,000 kW-hr, (in 2004 667,568,000,000 kW-hr); hard coal in 2005–06 407,040,000 metric tons, (in 2004 404,691,000 metric tons); lignite in 2005–06 30,360,000 metric tons, (in 2004 30,028,000 metric tons); crude petroleum in 2004–05 257,900,000 barrels, (in 2004 970,900,000 barrels); petroleum products in 2004–05 111,970,000 metric tons, (in 2004 84,734,000 metric tons); natural gas in 2004–05 31,763,000,000 cubic metres, (in 2004 30,654,000,000 cubic metres).

Land use as % of total land area (2003): in temporary crops 53.6%, in permanent crops 3.4%, in pasture 3.6%; overall forest area (2005) 22.8%.

Population economically active (2001): total 402,234,724; activity rate of total population 39.1% (participation rates: ages 15–69, 60.2%; female 31.6%; unemployed [2005] 9.9%).

Household income and expenditure: Average household size (2004) 5.4; sources of income: n.a.; expenditure (2003): food and nonalcoholic beverages 50.0%, housing and energy 11.2%, clothing and footwear 7.8%, health 6.7%, transportation 4.1%, tobacco and intoxicants 2.3%.

Service enterprises (net value added in Rs '000,000,000; 1998–99): wholesale and retail trade 1,562; finance, real estate, and insurance 1,310; transport and storage 804; community, social, and personal services 763; construction 545.

Selected balance of payments data. Receipts from
(US$'000,000): tourism (2003) 3,887; remittances (2006)
26,900; foreign direct investment (FDI: 2001–05 avg.)
5,551; official development assistance (2005) 2,819[12].
Disbursements for (US$'000,000): tourism (2003) 3,510;
remittances (2005) 1,008; FDI (2001–5 avg.) 1,558.

Foreign Trade[13]

Imports (2004–05): US$107,066,100,000 (crude petroleum
and petroleum products 27.9%; gold and silver 10.1%;
electronic goods [including computer software] 9.7%;
precious and semiprecious stones 8.8%; nonelectrical
machinery and apparatus 6.1%; organic and inorganic
chemicals 5.0%).
Major import sources: China 6.3%; US 5.9%; Switzerland
5.4%; United Arab Emirates 4.3%; Belgium 4.3%;
Australia 3.3%; UK 3.2%; South Korea 3.0%; Japan 2.8%.
Exports (2004–05): US$79,247,000,000 (engineering goods
20.7%; gems and jewellery 17.3%; chemicals and chemical
products 15.0%; food and agricultural products 10.1%;
petroleum products 8.6%; ready-made garments 7.6%;
cotton yarn, fabrics, and thread 4.0%).
Major export destinations: US 16.7%; United Arab Emirates
9.0%; China 5.8%; Singapore 4.8%; Hong Kong 4.6%; UK
4.5%; Germany 3.3%; Belgium 3.1%; Italy 2.7%; Japan 2.5%.

Transport

Railways (2002): length 89,879 miles (144,647
kilometres); passenger-miles 581,625,310,690 (passenger-
kilometres 936,037,000,000[14]); cargo 371,091,282,520
short ton-mile (541,783,000,000 metric ton-kilometres
cargo[15]). Roads (2002): total length 2,062,737 miles

(3,319,644 kilometres) (paved 46%). Vehicles (2003): passenger cars 8,619,000; trucks and buses 4,215,000. Air transport (2004–05): passenger-miles 26,373,428,280 (passenger-kilometres 42,444,000,000); cargo 519,872,496 short ton-mile (759,000,000 metric ton-kilometres).

Communications
Daily newspaper circulation (2005) 78,700,000; television receivers (2003) 88,876,000; telephones (2006), main lines 40,770,00, mobile telephone subscribers 166,050,000; personal computers (2005) 17,000,000 units; internet (2005) 60,000,000 users, 2,300,000 broadband subscribers.

Education
Primary (ages 6–10; 2004): schools 651,382[15]; teachers 3,038,204; students; 125,568,597; student/teacher ratio 41.3.
Secondary (age 11–17; 2004): schools 382,481[15]; teachers 2,507,357; students 80,339,753; student/teacher ratio 32.0.
Higher (2004): schools 42,057[16]; teachers 428,078; students 11,295,041; student/teacher ratio 26.4.
Literacy (2003): percentage of total population age 15 and over literate 59.5%; males literate 70.2%; females literate 48.3%.

Health
Physicians (2005) 767,500 (1 per 1,425 persons); hospital beds (2003) 963,720 (1 per 1,111 persons); infant mortality rate per 1,000 live births (2005) 56.3.
Food (2005): daily per capita caloric intake 2,529

(vegetable products 92%, animal products 8%); 139% of FAO recommended minimum requirement.

Military

Total active duty personnel (March 2006): 1,325,000 (army 83.0%, navy 4.2%, air force 12.8%); personnel in paramilitary forces 1,089,700. Military expenditure as percentage of GDP (2003): 2.1%; per capita expenditure US$12.

Notes

1 Council of States can have a maximum of 250 members; a maximum of 12 of these members may be nominated by the President.
2 House of the People can have a maximum of 552 members; this number includes 2 nonelective seats.
3 Excludes 46,660 sq miles (120,849 sq kilometres) of territory claimed by India as part of Jammu and Kashmir but occupied by Pakistan or China; inland water constitutes 9.6% of total area of India (including all of Indian-claimed Jammu and Kashmir).
4 Within Delhi urban agglomeration.
5 Mother tongue unless otherwise noted.
6 1981.
7 As of 2001 census.
8 2000 estimate
9 Data apply to the workers employed in the "organized sector" only (27.8 million in 2001, of which 19.1 million were employed in the public sector and 8.7 million were employed in the private sector); few legal protections exist for the more than 370 million workers in the "unorganized sector."
10 Crimes reported to National Crime Records Bureau by police authorities of state governments.
11 Metal content.
12 Figure represents commitments.
13 Fiscal year beginning April 1.
14 Includes Indian Railways and 15 regional railways.
15 Includes Indian Railways and 9 regional raliways.
16 2003.
17 2002.

Internet Resources for Further Information

India Portal: Directory of Government Web Sites http://www.india.gov.in

Census of India http://www.censusindia.net

Reserve Bank of India http://www.rbi.org.in/home.aspx

Ministry of Statistics and Programme Implementation http://mospi.nic.in

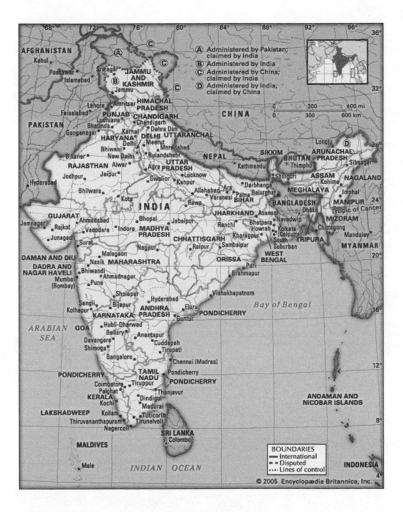

Political Map of India

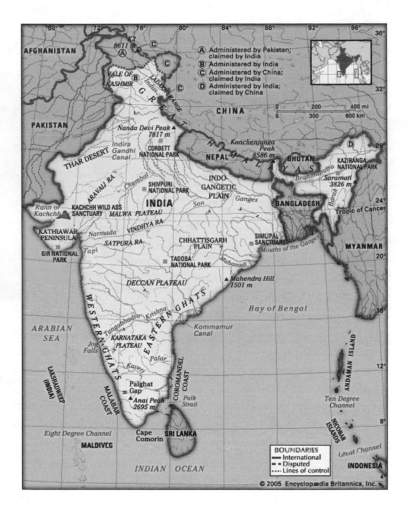

Physical Map of India

I

THE PLACE AND THE PEOPLE

India, a country that occupies the greater part of South Asia and in area the seventh largest country in the world, has roughly one-sixth of the world's total population and is the world's second most populous country after China. It is a constitutional republic consisting of 28 states, each with a substantial degree of control over its own affairs; 6 less fully empowered union territories; and the Delhi national capital territory, which includes New Delhi, India's capital.

India is a large and diverse polyglot nation whose tempo of life varies from region to region and from community to community. By the early twenty-first century the lifestyle of middle-class and affluent urban families differed little from that of urbanites in Europe, East Asia, or the Americas. For the most part, however, the flow of rural life continued much as it always had. Many small villages remained isolated from most forms of media and communications, and work was largely done by hand or by the use of animal power. Traditional forms of work and recreation only slowly have given way to habits and pastimes imported from the outside world.

While the pace of globalization was slow in much of rural India, even in urban areas western tastes in food, dress, and entertainment were adopted with discrimination. Indian fashions have remained the norm; Indians have continued to prefer traditional cuisine to western fare; and although Indian youths are as obsessed as those in the West with pop culture, Indians produce their own films and music (albeit strongly influenced by western styles), which have been extremely popular domestically and have been successfully marketed abroad. Custom and religious ritual are still widely observed and practised.

Throughout the centuries, residents of the subcontinent have developed a rich intellectual life in such fields as mathematics, astronomy, and architecture. It is known from archaeological evidence that a highly sophisticated, urbanized culture – the Indus civilization – dominated the northwestern part of the subcontinent from about 2600 to 2000 BCE. From that period on, India functioned as a virtually self-contained political and cultural arena, giving rise to a distinctive tradition that was associated primarily with Hinduism. However, throughout its history, India was intermittently disturbed by incursions from beyond the northern mountain wall. Especially important was the coming of Islam, beginning in the early eighth century CE. By the thirteenth century, much of the subcontinent was under Muslim rule. Muslim control declined as the subcontinent was absorbed into the British Empire. Direct administration by the British, from 1858 to 1947, effected a political and economic unification of the subcontinent. After the British left, the subcontinent was partitioned into two separate countries: India, with a majority of Hindus, and a predominantly Muslim Pakistan. Many British institutions stayed in place (such as the parliamentary system of government);

English continued to be a widely used lingua franca; and India remained within the Commonwealth. Hindi became the official language (and a number of other local languages achieved official status), while a vibrant English-language intelligentsia thrived.

India remains one of the most ethnically diverse countries in the world. Apart from its many religions and sects, India is home to innumerable castes and tribes, as well as to more than a dozen major and hundreds of minor linguistic groups from several language families unrelated to one another. Religious minorities, including Muslims, Christians, Sikhs, Buddhists, and Jains, still account for a significant proportion of the population; collectively, their numbers exceed the populations of all countries except China. Social legislation has done much to alleviate the disabilities previously suffered by formerly "untouchable" castes, tribal populations, women, and other traditionally disadvantaged segments of society. The country has also played an increasing role in global affairs.

Contemporary India's increasing physical prosperity and cultural dynamism are seen in its well-developed infrastructure and a highly diversified industrial base, in its pool of scientific and engineering personnel (one of the largest in the world), in the pace of its agricultural expansion, and in its rich and vibrant cultural exports of music, literature, and cinema. Though the country's population remains largely rural, India has three of the most populous and cosmopolitan cities in the world – Mumbai (Bombay), Kolkata (Calcutta), and Delhi. Three other Indian cities – Bangalore (Bengaluru), Chennai (Madras), and Hyderabad – are among the world's fastest-growing high-technology centres, and most of the world's major information technology and software companies now have offices in India.

The country

Set off from the rest of Asia by the northern mountain rampart of the Himalayas and by adjoining mountain ranges to the west and east, much of India's territory lies within a large peninsula, surrounded by the Arabian Sea to the west and the Bay of Bengal to the east. India has two union territories composed entirely of islands: Lakshadweep, in the Arabian Sea, and the Andaman and Nicobar Islands, which lie between the Bay of Bengal and the Andaman Sea.

It is now generally accepted that India's geographic position, continental outline, and basic geologic structure resulted from a process of plate tectonics – the shifting of enormous, rigid crustal plates over the Earth's underlying layer of molten material. The subcontinent's landmass, which forms one of these plates, has been moving northward, its leading edge forced under (subducted) and raising up the southern part of the Eurasian plate. India's present-day relief features have been superimposed on three basic structural units: the Himalayas in the north, the Deccan (plateau region) in the south, and the Indo-Gangetic Plain (lying over the subsidence zone) between the two.

The Himalayas (from the Sanskrit words *hima*, "snow," and *alaya*, "abode"), the loftiest mountain system in the world, form the northern limit of India. This great, geologically young mountain arc is about 1,550 miles (2,500 kilometres) long. Within India the Himalayas are divided (from south to north, respectively) into three longitudinal belts, called the Outer, Lesser, and Great Himalayas. At each extremity there is a great bend in the system's alignment, from which a number of lower mountain ranges and hills spread out. Those in the west lie wholly within Pakistan and Afghanistan, while those to the east straddle India's border with Myanmar (Burma). North of the Himalayas are the Plateau of Tibet and various Trans-Himalayan ranges, only a small part of which, in the Ladakh region of Jammu and Kashmir state, are within the territorial limits of India.

Because of the continued subduction of the Indian peninsula against the Eurasian plate, the Himalayas and the associated eastern ranges remain tectonically active. As a result the mountains are still rising, and earthquakes – often accompanied by landslides – are common. Several since 1900 have been devastating, including one in 1934 in what is now Bihar state that killed more than 10,000 persons. In 2000 another tremor, farther from the mountains, in Gujarat state, was less powerful but caused extensive damage, taking the lives of more than 20,000 people and leaving more than 500,000 homeless.

Between the Great and Lesser Himalayas are several fertile longitudinal vales; in India the largest is the Vale of Kashmir, an ancient lake basin with an area of about 1,700 square miles (4,400 square kilometres). The Great Himalayas, which lie mostly above the line of perpetual snow and contain most of the Himalayan glaciers, include some of the world's highest peaks. The highest, Mount Everest (at 29,035 feet; 8,850 metres), is on the China–Nepal border, but India also has many lofty peaks, such as Kanchenjunga (28,169 feet; 8,586 metres) on the border of Nepal and the state of Sikkim, and Nanda Devi (25,646 feet; 7,817 metres), Kamet (25,446 feet; 7,755 metres), and Trisul (23,359 feet; 7,120 metres) in Uttaranchal.

Various regional ranges and hills run parallel to the Himalayas' main axis. These are especially prominent in the north-west, where the Zaskar Range and the Ladakh and Karakoram ranges, all in Jammu and Kashmir state, run to the north-east of the Great Himalayas. Also in Jammu and Kashmir is the Pir Panjal Range which, extending along the south-west of the Great Himalayas, forms the western and southern flanks of the Vale of Kashmir.

At its eastern extremity, the Himalayas give way to a number of smaller ranges running north-east to south-west – including the heavily forested Patkai Range and the Naga and Mizo Hills – which extend along India's borders with Myanmar and the south-eastern panhandle of Bangladesh. Within the Naga Hills, the reedy Logtak Lake in the Manipur river valley is an important feature. Branching off from these hills to the north-west are the Mikir Hills, and to the west are the Jaintia, Khasi, and Garo Hills, which run just north of India's border with Bangladesh. Collectively, the latter group is also designated as the Shillong (Meghalaya) Plateau.

The second great structural component of India, the Indo-Gangetic Plain (also called the North Indian Plain), lies between the Himalayas and the Deccan. The plain stretches from the Pakistani provinces of Sind and Punjab in the west – where it is watered by the Indus river and its tributaries – eastward to the Brahmaputra river valley in Assam state. The Ganges (*Ganga*) river basin (mainly in Uttar Pradesh and Bihar states) forms the central and principal part of this plain. The eastern portion is made up of the combined delta of the Ganges and Brahmaputra rivers which, though mainly in Bangladesh, also occupies a part of the adjacent Indian state of West Bengal. This deltaic area is characterized by annual flooding attributed to intense monsoon rainfall, an exceedingly gentle gradient, and an enormous discharge that the alluvium-choked rivers cannot contain within their channels. The Indus river basin, extending west from Delhi, forms the western part of the plain; the Indian portion is mainly in the states of Haryana and Punjab.

The overall gradient of the plain is virtually imperceptible, averaging only about 6 inches per mile (95 millimetres per kilometre) in the Ganges basin and slightly more along the Indus and Brahmaputra. An exception to the largely monotonous relief is encountered in the south-western portion of the plain, where there are gullied badlands centring on the Chambal river. That area has long been famous for harbouring *dacoits* (violent gangs of criminals), who find shelter in its many hidden ravines. The Great Indian, or Thar, Desert forms an important southern extension of the Indo-Gangetic Plain. Although it is mainly an area of gently undulating terrain, within it are several areas dominated by shifting sand dunes and numerous isolated hills.

The remainder of India is designated, not altogether accurately, as either the Deccan plateau or peninsular India. This land is the oldest and most stable in the country. The plateau is mainly between 1,000 and 2,500 feet (300 to 750 metres) above sea level, and its general slope descends toward the east. A number of the hill ranges of the Deccan have been eroded and rejuvenated several times, and only their remaining summits testify to their geologic past.

The western edge of the Deccan plateau region is delineated by the Western Ghats, also called the Sahyadri, a north–south chain of mountains or hills. They rise abruptly from the coastal plain as an escarpment of variable height, but their eastern slopes are much more gentle. The hill station (resort) of Mahabaleshwar, located on a laterite plateau, is one of the highest elevations in the northern half, rising to 4,700 feet (1,430 metres). The chain attains greater heights in the south, where the mountains terminate in several uplifted blocks bordered by steep slopes on all sides. These include the Nilgiri Hills and the Anaimalai, Palni, and Cardamom Hills, all three of which radiate from the highest peak in the Western Ghats, Anai Peak (Anai Mudi – 8,842 feet; 2,695 metres). The Western Ghats receive heavy rainfall, and several major rivers

– most notably the Krishna (*Kistna*) and the two holy rivers, the Godavari and the Kaveri (*Cauvery*) – have their head-waters there.

The Eastern Ghats are a series of discontinuous low ranges running generally north-east to south-west, parallel to the coast of the Bay of Bengal. The largest single sector, in the Dandakaranya region between the Mahanadi and Godavari rivers, has a central ridge, the highest peak of which is Arma Konda (5,512 feet; 1,680 metres). The hills become subdued farther south-west. Still farther south-west, beyond the Krishna river, the Eastern Ghats appear as a series of low ranges and hills, including the Erramala, Nallamala, Velikonda, and Palkonda. South-west of the city of Chennai (Madras), the Eastern Ghats continue as the Javadi and Shevaroy Hills, beyond which they merge with the Western Ghats.

Most of the coast of India flanks the Eastern and Western Ghats. In the north-west, however, much of coastal Gujarat lies to the north-west of the Western Ghats, extending around the Gulf of Khambhat (Cambay) and into the salt marshes of the Kathiawar and Kachchh (*Kutch*) peninsulas. The area farther south, especially the stretch from Daman to Goa (known as the Konkan coast), is indented with *rias* (flooded valleys) extending inland into narrow riverine plains. These plains are dominated by low-level lateritic plateaus and are marked by alternating headlands and bays, the latter often sheltering crescent-shaped beaches. From Goa south to Cape Comorin (the southernmost tip of India) is the Malabar coastal plain, which was formed by the deposition of sediment along the shoreline. This plain, varying between 15 and 60 miles (25 to 100 kilometres) wide, is characterized by lagoons and brackish, navigable backwater channels.

The predominantly deltaic eastern coastal plain contains the major deltas of the Kaveri, the Krishna-Godavari, the Mahanadi, and the Ganges-Brahmaputra rivers. The last of these is some 190 miles (300 kilometres) wide, but only about one-third of it lies within India. Traversed by innumerable distributaries, the Ganges delta is an ill-drained region, and the western part within Indian territory has become moribund because of shifts in the channels of the Ganges. Tidal incursions extend far inland, and any small temporary rise in sea level could submerge Kolkata (Calcutta), located about 95 miles (155 kilometres) from the head of the Bay of Bengal. The eastern coastal plain includes several lagoons.

Several archipelagoes in the Indian Ocean are politically a part of India. The union territory of Lakshadweep is a group of small coral atolls in the Arabian Sea to the west of the Malabar Coast. Far off the eastern coast, separating the Bay of Bengal and the Andaman Sea, lie the considerably larger and hillier chains of the Andaman and Nicobar Islands.

The Ganges and Brahmaputra rivers, together with their tributaries, drain about one-third of India. The Ganges (*Ganga*), the longest river course in India and considered sacred by the Hindu population, is 1,560 miles (2,510 kilometres) long. Although the total length of the Brahmaputra (about 1,800 miles; 2,900 kilometres) exceeds that of the Ganges, only 450 miles (725 kilometres) of its course lies within India. A substantial part of north-western India is included in the Indus drainage basin, which India shares with China, Afghanistan, and Pakistan. The Indus rises in the trans-Himalayan region of Tibet, passing through the Pakistani-administered portion of the Kashmir region, and then south-west through Pakistan until it reaches the Arabian Sea. The area through which the five Indus tributaries flow has traditionally been called the Punjab (the area is in the Indian state of Punjab and the Pakistani province of Punjab), and despite low rainfall in the Punjab plains the moderately high runoff from the Himalayas ensures a year-round flow in the Indus and its tributaries, which are extensively utilized for canal irrigation.

Farther to the south, another notable river flowing into the Arabian Sea is the Luni of southern Rajasthan, which in most years has carried enough water to reach the Great Rann of Kachchh marshlands in western Gujarat. Also flowing through Gujarat is the Mahi river, as well as the two most important west-flowing rivers of peninsular India – the Narmada (which, with its basin, has been undergoing large-scale multipurpose development) and the Tapi.

For such a large country, India has few natural lakes. Most of the lakes in the Himalayas were formed when glaciers either dug out a basin or dammed an area with earth and rocks. By contrast, Wular Lake in Jammu and Kashmir, the largest natural freshwater lake in India, is the result of a tectonic depression.

Inland drainage in India is mainly ephemeral and almost entirely in the arid and semiarid part of north-western India, particularly in the Great Indian Desert of Rajasthan, where there are several ephemeral salt lakes – most prominently Sambhar Salt Lake, the largest lake in India. Many of India's largest lakes are reservoirs formed by damming rivers.

The climate

India provides the world's most-pronounced example of a monsoon climate. The wet and dry seasons of the monsoon system, along with the annual temperature fluctuations, produce (with some variations) three general climatic periods over much of the country: (i) hot, wet weather from about mid-June to the end of September, (ii) cool, dry weather from early October to February, and (iii) hot, dry weather (though normally with high atmospheric humidity) from about March to mid-June.

In India the wet season, called the "south-west monsoon," occurs from about mid-June to early October, when winds from the Indian Ocean carry moisture-laden air across the subcontinent, causing heavy rainfall and often considerable flooding. Usually about three-quarters of the country's total annual precipitation falls during those months. During the driest months (the "retreating monsoon"), especially from November to February, this pattern is reversed, as dry air from the Asian interior moves across India toward the ocean. October and March to May, by contrast, are typically periods of desultory breezes with no strong prevailing patterns.

Although the winds of the rainy season are called the south-west monsoon, they actually follow two generally distinct branches, one initially flowing eastward from the Arabian Sea and the other northward from the Bay of Bengal. Annual precipitation in parts of the Western Ghats exceeds 100 inches (2,540 millimetres) and is as high as 245 inches (6,250 millimetres) at Mahabaleshwar on the crest of the region. In the Shillong (Meghalaya) Plateau in eastern India, at Cherrapunji the average annual rainfall is 450 inches (11,430 millimetres), one of the heaviest in the world. In the Gangetic Plain the two branches of the monsoon merge into one and by the time they reach the Punjab their moisture is largely spent. The gradual reduction in the amount of rainfall toward the west is evidenced by the decline from 64 inches (1,625 millimetres) at Kolkata to 26 inches (660 millimetres) at Delhi and to desert conditions still farther west.

Much of India experiences infrequent and relatively feeble precipitation during the retreating monsoon. An exception to this rule occurs along the south-eastern coast of India and for some distance inland. From October to December the coast of

Tamil Nadu state receives at least half of its roughly 40 inches (1,000 millimetres) of annual precipitation. This rainy extension of the generally dry retreating monsoon is called the "north-east monsoon," or "winter monsoon." Another type of winter precipitation occurs in northern India, which receives weak cyclonic storms originating in the Mediterranean basin. In the Himalayas these storms bring weeks of drizzling rain and cloudiness, and are followed by waves of cold temperatures and snowfall. The state of Jammu and Kashmir in particular receives much of its precipitation from these storms.

Fierce tropical cyclones occur in India during what may be called the "premonsoon," the "early monsoon," or the "postmonsoon" periods. Originating in both the Bay of Bengal and the Arabian Sea, tropical cyclones often attain velocities of more than 100 miles (160 kilometres) per hour and are notorious for causing intense rain and storm tides (surges) as they cross the coast of India. The Andhra Pradesh, Orissa, and West Bengal coasts are especially susceptible to such storms.

Monsoons play a pivotal role in Indian agriculture, and the substantial year-to-year variability of rainfall, in both timing and quantity, introduces much uncertainty in the country's crop yield. Good years bring bumper crops, but years of poor rain may result in total crop failure over large areas, especially where irrigation is lacking. Large-scale flooding can also cause damage to crops.

Temperatures in India generally are the warmest in May or June, just prior to the cooling downpours of the south-west monsoon. A secondary maximum often occurs in September or October when precipitation wanes. The temperature range tends to be significantly less along the coastal plains than in interior locations. The range also tends to increase with latitude. Near India's southern extremity the seasonal range is no more than a few degrees; for example, at Thiruvanantha-puram (Trivandrum) in Kerala there is an average fluctuation of just 4.3°F (2.4°C) around an annual mean temperature of 81°F (27°C). In the north-west, however, the range is much greater as, for example, at Ambala in Haryana where the temperature fluctuates from 56°F (13°C) in January to 92°F (33°C) in June. Temperatures are also moderated wherever elevations are significant, and many Himalayan resort towns (known as "hill stations", a legacy of British colonial rule) afford welcome relief from India's sometimes oppressive heat.

Plant and animal life

The flora of India largely reflects the country's distribution of rainfall. Tropical broad-leaved evergreen and mixed, partially evergreen forests grow in areas with high precipitation; in successively less rainy areas are found moist and dry deciduous forests, scrub jungle, grassland, and desert vegetation. Coniferous forests are confined to the Himalayas. There are about 17,000 species of flowering plants in the country. The subcontinent's physical isolation, caused by its relief and climatic barriers, has resulted in a considerable number of endemic flora.

Roughly a quarter of the country is forested. However, beginning in the late twentieth century, forest depletion accelerated considerably to make room for more agriculture and urban-industrial development. This has taken its toll on many Indian plant species. About 20 species of higher-order plants are believed to have become extinct, and already some 1,300 species are considered to be endangered.

Tropical evergreen and mixed evergreen-deciduous forests generally occupy areas with more than 80 inches (2,000 millimetres) of rainfall per year, mainly in upper Assam, the Western Ghats (especially in Kerala), parts of Orissa, and the Andaman and Nicobar Islands. Common trees include species of Mesua, Toona ciliata, Hopea, and Eugenia, as well as gurjun (*Dipterocarpus turbinatus*), which grows to over 165 feet (50 metres) on the Andaman Islands and in Assam. The mixed evergreen-deciduous forests of Kerala and the Bengal Himalayas have a large variety of commercially valuable hardwood trees.

Tropical moist deciduous forests generally occur in areas with 60 to 80 inches (1,500 to 2,000 millimetres) of rainfall, such as the northern part of the Eastern Ghats, east-central India, and western Karnataka. Dry deciduous forests, which grow in places receiving less than 60 inches (1,500 millimetres) of precipitation, characterize the subhumid and semiarid regions of Gujarat, Madhya Pradesh, eastern Rajasthan, central Andhra Pradesh, and western Tamil Nadu. Teak, sal (*Shorea robusta*), axle-wood (*Anogeissus latifolia*), tendu, ain, and Adina cardifolia are some of the major deciduous species.

Tropical thorn forests occupy areas in various parts of the country, though mainly in the northern Gangetic Plain and southern peninsular India. The important commercial species include teak and sal. Other species with commercial uses are sandalwood (*Santalum album*), the fragrant wood that is perhaps the most precious in the world, and rosewood, an evergreen used for carving and furniture.

Other species are noteworthy because of the special ecological niches they occupy. Deltaic areas are fringed with mangrove forests. Conspicuous features of the tropical landscape are the palms, which are represented in India by some 100 species. Coconut and betel nut (the fruit of which is chewed) are cultivated mainly in coastal Karnataka and Kerala. Among the common, majestic-looking trees found throughout much of India are the mango, the pipal (famous as the Bo tree of Buddha), and the banyan. Many types of bamboo (members of the grass family) grow over much of the country, with a concentration in the rainy areas. Vegetation in the Himalayas, divided into a number of elevation zones, includes mixed evergreen-deciduous forests in the foothills; then subtropical pine forests; the Himalayan moist-temperate forests of oak, fir, deodar (*Cedrus deodara*), and spruce; and, at the highest tree zone, alpine shrubs. Rhododendrons are common at 12,000 feet (3,700 metres), above which occasional junipers and alpine meadows are encountered.

India's fauna are numerous and quite diverse. Wild herds of Indian elephants (*Elphas maximus*) can be observed in several areas, particularly in such renowned national parks as Periyar Wildlife Sanctuary in Kerala and Bandipur in Karnataka. The great one-horned Indian rhinoceros is protected at Kaziranga National Park and Manas Wildlife Sanctuary in Assam. Other ruminant species include the wild Indian bison, or gaur (*Bos gaurus*), which inhabits peninsular forests; Indian buffalo; and various antelope and deer, such as the rare Kashmir stag (*hangul*), the brow-antlered deer (*Cervus eldi eldi*, an endangered species known locally as the *sangai* or *thamin*), and mouse deer. Rhesus monkeys and grey, or Hanuman, langurs (*Presbytis entellus*) are found in forested areas and near human settlements. The only ape found in India, the hoolock gibbon, is confined to the rainforests of the eastern region. Lion-tailed macaques of the Western Ghats, with halos of hair around their faces, are becoming rare because of poaching.

Among the animals of prey, the Asiatic lion – now confined to the Gir Forest National Park, in the Kathiawar Peninsula of Gujarat – is the only extant subspecies of lion found outside Africa. The majestic Indian or Bengal tiger (*Panthera tigris*

tigris), the national animal of India, is the most numerous of the world's tiger subspecies. Once on the verge of extinction, Indian tigers have increased to several thousand, thanks largely to Project Tiger which has established reserves in various parts of the country. The Great Himalayas have notable fauna that includes wild sheep and goats, markhor (*Capra falconeri*), and ibex. Lesser pandas and snow leopards are also found in the upper reaches of the mountains.

India has more than 1,200 species of birds and perhaps 2,000 subspecies, although some migratory species are found in the country only during the winter. This avian diversity, made possible by the wide variety of habitats, represents roughly one-eighth of the world's species. Many smaller rivers drain internally and end in vast saline lakes that are important breeding grounds for such birds as black-necked cranes (*Grus nigricollis*), barheaded geese (*Anser indicus*), and great crested grebes, as well as various kinds of terns, gulls, plovers, and sandpipers. Herons, storks, ibises, and flamingos are well represented, and many of these birds frequent Keoladeo National Park, near Bharatpur, Rajasthan (designated a UNESCO World Heritage site in 1985). The Rann of Kachchh forms the nesting ground for one of the world's largest breeding colonies of flamingos.

Birds of prey include hawks, vultures, and eagles. Peacocks (peafowl), India's national bird, are also common, especially in Gujarat and Rajasthan, where they are kept as pets. Other notable birds in India include the Indian crane, commonly known as the sarus (*Grus antigone*), a large grey bird with crimson legs which stands as tall as a human. Bustards inhabit India's grasslands. The mainly nonmigratory kingfisher, living close to water bodies, is considered sacred in many areas. Hornbills, barbets, and woodpeckers also are common, as are larks, crows, babblers, and thrushes.

Reptiles are also well represented in India, with crocodiles and (in the north) the crocodile-like gavial inhabiting the country's rivers, swamps, and lakes. There are nearly 400 species of snakes, one-fifth of which are poisonous, including king cobras which often grow to at least 12 feet (3.6 metres) long. Of some 2,000 species of fish in India, about one-fifth live in fresh water. Common edible freshwater fish include catfish and several members of the carp family. Commercially valuable marine species include shrimps, prawns, crabs, lobsters, pearl oysters, and conchs. Among the commercially valuable insects are silkworms, bees, and the lac insect (*Laccifer lacca*), the latter secreting a sticky, resinous material, from which shellac and a red dye are produced.

The movement for the protection of forests and wildlife is strong in India. A number of species, including the elephant, rhinoceros, and tiger, have been declared endangered. Legislative measures have declared certain animals protected species, and areas with particularly rich floral diversity have been adopted as biosphere reserves.

The people

India is a diverse, multiethnic country that is home to thousands of small ethnic and tribal groups. This complexity developed from a lengthy and involved process of migration and intermarriage. The great urban culture of the Indus civilization, thought to have been Dravidian-speaking, thrived from roughly 2500 to 1700 BCE. An early Aryan civilization – dominated by peoples with linguistic affinities to peoples in Iran and Europe – came to occupy north-western and then north-central India over the period from roughly 2000 to 1500 BCE, and subsequently spread south-westward and eastward at the expense of other indigenous groups. Among the documented invasions that added significantly to the Indian ethnic mix are those of Persians, Scythians, Arabs, Mongols, Turks, and Afghans.

Broadly speaking, the peoples of north-central and northwestern India tend to have ethnic affinities with European and Indo-European peoples from southern Europe, the Caucasus region, and South-west and Central Asia. In north-eastern India, West Bengal (to a lesser degree), the higher reaches of the western Himalayan region, and Ladakh (in Jammu and Kashmir state), much of the population more closely resembles peoples to the north and east – notably Tibetans and Burmans. Many aboriginal ("tribal") peoples in the Chota Nagpur Plateau (north-eastern peninsular India) have affinities to such groups as the Mon, who have long been established in mainland South-east Asia. Much less numerous are southern groups who appear to be descended, at least in part, either from peoples of East African origin (some of whom settled in historical times on India's western coast) or from a population commonly designated as Negrito, now represented by numerous small and widely dispersed peoples from the Andaman Islands, the Philippines, New Guinea, and other areas.

There are probably hundreds of major and minor languages and many hundreds of recognized dialects in India, whose languages belong to four different language families: Indo-Iranian (a subfamily of the Indo-European language family), Dravidian, Austroasiatic, and Tibeto-Burman (a subfamily of Sino-Tibetan). There are also several isolate languages, such as Nahali, which is spoken in a small area of Madhya Pradesh state. The overwhelming majority of Indians speak Indo-Iranian or Dravidian languages.

Languages within India have adopted words and grammatical forms from one another, and vernacular dialects within languages often diverge widely. Over much of India, and especially the Indo-Gangetic Plain, there are no clear boundaries between one vernacular and another.

In the mountain fringes of the country, especially in the north-east, spoken dialects are often sufficiently different from one valley to the next to merit classifying each as a truly distinct language. There were at one time, for example, no fewer than 25 languages classified within the Naga group, not one of which was spoken by more than 60,000 people. Although many tribal communities are gradually abandoning their tribal languages, scores of such languages survive. Few, however, are still spoken by more than a million persons, with the exception of Bhili (Indo-European) and Santhali (of the Munda branch of the Austroasiatic family), which are both estimated as having more than five million speakers.

Lending order to this linguistic mix are a number of written, or literary, languages used on the subcontinent, each of which often differs markedly from the vernacular with which it is associated. Many people are bilingual or multilingual, knowing their local vernacular dialect ("mother tongue"), its associated written variant and, perhaps, one or more other languages. The official national language is Hindi, but there are 22 (originally 14) so-called "scheduled languages" recognized in the Indian constitution that may be used by states in official correspondence. Of these, 15 are Indo-European (Assamese, Bengali, Dogri, Gujarati, Hindi, Kashmiri, Konkani, Maithili, Marathi, Nepali, Oriya, Punjabi, Sanskrit, Sindhi, and Urdu), 4 are Dravidian (Kannada, Malayalam, Tamil, and Telugu), 2 are Sino-Tibetan (Bodo and Manipuri), and 1 is Austroasiatic (Santhali). These languages have become increasingly standardized since independence because of improved education and the influence of mass media. Most Indian languages are written using some variety of Devanagari script, but other scripts are used. Sindhi, for instance, is written in a Persianized form of Arabic script, but it is also sometimes written in the Devanagari or Gurmukhi scripts.

The Indo-Iranian branch of the Indo-European family is the largest language group in the subcontinent. By far the most widely spoken Indo-Iranian language is Hindi, which is used in one form or another by some three-fifths of the population. Apart from its nationally preeminent position, Hindi has been adopted as the official language by each of a large contiguous bloc of northern states – Bihar, Chhattisgarh, Haryana, Himachal Pradesh, Jharkhand, Madhya Pradesh, Rajasthan, Uttaranchal, and Uttar Pradesh – as well as by the national capital territory of Delhi.

Other Indo-European languages have been given official status in individual states: Assamese in Assam; Bengali in West Bengal and Tripura; Gujarati in Gujarat; Kashmiri in Jammu and Kashmir; Konkani in Goa; Marathi in Maharashtra; Nepali in portions of northern West Bengal; Oriya in Orissa; and Punjabi in Punjab. Urdu, the official language of Pakistan, is also the language of most Muslims of northern and peninsular India as far south as Chennai (Madras). Sindhi is spoken mainly by inhabitants of the Kachchh district of Gujarat, which borders the Pakistani province of Sind, as well as in other areas by immigrants (and their descendants) who fled Sind after the 1947 partition.

Dravidian languages are spoken by about a quarter of all Indians, overwhelmingly in southern India. The four constitutionally recognized Dravidian languages also enjoy official state status: Kannada in Karnataka; Malayalam in Kerala; Tamil (the oldest of the main Dravidian tongues) in Tamil Nadu; and Telugu in Andhra Pradesh. Manipuri and other Sino-Tibetan languages are spoken by small numbers of people in north-eastern India.

The two major lingua francas in India are Hindustani and English, a remnant of British colonial rule. Hindustani is based on an early dialect of Hindi which came to be used as a lingua franca throughout the Empire during the Mughal period (early sixteenth to mid-eighteenth century). In the nineteenth century two literary languages arose from this colloquial tongue – among Hindus, the modern form of Hindi, which derives its vocabulary and script (Devanagari) mainly from Sanskrit; and among Muslims, Urdu, which, though grammatically identical with Hindi, draws much of its vocabulary from Persian and Arabic and is written in the Perso-Arabic script. Despite this rift, Hindi and Urdu remain mutually intelligible, while their Hindustani progenitor still serves as a lingua franca in many parts of the subcontinent, particularly in the north.

The great size of India's population makes it one of the largest English-speaking communities in the world, although English is claimed as the mother tongue by only a small number of Indians and is spoken fluently by less than 5 per cent of the population. English, an "associate" official language, serves as the language linking the central government with the states and is the principal language of commerce and the language of instruction in almost all of the country's prestigious universities and private schools. The English-language press remains highly influential; scholarly publication is predominantly in English (almost exclusively so in science); and many Indians are devotees of literature in English (much of it written by Indians), as well as of English-language film, radio, television, popular music, and theatre.

Town and country

Only a tiny fraction of India is uninhabited. More than half of it is cultivated, and most of the area classified as forest – roughly one-fifth of the total – is used for grazing, gathering firewood and other forest products, commercial forestry and, in tribal areas, for shifting cultivation (often in defiance of the law) and hunting. The areas too dry for growing crops without irrigation are largely used for grazing. Although India's population is overwhelmingly rural, the country has three of the largest urban areas in the world – Mumbai, Kolkata, and Delhi – and these and other large Indian cities have some of the world's highest population densities.

Most Indians reside in the areas of continuous cultivation, including the towns and cities they encompass. Within such areas, differences in population density are largely a function of water availability (whether directly from rainfall or from irrigation) and soil fertility. More than three-fifths of the total population lives either on the fertile alluvial soils of the Indo-Gangetic Plain and the deltaic regions of the eastern coast or on the mixed alluvial and marine soils along India's western coast. Within those agriculturally productive areas – for example, parts of the eastern Gangetic Plain and of the state of Kerala – densities exceed 2,000 persons per square mile (800 persons per square kilometre).

The rural population lives in villages. Such settlements generally are divided by caste into distinct wards and grow outward from a recognizable core area. The dominant and higher castes tend to live in the core area, while the lower artisan and service castes, as well as Muslim groups, generally occupy more peripheral localities. When the centrally located castes increase in population, they cither subdivide their existing, often initially large, residential compounds; add second and even third storeys to their existing houses (a common expedient in Punjab); leapfrog over lower-caste wards to a new area on the village periphery; or, in rare cases where land is available, found a completely new village.

There are usually a few open spaces in these villages where people gather: adjacent to a temple or mosque, at the main village well, in areas where grain is threshed or where grain and oilseeds are milled, and in front of the homes of the leading families. In such spaces might be found the pancayat (village council) hall, a few shops, a tea stall, a public radio hooked up to a loudspeaker, a small post office, or perhaps a free guesthouse for travellers (*dharmshala*). The village school is usually on the edge of the village in order to provide pupils with adequate playing space. Another common feature along the margin of a village is a grove of mango or other trees, which provides shade for people and animals and often contains a large well.

There are, however, many regional variants from the simple agglomerated-villages pattern. Hamlets, each containing only one or a few castes, commonly surround villages in the eastern Gangetic Plain, for instance, and in Tamil Nadu and Gujarat villages have a more planned layout, with streets running north-south and east-west in straight lines. In particularly aquatic environments, such as the Gangetic delta and the tidal backwater region of Kerala, most rural families live singly or in clusters of only a few households on their individual plots of owned or rented land.

Most village houses are small, simple one-storey mud (*kacha*) structures, housing both people and livestock in one or just a few rooms. Roofs typically are flat and made of mud in dry regions, but in areas with considerable precipitation they generally are sloped for drainage and made of rice straw, other thatching material, or clay tiles. The houses usually are windowless and contain a minimum of furniture, a storage space for food, water, and implements, a few shelves and pegs for other possessions, a niche in the wall to serve as the household altar, and often a few decorations, such as pictures of gods and family photographs. In one corner of the house or in an exterior court is the earthen hearth on which all meals are cooked. Electricity, running water, and toilet facilities generally are absent. Relatively secluded spots on the edge of the village serve the latter need.

Dwellings of more affluent households are larger and usually built of more durable (*pakka*) materials, such as brick or stone; the number of rooms, the furnishings, and the interior and exterior decor, especially the entrance gate, generally reflect the wealth of the family. Within the compound there may be a private well or even a hand pump, an area for bathing, and a walled latrine enclosure, which is periodically cleaned by the village sweeper. Animal stalls, granaries, and farm equipment are in spaces distinct from those occupied by people.

Nomadic groups may be found in most parts of India. Some are small bands of wandering entertainers, ironworkers, and animal traders. A group variously known as the Banjari or Labhani, originally from Rajasthan and related to the Roma (Gypsies) of Europe, roams over large areas of central India and the Deccan, largely as agricultural labourers and construction workers. Many tribal peoples practise similar occupations seasonally. Shepherds, largely of the Gujar caste, practise transhumance in the western Himalayas. In the semi-arid and arid regions, where agriculture is either impossible or precarious, herders of cattle, sheep, goats, and camels live in a symbiotic relationship with local or nearby cultivators.

Although only about a quarter of India's people live in towns and cities, more than 4,500 places are classified as urban. For many years large cities have been growing at faster rates than small cities and towns. In many cities dating from the precolonial period, such as Delhi and Agra, the urban core is an exceedingly congested area within an old city wall, portions of which may still stand. In these "old cities" residential segregation by religion and caste and the layout of streets and open places are, except for scale, not greatly dissimilar from villages. Specialized bazaar streets selling sweets, grain, cloth, metalware, jewellery, books, stationery, and other commodities are characteristic of the old city. Cities that developed during the British occupation, such as Kolkata, Mumbai, and Chennai, usually have a few broad major thoroughfares, some degree of regularity to the street pattern, space reserved for parks, and a central business district, including old government offices, high-rise commercial office buildings, banks, elite shopping establishments, restaurants, hotels, museums, a few churches, and other reminders of the former colonial presence.

Associated with a great many cities are special sections created originally for the needs of the British: largely residential areas known as "civil lines," where the families of resident European administrators occupied spacious bungalows, with adjoining outbuildings for their servants, nearby shopping facilities, and a sports and social club (*gymkhana*); cantonments, where military personnel of all ranks were quartered, together with adjacent parade grounds, polo fields, and firing ranges; and industrial zones, including not only the modern mills but also the adjacent "factory lines," reminiscent of nineteenth-century company housing in Britain but even more squalid.

British rule also gave rise to the hill stations, such as Shimla (Simla) and Darjiling (Darjeeling) – cool retreats for the dependants of Europeans stationed in India and, in the summer months, seasonal capitals of the central or provincial governments. Hotels, guesthouses, boarding schools, clubs, and other recreational facilities characterize these settlements. Since independence, affluent Indians have come to depend on the hill stations no less than did the British.

In the post-independence period, with the acceleration of urban growth and the consequent need for urban planning, many "model" (planned) towns on the edges of the existing cities arose. The subsequent steady influx of job seekers, together with the natural growth of the already settled population, gave rise to many planned residential areas, typically called "colonies," usually consisting of four- or five-storey apartment blocks, a small shopping centre, schools, and playgrounds and other recreational spaces. Poorer immigrants moved into slum flats or found shelter in *basti*s (shantytowns), clusters of anywhere from a few to many hundreds of makeshift dwellings or, if they could not afford even that, became street dwellers.

Population

A population explosion in India followed the great influenza epidemic of 1918–19. In subsequent decades there was a steadily accelerating rate of growth up to the census of 1961, after which the rate levelled off (though it remained high). The total population in 1921 within the present borders of India was 251 million; in 1947, at the time of independence, it was about 340 million. India's population doubled between 1947 and the 1981 census, and by the 2001 census it had surpassed one billion. Although there has been a considerable drop in the birth rate, a much more rapid decline in the death rate has accounted for the rise in the country's rate of population growth. Moreover, the increasing proportion of females attaining and living through their childbearing years continues to inhibit a marked reduction in the birth rate.

The effect of emigration from or immigration to India on the overall growth of population has been negligible throughout modern history. Within India, however, migration from relatively impoverished regions to areas, especially cities, that offer some promise of economic betterment has been largely responsible for the differential growth rates from one state or region to another. In general, the larger a city, the greater its proportion of migrants to the total population and the more cosmopolitan its population mix. The rates of migration to Indian cities severely tax their capacity to provide housing, safe drinking water and sanitary facilities, and other amenities. The result is that many migrants live in conditions of appalling squalor. Refugees from the 1947 partition of India, from the violent separation in 1971 of Bangladesh from Pakistan, and from the communal violence and other forms of ethnic strife that periodically beset many parts of India are an additional source of population pressure in urban areas.

PART TWO

HISTORY

2

EARLY CIVILIZATIONS TO THE FALL OF THE MUGHAL EMPIRE (8000 BCE–1800)

Introduction

The Indian subcontinent is the home of one of the world's oldest and most influential civilizations. The expansive alluvial plain of the Indus and Ganges river basins provided the environment and focus for the rise of two great phases of city life: the Indus civilization during the third millennium BCE; and, during the first millennium BCE, the civilization of the Ganges.

Prior to this there is archaeological evidence of earlier peoples. The oldest artifacts found on the subcontinent – quartzite pebble tools and flakes – date to about two million years ago and represent a pre-hand-axe industry of a type that appears to have persisted for an extensive period thereafter. The Great India (Thar) Desert contains numerous archaeological sites, including those associated with a prolonged humid phase (140,000 to about 25,000 years ago) when the region provided a rich environment for hunting; as do the Rohri

Hills, where *chert* (a type of stone that is a principal raw material for making tools and weapons) has been found. This was followed by a drier period after about 25,000 years ago, marked by the production of parallel-sided blades with adaptations for working particular materials, such as leather, wood, and bone.

The Indian Mesolithic period saw a great proliferation of cultures throughout India that exhibited a wide variety of subsistence patterns, including hunting and gathering, fishing, and, at least for part of the period, some herding and small-scale agriculture. From about 5000 BCE, increasing numbers of settlements began to appear throughout the Indo-Iranian borderlands. These were village communities of settled agriculturalists, employing common means of subsistence in the cultivation of wheat, barley, and other crops and in the keeping of cattle, sheep, and goats.

The first evidence of agriculturalists and pastoralism dates from the eighth millennium BCE to the fouth (and possibly third) millennium, at early settlements at Mehrgarh and elsewhere. There was increasing cultivation of wheat and barley, and domestication of sheep and goats; later cattle came to predominate. A type of granary building, suggesting crop surpluses, first appeared then. The use of seashells and of various semiprecious stones, including turquoise and lapis lazuli, indicates the existence of trade networks. From the fifth to the third millennium, the remains of several massive brick walls and platforms suggest something approaching monumental architecture, and there is evidence of new crafts, including the first examples of the use of copper and ivory.

In peninsular India, pastoralists using stone axes appear to have spread southward to many parts from northern Karnataka during the second millennium BCE. Probably toward the middle of the fourth millennium BCE, agricultural settlements began to spread more widely in the Indus valley itself.

In the Early Harappan Period (from the mid-fourth to the mid-third millennium BCE), a number of substantial walled towns, including those at Amri, Kot Diji (in present-day Sind province, Pakistan) and Rehman Dheri (near Dera Ismail Khan) were established. The regular appearance of a stone-blade industry, far from any stone-producing region, implies that raw materials must have been imported. Incised or painted marks on pottery suggest that the need for a script was beginning to arise. Some of the painted decorations also appear to carry a distinctly religious symbolism.

The Indus civilization

The Indus (or Harappan) civilization, which emerged between 2600 and 2500 BCE, ran in full glory to about 2000 BCE, and in its late stage probably continued until about 1700 BCE; it has sometimes been considered the basis of modern Indian culture. Evidence of this can be seen not only in the Indus valley script found on seals but in the attention paid to domestic bathrooms, the drains, and the Great Bath at Mohenjo-daro – all of which can be compared to elements in the later Indian civilization. The bullock carts with a framed canopy (*ikka*s) and boats are little changed to this day. The absence of pins and the love of bangles and of elaborate nose ornaments are all peculiarly South Asian. The religion of the Indus also is replete with suggestions of traits known from later India. The significance of the bull, the tiger, and the elephant; the composite animals; the seated yogi god of the seals; the tree spirits and the objects resembling the Shiva *linga* (a phallus symbolic of the god Shiva) of later times – all these are suggestive of enduring forms in later Indian civilization.

It is still impossible to do more than guess at the social organization or the political and administrative control implied by this vast area of cultural uniformity. The evidence of widespread trade in many commodities, the apparent uniformity of weights and measures, the common script, and the uniformity – almost common currency – of the seals all indicate some measure of political and economic control, and point to the great cities Mohenjo-daro and Harappa as their centres. The presence of great granaries on citadel mounds in these cities and of the citadels themselves suggests the existence of priest-kings, or at least a priestly oligarchy, that controlled the economy and civil government.

Evidence suggests that the area occupied by the civilization is a little less than about 500,000 square miles (1,300,000 square kilometres). Within this area, several hundred sites, ranging from extensive cities to small villages or outposts, have been identified, the great majority of which are on the plains of the Indus or its tributaries or on the now dry course of the ancient Saraswati river, which flowed south of the Sutlej river and then, perhaps, southward to the Indian Ocean, east of the main course of the Indus itself.

The two largest sites are Mohenjo-daro and Harappa, each with a great fortified citadel mound to the west, protected by a defensive wall of brick, and a larger lower city to the east. A similar layout is also discernible in the somewhat smaller town of Kalibangan and in several other major settlements. In all three cases the city was situated near a river, and the lower city was laid out in a grid pattern of streets. Apart from domestic structures, a wide range of shops and craft workshops have been encountered, including potters' kilns, dyers' vats, and the shops of metalworkers, shellworkers, and beadmakers. The size of houses varies considerably, from single-roomed barracks to large houses around a central courtyard or sometimes with a set of intersecting courtyards, each with its own adjoining rooms.

The Indus civilization seems to have had a closely knit and integrated administration and to have had internal trade within the state. This is supported by the wide diffusion of *chert* blades, made of the characteristic Sukkur stone, and the enormous scale of the factory at the Sukkur site and the almost identical bronze carts discovered at Chanhu-daro (another major site) and Harappa. The wide range of crafts and special materials employed must also have caused the establishment of economic relations with peoples living outside the Harappan state. Such trade may be considered to be of two kinds: first, the obtaining of raw materials and other goods from the village communities or forest tribes in regions adjoining the Indus culture area; and second, trade with the cities and empires of Mesopotamia.

Gold was almost certainly imported from the group of settlements that sprang up in the vicinity of the goldfields of northern Karnataka, and copper could have come from several sources – principally from Rajasthan. Lead may have come from Rajasthan or elsewhere in India. Lapis lazuli, alabaster, and turquoise were probably imported from Iran. There is little evidence of what the Harappans gave in exchange for these materials – possibly nondurable goods such as cotton textiles and probably various types of beads, and perhaps tools or weapons of copper.

For the trade with Mesopotamia there is both literary and archaeological evidence. Timber and precious woods, ivory, lapis lazuli, gold, and luxury goods such as carnelian beads, pearls, and shell and bone inlays, including the distinctly Indian kidney shape, were among the goods sent to Mesopotamia in exchange for silver, tin, woollen textiles, and grains and other foods. Copper ingots appear to have been imported to Lothal. Other probable trade items include products originating exclusively in each respective region, such as bitumen, occurring naturally in Mesopotamia, and cotton textiles and chickens, major products of the Indus region that were not native to Mesopotamia.

In addition to instituting a uniform system of weights and measures, the Indus civilization seems to have used a lingua franca throughout the region (though the Harappan script in which it was written has long defied attempts to read it). Excavations of the Indus cities have also produced much evidence of artistic activity. Sculpted stone figures, apparently intended as images for worship, include seated men, recumbent composite animals or – in unique instances (from Harappa) – a standing nude male and a dancing figure. There is also a small but notable repertoire of cast-bronze figures, including dancing girls, small chariots, carts, and animals. The popular art of the Harappans was in the form of terracotta figurines: standing females, often heavily laden with jewellery, and standing males, some with beard and horns. These figures are largely deities (perhaps a Great Mother and a Great God), but some small figures of mothers with children or of domestic activities are probably toys. Painted pottery is the only evidence that there was a tradition of painting. The steatite seals, which probably also functioned as amulets, form the most extensive series of objects of art, the great majority showing a humpless "unicorn" or bull in profile, while others show the Indian humped bull, elephant, bison, rhinoceros, or tiger.

Religious beliefs can be deduced from the buildings identified as temples or as possessing a ritual function, such as the Great Bath at Mohenjo-daro, and the stone sculptures typically found with these buildings, as well as the terracotta figures and the seals and amulets that depict scenes with mythological or religious content. It is assumed that there was a Great God, who had many of the attributes later associated with the Hindu god Shiva, and a Great Mother, who was the Great God's spouse and shared the attributes of Shiva's wife, Durga-Parvati. Evidence also exists of some sort of animal cult, related particularly to the bull, the buffalo, and the tiger. Some seals suggest influence from (or at least traits held in common with) Mesopotamia, including the Gilgamesh (Mesopotamian epic) motif. Other seals depict cult scenes or symbols; a god, seated in a yogic (meditative) posture and surrounded by beasts, with a horned headdress and erect phallus; the tree spirit with a tiger standing before it; the horned tree spirit confronted by a worshipper; a composite beast with a line of seven figures standing before it; the pipal leaf motif; and the swastika (a symbol still widely used by Hindus, Jains, and Buddhists). Many burials have been discovered, giving clear indication of belief in an afterlife.

There is no general agreement regarding the causes of the breakdown of Harappan urban society. Theories on the causes include gradual environmental change, such as a shift in climatic patterns and consequent agricultural disaster; precipitous environmental change, such as tectonic events leading to the flooding of Mohenjo-daro; human activities, such as possible invasions of tribespeople that may have contributed to the breakdown of Indus trade links or disrupted the cities; or an epidemic or a similar agent of devastation. Whatever the cause, the decline probably occurred in several stages, perhaps over a century or more between about 2000 and 1750 BCE. After that date the cities disappear.

During the succeeding Post-Harappan (or "Post-Urban") period, which lasted until about 750 BCE, there is an increase in the number of settlements, but they are all small. Toward the end of the second millennium there appears to have been a further deterioration in the environment throughout the Indus system. Many of the Post-Urban settlements seem to have been abandoned, and traces are found of temporary settlements that were probably associated with nomadic pastoral groups and distinguished by the poverty of their material culture. To the north, in Punjab, Haryana, and the upper Gangetic Plain, such deterioration is less apparent, and there is a spread of settlements toward the east into the upper Ganges-Yamuna valleys which, by the second quarter of the first millennium BCE, gave rise to the first cities of the Ganges system. Another factor in the process of change undoubtedly was the spread of iron-working, probably beginning about 1200 to 1100 BCE. During this period an increasingly marked contrast may be observed between the growing number of cities across the north and the relatively less-developed settlement pattern of peninsular India, where a mixture of small-scale agriculture and pastoralism coincided with the appearance of the various types of Megalithic graves and monuments.

A considerable change becomes noticeable from 2000 to 1000 BCE, as centralized state governments give way gradually to decentralized administration and to what has been called a feudalistic pattern in the post-Gupta period (i.e. from the seventh century CE), with caste and village assemblies. The pendulum of politics swung from large to small kingdoms, with the former attempting to establish empires – the sole successful attempt being that of the Mauryan dynasty. The transition from tribal to peasant society was a continuing process, with the gradual clearing of wasteland and the expansion of the village economy based on plough agriculture. Recognition of the importance of land revenue coincided with the emergence of the imperial system in the fourth century BCE; and from this period onward, although the imperial structure did not last long, land revenue became central to the administration and income of the state.

The urban economy was crucial to the rise of civilization in the Indus valley (*c.*2600–2000 BCE). Later the first millennium BCE saw an urban civilization in the Ganges (*Ganga*) valley and still later in coastal south India. The emergence of towns was based on administrative needs, the requirements of trade, and pilgrimage centres. In the first millennium CE, when commerce expanded to include trade with western Asia, the eastern Mediterranean, and Central and South-east Asia, revenue from trade contributed substantially to the economies of the participating kingdoms. Gold coins were issued for the first time by the Kushan dynasty, and in large quantity by the Guptas; both kingdoms were active in foreign trade. Expanding trade encouraged the opening up of new routes, and this, coupled with the expanding village economy, led to a marked increase of knowledge about the subcontinent during the post-Mauryan period. With increasing trade, guilds became more powerful in the towns. Members of the guilds participated in the administration, were associated with politics, and controlled the development of trade through merchant embassies sent to places as far afield as Rome and China. Not least, guilds and merchant associations held envied and respectable positions as donors of religious institutions.

Migrations of peoples both within the subcontinent and from outside encouraged social mobility and change. The nucleus of the social structure in Indian society was the family. In the main, there were three levels of religious expression: worship of local cult deities; the more puritanical sects of Buddhism and Jainism and the *bhakti* (devotional) tradition of Hinduism; and classical Hinduism and more abstract levels of Buddhism and Jainism, with an emphasis on the major deities in the case of the first and on the teachings of the founders in the case of the latter two. It was this level, endorsed by affluent patronage, that provided the base for the initial institutionalization of religion. Sanskrit literature and the building of Hindu and Buddhist temples and sculpture both reached apogees in this period. It is also in this period, between 1500 and 800 BCE, that the earliest literary record of Indian culture, the *Vedas*, were composed; written in archaic, or Vedic, Sanskrit, they were transmitted orally.

From 1000 BCE to 1200 CE

By about 1500 BCE an important change began to occur in the northern half of the Indian subcontinent, as a new thrust toward a more lasting urbanization came from the migration of peoples from the Punjab into the Ganges valley. The Vedic period, from about 2000–500 BCE, witnessed the inward migration of Indo-European speakers from Central Asia and Iran and the transition from nomadic pastoralism to settled village communities, intermixing pastoral and agrarian economies. By the end of the period, clan identity had changed gradually to territorial identity, and the areas of settlement came eventually to form states. Some of these settlements along the rivers evolved into towns. By the mid-first millennium BCE the second urbanization – this time in the Ganges valley – was under way.

It was at this time that the notion of caste arose. A hymn in the *Rigveda* (one of the four groups of Vedic texts) refers to the emergence of four groups from the body of the god Prajapati – the Brahmans (*Brahmanas*; those possessing magical or divine knowledge), Kshatriyas (*Ksatriyas*; those having power or sovereignty), Vaishyas (*Vaisyas*; those settled on the land or members of the clan), and Sudras (*Sudras*; members of the group born to serve the other three). This is clearly a mythologized attempt to describe the origin of the four *varnas*, which came to be regarded as the four major classes in Indian society. In the course of time the Brahmans became the preeminent priestly group; the Kshatriyas, who were to become the landowning families, assumed the role of military leaders and of the natural aristocracy having connections with royalty; and the Vaishyas, who were more subservient, appear to have been crucial to the economy. The traditional view of the Sudras is that they were non-Aryan cultivators who came under the domination of the Aryans, and in many cases were enslaved and therefore had to serve the upper three groups.

By about 500 BCE, Buddhist and other writings mention 16 major states (*mahajanapada*) dominating the northern part of the subcontinent, some newly created, with monarchical government or a type of representative government that variously has been called republican or oligarchic. An increase in urban settlements and trade, and the formation of guilds, is evident not only from references in the literary sources but also from the introduction of two characteristics of urban civilization – a script and coinage. There was a sizable heterodox tradition, with speculation ranging from idealism to materialism. Among the various sects practised, Jainism and Buddhism, both founded in the sixth–fifth century BCE, acquired the status of major religions. The Jains participated widely as the middlemen in financial transactions, and in later centuries became the great financiers of western India.

Political activity in the sixth–fifth century BCE centred on the control of the Ganges valley, from which the Magadha king, Bimbisara (*c.*543–491 BCE) emerged victorious. He conquered Anga, which gave him access to the Ganges delta – a valuable asset in terms of the nascent maritime trade. His son, Ajatashatru, implemented his father's intentions within about 30 years. He built a small fort on the Ganges at Pataligrama, which was to become the famous capital Pataliputra (modern

Patna). He also established a rudimentary land-revenue and tax system. After Ajatashatru's death (*c*.459 BCE) and a series of ineffectual rulers, Shaishunaga founded a new dynasty, which lasted for about half a century until ousted by Mahapadma Nanda. The north-western part of India witnessed the military campaign of Alexander the Great of Macedon, who campaigned successfully across the Punjab as far as the Beas river.

Candra Gupta Maurya (reigned *c*.321–297 BCE), the first Mauryan emperor, overthrew the Nanda power and then campaigned in central and northern India, eventually inaugurating what was to become the first pan-Indian empire. The Mauryan dynasty was to rule almost the entire subcontinent (except the area south of present-day Karnataka) as well as substantial parts of present-day Afghanistan — perhaps as many as 50 million people – as a single political unit and to maintain an imperial system for almost 100 years. The Mauryan Empire reached its zenith during the reign of Ashoka, a great patron of Buddhism, but then began a steady decline.

In 185 BCE the last of the Mauryas, Brihadratha, was assassinated by his Brahman commander in chief, Pushyamitra, who founded the Shunga dynasty. The Shunga lasted for about a century, until it was replaced by the Kanva dynasty, which ruled for the next 45 years. The disintegration of the Mauryan Empire gave rise to a number of small kingdoms. The Punjab and Kashmir regions were drawn into the orbit of Central Asian politics. In the northern Deccan there arose the first of many important kingdoms that were to serve as the bridge between the north and the south. In the extreme south the prestige and influence of the Cera, Cola, and Pandya kingdoms continued unabated. Yet in spite of political fragmentation, this was a period of economic prosperity, resulting partly from a new source of income – trade, both within the subcontinent and with distant places in Central Asia, China, the eastern Mediterranean, and South-east Asia.

There were a number of incursions into India from foreign states during the next two centuries. The Bactrian king, Demetrius (reigned c.190–c.167 BCE), took his armies into the Punjab and finally down the Indus valley, gaining control of north-western India and introducing a period of Indo-Greek rule. The Scythians, known in Indian sources as the Shakas, attacked the kingdom of Bactria and subsequently moved into India, sweeping through Parthia and into the Indus valley in the first century BCE. Kujula Kadphises, the Yuezhi chief, conquered northern India in the first century CE. He was succeeded by his son, Vima, after whom came Kanishka, the most powerful among the Kushan kings, as the dynasty came to be called. The Kushan kingdom was essentially oriented to the north, with its capital at Purusapura (near present-day Peshawar), although it extended southward as far as Sanchi and into the Ganges valley as far as Varanasi. Between the Indus and Ganges valleys, in Punjab and Rajasthan, there were also a number of oligarchies, or tribal republics – the Andhras in north-western Deccan, for instance – whose local importance rose and fell in inverse proportion to the rise and fall of larger kingdoms.

There was also contact between the north and the Tamil region, then centred on present-day Chennai. The three major chiefdoms of Tamilakam were those of the Pandya dynasty (Madurai), the Ceras (Cheras; Malabar Coast and the hinterland), and the Colas (Cholas; Thanjavur and the Kaveri valley), founders of the Cola dynasty. Ultimately all the chiefdoms suffered at the hands of the Kalvar, or Kalabras, who came from the border to the north of Tamilakam and were described as evil rulers. They were overthrown in the fifth century CE with the rise of the Calukya (Chalukyas) and

Pallava dynasties. Trade with the northern parts of the sub-continent provided considerable economic momentum for the southern Indian states.

In addition, trade increased beyond Indian shores. Unification of the Mediterranean and western Asian world at the turn of the first century CE under the Roman Empire brought Roman trade into close contact with India – overland with northern India and by sea with peninsular India. The route connecting China with Bactria via Central Asia, which would shortly become famous as the Silk Road, linked the oases of Kashgar, Yarkand, Khotan, Miran, Kucha, Karashahr, and Turfan, in all of which Indian merchants established trading stations. The Central Asian route brought Chinese goods in large quantities into the Indian and western Asian markets. It is thought that the prosperity resulting from this trade enabled the Kushans to issue the first Indian gold coins. Another consequence was the popularity of horsemanship.

The Gupta period (c.320–540) was once regarded as the classical age of India, the period during which the norms of Indian literature, art, architecture, and philosophy were established. The Guptas, a comparatively unknown family from Magadha or eastern Uttar Pradesh, through conquest over some decades came to rule over the northern half and central parts of the subcontinent, in addition to Nepal and Sinhala (Sri Lanka). By the mid-sixth century, however, when the Gupta dynasty apparently came to an end, northern India and parts of central India were in the hands of the Hunas. The Guptas by then held just Kashmir and Punjab, while a number of smaller kingdoms arose as inheritors of Gupta territories. At the same time, a number of Central Asian tribes migrated into India.

The political pattern of this time reveals a rebirth of re-gionalism and of new political and economic structures. In the eighth century the rising power in western India was that of the

Gurjara-Pratiharas. The Tomara Rajputs (Tomara dynasty), originally their feudatories, founded the city of Dhillika (modern Delhi) in 736. A new power base was also established briefly with the arrival of the Arabs in Sind, who by 724 had established direct rule, with a governor representing the Muslim caliph.

In the Deccan there was a succcession of ruling families, from the Vakataka dynasty in the fourth century to the Calukyas (Chalukyas) whose power reached its zenith during the reign of Pulakeshin II (610–42). It was he who established good relations with the Persians, which later led to persecuted Zoroastrians seeking asylum in India and settling in the Deccan; their descendants today constitute the Parsi community.

The southern part of the peninsula split into many kingdoms, each fighting for supremacy. Cera power relied mainly on a flourishing trade with western Asia. The Colas retired into insignificance in the Uraiyur (Tiruchchirappalli) area. The Pandyas were involved in fighting the rising power of the Pallavas, and occasionally they formed alliances with the Deccan kingdoms.

During this period Buddhist temples and monasteries became larger and more complex, and the decorative arts of mural painting and sculpture flourished. Early examples of mural painting occur at Bagh and Sittanvasal (now in Tamil Nadu), and the tradition reached its apogee in the murals at the Ajanta Caves (Maharashtra) during the Vakataka and Calukya periods. There was also a flowering of classical Sanskrit and Tamil literature. A less common genre of literature in the Gupta period was the *Kama-sutra* of Vatsyayana, a manual on the art of love. This was a collation and revision of earlier texts and displays a remarkable sophistication and urbanity. Mathematics and astronomy were probably more advanced than anywhere in the world at the time; Indian numerals were later borrowed by the Arabs and introduced to Europe as Arabic numerals.

The eighth and ninth centuries were a time of struggle for control over the central Ganges valley among the Gurjara-Pratihara, the Rashtrakuta, and the Pala dynasties. Sporadic campaigns against the Pratiharas, the Eastern Calukyas, and the Colas (the new power of the south) continued, and at the end of the tenth century the Later Calukyas clashed with the ambitious Colas. Campaigns between the two dynasties would continue until the twelfth century. In the eleventh century the Colas were to become by far the most important dynasty in the subcontinent, controlling the Maldive Islands, the Malabar Coast, and northern Sri Lanka, all of which were essential for trade with Southeast Asia, Arabia and eastern Africa. Later they campaigned along the east coast as far as Bengal and then north to the Ganges river. Meanwhile, in Rajasthan and central India there arose a number of small kingdoms ruled by dynasties that came to be called the Rajputs (from Sanskrit *raja-putra*, "son of a king").

The twelfth and thirteenth centuries saw a gradual decline in Cola power, accelerated by the rise of the Hoysalas to the west and the Pandyas to the south. The dynasty left a legacy of bronze sculpture, mainly of Shaiva and Vaishnava deities and saints, the severe beauty and elegance of which remains unsurpassed. Also of note was a new genre of painting that rose to popularity in Nepal, eastern India, and Gujarat: the illustration of Buddhist and Jain manuscripts with miniature paintings.

The early Muslim period

The first Muslim raids in the subcontinent were made by Arabs on the western coast and in Sind during the seventh and eighth centuries, and there had been Muslim trading communities in India at least since that time. The significant and permanent military movement of Muslims into northern India, however, dates from the late twelfth century, when the Ghurid Turks, led by Muhammad of Ghur, invaded northern India.

The conquest of the Rajputs was not easy, and they suffered a number of defeats, but by the beginning of the thirteenth century Muhammad's slave and lieutenant, Qutb al-Din Aybak, was in control of Varanasi, Badaun, Kannauj, and Kalinjar, as well as Delhi. Although there was a setback in 1205 and a short-lived rebellion by some of the sultan's followers in the Punjab, by his death in 1210 Qutb al-Din had managed to establish the foundation of an Indian Muslim state.

Iltutmish, Qutb al-Din's successor, was faced with three problems: defence of his western frontier, control over the Muslim nobles within India, and subjugation of the many Hindu chiefs who still exercised a large measure of independent rule. His relative success in all three areas gives him claim to the title of founder of the independent Delhi sultanate. By 1236, the year Iltutmish died, the Delhi sultanate was established as the largest and most powerful of a number of competing states in north India. After his death, the new state survived severe factional disputes. The period was characterized by almost continuous struggles to maintain Delhi's position against the revived power of the Hindu chiefs (principally Rajputs), and by vigilance against the strife-ridden but dangerous Mongols in the west.

During succeeding years, the sultans continually campaigned against the Hindu chiefs, seeking to establish their dominance over Indian territory. Following Balban, who had assumed the sultanate in 1266 and consolidated Turkish rule, the sultans undertook a number of successful expansionist campaigns. During the reign of 'Ala' al-Din Khalji, the sultanate briefly assumed the status of an empire, extorting heavy agrarian and land taxes and using plunder from 'Ala' al-Din's victories for his state-building plans and to purchase the support of disaffected Turkish nobles. His successful campaigns in Rajasthan opened the way for further raids into south India. He was also one of the first rulers to extend limited political participation to the non-Turkish Muslim nobility and to Hindus.

During the late thirteenth and early fourteenth centuries the economy flourished, and Delhi became one of the largest cities in the whole of the Islamic world. Bengal and Gujarat developed into centres of fabric production. The production of paper gave rise to increased record keeping in government offices and to widespread use of bills of exchange (*hundis*). Horses were imported in large numbers to supply the cavalry. The unification of the Central Asian steppes opened up a new and secure trade route from India to China and the Black Sea.

Within five years of 'Ala' al-Din's death (1316), the Khaljis lost their power. Muhammad ibn Tughluq took control in 1325, and within ten years there were few places in the subcontinent where the sultan's authority could be seriously challenged. But by his death in 1351, southern India had been lost and much of the north was in rebellion. Uprisings by Hindu chiefs resulted in the formation of several new states. The former rural elite began to reappear, and the Rajputs claimed power and perquisites, at least at the local level.

Muhammad ibn Tughluq's successor, Firuz Tughluq (reigned 1351–88), built an army from among the huge corps of slaves (*mamluks*) plundered from throughout the sultanate, but by his death in 1388 the decline of the sultanate was imminent; subsequent succession disputes and palace intrigues only accelerated its pace. By the time Timur (the Tamerlane of western literature) invaded India in 1398, Gujarat had declared independence. Already in possession of a vast empire in the Middle East and Central Asia, Timur sacked Delhi, apparently ordering the execution of at least 50,000 captives before the battle and removing practically everything of value – including those inhabitants who were not killed.

During the fifteenth and early sixteenth centuries, no paramount power enjoyed effective control over most of north India and Bengal. Delhi became merely one of the regional principalities of north India, competing with the emerging Rajput and Muslim states.

In southern India, sultanate forces had been compelled to withdraw from the Deccan between 1330 and 1347, as Hindu chiefs and some Muslim nobles established several rebel principalities and the two strongest states of the south: the Muslim-ruled Bahmani kingdom and the Hindu-ruled Vijayanagar Empire. The Bahmani Muhammad Shah I (reigned 1358–75) began a struggle with Vijayanagar that was to outlast the Bahmani sultanate and continue, as a many-sided conflict, into the seventeenth century.

The Bahmani state, which saw the immigration of large numbers of Arabs, Turks, and particularly Persians, was torn by rivalries between the old guard from Deccan and the newcomers. Temporary alliances formed, giving rise to five successor states to the sultanate. The Hindu Vijayanagar Empire, founded in 1336, was the dominant power in south India for two centuries, but after 1446, when the centralized power of the state declined, a considerable amount of territory along both coasts was lost to the Bahmani and to the suddenly powerful Gajapati ruler of Orissa. Beginning in 1470, the Bahmanis, under the vizier Mahmud Gawan, began a campaign that succeeded in taking much of the west coast and the northern Karnataka from Vijayanagar. Saluva Narasimha (reigned 1485–90), a former Vijayanagar general, regained some of the territories and by 1485 had put together a large dominion under his independent control. His successor, his chief minister, Narasa Nayaka, campaigned in the south to restore effective control, and during the reign of his son Krishna Deva Raya (reigned 1509–29), generally regarded as the greatest of the Vijayanagar kings, the kingdom became more powerful than ever before, internal consolidation reached a new peak, and large parts of Orissa were conquered.

In the late 1530s a power struggle in Vijayanagar precipitated civil war, with Rama Raya, the former chief minister, eventually assuming control. It is likely that the sultans of Golconda and Ahmadnagar, two of the strongest and best organized of the Bahmani successor states (who had lost much at the hands of Rama Raya), were primarily responsible for the formation of an alliance that destroyed Vijayanagar's power forever. A temporary but fruitful coalition among the Bahmani successor states resulted in the crushing defeat of Vijayanagar's powerful forces at the Battle of Talikota in 1565 which, though it did not destroy the Hindu kingdom, ultimately helped the expansionist ambitions of Bijapur and Golconda.

During the battle Rama Raya was captured and killed, but his brother Tirumala escaped; in 1570 he had himself crowned, thus establishing the fourth and last dynasty of the Vijayanagar. However, much of the south and south-east had been lost, and rebellions and banditry arose in many areas. Rulers of the fourth dynasty attempted to rebuild the kingdom; but although Venkata II (reigned 1585–1614) to some extent reestablished the dynasty, rivalries among the nobility, the murder of his successor, and civil war rapidly led to further deterioration of the state.

In the meantime, the Mughal Empire, already powerful in the north, had begun its southward expansion under Akbar (reigned 1556–1605) with a successful onslaught against Ahmadnagar. It was to end with the annexation of Bijapur (1686) and Golconda (1687), during the reign of Aurangzeb (reigned 1658–1707). By 1617, when surviving member of the Vijayanagar dynasty, Rama Deva Raya, finally ascended the throne, real political power resided at the level of chieftains and provincial governors, who were carving out their own principalities. The combined forces of Bijapur and Golconda, taking advantage of the state's decline, made advances into the kingdom. Venkata's nephew, Shriranga, at first sided with Bijapur against his uncle but hearing that his uncle was dying he deserted them and had himself crowned. While he originally held off opposing forces, in 1645 Bijapur and Golconda, with the blessings of the Mughal emperor at Delhi, defeated him. By 1652 the Muslim sultans had seized control.

The Mughal Empire, 1526–1761

The Mughal Empire at its zenith commanded resources unprecedented in Indian history, and covered almost the entire subcontinent. From 1556 to 1707, during the heyday of its fabulous wealth and glory, the Mughal Empire was a fairly efficient and centralized organization, with a vast complex of personnel, money, and information dedicated to the service of the emperor and his nobility. Much of the Empire's expansion was attributable to India's growing commercial and cultural contact with the outside world. The sixteenth and seventeenth centuries brought the establishment and expansion of European and non-European trading organizations in the subcontinent, principally for the procurement of Indian goods in demand abroad. Indian regions drew close to each other by means of an enhanced overland and coastal trading network.

New ideologies and technologies arrived to challenge and enrich the imperial edifice.

The Empire itself, however, was a purely Indian historical experience. Mughal culture blended Perso-Islamic and regional Indian elements into a distinctive but variegated whole. The individual abilities and achievements of the early Mughals – Babur, Humayun, and later Akbar – largely charted this course. The foundation of the Empire was laid in 1526 by Zahir al-Din Muhammad Babur, a Chagatai Turk, who in 1534 inherited his father's principality in Fergana at a young age. After conquering Kabul and Ghazni in 1504 and then Samarkand in 1511, he turned to the south-east toward India to have an empire of his own. As a Timurid, Babur had an eye on the Punjab, part of which had been Timur's possession.

Having secured the Punjab, Babur advanced toward Delhi, garnering support from many Delhi nobles. Babur's knowledge of western and central Asian war tactics and his brilliant leadership proved decisive. By April 1526 he was in control of Delhi and Agra, and held the keys to conquer Hindustan. In the following years, until his death in 1530, he continued to pursue his campaign against the Afghans, who held important towns in what is now eastern Uttar Pradesh and Bihar, and the Rajputs, crushing opposing forces near Fatehpur Sikri (March 1527), Chanderi, and (in 1529) at Ghagra, near Varanasi.

Babur's son, Humayun, became entangled in a quarrel with Sher (or Shir) Khan (later Sher Shah of Sur, founder of the Sur dynasty), the new leader of the Afghans in the east, and fought a series of unsuccessful battles against him – unable even to hold the lands he gained. Having lost control of Agra to his brother Hindal, he fled (July 1543) to Iran to seek military assistance from its ruler, but this was only promised if Humayun became a Shi'ite Muslim and agreed to return Kandahar to Iran in the event of his successful acquisition of that fortress. In the meantime, in Humayun's absence, Sher Shah had established a vast and powerful empire.

After Sher Shah's death in 1545 and then the death of his son, Islam Shah, in 1553, following which the Mughal Empire fractured into several parts, Humayan prepared to recover his throne. Following the capture of Kandahar and Kabul from his brothers, he had reasserted his unique royal position and in December 1554 he crossed the Indus river to regain the throne of Delhi after an interval of 12 years. He did not live long enough to recover the whole of the lost Empire.

Humayun's son Akbar (ruled 1556–1605) was proclaimed emperor amid gloomy circumstances. Delhi and Agra were threatened by Hemu (the Hindu general of the Sur ruler, 'Adil Shah) and Mughal governors were being driven from all parts of northern India. Akbar's hold over a fraction of the Punjab – the only territory in his possession – was disputed by Sikandar Sur and was precarious. There was also disloyalty among Akbar's own followers. The task before Akbar was to reconquer the Empire and consolidate it by ensuring control over its frontiers and, moreover, by providing it with a firm administrative machinery.

Until 1560 the administration of Akbar's truncated Empire was in the hands of his loyal regent, Bayram Khan. By the end of the regency the Mughal dominion embraced the whole of the Punjab, the territory of Delhi, what are now the states of Uttar Pradesh and Uttaranchal in the north (as far as Jaunpur in the east), and large tracts of what is now Rajasthan in the west. Akbar's marriage in 1562 to a Rajput princess, the daughter of Raja Bharmal of Amber, led to a firm alliance between the Mughals and the Rajputs. The same year, shaping his own policies but leaving them to be implemented by his agents, Akbar embarked on a policy of conquest. He established control over Jodhpur, Bhatha (present-day Rewa), and the Gakkhar country between the Indus and Beas rivers in the Punjab. Next he made inroads into Gondwana. He now commanded the entire area of Humayun's Indian possessions.

During this period he ended discrimination against the Hindus by abolishing pilgrimage taxes in 1563, and the hated poll tax on non-Muslims (*jizyah*) in 1564. By the mid-1560s he had also developed a new pattern of king-noble relationship that suited the current need of a centralized state to be defended by a nobility of diverse ethnic and religious groups. In order to strike a balance in the ruling class, he promoted the Persians (Irani), the Indian Muslims, and the Rajputs in the imperial service, placed eminent clan leaders in charge of frontier areas, and staffed the civil and finance departments with relatively new non-Turani recruits. The revolts in 1564–74 by the members of the old guard – the Uzbeks, the Mirzas, the Qaqshals, and the Atgah Khails – showed the intensity of their indignation over the change; Akbar crushed the opposition ruthlessly.

Rajasthan occupied a prominent place in Akbar's scheme of conquest; without establishing his suzerainty over that region, he would have no title to the sovereignty of northern India. The fall of Chitor, in February 1568, and then of Ranthambor (1569) brought almost all of Rajasthan under Akbar's suzerainty. Akbar's next objective was the conquest of Gujarat and Bengal, which had connected Hindustan with the trading world of Asia, Africa, and Europe. He conquered Gujarat, a haven of the refractory Mughal nobles, at his second attempt in 1573 and celebrated by building a victory gate, the lofty Buland Darwaza ("High Gate"), at his new capital, Fatehpur Sikri. The conquest of Gujarat pushed the Mughal Empire's frontiers to the sea, and by July 1576 he had brought the other gateway to his empire's international trade – namely, Bengal – under his firm control.

On the north-west frontier Kabul, Kandahar, and Ghazni were not simply strategically significant; these towns linked India through overland trade with central and western Asia and were crucial for securing horses for the Mughal cavalry. Akbar strengthened his grip over these outposts in the 1580s and 1590s. Further conquests in the east added Orissa, Cooch Behar, and a large part of Bengal, while Kathiawar, Asirgarh, and the northern territory of the Nizam Shahi kingdom of Ahmadnagar ensured a firm command over Gujarat and central India. At Akbar's death in October 1605, the Mughal Empire extended to the entire area north of the Godavari river, with the exceptions of Gondwana in central India and Assam in the north-east.

More than for its military victories, the Empire under Akbar is noted for a sound administrative framework and a coherent policy that gave the Mughal regime a firm footing and sustained it for about 150 years. Akbar's central government consisted of four departments, each presided over by a minister appointed, promoted, and dismissed by the emperor, and their duties were well defined. The Empire was divided into 15 provinces (*subahs*); each with a governor, a finance minister (*diwan*), a military commander (*bakhshi*), a religious administrator (*sadr*), and a judge (*qadi*) and agents who supplied information to the central government. Separation of powers among the various officials was a significant operating principle in imperial administration.

The recruitment of Hindu Rajput leaders into the Mughal nobility was also significant. The Rajputs were given high rank, pay, perquisites, and an assurance that they could retain their age-old customs, rituals, and beliefs as Hindu warriors, and in return they not only publicly expressed their allegiance but also offered active military service to the Mughals. Akbar thus obtained a wide base for Mughal power among thousands of Rajput warriors who controlled large and small parcels of the countryside throughout much of his empire. In order to organize his civil and military personnel, Akbar devised a system of ranks (*mansab*s); although they fell under the jurisdiction of the *mir bakhshi* (paymaster general), each owed direct subordination to the emperor.

A remarkable feature of the Mughal system under Akbar was his revenue administration. In 1580 he obtained the previous ten years' local revenue statistics and then demanded revenue of one-third to one-half of production value, payable in copper coin (*dam*s). The peasants thus had to enter the market and sell their produce in order to meet the assessment, and the new system encouraged rapid economic expansion. Akbar also reformed Mughal currency, aiming to establish a uniform coinage throughout his empire.

Mughal society was predominantly non-Muslim. Akbar therefore had not simply to maintain his status as a Muslim ruler but also to be liberal enough to elicit active support from non-Muslims. He abolished both the *jizyah* and the practice of forcibly converting prisoners of war to Islam, and encouraged Hindus as his principal confidants and policy makers. To legitimize his nonsectarian policies, he issued in 1579 a public edict (*mahzar*) declaring his right to be the supreme arbiter in Muslim religious matters. At his famous religious assembly at Fatehpur Sikri he threw open the meetings to non-Muslim religious experts and, convinced that there was truth in all faiths but that no one of them possessed absolute truth, disestablished Islam as the religion of the state and adopted a theory of rulership as a divine illumination incorporating the acceptance of all, irrespective of creed or sect. He repealed discriminatory laws and amended the personal laws of both Muslims and Hindus so as to provide as many common laws as possible. The emperor created a new order commonly called the Din-e Ilahi ("Divine Faith"), with the object of forging the diverse groups in the service of the state into one cohesive political community.

The Mughal Empire in the seventeenth century continued its conquest and territorial expansion, with a dramatic increase in the numbers, resources, and responsibilities of the Mughal nobles and *mansabdar*s (rank holders). There were also attempts at tightening imperial control over the local society and economy. These centralizing measures imposed increasing demands upon both the Mughal officials and the local magnates, and therefore generated tensions expressed in various forms of resistance. The century witnessed the rule of the three greatest Mughal emperors – Jahangir (ruled 1605–27), Shah Jahan (1628–58), and Aurangzeb (1658–1707) – but also saw the unmistakable symptoms of Mughal decline.

Political unification and the establishment of law and order over extensive areas, together with extensive foreign trade and the ostentatious lifestyles of the Mughal elites, encouraged the emergence of large centres of commerce and crafts. Lahore, Delhi, Agra, and Ahmedabad, linked by roads and waterways to other important towns and the key seaports, were among the leading cities of the world at the time. The Mughal system of taxation had expanded both the degree of monetization and commodity production, which in turn promoted a network of grain markets (*mandi*s), bazaars, and small fortified towns (*qasbah*s), supplied by a highly differentiated peasantry in the countryside.

Within a few months of his accession, Jahangir had to put down the rebellion of his eldest son, Khusraw, who was reportedly supported by, among others, the Sikh Guru Arjun. The subsequent execution of the Sikh Guru permanently estranged the Sikhs from the Mughals. Jahangir's most significant political achievement was the cessation of the Mughal-

Mewar conflict, following three consecutive campaigns and his own arrival in Ajmer in 1613. Prince Khurram (later Shah Jahan) was given supreme command of the army, and in 1615 Rana Amar Singh negotiated peace. Jahangir also subjugated the last Afghan domains in eastern Bengal (1612) and Orissa (1617).

There were also difficulties with the Deccan territories. Jahangir, backed by the local Marathas, had two successive Mughal victories against the combined Deccani armies (1618 and 1620). However, he was then compelled to turn his attention to the ploys of his queen, Nur Jahan, to secure the prince of her choice as successor and to the rebellion of Prince Khurram. In 1622 Shah 'Abbas I of Iran took Kandahar. Although Jahangir had sent Prince Khurram to relieve the fortress, the prince instead rebelled against his father.

After failing to take Fatehpur Sikri in April 1623, and under pursuit from Mahabat Khan who was deputed to subdue him, Prince Khurram retreated, submitted to his father unconditionally (1626), and was forgiven. The ordeal greatly impaired the emperor's health, and he died in November 1627. On his accession, Khurram assumed the title Shah Jahan. Shahryar, his younger and only surviving brother, had contested the throne but was soon blinded and imprisoned. Shah Jahan's father-in-law, Asaf Khan (appointed prime minister), was instructed to slay all other royal princes, the potential rivals for the throne.

Shah Jahan was, on the whole, a tolerant and enlightened ruler, patronizing scholars and poets of Sanskrit and Hindi as well as Persian, but his reign was marred by rebellions: first, that of Khan Jahan Lodi, governor of the Deccan, who was defeated in December 1629; then that of Jujhar Singh, a Hindu chief of Orchha in Bundelkhand, who commanded the crucial passage to the Deccan and was defeated and murdered in

1634. Seeking a comprehensive solution to the Deccan problem, Shan Jahan offered a military alliance to Bijapur, and after the total annihilation of Ahmadnagar, Bijapur was granted one-third of its southern territories. Bijapur agreed not to interfere with Golconda, which became a tacit ally of the Mughals. The treaty limited further Mughal advance in the Deccan and gave Bijapur and Golconda respite to conquer the warring Hindu principalities in the south. At the same time, the Mughals extended their eastern position on the Assamese border (1639) and also in Bengal.

In 1648 Shah Jahan moved his capital from Agra to Delhi in an effort to consolidate his control over the north-western provinces of the Empire. The Mughal attitude of benevolent neutrality toward the Deccan states now changed, culminating in the invasion of Golconda and Bijapur in 1656 and 1657. Bijapur was compelled to surrender the Ahmadnagar areas it had received in 1636, and Golconda was to cede to the Mughals the rich and fertile tract on the Coromandel Coast, now important as a centre for the export of textiles and indigo. Following in the footsteps of his predecessors, Shah Jahan also hoped to conquer Samarkand, the original homeland of his ancestors, and in 1646, responding to the Uzbek ruler's appeal for aid in settling an internal dispute, he sent a huge army to the north-west. The campaign cost the Mughals heavily, and an alliance between the Uzbeks and the shah of Iran complicated the situation. Kandahar was again taken by Iran, even though the Mughals reinforced their hold over the other frontier towns.

The events at the end of Shah Jahan's reign did not augur well for the future of the Empire. The emperor fell ill in September 1657, and rumours of his death spread. He executed a will bequeathing the Empire to his eldest son, Dara, but his other sons, Shuja', Aurangzeb, and Murad, decided to contest the throne. From the war of succession in 1657–59 Aurangzeb emerged the sole victor. He then imprisoned his father in the Agra fort (where he died in 1666), and declared himself emperor. Shah Jahan's remains were buried alongside those of his queen, Mumtaz Mahal, in the tomb he had built for her – the Taj Mahal, outside Agra.

The Empire under Aurangzeb experienced further growth but also manifested signs of weakness. For more than a decade, Aurangzeb appeared to be in full control. The Mughals suffered a bit in Assam and Cooch Behar, but they gainfully invaded Arakanese lands in coastal Myanmar (Burma), captured Chittagong, and added territories in Bikaner, Bundelkhand, Palamau, Assam, and elsewhere. Soon, however, regional disturbances again rocked the Empire: between 1669 and 1675 there were uprisings from Mathura, the tribal Pathans, the Satnami sect in Narnaul, and the Sikhs in the Punjab.

The most prolonged uprising, however, was the Rajput rebellion, sparked by Aurangzeb's annexation of the Jodhpur state and his seizure of its ruler's posthumous son, Ajit Singh, with the alleged intention of converting him to Islam. The war came to an end (June 1681) because Aurangzeb had to pursue the emperor's third son Akbar to the Deccan, where the prince had joined the Maratha king Sambhaji. Jodhpur remained in a state of rebellion for 27 years more, and Ajit Singh occupied his ancestral dominion immediately after Aurangzeb's death. Aurangzeb spent the last 25 years of his reign in the Deccan, fighting for control of his rebellious subjects. He annexed Bijapur (1686) and Golconda (1687), but Maratha resistance proved so stubborn that even after nearly two decades of struggle Aurangzeb failed to subdue them completely. The aged emperor died on March 3, 1707.

Aurangzeb had deliberately reversed the policy of his predecessors toward non-Muslim subjects by trying to enforce the principles and practices of the Islamic state. He reimposed the *jizyah* on non-Muslims and saddled them with religious, social, and legal disabilities, and forbade their building new temples. In the regions that experienced economic growth, the local power-mongers and their followers in the community felt increasingly confident to stand on their own. The abundant commissioning of *mansabdar*s with which the leadership addressed this situation far outstripped the Empire's growth in area or revenues. The Mughal centre thus began to collapse under its own weight. When Aurangzeb died, serious threats from the peripheries had begun to accentuate the problems at the core of the Empire, and in the eighteenth century the Mughal Empire gradually declined.

The new emperor, Bahadur Shah I (or Shah 'Alam; ruled 1707–12), followed a policy of compromise, pardoning all nobles who had supported his dead rivals and granting them appropriate postings. In the beginning he tried to gain greater control over the Rajput states of the rajas of Amber (later Jaipur) and Jodhpur but, when his attempt met with firm resistance, he realized the necessity of a settlement. Because Rajput demands for high *mansab*s and important governorships were never conceded, however, the settlement did not restore them to fully committed warriors for the Mughal cause. The emperor's policy toward the Marathas was also that of halfhearted conciliation. They continued to fight among themselves as well as against the Mughals in the Deccan.

There was also a Sikh challenge to Mughal royalty. After the death of the Guru Gobind Singh, the Sikhs raised the banner of revolt in the Punjab under the leadership of Banda Singh Bahadur. Practically the entire territory between the Sutlej and the Jamuna rivers, reaching the immediate vicinity of Delhi, was soon under the Sikhs, who were aided by the Himalayan Rajput chiefs. The imperial forces under Bahadur Shah captured some important Sikh strongholds but could not crush the movement; they only swept the Sikhs from the plains back into the Himalayan foothills. However, in 1715, during Farrukh-Siyar's reign, Banda Singh Bahadur and hundreds of his followers were captured by the governor of the Punjab. They were all executed in Delhi.

New elements now entered Mughal politics: ambitious nobles now became direct aspirants to the throne and regional aspirations became increasingly powerful. The leading contender to succeed Bahadur Shah was his second son, ʿAzim al-Shan, but Zulfiqar Khan (Dhu al-Fiqar Khan), a powerful Iranian noble who was the chief *bakhshi* of the Empire and the viceroy of the Deccan, assumed the executive direction of the Empire as imperial vizier by allying himself with Jahandar Shah, the most pliable of 'Azim's three brothers. Zulfiqar believed that it was necessary to establish friendly relations with the Rajputs and the Marathas, and to conciliate the Hindu chieftains in general in order to save the Empire. He reversed the policies of Aurangzeb. The hated *jizyah* was abolished. Zulfiqar Khan made several attempts at reforming the economic system but, in the brief course of his ascendancy, he could do little to redress imperial fiscal decay. When Farrukh-Siyar, son of the slain prince 'Azim al-Shan, challenged Jahandar Shah and Zulfiqar Khan with a large army and funds from Bihar and Bengal, the rulers found their coffers depleted. In desperation they looted their own palaces, even ripping gold and silver from the walls and ceilings, in order to finance an adequate army.

Farrukh-Siyar (ruled 1713–19) owed his victory and accession to the Sayyid brothers, ʿAbd Allah Khan and Husayn ʿAli

Khan Baraha, and they became vizier and chief *bakhshi* and acquired control over the affairs of state. They promoted the policies initiated earlier by Zulfiqar Khan. In addition to the *jizyah*, other similar taxes were abolished. The brothers finally suppressed the Sikh revolt and tried to conciliate the Rajputs, the Marathas, and the Jats. However, this policy was hampered by divisiveness between the vizier and the emperor, as the groups tended to ally themselves with one or the other. Finally, in 1719, the Sayyid brothers brought Ajit Singh of Jodhpur and a Maratha force to Delhi to depose the emperor.

The murder of Farrukh-Siyar created a wave of revulsion against the Sayyids among the various factions of nobility. In Farrukh-Siyar's place the brothers raised to the throne three young princes in quick succession within eight months in 1719. Two died of consumption, and the third, who assumed the title Muhammad Shah (ruled 1719–48), set about freeing himself from the brothers' control. However, although the Sayyid brothers were dislodged in 1720, individual interests of the nobles had come to guide the course of politics and state activities, and a succession of viziers were appointed with little involvement from the emperor. The nobles in control of the central offices maintained an all-Empire outlook, even if they were more concerned with the stability of the regions where they had their *jagir*s (assignments of land from which they could collect revenues). *Farman*s, (mandates granting certain rights or special privileges to *fowjdar*s (military officers whose duties roughly corresponded to those of a collector) and to other local officials were sent, in conformity with tradition, in the name of the emperor.

The steadily increasing vulnerability of the centre in the face of agrarian unrest, combined with the aforementioned irregularities, set in motion a new type of provincial government. Nobles with ability and strength sought to build a regional base for themselves. The vizier himself, Chin Qilich Khan, showed the path. Having failed to reform the administration, he relinquished his office in 1723, and in October 1724 marched south to found the state of Hyderabad in the Deccan. In the east, Murshid Quli Khan had long held Bengal and Orissa, which his family retained after his death in 1726. In the heartland of the Empire, the governors of Ayodhya and the Punjab became practically independent.

Seizing upon the disintegration of the Empire the Marathas now began their northward expansion, and overran Malwa, Gujarat, and Bundelkhand. Then, in 1738–39, Nadir Shah, who had established himself as the ruler of Iran, invaded India for plunder and spoil. Nadir captured Ghazni and Kabul, occupied Lahore virtually unopposed. With the faction-ridden nobles unable to agree on a strategy, he defeated the Mughals at the Battle of Karnal (February 1739), took the emperor Muhammad Shah prisoner, and marched to Delhi. The invader left Delhi in May laden with booty, including the famous Koh-i-noor diamond and the jewel-studded Peacock Throne of Shah Jahan. He compelled Muhammad Shah to cede to him the province of Kabul.

The Iranian invasion paralysed Muhammad Shah and his court. Maratha raids on Malwa, Gujarat, Bundelkhand, and the territory north of these provinces continued as before; Katehar (Rohilkhand) was seized by an adventurer, 'Ali Muhammad Khan Ruhela. The loss of Kabul opened the Empire to the threat of invasions from the north-west. The Punjab was again invaded, this time by Ahmad Shah Durrani (Abdali), an Afghan lieutenant of Nadir Shah's forces, who became king of Kabul after Nadir's death (June 1747). Ahmad Shah sacked Lahore and, even though a Delhi army compelled him to retreat, his repeated invasions eventually devastated the Empire.

Within the next 11 years after Muhammad Shah's death in April 1748, four princes ascended the Mughal throne. The period saw a fierce struggle between the Marathas and the Afghans for control over Delhi and northern India. The final battle, in which the forces of Ahmad Shah Durrani routed the Marathas, was fought near Panipat on January 14 1761. This defeat shattered the Maratha dream of controlling the Mughal court and thereby dominating the whole of the Empire. Durrani did not, however, found a new kingdom in India. The Afghans could not even retain the Punjab, where a regional confederation was emerging again under the Sikhs. With Shah 'Alam II away in Bihar, the throne in Delhi remained vacant from 1759 to 1771. During most of this period, the Afghan Najib al-Dawlah was in charge of the dwindling Empire, which was now effectively a regional kingdom of Delhi.

The rise of the regional states

The decline of Mughal central authority witnessed a resurgence of regional identity that promoted both political and economic decentralization, and prepared the way for the future dominance of British imperial power. The single most important power to emerge was the Maratha confederacy. Initially deriving from the western Deccan, the Marathas were a peasant warrior group that rose to prominence during the rule in that region of the sultans of Bijapur and Ahmadnagar. In the reign of Shahu (1708-49), the Citpavan Brahman *peshwa* (chief minister) virtually came to control central authority in the Maratha state. By the close of his reign, they had developed sophisticated networks of trade, banking, and finance throughout their territories and had access to the

Angria clan's fleet of vessels on the west coast. These ships posed a threat not only to the new English settlement of Bombay (Mumbai), but to the Portuguese at Goa, Bassein, and Daman.

There also emerged a far larger domain of activity away from the original heartland of the Marathas, which was either subjected to raiding or given over to subordinate chiefs. Of these chiefs, the most important were the Gaekwads (Gaikwars), the Sindhias, and the Holkars. The role of the Gaekwads, who came to prominence in the 1720s with the incursions of Damaji and Pilaji Gaekwad into Gujarat, was largely confined to the collection of the *cauth* levy. By the early 1750s, the rights of the family to an extensive portion of the revenues of Gujarat were recognized. In the late 1770s and early 1780s Fateh Singh (ruled 1771–89) negotiated a settlement with the English East India Company, which eventually led to increased British interference in his affairs. By 1800 the British were the final arbiters in determining succession among the Gaekwad, who became subordinate rulers under them in the nineteenth century.

From petty local power brokers, the Holkars emerged by the 1730s into a position in which Malhar Rao Holkar could be granted a large share of the *cauth* collection in Malwa, eastern Gujarat, and Khandesh. Within a few years, Malhar Rao consolidated his own principality at Indore, from which his successors controlled important trade routes as well as the crucial trading centre of Burhanpur. After him, control of the dynastic fortunes fell largely to his son's widow, Ahalya Bai, who ruled from 1765 to 1794 and brought Holkar power to its apogee.

The Sindhias, based largely in central India, carved a prominent place for themselves in north Indian politics during the long reign of Mahadaji Sindhia (1761–94). Mahadaji, an effective and innovative military commander, intervened in the Mughal court during the reign of Shah ʿAlam II, who made him the "deputy regent" of his affairs in the mid-1780s. His shadow fell not only across the provinces of Delhi and Agra but also on Rajasthan and Gujarat, making him the most formidable Maratha leader of the era. The momentum generated by Mahadaji could not be maintained, however, and his successor was defeated by the British and forced under the Treaty of Surji-Arjungaon (1803) to surrender his territories both to the north and to the west.

The origins of the Sikhs lie in the Punjab in the fifteenth century with Guru Nanak (1469–1539), a wandering preacher who settled at Kartarpur in the Punjab. The last of the Gurus, Gobind Singh (1675–1708), gave battle to Mughal forces, and after his death the Sikh threat to Mughal dominance increased. In the 1720s and 1730s, when Amritsar emerged as a centre of Sikh activity, Kapur Singh, the most important of the Sikh leaders of the time, operated from its vicinity and gradually set about consolidating a revenue-cum-military system. By the mid-1760s Sikh authority over Lahore had been established, and within a decade there was a confederation of about 60 Sikh chieftains, some of whom founded what were to remain princely states under the British – such as Nabha and Patiala. One chief, Ranjit Singh, eventually welded these principalities into a larger entity, centred on Lahore, which he captured in 1799. His rule lasted four decades, to 1839, and was realized in a context already dominated by the growing power of the English East India Company. Having gained control of the trade routes, he imposed monopolies on the trade in salt, grain, and textiles from Kashmir to enhance his revenues. He used the cash raised to build up an army of 40,000 cavalry and infantry, and by 1809 he was undisputed master of most of Punjab. Within ten years of his death, the British had annexed Punjab.

Such relatively ephemeral successes at state building as that of Ranjit Singh are rare. In the north, consolidation of power in Rajasthan in the eighteenth century was rapidly followed by reversal. From the sixteenth century the Kachwahas had controlled the Rajput prinicipality of Jaipur, under the Mughals. In the early eighteenth century the ruler Jai Singh Sawai took steps to greatly increase his power by arranging to have his *jagir* assignment in his home territories, and by taking on parcels of land in which the tax rights were initially rented from the state and then gradually made permanent. By the time of his death in 1743, Jai Singh (for whom Jaipur came to be named) had emerged as the single most important Rajput ruler. In the 1750s Suraj Mal adopted a modified form of Mughal revenue administration, but the Jaipur kingdom came under threat from the Marathas. Recourse had to be taken more and more to short-term fiscal exactions, a series of crop failures produced an economic depression, and Jaipur's political power declined.

In south India several states made a determined bid in this period to consolidate their power by the use of maritime outlets. Principal among these were Travancore in Kerala under Martanda Varma and Rama Varma, and Mysore under Hyder Ali and Tippu Sultan. In the southern Kerala state of Venad (Travancore), Martanda Varma (ruled 1729–58) built a substantial standing army of about 50,000, reduced the power of the Nayar aristocracy on which rulers of the area had earlier been dependent militarily, and fortified the northern limits of his kingdom at the so-called "Travancore line." He also extended patronage to the Syrian Christians, a large trading community within his domains, as a means of limiting European involvement in trade. These policies were continued in large measure by Martanda's successor, Rama Varma (ruled 1758–98), who was able, moreover, to defend his kingdom successfully against a dangerous new rival power – Mysore.

The rise of Mysore to importance dates to the mid-seventeenth century, when rulers of the Vadiyar dynasty extended their control to parts of what is now interior Tamil Nadu. Until the second half of the eighteenth century, however, Mysore was a landlocked kingdom dependent on trade and military supplies brought through the ports of the Indian east coast. As these ports came increasingly under European control, Mysore's vulnerability increased. Then Hyder Ali (who assumed effective power in 1761), and, after 1782, his son, Tippu Sultan, made attempts to consolidate Mysore and make it a kingdom with access to both coasts of peninsular India. Coastal Karnataka and northern Kerala came under their sway, enabling Tippu to open diplomatic and commercial relations on his own account with the Middle East. Tippu's ambitions greatly exceeded those of his father, but by the 1770s Mysore faced a formidable military adversary in the form of the English East India Company. It was the English who denied Mysore access to the relatively rich agricultural lands and ports of the Coromandel coastal plain in eastern India and, equally as significant, it was at the hands of an English attacking force that Tippu was killed in 1799 during the fourth of the Mysore Wars.

3

EUROPEAN EXPANSION AND
BRITISH IMPERIAL POWER (1750–1947)

Early European expansion

The year 1765, when Robert Clive (later 1st Baron Clive of Plassey) arrived in India, can be said to mark the real beginning of the British Empire in India as a territorial dominion. By the year 1857 the British would have complete political control of the Indian subcontinent. Eventually they did more to transform India than did any previous ruling power. Yet, the onset of British influence in India differed from that of other historical invasions. The British came neither as migrating hordes seeking new homes nor, originally, as armies seeking plunder or empire.

Neither was the regime that Clive established a British colony. It was really a private dominion of the English East India Company, and it fitted into the highly flexible structure of the dying Mughal Empire. The structure of the administration was Mughal, not British, and its operators were Indian, personified by the deputy *nawab* Muhammad Rida Khan. It was in fact a continuation of the traditional state under British control.

The origins of British India can be traced to the growth of European influence from the fifteenth century when the Portuguese navigator Vasco da Gama landed at Calicut (now Kozhikode) in 1498. Over the next two centuries, navigating European powers – first the Portuguese and then, when they lost control of the route to the East in the late sixteenth century, the Dutch and the English – established their empires there to exploit the spice trade. They made their bases in the East Indies (Indonesia), at Goa in western India, in southern India and Ceylon (Sri Lanka).

The European powers fought for control of the eastern seas. For a while, in the fifteenth century, the Dutch held sway, ousting the Portuguese from most strongholds – although the Portuguese retained their capital, Goa (they did not cede the area to India until 1961) – and virtually excluding the English from the East Indies. The Dutch East India Company instituted a triangular trade, buying the textiles needed to purchase spices in Indonesia from India and China. The English likewise traded through the (English) East India Company, which received its monopoly rights of trade in 1600. Then, in the seventeenth century, the English secured the right from the Mughal court to trade and to establish factories in return for becoming the virtual naval auxiliaries of the Mughal Empire. In 1708–09 the company was reestablished under the name of the United Company of Merchants of England Trading to the East Indies, and trade expanded. Madras (now Chennai) and Gujarat supplied cotton goods, and Gujarat supplied indigo as well; silk, sugar, and saltpetre (for gunpowder) came from Bengal, while there was a spice trade along the Malabar Coast from 1615 on a competitive basis with the Dutch and Portuguese. Opium was shipped to East Asia, where it later became the basis of the Anglo-Chinese tea trade. Fortified factories (trading houses) were established, and by the end of the seventeenth century the company had three centres of Indian power, at Bombay (now Mumbai), Madras, and Calcutta (now Kolkata).

The French East India Company, launched in 1664, acquired Pondicherry (now Puducherry), in 1674 and Chandernagore (now Chandannagar), in 1690–92, and began to prosper. Although it encountered a setback when it lost territory and trade to the Dutch, its trade expanded in the eighteenth century and new stations were opened. Other enterprises in India included a Danish East India Company, which operated intermittently from 1616, and the Ostend Company of Austrian Netherlands merchants from 1723, a serious rival until eliminated by diplomatic means in 1731.

Each enterprise was trading peaceably, until the War of the Austrian Succession in Europe precipitated an Anglo-French struggle in India resulting in the Treaty of Aix-la-Chapelle (1748). Madras was now recognized as British, and this was accepted by one of the rival Indian chiefs. A secondary dispute in Hyderabad, after the nizam there died, saw the French placing the late nizam's third son, Salabat Jang, on the Hyderabad throne, with Frenchman Charles, Marquis de Bussy-Castelnau beside him using the revenues of the Northern Sarkars (six coastal districts) to support his army.

The British response to this was to support for the Carnatic nawabship the late *nawab*'s son, Muhammad 'Ali, who had taken refuge at Trichinopoly (now Tiruchchirappalli). The French supported Chanda Sahib for the nawabship. There thus developed what was really a private war between the two companies. In 1751 Robert Clive, a discontented young British factor who had left the countinghouse for the field, seized the fort of Arcot, political capital of the Carnatic. This daring stroke had the hoped-for effect of diverting half of Chanda Sahib's army to its recovery. Clive's successful 50-day defence permitted Muhammad 'Ali to procure allies from Tanjore and the Marathas. The French were worsted, and they were eventually forced to surrender in June 1752.

The respite was brief. When the Seven Years' War broke out in Europe in 1756, in which Britain and France were once more on opposite sides, both sides sent armaments to the East. The first British force was diverted to Bengal, so that the French general Thomas-Arthur Lally had an advantage on his arrival in 1758. But Lally's attack on Madras (1758–59) miscarried, and when Sir Eyre Coote arrived with reinforcements, the British defeated Lally decisively. Lally retreated to Pondicherry where, after an eight-month siege made tense by bitter recrimination, he surrendered in January 1761.

Meantime, Clive was occupied with revolution in Bengal. Succession troubles there had combined with British mercantile incompetence to produce a crisis. The *nawab* and virtual ruler of Bengal died in April 1756, leaving his power to his young grandson Siraj al-Dawlah, who was both headstrong and vacillating. On an exaggerated report that the British were fortifying Calcutta, he attacked and took the city after a four-day siege, on June 20 1756. The flight of the British governor and several councillors added ignominy to defeat. The survivors were held for a night in the local lockup, known as the Black Hole of Calcutta; many were dead the next morning. News of this disaster caused consternation among the British, and forces were diverted to Clive, giving him an army of 900 Europeans and 1,500 Indians. He relieved the Calcutta survivors and recovered the city on January 2 1757. An indecisive engagement led to a treaty with Siraj al-Dawlah on February 9, which restored the company's privileges, gave permission to fortify Calcutta, and declared an alliance.

This was a decisive point in British Indian history. According to plan, Clive should have returned to Madras to pursue the campaign against the French; but he did not. He sensed both the hostility and insecurity of Siraj al-Dawlah's position and began to receive overtures to support a military coup. Intent on installing a friendly and dependent *nawab*, Clive chose Mir Ja'far, an elderly general with much influence in the army. The conflict with Siraj al-Dawlah at Plassey (June 23 1757) was followed by the flight and execution of Siraj al-Dawlah; the occupation of Murshidabad, the capital; and the installation of Mir Ja'far as the new *nawab*. Clive now controlled a sponsored state, and this would eventually evolve into a virtually annexed state by 1765.

By the time Clive left Calcutta on February 25 1760, at the height of his fame and aged only 34, the *nawab* was completely dependent on the British, to whose trade it seemed that the rich resources of Bengal were now open. However, two measures undermined the plan of a sponsored state, leading to the company's bankruptcy on the one hand and to the virtual annexation of Bengal on the other. The first of these was an understanding with Mir Ja'far that personal domestic trade (trade within India) of company employees would be exempted from the usual tolls and customs duties. This was a fiscal disaster: local Indian traders were soon unable to compete against rivals with such an advantage, and the company itself was soon out-positioned by its own employees, many of whom employed agents who used the British name to terrorize the countryside and infringe on the company's monopoly. The second measure was the acceptance of gifts. Though not forbidden by the company, this opened the floodgates of corruption. On the strength of rumours regarding the vast sum of the Murshidabad treasury – which later proved to be hugely exaggerated, so that the *nawab* had to sell jewels, goods, and furniture to meet his obligations – large amounts were paid to the armed forces and to the company leaders following the city's capitulation. In addition, Clive obtained a further Mughal title and then claimed a *jagir* for its upkeep. The company's directors in London, with relatives and connections on the spot, preferred verbal denunciations to any resolute or sustained action.

The departure of Clive signalled the release of acquisitive urges by the company's Bengal servants, who suddenly found themselves with real but undefined authority over the whole of a large and rich province. The governor, Henry Vansittart (served 1760–64), was unable to control them. The first step was to supplant the *nawab* Mir Ja'far on the grounds of old age and incompetence with his son-in-law, Mir Qasim, after the latter had paid a large gratuity to the company and to Vansittart personally. He also ceded to the British the districts of Burdwan, Midnapore, and Chittagong. Both sides wanted power, and both sides were short of money. The *nawab* had lost substantial land revenue and the lucrative tolls on the British merchants' private trade; the company was receiving no remittances from Britain, because the directors considered that Bengal should pay for itself. A clash was inevitable.

Mir Qasim removed his capital to distant Monghyr where he could not be so easily overseen, asserted his authority in the districts, and raised a disciplined force. He then negotiated a settlement with Vansittart, by which the company's merchants were to pay an *ad valorem* duty of 9 per cent, against an Indian merchant's duty of 40 per cent. The Calcutta council revolted, reducing the company's duty to 2.5 per cent and on salt only. The breach came in 1763 when Mir Qasim, after defeat in four pitched battles, murdered his Indian bankers and British prisoners and fled to Avadh. The next year Mir Qasim returned with the emperor Shah 'Alam II and his minister

Shuja' al-Dawlah to be finally defeated at the Battle of Buxar (Baksar). That conflict, rather than Plassey, was the decisive battle that gave Bengal to the British.

These events had been viewed with growing alarm in London. Clive, having appointed himself governor, arrived back in India in May 1765 to find Mir Ja'far restored to power and British merchants and their agents the unresisted predators of the Bengal economy.

Within four days of arrival he had set up a Select Committee; and, when he left less than two years later, he had effected another revolution. He fixed his frontier at the borders of Bihar and Avadh. Shah 'Alam was given the districts of Kora and Allahabad, and Shuja' al-Dawlah received back Avadh, with a guarantee of its security, in return for paying the troops involved and a cash indemnity. These two were to be buffers between the company and the Marathas and possible marauders from the north. The actual administration remained in Indian hands, but the company, acting in the name of the emperor and using Indian personnel and the traditional apparatus of government, now ruled Bengal.

Within the company, Clive enforced his authority by accepting some resignations and enforcing others. Gifts were restricted to those worth less than 4,000 rupees and then only allowed with official consent. Clive formed a Society of Trade, which operated the salt monopoly, to provide salaries on a graduated scale; but two years later the company directors replaced this by commissions on the revenue. Finally, Clive dealt with overgrown military allowances, and used a legacy from Mir Ja'far to start a pension fund for the Indian army. The structure of the administration which he established continued in essence until the early nineteenth century.

The East India Company

When Warren Hastings became governor of Bengal in 1772, he instituted a period of reform. Corruption had crept in again, and his first step was to abolish the free passes (*dastak*s) and to introduce a tariff of 2.5 per cent on all internal trade. Private trade by the company's servants continued, but within enforceable limits. He substituted British for Indian collectors working under a Board of Revenue, which allowed any irregularities to be more easily dealt with. Finally, Hastings instituted a network of civil and criminal courts in place of the deputy *nawab*'s. But Hastings' reforms were too late to avoid state intervention.

The return to Britain of the East India Company's servants with lavish fortunes had had two results: shareholders demanded increased dividends, and the directors saw the necessity of disciplining its servants in order to secure some profit for the company. The close personal connection between the "direction" and the company's servants themselves, however, stultified the directors' efforts, as employees dismissed for irregularities by one faction were reinstated by another. Meanwhile, the increase in dividends brought the company to the brink of bankruptcy. In 1772 the company's request for a loan to avert bankruptcy provoked parliamentary opposition, and subsequent committees of inquiry revealed malpractices. The British government gave a substantial loan, but its price was the Regulating Act (1773), which controlled directors' terms of engagement and ended the soliciting of votes for the control of policy by private interests. The governor-generalship of Fort William in Bengal was established, with supervisory control over the other Indian settlements and Warren Hastings as its first incumbent.

Hastings was given four named councillors, but future appointments were to be made by the company, and the governor-general possessed no veto in his council. This led to Hastings' virtual supersession by the majority for two years. Hastings used the energy in fighting his council that should have gone to reforming Bengal. The conviction and hanging of an Indian official, Nand Kumar (Nandakumar), for perjury – an offence not recognized as being capital in any Indian code – by a supreme court that had decided to administer English law not only to all the British in Bengal but also to all Indians connected with them, also exposed the moral weakness of the council and convinced Indians of Hastings' overriding power.

Hastings' subsequent impeachment – for acts such as the dunning (demands for money) of Raja Chait Singh of Varanasi and his deposition in 1781 and the pressuring of the Begums of Avadh for the same reason – although it ended in his acquittal, served notice that the company's servants were responsible for their actions toward those they governed, and for these actions they were answerable to Parliament.

In 1784, Prime Minister William Pitt the Younger's India Act introduced dual control of British India. The directors were left in charge of commerce and as political executants, but they were politically superintended by a new Board of Control, the president of which, in the person of Henry Dundas, soon became the virtual minister for India. The directors dealt with the board through a secret committee of three, but their dispatches to India could be altered, vetoed, and dictated by the board. The governor-general could be recalled by the crown. In India the governor's council was reduced to three, including the commander in chief, and by an amending act he acquired the veto. Finally, there was to be a parliamentary inquiry before each 20-year renewal of the company's charter. In 1813 the company was deprived of its monopoly on trade. By the Act of 1833 it lost its trade altogether and was thenceforth a governing corporation under increasing state surveillance. The last case of the recall of a governor-general by the company was that of Lord Ellenborough in 1844; this was the real swan song of the company, because it was recognized that such a thing could never happen again. The company had become a managing agency of the British government.

For Hastings and succeeding governor-generals, a major role was to preserve the company's dominion. For several years in the late eighteenth century Hastings was involved in the Maratha Wars, first safeguarding Bengal from the reviving power of the Marathas in 1771 and then drawn into a succession struggle in Pune. In the 1780s he also found himself having to contain the Marathas' progress in the Carnatic. Pitt's Act of 1784 reiterated the company's own intentions by forbidding aggressive wars and annexations. Lord Cornwallis and his successor Sir John Shore (governor-general 1793–98) were eager to comply, but Cornwallis nevertheless found himself involved in the third Mysore war (1790–92) with Tippu Sultan.

There was now, however, a growing body of opinion that only British control of India could end the constant wars and provide really satisfactory conditions for trade; full dominion would be economical as well as salutary. A new French threat to India also emerged with Napoleon I's Egyptian expedition of 1798–99. The next governor-general, Lord Mornington (later Richard Colley Wellesley, Marquess Wellesley), combined the convictions of the imperialist group with a mandate to deal with the French. His term of office (1798–1805) was therefore a decisive period in the rise of the British dominion.

Wellesley decided first to strike at Mysore. The nizam, hard pressed by the Marathas, was persuaded to disband his contingent of French-trained troops in return for a promise of protection. This was the first of Wellesley's subsidiary treaties.

Next the British successfully stormed Tippu Sultan's forces at Seringapatam in May 1799. Wellesley tempered his imperialism with diplomacy by restoring the child head of the old Hindu reigning family as the ruler of half of Tippu Sultan's dominions; the other half was divided between the nizam and the company. In the next three years Wellesley used the subsidiary treaty – by which the company undertook to protect a state from external attack in return for control of its foreign relations (the company's forces being funded by means of a subsidy from the state, often commuted into ceding territory) – to subject independent states to British control. By this means he took over Carnatic territories, Tanjore (1799), the port city of Surat, and the Mughal successor state of Avadh in northern India, the latter of which had been in treaty relationship with the company since 1765.

Wellesley next turned to the Marathas – one of the few remaining bastions of Indian independence. Under the Treaty of Bassein (December 31 1802), British troops were stationed at Pune, at the price of a cession of territory, and the *peshwa* was reduced to dependency on the British. This action provoked the Second Maratha War. Although the British at first won resounding victories, they were later forced to retreat, and Delhi was besieged. Wellesley was recalled.

During the next ten years Lord Minto (governor-general 1807–13) was occupied with the revived French danger, which was once again serious with the Treaty of Tilsit (1807) and Napoleon I's resulting alliance with Russia. A British mission to Ranjit Singh, the Sikh ruler of the Punjab, resulted in the Treaty of Amritsar (1809) and defined British and Sikh spheres of influence and settled relations for a generation. The end of the Napoleonic Wars in 1815 opened a new era in India by strengthening the commercial and economic arguments for completing supremacy and by removing all fear of the French.

The final act was directed by Francis Rawdon-Hastings, 1st Marquess of Hastings (governor-general 1813–23). He first had to deal in 1814–16 with the Gurkhas of the northern kingdom of Nepal, who inflicted a series of defeats on a Bengal army unprepared for mountain warfare. The resulting Treaty of Segauli (1816) gave the British the tract of hill country where Shimla (Simla), the site of the future summer capital of British India, was situated, and it settled relations between Nepal and British India for the rest of the British period. Lord Hastings then turned to the Pindaris. Holkar's state was in disorder and was easily defeated. The East India Company was thus the undisputed master of India, as far as the Sutlej river in the Punjab. This episode was completed by the acceptance of British suzerainty by the Rajput chiefs of Rajasthan, central India, and Kathiawar. Thus, in the year 1818, the British Empire in India became the British Empire of India.

British India 1818–58

The diplomatic settlement of 1818, except for a few annexations before 1857, remained in force until 1947. Having controlled the larger states by its subsidiary forces (for which they paid), the East India Company was content with tribute from the remainder, with control posts at strategic points. About half of India remained under Indian rulers, robbed of any power of aggression and deprived of any opportunity of cooperation.

The realization of supremacy made urgent the problem of the organization of and determination of policy for British India. So far only Bengal had been deliberately organized; the extensive areas annexed after 1799 in the north and the south were still under provisional arrangements. The *peshwa*'s dominions in the west awaited settlement.

Lord Cornwallis had been charged by Pitt with the reorganization of Bengal under the new act, and set about establishing a new regime for the company under what came to be known as the Cornwallis Code. Discipline among the company's servants was enforced at the price of dismissal; private trade forbidden to all government officers; and the service was divided into administrative and commercial branches. A generous salary system removed the temptation to corruption.

Cornwallis also built up the Bengal system. Its first principle was Anglicization. All posts worth more than £500 a year were reserved for the company's covenanted servants. The 23 districts each had a British collector with magisterial powers and two assistants, who were responsible for revenue collection. The judicial system was organized with district judges for both civil and criminal cases. Criminal justice was taken over from the *nawab*'s deputy. A new police force replaced the former local constables of the *zamindar*s (superior landright holders). All governmental acts were answerable in the ordinary courts of law. Though hardly noticed at the time by Indians, this charter of civil – as distinct from political – liberty was a radical innovation with far-reaching effects.

Cornwallis's permanent settlement of the land revenue is the measure that most deeply affected the life and structure of Indian society, three-quarters of the revenue coming from the land. In 1793 he stabilized the revenue demand at a fixed annual figure, with a commission to the *zamindar* for collection; the *zamindar* was also regarded as the owner of his *zamindari* (land held by a *zamindar*). Thus, the land revenue collector became a landlord, with the Achilles' heel that the lands he administered could be sold for arrears, while the tiers of lesser landholders became his tenants and lost their occupancy rights.

At first the Bengal system was thought to provide the key to Indian administration, but doubts multiplied with the years. In Madras, Sir Thomas Munro introduced a radically differing method of revenue management, known as the *ryotwari* system, in which the settlement was made directly with the cultivator, each field being separately measured and annually assessed. In western India, Mountstuart Elphinstone retained Indian agency as far as possible and also used the *ryotwari* method of assessing land revenue. In the north, Sir Charles Metcalfe attempted to preserve the largely autonomous village with its joint ownership and cultivation by caste oligarchies that he found there.

The resulting system of administration of British India was still largely Indian in pattern, though it was now British in direction and superintendence. But there were also large changes. The British established the idea of property in land, and the resulting buying and selling caused large class changes. Their new security benefited the commercial classes, but the deliberate sacrifice of Indian industry to the claims of the new machine industries of Britain ruined such ancient crafts as cotton and silk weaving. The new legal system proved efficient on the criminal justice side, but was heavily overloaded on the civil. This created a demand for increased Indian agency and caused the first breaches in the British monopoly of higher office.

In the early nineteenth century a great debate went on in Britain about the nature of the government in India. While the company wanted India to be regarded as a field for British commercial exploitation, Whig voices, led by Edmund Burke, demanded that the Indian government must be responsible for the welfare of the governed. Evangelicals in England argued that Britain was responsible for India's spiritual and moral welfare and wanted English education instituted there. Radical rationalists wanted to introduce a doctrine of human rights into India. And a body of British merchants and manufacturers saw in India both a market and a profitable theatre of activity, and chafed at the restraints of the East India Company's monopoly.

The result of all this was that in 1813 the East India Company lost its monopoly of trade and was compelled to allow free entry of missionaries. British India was declared to be British territory, and money was to be set aside annually for the promotion of both eastern and western learning. But the real breakthrough came with the reforms under the governor-generalship of Lord William Bentinck (served 1828–35). In Bengal the collector was made the real head of his district by the addition of civil judgeship to his magistracy. The judiciary was also overhauled. Bentinck took the first steps in Indianizing the higher judicial services, while suppressing the ritual practices of *suttee* (in which a widow burns herself to death on the funeral pyre of her husband), child sacrifice (on Sagar Island in the Ganges delta), and ritual murder and robbery by gangs of thugs (*thagi*). He also substituted English for Persian as the language of record for government and the higher courts, and he declared that government support would be given primarily to the cultivation of western learning and science through the medium of English.

The place of the Indian states in British India was also subject to discussion. On the whole, the argument for sub-ordinate isolation held, and no great change occurred in their status until after the revolt of 1857. Out of the discussions, however, came the principle of British paramountcy, which was increasingly assumed though not openly proclaimed. The only important change before 1840 was the takeover of

Mysore in 1831 on the ground of misgovernment; it was not annexed, but it was administered on behalf of the raja for the next 50 years.

After the settlement of 1818, the only parts of India beyond British control were a fringe of Himalayan states to the north, the valley and hill tracts of Assam to the east, and a block of territory in the north-west covering the Indus valley, the Punjab, and Kashmir. Nepal and Bhutan remained nominally independent throughout the British period, though both eventually became British protectorates – Nepal in 1815 and Bhutan in 1866. Sikkim came under British protection in 1890; earlier it had ceded the hill station of Darjiling (Darjeeling) to the British. The valley and hill tracts of Assam were taken under protection to save them from attack by Burmans from Myanmar (Burma). After the Battle of Miani (1843), Sind was annexed to the Bombay Presidency. A sharp and bloody war in the Punjab after Ranjit Singh's death, when the state had fallen into disarray, ended with British victory at the Battle of Sobraon in February 1846. By the Treaty of Lahore the British took Kashmir and its dependencies, then sold it to the Hindu chief Gulab Singh of Jammu. Two years later another brief and still bloodier war ended with their surrender in March 1849 and the British annexation of the state.

By the year 1857 the British had thus established complete political control of India, which they ruled directly or through subordinate princes. The average Indian was far more secure than before (except for famine), but generally was not much more prosperous. From 1836 tea was grown in Assam, and coffee was cultivated in the south. Coal mining and the jute and cotton machine industries were begun. However, the East India Company, with its bias in favour of British merchants, had diverted trade from their Indian counterparts. The revenue figure fixed under the permanent settlement of 1793 was in many cases too high for the existing cultivation; by 1820 more than one-third of the estates had changed hands through sale for arrears of land tax.

While some Indians rejected all things western, others sought to incorporate in their own society anything that seemed desirable. Between the complete westernizers and the careerists was a third group, which found a leader of genius in Ram Mohun Roy. It advocated reforms in Hindu society, such as the banning of *suttee*; denounced idolatry and monotheism; and promoted the acceptance of some features of western thought and English education as a means of bringing western knowledge to India. Laying the foundations of a modernized Hinduism, its ideas would later find political expression in the Indian National Congress.

When soldiers of the Bengal army mutinied in Meerut on May 10 1857, tension had been growing for some time. The immediate cause of military disaffection was the deployment of the Enfield rifle, the cartridge of which was purportedly greased with pork and beef fat. When Muslim and Hindu troops learned that the tip of the Enfield cartridge had to be bitten off to prepare it for firing, a number of troops refused. These recalcitrant troops were placed in irons, but their comrades soon came to their rescue. They shot the British officers and made for Delhi, 40 miles (65 kilometres) distant, where there were no British troops. The Indian garrison at Delhi joined them, and by the next nightfall they had secured the city and Mughal fort, proclaiming the aged titular Mughal emperor, Bahadur Shah II, as their leader. There at a stroke was an army, a cause, and a national leader – the only Muslim who appealed to both Hindus and Muslims.

There were various underlying factors involved in turning what was initially a military mutiny into a popular revolt. The Bengal army of some 130,000 Indian troops may have contained as many as 40,000 Brahmans as well as many Rajputs. The British had accentuated caste consciousness by careful regulations, had allowed discipline to grow lax, and had failed to maintain understanding between British officers and their men. In addition, the General Service Enlistment Act of 1856 required recruits to serve overseas if ordered, a challenge to the castes who composed so much of the Bengal army. At the same time, the British garrison in Bengal had been reduced to 23,000 men because of troop withdrawals for the Crimean and Persian wars. In addition, the wars against the Afghans and the Sikhs and then the annexations of Dalhousie alarmed and outraged the Indian princes. Western innovations, such as the institution of English as the official language; interventions in Hindu customs, such as *suttee*; and the activity of Christian missionaries were widely resented.

The dramatic capture of Delhi turned mutiny into full-scale revolt. From Delhi the revolt spread to Kanpur (Cawnpore) and Lucknow. The surrender of Kanpur, after a relatively brief siege, was followed by a massacre of virtually all British citizens and loyal Indian soldiers. The Lucknow garrison held out in the residency from July 1. The campaign then settled down to British attempts to take Delhi and relieve Lucknow. Some 10,000 British troops, supported by Sikhs hostile to the Muslims, stormed and captured Delhi on September 20.

Five days later, Sir Henry Havelock fought through Kanpur to the Lucknow residency, where he was besieged in turn. But the back of the rebellion had been broken and time gained for reinforcements to restore British superiority. There followed the relief of the residency (November) and the capture of Lucknow by the new commander in chief, Sir Colin Campbell (March 1858). By a campaign in Avadh and Rohilkhand, Campbell cleared the countryside. The next phase was the central Indian campaign of Sir Hugh Rose, who achieved the

British recovery of Gwalior on June 20 1858. Although mopping-up operations lasted until the British capture of rebel leader Tantia Topi in April 1859, the revolt was over.

British imperial power

On August 2 1858, less than a month after Canning proclaimed the victory of British arms, Parliament passed the Government of India Act, transferring British power over India from the East India Company (whose ineptitude was primarily blamed for the mutiny) to the crown. The merchant company's residual powers were vested in the secretary of state for India, a minister of Great Britain's cabinet, who would preside over the India Office in London and be assisted and advised, especially in financial matters, by a Council of India. Though some of Britain's most powerful political leaders became secretaries of state for India in the latter half of the nineteenth century, actual control over the government of India remained in the hands of British viceroys and their "steel frame" of approximately 1,500 Indian Civil Service (ICS) officials.

On November 1 1858, Lord Canning announced Queen Victoria's proclamation to "the Princes, Chiefs and Peoples of India," which unveiled a new British policy of perpetual support for "native princes" and nonintervention in matters of religious belief or worship within British India. The announcement reversed Lord Dalhousie's prewar policy of political unification through princely state annexation, and princes were left free to adopt any heirs they desired so long as they all swore undying allegiance to the British crown. In 1876, at Prime Minister Benjamin Disraeli's prompting, Queen Victoria added the title Empress of India to her regality.

British fears of another mutiny and consequent determination to bolster Indian states as "natural breakwaters" against any future tidal wave of revolt thus left more than 560 enclaves of autocratic princely rule to survive, interspersed throughout British India, for the entire nine decades of crown rule.

British officials who went to India during this period lived as super-bureaucrats, "Pukka Sahibs," remaining as aloof as possible from "native contamination" in their private clubs and well-guarded military cantonments (called camps), which were constructed beyond the walls of the old, crowded "native" cities in this era. After 1869, when the opening of the Suez Canal shortened the sea passage between Britain and India to only three weeks, British officials and their wives returned home during furloughs rather than tour India as their predecessors had done. British contacts with Indian society diminished and British sympathy for and understanding of Indian life and culture were, for the most part, replaced by suspicion, indifference, and fear.

From 1858 to 1909 the government of India was an increasingly centralized paternal despotism and the world's largest imperial bureaucracy. The Indian Councils Act of 1861 transformed the viceroy's Executive Council into a miniature cabinet with each of the five members in charge of a distinct department of Calcutta's government – home, revenue, military, finance, and law. The military commander in chief sat with this council as an extraordinary member. A sixth ordinary member was assigned to the viceroy's Executive Council after 1874, initially to preside over the Department of Public Works, which after 1904 came to be called Commerce and Industry. The viceroy, also in charge of the Foreign Department, was empowered to overrule his councillors if ever he deemed that necessary.

From 1854 additional members met with the viceroy's Executive Council for legislative purposes, and by the Act of

1861 their permissible number was raised to between six and twelve, no fewer than half of whom were to be nonofficial. While the viceroy appointed all such legislative councillors and was empowered to veto any bill passed on to him by this body, its debates were to be open to a limited public audience, and several of its nonofficial members were Indian nobility and loyal landowners. The legislative council sessions thus served as a crude public-opinion barometer and the beginnings of an advisory "safety valve" that provided the viceroy with early crisis warnings at the minimum possible risk of parliamentary-type opposition. The Act of 1892 further expanded the council's permissible additional membership to sixteen, of whom ten could be nonofficial, and increased their powers, though only to the extent of allowing them to ask questions of government and to criticize formally the official budget.

Economically, this was an era of increased commercial agricultural production, rapidly expanding trade, early industrial development, and severe famine. The major source of government income throughout this period remained the land revenue, which usually amounted to about half of British India's gross annual revenue. The second most lucrative source of revenue at this time was the government's continued monopoly over the flourishing opium trade to China; the third was the tax on salt. An individual income tax was introduced for five years to pay off the war deficit, but urban personal income tax was not added as a regular source of Indian revenue until 1886.

Bombay's textile industry now had more than 80 power mills, competing directly with England's Lancashire mills for the vast Indian market. In 1894 the value of silver fell so precipitously on the world market that the government of India was forced to reinstate duty on British cotton goods by adding enough rupees to its revenue to make ends meet,

Britain's mill owners forced the government of India to impose an "equalizing" 5 per cent excise tax on all cloth manufactured in India, thereby convincing many Indian mill owners and capitalists that their best interests would be served by contributing financial support to the Indian National Congress.

Britain's major contribution to India's economic development throughout the era of crown rule was the railway network that spread swiftly across the subcontinent. By 1869 more than 5,000 miles (8,000 kilometres) of steel track had been completed by British railway companies, and by the start of the First World War (1914–18) the total reached 35,000 miles (56,000 kilometres). The railways served both to accelerate the pace of raw-material extraction from India and to speed up the transition from cultivating subsistence food to commercial crops. When the Indian market collapsed, however, millions of peasants were unable to convert their commercial agricultural surplus back into food during depression years, and from 1865 to 1900 India experienced a series of protracted famines. As a result, though the population of the subcontinent increased dramatically from about 200 million in 1872 (the year of the first almost universal census) to more than 319 million in 1921, the population may have declined slightly between 1895 and 1905. The spread of railways also accelerated the destruction of India's indigenous handicraft industries, for trains filled with cheap competitive manufactured goods shipped from England now rushed to inland towns for distribution to villages, underselling the rougher products of Indian craftsmen. By the end of the nineteenth century a larger proportion of India's population (perhaps more than three-quarters) depended directly on agriculture for support than at the century's start.

The rich coalfields of Bihar began to be mined during this period to help power the imported British locomotives, and coal production jumped from roughly 500,000 tons in 1868 to some 6,000,000 tons in 1900 and more than 20,000,000 tons by 1920. The Tata Iron and Steel Company, which launched India's modern steel industry, started production in 1911 and by the Second World War had become the largest steel complex in the British Commonwealth. The jute textile industry developed in the wake of the Crimean War (1853–56), and by 1882 there were 20 mills, employing more than 20,000 workers.

The most important plantation industries of this era were tea, indigo, and coffee. British tea plantations were started in north India's Assam Hills in the 1850s and in south India's Nilgiri Hills some 20 years later. By 1871 there were more than 300 tea plantations, producing some 3,000 tons of tea annually. By 1900 India's tea crop was large enough to export 68,500 tons to Britain. The flourishing indigo industry of Bengal and Bihar was threatened with extinction during the "Blue Mutiny" (violent riots by cultivators in 1859–60), but India continued to export indigo to European markets until the end of the nineteenth century, when synthetic dyes made that natural product obsolete. Coffee plantations flourished in south India from 1860 to 1879, after which disease blighted the crop and sent Indian coffee into a decade of decline.

Politically, British India expanded beyond its company borders to both the north-west and the north-east during crown rule. Lord Canning (governed 1856–62) and Lord Lawrence (governed 1864–69) pursued a punitive expedition policy (commonly called "butcher and bolt"), which was generally regarded as the simplest, cheapest method of "pacifying" the Pathan raiders on the north-western frontier. In 1878, when Russia's General Stolyetov was admitted to Kabul while the viceroy Lord Lytton's envoy, Sir Neville Chamberlain, was turned back at the border by Afghan troops, Lytton launched the Second Afghan War. A treaty was concluded with Ya'qub Khan, but two months later the British resident in Kabul was assassinated. British troops removed Ya'qub from the throne, which remained vacant until July 1880, when 'Abd al-Rahman Khan became emir until his death in 1901.

In 1896 Lord Lansdowne (governed 1888–94) negotiated the delimitation of the Indo-Afghan border, which became known as the Durand Line, and added the tribal territory of the Afridis, Mahsuds, Waziris, and Swatis as well as the chieftainships of Chitral and Gilgit, to the domain of British India. Lord Curzon (governed 1899–1905), however, recognized the impracticality of trying to administer the turbulent frontier region as part of the large Punjab province, and in 1901 created a new North-West Frontier Province under a British chief commissioner responsible directly to the viceroy.

British India's conquest of Burma (Myanmar) was also completed during this period. The Second Anglo-Burmese War (1852) had left the kingdom of Ava (Upper Burma) independent of British rule. Lord Dufferin (governed 1884–88), impatient with King Thibaw for delaying a treaty with British India, goaded to action by British traders in Rangoon, and provoked by fears of French intervention in Britain's "sphere," sent an expedition of some 10,000 troops up the Irrawaddy in November 1885. The Third Anglo-Burmese War ended in less than a month, and on January 1 1886, Upper Burma was annexed by proclamation to British India.

The rise of Indian nationalism

In India itself, nationalism began to emerge both in emulation of and as a reaction against the consolidation of British rule and the spread of western civilization there. It had two strands:

the Indian National Congress, which held its first meeting in December 1885 in Bombay and led eventually to the birth of India; and a smaller Muslim movement, which acquired its organizational skeleton with the founding of the Muslim League in 1906 and led to the creation of Pakistan.

Many English-educated young Indians of the post-mutiny period emulated their British mentors by seeking employment in the ICS, the legal services, journalism, and education. They were convinced that with the education they had received and the proper apprenticeship of hard work, they would eventually inherit the machinery of British Indian government. Few Indians, however, were admitted to the ICS. Among the first handful who were admitted, one of the brightest, Surendranath Banerjea (1848–1925), was dismissed at the earliest pretext and turned to active nationalist agitation. In 1883 he convened the first Indian National Conference in Bengal, anticipating by two years the birth of the Congress on the opposite side of India.

During the 1870s young leaders in Bombay also established a number of provincial political associations, such as the Poona Sarvajanik Sabha (Poona Public Society), founded by Mahadev Govind Ranade. His brilliant disciple Gopal Krishna Gokhale (1866–1915) was elected president of the Congress in 1905. Gokhale's fellow teacher at Fergusson College in Poona (Pune), Bal Gangadhar Tilak (1856–1920), produced a vernacular newspaper entitled *Kesari* ("Lion"), which was the leading literary thorn in the side of the British. Tilak was devoted primarily to ousting the British from India by any means and restoring *swaraj* ("self-rule" or independence) to India's people. In the Punjab, Swami Dayananda Sarasvati's reformist Hindu society, the Arya Samaj (founded 1875) – which called on Hindus to reject the "corrupting" excrescences of their faith, including idolatry, the caste system, and infant marriage, and to return to the original purity of Vedic life and thought – became that province's leading nationalist organization.

The first Congress session was attended by representatives of virtually every province of British India. Fifty-four of the delegates were Hindu, only two were Muslim, and the remainder were mostly Parsi and Jain. The event essentially was a gathering of English-speaking middle-class intellectuals devoted to peaceful political action and protest on behalf of their nation in the making, but on its last day the Congress passed resolutions embodying the political and economic demands of its members. These included the addition of elected nonofficial representatives to the supreme and provincial legislative councils; equality of opportunity for Indians to enter the ICS by the introduction of simultaneous examinations in India and Britain; the reduction of "home charges" (that part of Indian revenue that went toward the India Office budget and the pensions of officials living in Britain in retirement); the reduction of military expenditure; retrenchment of administrative expenses; and reimposition of import duties on British goods.

Allan Octavian Hume (1829–1912), radical confidant of Lord Ripon (governed 1880–84) and a mystic reformer sympathetic to Indian civilization, was the only British delegate to the Congress. Most Britons in India either ignored the Congress and its resolutions as the action and demands of a "microscopic minority" of India's diverse millions, or considered them the rantings of disloyal extremists. Despite this, the Congress quickly won substantial Indian support and by 1888 had 1,248 delegates at its annual meeting. Still British officials continued to dismiss the significance of the Congress, and more than a decade later Viceroy Curzon claimed, perhaps wishfully, that it was "tottering to its fall."

The first partition of Bengal in 1905 brought that province to the brink of open rebellion. With some 85 million people,

Bengal was admittedly much too large for a single province but the dividing line drawn by Lord Curzon's government cut through the heart of the Bengali-speaking "nation," leaving western Bengal's *bhadralok* ("respectable people"), the intellectual Hindu leadership of Calcutta, tied to the much less politically active Bihari- and Oriya-speaking Hindus to their north and south. A new Muslim-majority province of Eastern Bengal and Assam was created, with its capital at Dacca (now Dhaka). The leadership of the Congress viewed this partition as an attempt to "divide and rule," and as proof of the government's vindictive antipathy toward the outspoken *bhadralok* intellectuals – especially since Curzon and his subordinates had ignored countless pleas and petitions signed by tens of thousands of Calcutta's leading citizens. Mass protest rallies before and after Bengal's division attracted millions previously untouched by politics of any variety.

The new tide of national sentiment born in Bengal rose to inundate India in every direction, and "Bande Mataram" ("Hail to Thee, Mother") became the Congress's national anthem. As a reaction against the partition, Bengali Hindus launched an effective boycott of British-made goods and dramatized their resolve to live without foreign cloth by igniting huge bonfires of Lancashire-made textiles. Instead of wearing foreign-made cloth, Indians vowed to use only domestic (*swadeshi*) cottons and other clothing made in India. The *swadeshi* movement soon stimulated indigenous enterprise in many fields, from Indian cotton mills to match factories, glassblowing shops, and iron and steel foundries. Demand for self-rule (*swaraj*), soon to become the most popular mantra of Indian nationalism, was first articulated in the presidential address of Dadabhai Naoroji as the Congress's goal at its Calcutta session in 1906.

While the Congress was calling for *swaraj* in Calcutta, the Muslim League held its first meeting in Dacca. In 1875 Sir Sayyid Ahmad Khan (1817–98), India's greatest nineteenth-century Muslim leader, had founded at Aligarh what became the intellectual cradle of the Muslim League and Pakistan – the Anglo-Muhammadan Oriental College (now Aligarh Muslim University). His successor, Sayyid Mahdi Ali (1837–1907), convened a deputation of some 36 Muslim leaders, headed by the Aga Khan III, that in 1906 called upon Lord Minto (viceroy from 1905–10) to articulate the special national interests of India's Muslim community. Minto promised that any reforms enacted by his government would safeguard their interests. Separate Muslim electorates, formally inaugurated by the Indian Councils Act of 1909, were thus vouchsafed by viceregal fiat in 1906. Encouraged by the concession, the Aga Khan's deputation issued an expanded call during the first meeting of the Muslim League "to protect and advance the political rights and interests of Mussalmans of India."

In Great Britain the Liberal Party's electoral victory of 1906 marked the dawn of a new era of reforms for British India. The new secretary of state for India, John Morley, appointed two Indian members to his council at Whitehall: one a Muslim, Sayyid Husain Bilgrami, who had taken an active role in the founding of the Muslim League; the other a Hindu, Krishna G. Gupta, the senior Indian in the ICS. Morley also persuaded a reluctant Lord Minto to appoint to the viceroy's executive council the first Indian member, Satyendra P. Sinha (1864–1928), in 1909. Morley's major reform scheme, the Indian Councils Act of 1909, directly introduced the elective principle to Indian legislative council membership.

Minto and his officials in Calcutta and Simla watered down the reforms by writing stringent regulations for their imple-mentation and insisting upon the retention of executive veto power over all legislation. Elected members of the new councils were empowered, nevertheless, to engage in supplementary questioning, as well as in formal debate with the executive concerning the annual budget and to introduce legislative proposals. The liberal Congress leader Gokhale took immediate advantage of these new parliamentary procedures by introducing a measure for free and compulsory elementary education throughout British India. Although defeated, it was brought back again and again by Gokhale, who used the platform of the government's highest council of state as a sounding board for nationalist demands.

In 1907 the Congress split into two parties, which would not reunite for nine years. Young militants of Tilak's New Party wanted to extend the boycott movement to the entire British government, while moderate leaders like Gokhale cautioned against such "extreme" action, fearing it might lead to violence. Political violence by the militants indeed escalated, reaching its peak in Bengal between 1908 and 1910, as did the severity of official repression and the number of "preventive detention" arrests.

Minto's successor, the liberal Lord Hardinge (governed 1910–16), recommended the reunification of Bengal. In 1911 King George V journeyed to India for his coronation durbar in Delhi and there, on December 12, announced the revocation of the partition of Bengal, the creation of a new province, and the plan to shift the capital of British India from Calcutta to Delhi's distant plain. Reunification of Bengal indeed served somewhat to mollify Bengali Hindus, but political unrest continued, now attracting Muslim as well as Hindu acts of terrorist violence. In 1912 Edwin Samuel Montagu, parliamentary undersecretary of state for India, announced that the goal of British policy toward India would be to meet the just demands of Indians for a greater share in government.

Britain seemed to be awakening to the urgency of India's political demands – but European war now demanded Whitehall's attention.

The First World War and its aftermath

From 1914 to 1918 the world was at war. Indian princes volunteered their men, money, and personal service, while leaders of the Congress were allied in backing the war effort. Only India's Muslims, many of whom felt a strong religious allegiance to the Ottoman caliph, seemed ambivalent. Support from the Congress was primarily offered on the assumption that Britain would repay such loyal assistance with substantial political concessions – if not immediate independence or at least dominion status following the war, then surely its promise would be soon after the Allies achieved victory.

Although anti-British terrorist activity from Sikhs and Muslims started soon after the war began, India's military support was of vital importance. In the early months of the war, Indian troops were rushed to eastern Africa and Egypt, and by the end of 1914 more than 300,000 officers and men of the British Indian Army had been shipped to overseas garrisons and battlefronts. The British Indian Army bolstered the Allies on the Western Front, but its most ambitious, though doomed, campaign was against the Turks in Mesopotamia. After the disastrous campaign ended in retreat, Edwin Montagu, India's newly appointed secretary of state, informed the British House of Commons on August 20 1917 that the policy of the British government toward India was thereafter to be one of "increasing association of Indians in every branch of the administration . . . with a view to the progressive realization of responsible government in India as an integral part of the

Empire." During a subsequent tour of India, Montagu conferred with his new viceroy, Lord Chelmsford (governed
1916–21), and their lengthy deliberations bore fruit in the
Montagu-Chelmsford Report of 1918, the theoretical basis for
the Government of India Act of 1919.

The deaths of Gokhale and of the Bombay political leader
Sir Pherozeshah Mehta in 1915 removed the most powerful
moderate leadership from the Congress and cleared the way
for Tilak's return to power in that organization after its
reunification in 1916 at Lucknow. The Congress and the
Muslim League's leaders, including Mohammad Ali Jinnah
(1876–1949), briefly agreed to set aside doctrinal differences
and work together toward the attainment of national freedom
from British rule. The Lucknow Pact, which they formed in
1916, called for the creation of expanded provincial legislative
councils, four-fifths of whose members should be elected
directly by the people on as broad a franchise as possible.
The rapprochement between the Congress and the Muslim
League was short-lived, however, and by 1917 communal
tensions and disagreements once again dominated India's
faction-ridden political scene.

By Armistice Day, November 11 1918, more than a million
Indian troops had been shipped overseas to fight or serve as
noncombatants behind the Allied lines on every major front.
There were nearly 150,000 Indian battle casualties, more than
36,000 of them fatal. India had also made substantial material
and financial contributions to the war effort, including the
shipment of vast amounts of military stores and equipment,
jute and cotton goods, oils, minerals, and nearly five million
tons of wheat and a gift of £100 million (actually an imperial
tax) from the viceroy to the British government. Wartime
inflation was immediately followed by one of India's worst
depressions, which came in the wake of the devastating

influenza epidemic of 1918–19, a pandemic that took a far heavier toll of Indian life and resources than all the casualties sustained throughout the war. (Indians accounted for roughly half of the pandemic's total deaths worldwide.)

Despite the British promises, those returning to India after the war found nothing had changed. British officials returned to oust Indian subordinates acting in their stead, and Indian soldiers were no longer treated as invaluable allies but again as "natives." As many as half of the combatant troops shipped abroad had come from the Punjab, and it was here that the flashpoint of postwar violence occurred that shook India in the spring of 1919. The issue that served to rally millions of Indians was the government of India's hasty passage of the Rowlatt Acts – peacetime extensions of the wartime emergency measures – over the unanimous opposition of its Indian members, several of whom, including Jinnah, resigned in protest. Mohandas K. Gandhi, the Gujarati barrister who was recognized throughout India as one of the most promising leaders of the Congress, called upon all Indians to take sacred vows to disobey the Rowlatt Acts and launched a nationwide movement for their repeal.

Gandhi's appeal received the strongest popular response in the Punjab, where the nationalist leaders Kichloo and Satyapal addressed mass protest rallies both from the provincial capital of Lahore and from Amritsar. On April 10, Kichloo and Satyapal were arrested in Amritsar and deported from the district by Deputy Commissioner Miles Irving. When their followers tried to march to Irving's bungalow in the camp to demand the release of their leaders, they were fired upon by British troops. With several of their number killed and wounded, the enraged mob rioted through Amritsar's old city, burning British banks, murdering several Britons, and attacking two British women. General Reginald Edward Harry Dyer was sent with Gurkha (Nepalese) and Balochi troops from Jullundur to restore order.

Soon after Dyer's arrival, on the afternoon of April 13 1919, some 10,000 or more unarmed men, women, and children gathered in Amritsar's Jallianwala Bagh to attend a protest meeting, despite a ban on public assemblies. Dyer positioned his men at the sole, narrow passageway of the Bagh and ordered 50 soldiers to fire into the gathering, and for 10 to 15 minutes 1,650 rounds of ammunition were unloaded into the screaming, terrified crowd. According to official estimates, nearly 400 civilians were killed, and another 1,200 were left wounded with no medical attention.

Although Secretary of State Edwin Montagu appointed a commission of inquiry when he learned of the slaughter, and Dyer was subsequently relieved of his command, the Massacre of Amritsar turned millions of moderate Indians from patient and loyal supporters of the British raj into nationalists who would never again place trust in British "fair play." It thus marks the turning point for a majority of the Congress' supporters from moderate cooperation with the raj and its promised reforms to revolutionary noncooperation. Liberal Anglophile leaders, such as Jinnah, were soon to be displaced by the followers of Gandhi – who would launch, a year after that dreadful massacre, his first nationwide *satyagraha* ("devotion to truth") campaign as India's revolutionary response.

The lead-up to independence

For Gandhi, there was no dichotomy between religion and politics, and his unique political power was in great measure attributable to the spiritual leadership he exerted over India's masses, who viewed him as a *sadhu* (holy man) and worshipped him as a *mahatma* (in Sanskrit, "great soul"). With the weapons of *satya* ("truth") and *ahimsa* (nonviolence, or love), Gandhi assured his followers, unarmed India could bring the mightiest empire known to history to its knees. Gandhi's strategy was to call upon Indians to boycott all British-made goods, British schools and colleges, British courts of law, British titles and honours, British elections and elective offices and, should the need arise if all other boycotts failed, British tax collectors as well. The total withdrawal of Indian support would achieve the national goal of *swaraj*.

The Muslim quarter of India's population could hardly be expected to respond any more enthusiastically to Gandhi's *satyagraha* call than they had to Tilak's revivalism, but Gandhi laboured valiantly to achieve Hindu-Muslim unity by embracing the Ali brothers' Khilafat movement as the "premier plank" of his national programme. However, in December 1920 Mohammad Ali Jinnah, alienated by Gandhi's mass following of Hindi-speaking Hindus, left the Nagpur Congress.

The last quarter century of British crown rule was racked by increasingly violent Hindu-Muslim conflict and intensified agitation demanding Indian independence. British officials tried in vain to stem the rising tide of popular opposition by offering tidbits of constitutional reform, which proved either too little to satisfy both the Congress and the Muslim League or too late to avert disaster. More concerted efforts were made in 1919 and 1935 to wean minorities and India's educated elite away from revolution and noncooperation. Sikhs and Christians, for example, were given special privileges in voting for their own representatives comparable to those vouchsafed to Muslims. The Government of India Act of 1919 (also known as the Montagu-Chelmsford Reforms) increased the number of Indian members to the viceroy's

Executive Council to no fewer than three and transformed the Imperial Legislative Council into a bicameral legislature consisting of a Legislative Assembly (lower house) and a Council of State (upper house). The Legislative Assembly, with 145 members, was to have a majority of 104 elected, while 33 of the Council of State's 60 members were also to be elected. The total number of Indians eligible to vote for representatives to provincial councils was expanded to five million; just one-fifth of that number, however, were permitted to vote for Legislative Assembly candidates, and only about 17,000 elite were allowed to choose Council of State members.

The Government of India Act of 1935, the result of three Round Table Conferences held in London – Gandhi could not attend the first because he was imprisoned at the time, and was the only Congress representative at the second – gave all provinces full representative and elective governments, chosen by franchise extended now to some 30 million Indians. The viceroy and his governors retained veto powers over any legislation they considered unacceptable, but prior to the 1937 elections they reached a "gentleman's agreement" with the Congress's high command not to resort to that constitutional option, which was their last vestige of autocracy. The new provinces of Orissa and Sind (Sindh) also emerged from those official deliberations, and it was also decided that Burma should be a separate colony from British India.

In August 1932 Prime Minister Ramsay MacDonald's Communal Award expanded the separate-electorate formula reserved for Muslims to other minorities, including Sikhs and Indian Christians, distinct regional groups (such as the Marathas in the Bombay Presidency), and special interests (women, organized labour, business, landowners, and universities). The Congress was, predictably, unhappy at the extension of communal representation but became particularly outraged at the British offer of separate-electorate seats for "depressed classes" (meaning the so-called "untouchables"). Gandhi undertook a "fast unto death" against that offer, which he viewed as a nefarious British plot to wean more than 50 million Hindus away from their higher-caste brothers and sisters. Gandhi, who called the "untouchables" *Harijans* ("Children of God"), agreed after prolonged personal negotiations with Bhimrao Ramji Ambedkar (1891–1956), a leader of the "untouchables", to reserve many more seats for them than the British had promised, as long as they remained within the "Hindu" majority fold. Thus, the offer of separate-electorate seats for the "untouchables" was withdrawn.

Gandhi, promising his followers freedom in just one year, launched on August 1, 1920, his first nationwide *satyagraha* campaign, which he believed would bring the British raj to a grinding halt. After more than a year, and even with 60,000 "*satyagrahis*" in prison cells across British India, the raj remained firm. Gandhi therefore prepared to unleash his last and most powerful boycott weapon – calling upon the peasants of Bardoli in Gujarat to boycott land taxes. In February 1922, on the eve of that final phase of boycott, word reached Gandhi that in Chauri Chaura, United Provinces, 22 Indian police were massacred in their police station by a mob of *satyagrahis*, who set fire to the station and prevented the trapped police from escaping immolation. As a result he called a halt to the noncooperation movement. He was subsequently arrested, found guilty of "promoting disaffection" toward the raj, and sent to prison.

While Gandhi was behind bars, Motilal Nehru (1861–1931), one of northern India's wealthiest lawyers, started within Congress a new politically active "party," the Swaraj Party. Motilal Nehru shared the lead of this new party with C.R. (Chitta Ranjan) Das (1870–1925) of Bengal. The party sought by antigovernment agitation within the council chambers to disrupt official policy and derail the raj.

After Gandhi was released from jail in February 1924, he focused on his "constructive programme" of hand spinning and weaving and overall village "uplift," as well as on Hindu "purification" in seeking to advance the cause of the Harijans. Gandhi himself lived in village ashrams (religious retreats), which served more as models for his socioeconomic ideals than as centres of political power, though the leaders of the Congress flocked to his remote rural retreats for periodic consultation on strategy. In 1930 he mobilized India's peasant masses behind the Congress during his famous march against the salt tax, walking from his ashram near Ahmedabad to the sea at Dandi, where he illegally picked up salt from the sands on the shore. It was an ingeniously simple way to break a British law nonviolently, and before year's end jail cells throughout India were again filled with *satyagrahi*s.

Many of the younger members of the Congress, however, were eager to take up arms against the British, and some considered Gandhi an agent of imperial rule for having called a halt to the first *satyagraha* in 1922. Most famous and popular of these militant Congress leaders was Subhas Chandra Bose (1897–1945) of Bengal, a disciple of C.R. Das and an admirer of Hitler and Mussolini. Bose was so popular within Congress that he was elected its president twice (in 1938 and 1939) over Gandhi's opposition and the active opposition of most members of its central working committee. After being forced to resign the office in April 1939, Bose organized with his brother Sarat his own Bengali party, the Forward Bloc, which initially remained within the Congress fold. Jawaharlal Nehru (1889–1964), elected president of the Congress in December 1929 when it passed its Purna Swaraj ("Complete Self-Rule") resolution, emerged as Gandhi's designated successor to Congress leadership during the 1930s.

In the meantime, the Muslim quarter of India's population became increasingly wary of the Congress's promises. Hindu-Muslim riots in Malabar claimed hundreds of lives in 1924, and similar religious rioting spread to every major city in northern India. The older, more conservative leadership of the pre-First World War Congress found Gandhian *satyagraha* too radical to support, and liberals like Sir Tej Bahadur Sapru (1875–1949) organized their own party (eventually to become the National Liberal Federation), while others, like Jinnah, dropped out of political life entirely until he revitalized the Muslim League in the 1930s.

By 1930 a number of Indian Muslims had begun to think in terms of separate statehood for their minority community. One of Punjab's greatest Urdu poets, Sir Muhammad Iqbal (1877–1938), while presiding over the Muslim League's annual meeting in Allahabad in 1930, proposed that "the final destiny" of India's Muslims should be to consolidate a "North-West Indian Muslim state." The Muslim League and its president, Jinnah, did not join in the Pakistan demand until after the league's famous Lahore meeting in March 1940, as Jinnah, a secular constitutionalist by predilection and training, continued to hope for a reconciliation with the Congress. Such hopes virtually disappeared, however, when Nehru refused to permit the league to form coalition ministries with the Congress majority in the United Provinces and elsewhere after the 1937 elections, insisting that there were but "two parties" in India, the Congress and the British raj.

During 1937 to 1939, when the Congress actually ran most of British India's provincial governments, the Muslim League grew in popularity and power, for many Muslims soon viewed the new "Hindu raj" as biased and tyrannical. Thus, the lines of battle were drawn by the eve of the Second World War – which served only to intensify and accelerate the process of communal conflict and irreversible political division that would split British India.

On September 3 1939, the viceroy Lord Linlithgow (governed 1936–43) informed India's political leaders and populace that they were at war with Germany. To the Congress, which thought of itself as the viceroy's "partner", such autocratic declaration of war was viewed as "betrayal." Instead of offering loyal support to the British raj they demanded a prior forthright statement of Britain's postwar "goals and ideals." Nehru's outrage helped convince the Congress's high command to call on all its provincial ministries to resign. Jinnah was overjoyed at this decision and proclaimed Friday, December 22 1939 a Muslim "Day of Deliverance" from the tyranny of the Congress "raj." Jinnah assured the viceroy that he need not fear a lack of support from India's Muslims, and throughout the war, as the Congress moved farther from the British, the Muslim League in every possible way quietly supported the war effort.

The Lahore Resolution (March 1940), later known as the Pakistan Resolution, was passed by the largest gathering of league delegates just one day after Jinnah informed his followers that "the problem of India is not of an inter-communal but manifestly of an international character". The league resolved that any future constitutional plan proposed by the British for India would not be "acceptable to the Muslims" unless it was so designed that the Muslim-majority "areas" of India's "North-Western and Eastern Zones" were "grouped to constitute 'independent States' in which the constituent units shall be autonomous and sovereign." Pakistan was not mentioned until the next day's newspapers introduced that word in their headlines, and Jinnah explained that the resolution envisioned the establishment of not two separately administered Muslim countries but rather a single Muslim nation-state – namely, Pakistan.

The same year, in October 1940, Gandhi launched his first "individual *satyagraha*" campaign against the war. Vinoba Bhave, Gandhi's foremost disciple, publicly proclaimed his intent to resist the war effort and was sentenced to three months in jail. Nehru, the next to openly disobey British law, was sentenced to four years behind bars. By June 1941 more than 20,000 Congress *satyagrahi*s were in prisons.

It was also in 1941 that Bose fled to Germany, where he started broadcasting appeals to India urging the masses to "rise up" against British "tyranny." There were, however, few Indians in Germany, and he was eventually transported to Singapore, where Japan had captured at least 40,000 Indian troops. These captured soldiers became Netaji ("Leader") Bose's Indian National Army (INA) in 1943 and, a year later, marched behind him to Rangoon. Bose hoped to "liberate" first Manipur and then Bengal from British rule, but the British forces drove Bose and his army back down the Malay Peninsula. In August 1945 Bose escaped from Saigon, but died after his overloaded plane crashed onto the island of Taiwan (Formosa).

After Japan joined the Axis powers in late 1941, Britain feared that the Japanese would invade India. In March 1942 the war cabinet of British Prime Minister Winston Churchill sent the socialist Sir Richard Stafford Cripps, a close personal friend of Nehru, to New Delhi with a postwar proposal. The Cripps Mission offered full "dominion status" for India after the war's end, with the additional stipulation, as a concession primarily to the Muslim League, that any province could vote to "opt out" of such a dominion if it preferred to do so. Gandhi irately called the offer "a post-dated cheque on a bank that was failing," and Nehru was equally negative and angry at Cripps for his readiness to give so much to the Muslims. Cripps flew home empty-handed in less than a month, and soon afterward Gandhi planned his last *satyagraha* campaign, the Quit India movement. But Gandhi and all members of the Congress high command were arrested before the dawn of that movement in August 1942. In a few months at least 60,000 Indians filled British prison cells, and the raj unleashed massive force against Indian underground efforts to disrupt rail transport and to generally subvert the war effort. Many Indians were killed and wounded, but wartime resistance continued as more young Indians were recruited.

In mid-1943 Field Marshall Lord Wavell, who replaced Linlithgow as viceroy (1943–47), brought India's government fully under martial control for the war's duration. With the end of the war, London's primary concern was to find the political solution to the Hindu-Muslim conflict that would most expeditiously permit the British raj to withdraw. In the elections held in the winter of 1945–46 Jinnah's Muslim League won all 30 seats reserved for Muslims in the Central Legislative Assembly and most of the reserved provincial seats as well. The Congress was successful in gathering most of the general electorate seats, but it could no longer effectively insist that it spoke for the entire population of British India.

In 1946 Secretary of State Pethick-Lawrence personally led a three man cabinet deputation to New Delhi with the hope of resolving the Congress–Muslim League deadlock and, thus, of transferring British power to a single Indian administration. The Cabinet Mission Plan proposed a three-tier federation for India, integrated by a minimal central-union government in Delhi, which would be limited to handling foreign affairs, communications, defence, and those finances required to care for unionwide matters. The subcontinent was to be divided into three major groups of provinces: Group A, to include the Hindu-majority provinces of the Bombay Presidency, Madras, the United Provinces, Bihar, Orissa, and the Central Provinces (virtually all of what became independent India a year later); Group B, to contain the Muslim-majority provinces of the Punjab, Sind, the North-West Frontier, and Balochistan (the areas out of which the western part of Pakistan was created); and Group C, to include the Muslim-majority Bengal (a portion of which became the eastern part of Pakistan and in 1971 the country of Bangladesh) and the Hindu majority Assam. The group governments were to be virtually autonomous in everything but matters reserved to the union centre, and within each group the princely states were to be integrated into their neighbouring provinces. Local provincial governments were to have the choice of opting out of the group in which they found themselves, should a majority of their populace vote to do so.

Punjab's large and powerful Sikh population would have been placed in a particularly difficult and anomalous position, for Punjab as a whole would have belonged to Group B, and much of the Sikh community was anti-Muslim. By March 1946 many Sikhs demanded a Sikh nation-state, alternately called Sikhistan or Khalistan ("Land of the Sikhs" or "Land of the Pure"). The Cabinet Mission, however, had no time or energy to focus on Sikh separatist demands and found the Muslim League's demand for Pakistan equally impossible to accept.

As a pragmatist, Jinnah accepted the Cabinet Mission's proposal, as did Congress leaders. The early summer of 1946, therefore, saw a dawn of hope for India's future prospects, but that soon proved false when Nehru announced at his first press conference as the reelected president of the Congress that no constituent assembly could be "bound" by any prearranged constitutional formula. Jinnah read Nehru's remarks as a "complete repudiation" of the plan, which had to be accepted in its entirety in order to work. Jinnah then convened the league's Working Committee, which withdrew its previous agreement to the federation scheme and instead called upon the "Muslim Nation" to launch "direct action" in mid-August 1946. Thus began India's bloodiest year of civil war since the mutiny nearly a century earlier.

Lord Mountbatten (served March–August 1947) was sent to replace Wavell as viceroy, as Britain prepared to transfer its power over India to some "responsible" hands by no later than June 1948. Shortly after reaching Delhi, where he conferred with the leaders of all parties and with his own officials, Mountbatten resolved to opt for partition rather than risk further political negotiations while civil war raged and a new mutiny of Indian troops seemed imminent. Among the major Indian leaders, Gandhi alone refused to reconcile himself to partition and urged Mountbatten to offer Jinnah the premiership of a united India rather than a separate Muslim nation. Nehru, however, would not agree.

In July 1947, Britain's Parliament passed the Indian Independence Act, ordering the demarcation of the dominions of India and Pakistan by midnight of August 14–15, 1947, and dividing within a single month the assets of the world's largest empire. Two boundary commissions worked desperately to partition Punjab and Bengal in such a way as to leave the maximum practical number of Muslims to the west of the former's new boundary and to the east of the latter's – but, as soon as the new borders were known, roughly 15 million Hindus, Muslims, and Sikhs fled from their homes on one side of the newly demarcated borders to what they thought would be "shelter" on the other. In the course of that tragic exodus, as many as a million people were slaughtered in communal massacres.

4

THE REPUBLIC OF INDIA (1947–2007)

The Nehru era

India's first years of freedom were plagued by the tragic legacy of partition. Refugee resettlement, economic disruption and inadequate resources, continuing communal conflicts (as more than ten per cent of India's population remained Muslim) and, within a few months of independence, the outbreak of un-declared war with Pakistan over Kashmir were but a few of the major difficulties confronting the newborn dominion. Mount-batten remained in New Delhi to serve as India's first new governor-general, mostly a ceremonial job, while Nehru took charge of free India's responsible government as its first prime minister, heading a Congress cabinet whose second most powerful figure was Vallabhbhai Jhaverbhai Patel.

Gandhi, who accepted no office, chose to walk barefoot through the riot-torn areas of Bengal and Bihar, where he tried through his presence and influence to stop the communal killing. He then returned to Delhi, and there he preached nonviolence daily until he was assassinated by an orthodox

Hindu Brahman fanatic on January 30 1948. "The light has gone out of our lives," Prime Minister Nehru said, "and there is darkness everywhere." Yet Nehru carried on at India's helm and, owing in part to his secular, enlightened leadership, not only did India's flood of religious hatred and violence recede but also some progress was made toward communal reconciliation and economic development.

On January 26 1950, the Dominion of India was reborn as a sovereign democratic republic and a union of states. With universal adult franchise, India's electorate was the world's largest, but the traditional feudal roots of most of its illiterate populace were deep. Elections were to be held at least every five years, and the major model of government followed by India's constitution was that of British parliamentary rule, with a lower House of the People (*Lok Sabha*), in which an elected prime minister and his cabinet sat, and an upper Council of States (*Rajya Sabha*). Nehru led his ruling Congress Party from New Delhi's *Lok Sabha* until his death in 1964. The nominal head of India's republic, however, was a president, who was indirectly elected. India's first two presidents were Hindu Brahmans, Rajendra Prasad and Sarvepalli Radhakrishnan (the latter a distinguished Sanskrit scholar who had lectured at Oxford). Presidential powers were mostly ceremonial, except for brief periods of "emergency" rule.

India's federation divided powers between the central government in New Delhi and a number of state governments (crafted from former British provinces and princely states), each of which also had a nominal governor at its head and an elected chief minister with his cabinet to rule its legislative assembly. One of the Congress' long-standing resolutions had called for the reorganization of British provincial borders into linguistic states, where each of India's major regional languages would find its administrative reflection, while English and Hindi would remain joint national languages for purposes of legislation, law, and service examinations.

Pressure for such reorganization increased in 1953, after the former British province of Madras was divided into Tamil Nadu ("Land of the Tamils") and Andhra (from 1956 Andhra Pradesh), where Telugu, another Dravidian tongue, was spoken by the vast majority. Nehru thus appointed the States Reorganization Commission to redesign India's internal map, which led to a major redrawing of administrative boundaries, especially in southern India, by the States Reorganization Act, passed in 1956. Four years later, in 1960, the enlarged state of Bombay was divided into Marathi-speaking Maharashtra and Gujarati-speaking Gujarat. The Sikhs demanded that their language, Punjabi, be made the official tongue of Punjab, but it was refused; Nehru feared that such a concession might open the door to further "Pakistan-style" fragmentation.

Nehru served as his own foreign minister and throughout his life remained the chief architect of India's foreign policy. Partition, however, left India and Pakistan suspicious of one another's incitements to border violence and a little more than two months after independence the first undeclared war with Pakistan began. Prior to partition, princes were given the option of joining the new dominion within which their territory lay, and most of the princes agreed to do so, accepting handsome pensions (so-called "privy purses") as rewards for relinquishing sovereignty. Of some 570 princes, only 3 had not acceded to the new dominion or gone immediately over to Pakistan – those of Junagadh, Hyderabad, and Kashmir. The *nawab* of Junagadh and the nizam of Hyderabad were both Muslims, though most of their subjects were Hindus, and both states were surrounded, on land, by India. Junagadh, however, faced Pakistan on the Arabian Sea, and when its *nawab* followed Jinnah's lead in opting to join that Muslim nation,

India's army moved in and took control of the territory. The nizam of Hyderabad was more cautious, hoping for independence for his vast domain, but India refused to give him much more than one year and sent troops into the state in September 1948. Both invasions met little, if any, resistance, and both states were swiftly integrated into India's union.

Kashmir, lying in the Himalayas, presented a different problem. Its maharaja was Hindu, but about three-quarters of its population was Muslim. Maharaja Hari Singh tried at first to remain independent, but in October 1947 Pashtun (Pathan) tribesmen from the North-West Frontier of Pakistan invaded Kashmir in trucks, heading toward Srinagar. The invasion triggered India's first undeclared war with Pakistan and led at once to the maharaja's decision to opt for accession to India. Mountbatten and Nehru airlifted Indian troops into Srinagar, and the tribesmen were forced to fall back to a line that has, since early 1949, partitioned Kashmir into Pakistan-held Azad Kashmir (the western portion of Kashmir) and the Northern Areas (the northern portion of Kashmir, also administered by Pakistan) and India's state of Jammu and Kashmir, which includes the Vale of Kashmir and Ladakh. A UN-sponsored cease-fire was agreed to by both parties on January 1 1949.

India's foreign policy, defined by Nehru as nonaligned, was based on Five Principles (*Panch Shila*): mutual respect for other nations' territorial integrity and sovereignty; nonaggression; noninterference in internal affairs; equality and mutual benefit; and peaceful coexistence. These principles were, ironically, articulated in a treaty with China over the Tibet region in 1954, when Nehru still hoped for Sino-Indian "brotherhood" and leadership of a "Third World" of nonviolent nations, recently independent of colonial rule, eager to save the world from Cold War superpower confrontation and nuclear annihilation.

China and India, however, had not resolved a dispute over several areas of their border, most notably the section demarcating a barren plateau in Ladakh and the section bordered on the north by the McMahon Line, which stretched from Bhutan to Burma (Myanmar) and extended to the crest of the Great Himalayas. The latter area, designated as the North-East Frontier Agency (NEFA) in 1954, was claimed on the basis of a 1914 agreement between Arthur Henry McMahon, the British foreign secretary for India, and Tibetan officials but was never accepted by China. After China had reasserted its authority over Tibet in 1950, it began appealing to India – but to no avail – for negotiations over the border. This Sino-Indian dispute was exacerbated in the late 1950s after India discovered a road across Aksai Chin (a part of the Ladakh section) built by the Chinese to link its autonomous region of Xinjiang with Tibet. The tension was further heightened when, in 1959, India granted asylum to the Dalai Lama, Tibet's spiritual leader. Full-scale war blazed in October 1962 when a Chinese army moved easily through India's northern outposts and advanced virtually unopposed toward the plains of Assam before Beijing ordered their unilateral withdrawal.

The war was a blow to Nehru's most cherished principles and ideals, though as a result of swift and extensive US and British military support, including the dispatch of US bombers to the world's highest border, India soon secured its northern defences. India's "police action" of integrating Portuguese Goa into the union by force in 1961 represented another fall from the high ground of nonviolence in foreign affairs, which Nehru so often claimed for India in his speeches to the UN and elsewhere. During his premiership, Nehru tried hard to identify the country's foreign policy with anticolonialism and antiracism. He also tried to promote India's role as the peacemaker, which was seen as an extension of the policies of

Gandhi and as deeply rooted in its religious traditions. Like most foreign policies, India's was, in fact, based primarily on its government's perceptions of national interest and on security considerations.

The early years of the Republic were also dominated by attempts to improve India's economy, increase its industrial growth, and reduce rural poverty. As a Fabian Socialist, Nehru had great faith in economic planning and personally chaired his government's Planning Commission. India's First Five-Year Plan was launched in 1951, and most of its funds were spent on rebuilding war-shattered railways and on irrigation schemes and canals. Food grain production increased from 51 million tons in 1951 to 82 million tons by the end of the Second Five-Year Plan (1956–61). During that same decade, however, India's population grew from about 360 million to 440 million, which eliminated real economic benefits for all but large landowners and the wealthiest and best educated quarter of India's urban population. The landless and unemployed lower half of India's fast-growing population remained inadequately fed, ill-housed, and illiterate. It was not until the late 1960s that chemical fertilizers and high-yield food seeds brought the Green Revolution in agriculture to India. The results were mixed, however, as many poor or small farmers were unable to afford the seeds or the risks involved in the new technology, and as rice and wheat production increased, there was a corresponding decrease in other grain production.

Nehru's wisdom in keeping his nation nonaligned helped accelerate the country's economic development, as India received substantial aid from both sides of the Cold War, with the Soviet Union and Eastern Europe contributing almost as much in capital goods and technical assistance as did the United States, Great Britain, and West Germany. The growth of the iron and steel industries soon became a truly international example of coexistence, with the United States building one plant, the Soviet Union another, Britain a third, and West Germany a fourth. For the Third Five-Year Plan (1961–66), launched during Nehru's era, an Aid India Consortium of the major western powers and Japan provided some $5 billion in capital and credits. As a result, India's annual iron output rose to nearly 25 million tons by the plan's end, with about three times that amount of coal produced and almost 40 billion kilowatt-hours of electric power generated. India had become the world's tenth most advanced industrial country in terms of absolute value of output, though it remained per capita one of the least productive of the world's major countries.

As modernity brought added comforts and pleasure to India's urban elite, the gap between the larger industrial urban centres and the areas of extensive rural poverty became greater. Various schemes designed to reduce rural poverty were tried, many ostensibly in emulation of Gandhi's *sarvodaya* (rural "uplift") philosophy, which advocated community sharing of all resources for the mutual benefit and enhancement of peasant life. The social reformer Vinoba Bhave started a *bhoodan* ("gift-of-land") movement, in which he walked from village to village and asked large landowners to "adopt" him as their son and to give him a portion of their property, which he would then distribute among the landless. He later expanded that programme to include *gramdan* ("gift-of-village"), in which villagers voluntarily surrendered their land to a cooperative system, and *jivandan* ("gift-of-life"), the giving of all one's labour, the latter attracting volunteers as famous as the socialist J.P. (Jaya Prakash) Narayan, founder of the Janata ("People's") opposition to the Congress of the mid-1970s. The Ford Foundation, an American philanthropic organization, began a community development and rural extension programme in the early 1950s that encouraged young Indian college students and technical experts to focus their skills and knowledge on village problems. India's half million villages, however, were slow to change and, though a number of showcase villages emerged in the environs of New Delhi, Bombay, and other large cities, the more remote villages remained centres of superstition, poverty, caste division, and illiteracy.

Post-Nehru politics and foreign policy

At his death on May 27 1964, Nehru's only child and closest confidante, Indira Gandhi, was with him. She had accompanied her father the world over and had been the leader of his Congress Party's "ginger group" youth movement, as well as Congress president but, as a young mother and widow, she had not as yet served in parliament nor on her father's cabinet and, hence, did not put herself forward as a candidate for prime minister. Though it appeared that Nehru was grooming her as his successor, he had denied any such intention, and his party instead chose Lal Bahadur Shastri, who had devoted his life to party affairs and had served Nehru well both inside and outside his cabinet, as India's second prime minister.

Almost immediately after Shastri took office, India was faced with a threat of war from Pakistan. Pakistan's president, Mohammad Ayub Khan, had led a military coup in 1958 that put him in charge of his country's civil and military affairs, and his regime had received substantial military support from the United States. By 1965 Ayub felt ready to test India's frontier outposts, first in the Sindh (Sind) and then in Kashmir. The first skirmishes were fought in the Rann of Kachchh (*Kutch*) in April, and Pakistan's US-made tanks rolled to what seemed like an easy victory over India's counterparts. The Commonwealth prime ministers and the UN quickly prevailed on both sides to agree to a cease-fire and withdrawal of forces to the prewar borders. Pakistan, however, believed it had won and that India's army was weak, and in mid-August Pakistan launched "Operation Grandslam" with the hope of cutting across the only significant overland route to Kashmir before India could bring up its outmoded tanks. India's forces, however, moved a three-pronged tank attack aimed at Lahore and Sialkot across the international border in Punjab early in September. The great city of Lahore was in range of Indian tank fire by September 23, when a UN cease-fire was agreed on by both sides.

A Soviet-sponsored South Asian peace conference was held early in January 1966 at Tashkent, in what was then the Uzbek SSR, where Ayub and Shastri finally reached an agreement on January 10 to "restore normal and peaceful relations" between India and Pakistan. The next morning, however, Shastri was dead of a heart attack, and the Tashkent Agreement hardly outlived him. Before the month's end, Indira Gandhi, who had served in Shastri's cabinet as minister of information and broadcasting, had been elected by the Congress Party to become India's next prime minister. She easily defeated her only rival, Morarji Desai.

Indira Gandhi's soft-spoken, attractive personality masked her iron will and autocratic ambition, and most of her Congress contemporaries underestimated her drive and tenacity. During her first year in office she visited Washington, where she won substantial support for India's weakened economy, and her subsequent visit to Moscow reflected the continuation of her father's policy of nonalignment. Trying to defuse Sikh agitation, moreover, and as a reward for Sikh military service in the Kashmir war, she granted the long-standing Sikh demand of a Punjabi state, which required partition of the existing state of Punjab but left its newly designed capital of Chandigarh as shared administrative headquarters of the new states of Punjab, with a Sikh majority, and Haryana, with a slight Hindu majority.

Several years of poor monsoons had conspired with wartime spending to undermine India's economy, and Prime Minister Gandhi's subsequent decision to devalue the rupee cost her party considerable losses at the polls in India's fourth general elections in 1967. Although the Congress was still considerably larger than any of the various left- and right-wing opposition parties, her overall *Lok Sabha* majority was reduced from some 200 (which she had inherited) to fewer than 50. The Congress, moreover, lost most of the more than 3,400 elective seats in the state assemblies, and Gandhi felt obliged to invite Desai, a leader of Gujarat's wealthy banking and business elite, into her cabinet as deputy prime minister and finance minister in order to try to restore confidence in the government.

India's first Muslim president, Zakir Husain, was also elected in 1967, but his death two years later opened a wider rift in Congress leadership and gave Gandhi the opportunity of taking more power into her own hands, as she began rejecting the old guard, including Desai, whom she forced out of her cabinet. For president she backed her own candidate, Vice President V.V. (Varahagiri Venkata) Giri, against the majority of her party's leadership; she proved to be a skilful political manager for Giri, who was easily elected. Because of this, the old guard of the Congress Party expelled Gandhi for "indiscipline," but, refusing to be intimidated, she rallied most of the elected members of parliament to her "New Congress" standard and led a left-wing national coalition of communist and provincial Dravidian and Akali parties from Punjab and Tamil Nadu. Desai led the old guard, a minority of Congress members who remained as the prime minister's opposition in the *Lok Sabha* but who could not thwart any of her major legislation. Gandhi called new elections at the end of 1970, and – sweeping the polls the following March with the promise "Eliminate poverty!" – her party won 350 seats in a *Lok Sabha* of 515.

In December 1970 Pakistan held general elections, its first since independence. The Awami League, headed by East Pakistan's popular Bengali leader Mujibur Rahman (Sheikh Mujib), won a clear majority of seats, but West Pakistan's chief martial law administrator and president, General Agha Mohammad Yahya Khan, refused to honour the democratic choice of his country's majority. At the end of March 1971, after failed negotiations in which Mujib demanded virtual independence for East Pakistan, Yahya Khan ordered a military massacre in Dhaka (Dacca). Though Mujib was arrested and flown to prison in West Pakistan, he called on his followers to rise up and proclaim their independence as Bangladesh ("Land of the Bengalis").

Some ten million refugees fled across the border from East Pakistan to India in the ensuing eight months of martial rule and sporadic firing by West Pakistan's army. Soon after the monsoon stopped, India's army moved up to the Bangladesh border and by early December had advanced virtually unopposed to Dhaka, which was surrendered in mid-December. Mujib, released by President Zulfikar Ali Bhutto who had taken over from the disgraced Yahya Khan, flew home to a hero's welcome, and in January 1972 he became the first prime minister of the People's Republic of Bangladesh.

India's victory over Pakistan in the Bangladesh war was achieved in part because of Soviet military support and diplomatic assurances. The Treaty of Peace, Friendship, and Co-operation, signed in mid-1971 by India with the Soviet Union, gave India the arms it used in the war. With the birth of Bangladesh, India's already dominant position in South Asia was enhanced, and its foreign policy, which remained officially nonaligned, tilted further toward the Soviet Union. In a last-ditch but futile effort to support Pakistan, a nuclear-armed aircraft carrier of the US Pacific Fleet was sent to the Bay of Bengal, ostensibly to evacuate civilians from Dhaka, but the war ended before any such assistance could be rendered. Many Indians viewed the aircraft carrier's presence so close to their own shores as provocative "nuclear weapons rattling," and by 1972 India launched an atomic programme of its own, det-onating its first plutonium-armed device under the sands of Rajasthan in May 1974. The atomic explosion was felt in Pakistan's neighbouring Sind province and triggered that country's resolve to produce a bomb of its own as swiftly as possible. Pakistan subsequently forged stronger ties with China and with Muslim countries to the west, but found itself further diminished as a potential challenge to Indian he-gemony over South Asia.

The Bangladesh war raised Prime Minister Gandhi to virtual "mother goddess" stature at home. She was viewed as a brilliant military strategist and diplomat, and her popularity was never greater than in the years immediately after the war. By late 1974, however, Gandhi's golden image had tarnished for, despite her campaign rhetoric, poverty was hardly abol-ished in India. The situation was quite the contrary, with skyrocketing oil prices and consumer-goods inflation. India's unemployed and landless, as well as its large fixed-income labouring population, found itself sinking deeper into star-vation's grip and heavy debt. Student strikes and mass protest marches rocked Bihar and Gujarat, as Narayan and Desai joined forces in leading a new Janata Morcha ("People's Front") movement against government corruption and Gandhi's allegedly inept leadership. The mass movement gathered momentum throughout the first half of 1975 and reached its climax that June, when the Congress lost a crucial by-election in Gujarat and Gandhi herself was found guilty by Allahabad's High Court of several counts of malpractice during her last election campaign. The mandatory penalty for that crime was exclusion from holding any elective office for six years from date of conviction.

Opposition leaders threatened a civil disobedience campaign to force the prime minister to resign, and many of her oldest cabinet colleagues and Congress Party advisers urged her to step down pending an appeal to India's Supreme Court. Following instead the advice of her ambitious and energetic younger son, Sanjay, on June 26 1975 Gandhi persuaded President Fakhruddin Ali Ahmed to declare a national emergency, which empowered her to do whatever she considered best for the country for at least six months. The elite Central Reserve Police force, the prime minister's palace guard, was ordered to arrest Desai and the ailing and aged Narayan, as well as hundreds of others who had worked with her father and Mohandas Gandhi in helping India to win its freedom from British rule. She then blacked out the entire region of Delhi in which the press was published, and appointed Sanjay as her trusted personal censor of all future news leaders and editorials. Her minister of information and broadcasting, Inder K. Gujral, immediately resigned. "India is Indira, and Indira is India," was the call of Congress Party sycophants, and soon the country was plastered with her poster image. Practically every leader of India's political opposition was jailed or kept under house arrest for almost two years, and some of India's most prominent journalists, lawyers, educators, and political activists were muzzled or imprisoned.

Gandhi announced her Twenty-Point Programme soon after the emergency was proclaimed, most of its points aimed at reducing inflation and energizing the economy by punishing tax evaders, black marketeers, smugglers, and other criminals. Prices did come down, production indexes rose dramatically, and even the monsoon proved cooperative by bringing abundant rains on time two years in a row. At the same time, however, popular discontent was fostered by some of the emergency acts, such as a freeze on wage increases, pressure for increased worker discipline, and compulsory sterilization for families with more than two children.

It was perhaps because of the economic gains that the prime minister decided early in 1977 to call general elections, but she may also have believed what she read about herself in her controlled press or feared a military coup had she refused to seek a civil mandate. Most political prisoners were released, and Narayan immediately joined Desai in quickly revitalizing the Janata movement, whose campaign warned Indians that the elections might be their last chance to choose between "democracy and dictatorship." In the elections, held in February, Indira and Sanjay both lost their *Lok Sabha* seats, as did most of their loyal followers, and the Congress was reduced to just 153 seats, 92 of which were from four of the southern states. The Janata Party's 295 seats (of a total 542) gave it only a modest majority, but opposition candidates together represented more than two-thirds of the *Lok Sabha*.

At the age of 80, Desai took the post of prime minister. Although Narayan was too sick to accept any office, there were others in the Janata Party, especially Charan Singh, who considered themselves at least as worthy of becoming prime minister, and the petty squabbling over power kept the new leaders in Delhi so preoccupied that little time or energy was left with which to address the nation's needs. Freedom did return, however, including laissez-faire in all its worst forms, and inflation soon escalated, as did smuggling, black-marketing, and every form of corruption endemic to any poor country with underpaid bureaucrats and undereducated police. The high-spending regime soon also used up the substantial food surplus in food grains that Gandhi had amassed.

Politically, perhaps the worst error made by Desai was to insist on punishing Indira Gandhi and Sanjay Gandhi, both of whom were accused of many crimes, none of which would be easy to prove in any Indian court. In November 1978 Indira Gandhi had again been elected to the *Lok Sabha*, but this time as a member of the Congress (I) Party (the I stood for Indira), which she and her supporters had formed that year. She was expelled from the *Lok Sabha* the following month and then briefly imprisoned, but this action brought a strong backlash of sympathy for her from millions of Indians, many of whom a year earlier had feared her as a tyrant.

No major legislation was introduced by the new government, which in a year of inaction seemed incapable of solving any of India's problems and lost the confidence of most of the populace. In mid-July 1979 Desai resigned rather than face a no-confidence motion. Charan Singh was then elected prime minister, but just a few weeks later he too resigned. President Reddy, who had been elected along with Desai in 1977, called for new elections and dissolved parliament in the winter of 1979.

In January 1980 India's seventh general election returned Indira Gandhi to power over New Delhi's central government. The Congress (I) Party, which had run on the slogan "Elect a government that works," won 351 of the 525 contested *Lok Sabha* seats, as against 31 for Janata. Sanjay Gandhi also won election to the *Lok Sabha* and resumed his former post as head of the Congress's youth wing (the Youth Congress). Though

he remained outside his mother's cabinet, he personally selected half of the Congress's successful *Lok Sabha* candidates,
and it appeared that he was being groomed as her successor. In
June 1980, however, he was killed in the crash of a new stunt
plane he was flying. Indira Gandhi, who seemed never fully to
recover from the loss of Sanjay, immediately recruited her
elder son, Rajiv, into political life.

India's problems of poverty, pluralism, inequities in development and gross disparities in wealth and education, as well
as continuing provincial and communal violence, did not
disappear or diminish. The worst violence erupted in Punjab,
where as a result of new affluence brought by India's Green
Revolution of the late 1960s, a large gap had opened up
between many younger Sikhs lured by the gadgets and toys
of modernity and those who still held to older traditions and
religious values. Political divisions also remained. Though
Indira Gandhi had agreed in 1970 to transfer Chandigarh
to the recently divided Punjab as its sole capital, that simple act
had never been carried out, for Haryana's mainly Hindu
populace vigorously demanded adequate compensation if their
state were to be deprived of so valuable an asset. The prime
minister tried to appease Sikh frustrations by appointing a
Sikh, Zail Singh, as her home minister, yet most of the leaders
in Chandigarh and Amritsar distrusted him. In 1982 she
nominated Singh to be the first Sikh president of India, but
even elevation of a member of the small Sikh minority to the
highest office in India's secular republic failed to quell the
rising storm over Punjab.

By the early 1980s some Sikhs were calling for more than
mere separate provincial statehood, instead demanding nothing less than a nation-state of their own, an autonomous Sikh
Khalistan, or "Land of the Pure." More moderate Sikh leaders,
such as Harchand Singh Longowal, who was elected president

of the Akali Party in 1980, unsuccessfully attempted to avert civil war by seeking to negotiate a settlement of Sikh demands with New Delhi's Congress leaders. Extremists like Jarnail Singh Bhindranwale won the support of many younger devout Sikhs around Amritsar, who were armed with automatic weapons and launched a violent movement for Khalistan that took control of the Sikhs' holiest shrine, the Golden Temple (*Harimandir*), and its sacred precincts.

Gandhi and her government seemed unable to do anything to stop the growing number of politically motivated killings and acts of terror in Punjab, Haryana, and Delhi. She knew that nationwide elections would have to be called by January 1985, and the overwhelming Hindu majority of India's electorate would likely judge her government too weak to be retained. In 1984, therefore, Gandhi gave her generals permission to launch "Operation Bluestar" against the Golden Temple. Early in June, after a night of artillery fire, they moved tanks and troops into the temple precincts, and for four days and nights the battle raged, until Bhindranwale and most of his snipers were dead. Hundreds of innocent people were caught in the cross fire, and at least 100 soldiers died. In retaliation, on October 31 1984, Gandhi herself was shot dead by two of her own Sikh guards inside her garden in New Delhi. The next day mobs of bloodthirsty thugs began to roam the Sikh neighbourhoods in and around Delhi, where they set fire to cars, homes, and businesses and launched a massacre of Sikhs that left thousands dead and many more thousands wounded and homeless in the worst religious riot since partition.

The night Indira Gandhi died, her son flew back to New Delhi from West Bengal, where he had been on the campaign trail. President Zail Singh also flew home, from a visit to the Persian Gulf, and swore in the 40-year-old Rajiv Gandhi as prime minister, though he had not even been a member of his mother's cabinet. Several days later, on the eve of his mother's funeral, Rajiv decided to call out the army to stop the orgy of murder and terror in Delhi. Several well-known leaders of the Congress (I) Party in Delhi were accused by human-rights activists of having incited the Hindu mobs to violence, but none was ever accused in any court of law or sentenced to any jail term.

India since the mid-1980s

Rajiv Gandhi wisely opted to call for fresh elections nation-wide soon after taking office, and, reaping the sympathy vote for his mother's murder, won the December 1984 election by the largest majority ever amassed by any party leader in independent India. With the Congress (I) winning more than 400 seats in the *Lok Sabha*, Rajiv Gandhi could have passed virtually any legislative programme he wanted. He chose to work toward removing onerous licensing restrictions and other bureaucratic red tape relating to high-technology imports, and the establishment of foreign-funded factories and other businesses in India. The new prime minister hoped to lead India into the computer age and, departing from his grandfather's predisposition toward Great Britain and his mother's leaning toward the Soviet Union – which continued to bolster India's air and sea defences – Rajiv Gandhi looked more to the United States for help and to US technology as his favoured model for India's development. Though hundreds of millions remained unemployed or underemployed and illiterate, he stopped emphasizing the need to abolish or even diminish poverty, instead addressing himself more to the captains of Indian industry and commerce and advocating a trickle-down theory of economic growth.

Gandhi represented the ascension of a new generation to power and brought with him the hope of resolving some of India's long-standing problems. His initial popularity, however, began to diminish after his first two years in office, and charges of mismanagement became common. His greatest political challenge, though, resulted from problems with a member of his own cabinet, Minister of Finance V.P. Singh, who by 1987 had conducted investigations into the machinations of several of India's leading industrial and commercial families and houses whose reputations for tax evasion were notorious. In January of that year Singh found himself suddenly transferred to the Ministry of Defence, but his crusade against corruption continued in his new ministry, where he found signs of financial kickbacks in the procurement of arms, especially from the Swedish firm of Bofors. Political uproar followed and Singh, charging that the government was hindering his investigation, resigned from the cabinet in April.

By 1989 Gandhi, as well as the Congress (I), was still tainted by charges of corruption, and recent price increases on essential goods made the Congress (I) even more vulnerable to opposition parties, including the right-wing Bharatiya Janata ("Indian People's") Party (BJP), headed by L.K. Advani, and V.P. Singh's new Janata Dal. In the general elections held in November, Gandhi barely managed to retain his own *Lok Sabha* seat, as the Congress (I), winning only 193 seats, lost its majority. The Janata Dal (141 seats) emerged with the second largest block, and V.P. Singh, with the support of the BJP (88 seats) and the two main communist parties (44 seats), put together a coalition majority that took office in December.

Relations with the United States improved during the second half of the 1980s, with greater trade, scientific cooperation, and cultural exchanges. When civil rule resumed in Pakistan in 1988, India's relations with that country also reached a new level of friendship, though the South Asian thaw proved to be brief. In December 1985 Rajiv Gandhi had helped to launch the seven-nation South Asian Association for Regional Co-operation (SAARC), whose annual meetings thereafter offered the leaders of India and Pakistan, as well as their smaller neighbours, informal opportunities to discuss and resolve problems.

The problem of Kashmir was among the worst of these, though India had in the late 1980s also accused Pakistan of arming and then sending Pakistani agents across the Punjab border. In late 1989 strikes, terrorism, and unrest escalated, and by early 1990 Kashmir was rocked by a series of violent explosions and fierce exchanges of heavy fire along the line of control that separated the Indian- and Pakistani-administered sectors. A newly vitalized liberation front in Srinagar captured the allegiance of many young Kashmiri Muslims. New Delhi responded by proclaiming president's rule, suspending all local elected government, and rushing in additional troops until the entire state of Jammu and Kashmir was under curfew and martial law.

The Indian government was also confronted by unrest in Sri Lanka, where in the 1980s conflict between the island's Sinhalese Buddhist majority and its Tamil Hindu minority broke out into civil war. With a large, politically powerful Tamil community of its own, India viewed the unrest with particular concern. In 1987, after several SAARC meetings between Gandhi and Sri Lanka's president, J.R. Jayewardene, the two leaders signed a peace accord that provided the Tamils with an autonomous province within a united Sri Lanka. India agreed to prevent Tamil separatists from using its territory, notably Tamil Nadu, for training and shelter and agreed to send an Indian Peace-Keeping Force (IPKF) to disarm the Liberation Tigers of Tamil Eelam (Tamil Tigers) and other

Tamil forces. The IPKF, however, soon found itself embroiled in fighting the Tamil Tigers. The accord had never been popular among Tamils or Sinhalese, and by 1989 the Indian government was bowing to Sri Lankan pressure to pull out its troops. In March 1990, with its mission unaccomplished, the last of the IPKF had been withdrawn.

V.P. Singh's appointment of Haryana's Jat leader, Devi Lal (who had supported him for prime minister), as deputy prime minister raised fears in Punjab that another period of harsh Delhi rule was about to begin. Singh's first visit as prime minister, however, was to Amritsar's Golden Temple, where he walked barefoot to announce that he hoped to bring a "healing touch" to Punjab's sorely torn state. He promised a political solution for the region's problems but, reflecting the ambivalence in his new coalition, did not follow this up with the transfer of Chandigarh or state elections.

A similar ambivalence within the coalition was seen with respect to events in Ayodhya (in Uttar Pradesh), an ancient capital and – most orthodox Hindus believe – birthplace of the deity Rama. The Babri Masjid, a mosque built in 1528, was said to have been built over the very site of Rama's birthplace, where a more ancient Hindu temple, Ram Janmabhoomi, was supposed to have stood. In autumn 1990 a mass march of Hindus bearing consecrated bricks to rebuild "Rama's birth temple" won the support of most members of Advani's BJP, as well as of many other Hindus throughout India. V.P. Singh and his government, however, were committed to India as a secular nation and would not permit the destruction of the mosque, which Muslims considered one of their oldest and most sacred places. India's police were thus ordered to stop the more than one million Hindus, and Advani was arrested. On the same day, October 23, Singh lost his *Lok Sabha* majority, as the BJP withdrew its support for the coalition.

Singh had earlier come under severe attack from many upper-caste Hindus of northern India for sponsoring implementation of the 1980 Mandal Commission report, which recommended that more jobs in all services be reserved for members of the lower castes and ex-untouchable communities (officially called Scheduled Castes). After he announced in August 1990 that the recommendations would be enforced, many young upper-caste Hindus immolated themselves in protests across northern India. Singh's critics accused him of pandering to the lower castes for their votes, and many members of his own party deserted him, foremost among them Chandra Shekhar, who led a splinter group of Janata Dal dissidents out of Singh's coalition. On November 7 1990, V.P. Singh resigned after suffering a vote of no confidence.

Most of those who voted against the prime minister were members of Rajiv Gandhi's Congress (I) Party, for Gandhi retained the largest single block of party faithful in the *Lok Sabha*; however, Advani's BJP support also lined up against Singh. The smallest new party bloc in *Lok Sabha* belonged to Shekhar, whose Janata Dal (S) – the S stood for Socialist – gained the support of Gandhi and thus Shekhar came to be invited by President Ramaswamy Venkataraman to serve as prime minister. Devi Lal, who in August had been ousted by Singh, again became deputy prime minister. With fewer than 60 Janata (S) members in the *Lok Sabha*, however, the new prime minister's hold on power was tenuous and not expected to survive any longer than deemed expedient by Gandhi and the Congress (I) bloc. When the Congress (I) walked out of the *Lok Sabha* in March 1991, Shekhar had little choice but to resign.

The first round of the new elections took place on May 20, but the following day in Tamil Nadu, in a small town just south of Madras (now Chennai), Gandhi was assassinated in a suicide bomb attack. The other two rounds of the elections were postponed in respect for the young leader. After Sonia, Rajiv's Italian-born widow, declined an invitation by the Congress (I) to replace her husband as party president, the Congress (I) closed ranks behind P.V. (Pamulaparti Venkata) Narasimha Rao, a disciple of Mohandas Gandhi and of Nehru who had served as foreign minister under both Indira Gandhi and Rajiv Gandhi, and unanimously elected him Congress (I) president.

"The only way to exist in India is to coexist," Narasimha Rao told his pluralistic nation as election campaigning resumed in early June. Though the younger Gandhi's assassination apparently had ended the Nehru dynasty, the Nehru legacy of secular democratic development for India remained the Congress (I) policy. On June 20, after the Congress (I) won more than 220 of the 524 seats contested for the Lok Sabha, Narasimha Rao was able to form a minority government and became the first Indian prime minister from a southern state (he was born in Madras). The opposition in the Lok Sabha was led by Advani, whose BJP won some 120 seats, reaching a new peak in popularity, especially in the Hindi-speaking heartland of northern India, where it took control of India's most populous state, Uttar Pradesh. The Janata Dal gained fewer than 60 seats, just slightly more than the approximately 50 seats won by the two communist parties.

The Rao government's nearly five-year rule was marked by many challenges. In 1992 Advani's promise to resume his "sacred pilgrimage" to Ayodhya to erect Rama's temple became an immediate and potentially explosive issue when, despite promises of restraint from Hindu nationalist leaders, an army of Hindu protestors tore down the Babri Masjid in December of that year. The mosque's destruction ignited the country's worst interreligious rioting since partition and set the stage for severe clashes between Hindu and Muslim extremists during the rest of the decade. One of the worst incidents occurred two years later when Hindu-Muslim riots in Banga-lore, Karnataka, resulted in 27 deaths when the local television station broadcast news bulletins in Urdu, which was consid-ered to be the language of Muslims.

There were also allegations of corruption within the Rao government, and in 1992 a number of bankers, brokers, and political figures were indicted in a widescale stock market swindle. These financial misdealings took place in a frame-work of growing economic liberalization, deregulation, and privatization that had begun under the government of Rajiv Gandhi and continued unabated until the end of the century and beyond. India's move toward a more market-oriented economy was fuelled largely by an educational system that produced a huge number of graduates in technology and the sciences, and India experienced a dramatic growth in its high-technology and computer sectors.

In 1993 the finance minister, Manmohan Singh, declared that his objectives were to restructure trade and industrial policies, encourage efficiency through greater domestic com-petition, allow producers to have access to imports at reason-able rates of duty, encourage foreign investment, upgrade technology, and integrate the Indian economy with the world economy. In the first six months of that fiscal year, exports registered a 27 per cent increase. Foreign investment commit-ments were placed at $3 billion over an 18-month period. The International Monetary Fund reported that the Indian econ-omy was now the sixth largest in the world. In 1994 a rapprochement with China on the reduction of troops along the 2,500-mile (4,000-kilometres)-long line of control between the two countries led to an agreement between the two countries to expand trade and travel. The following year, both countries began withdrawing troops along the border.

Also in 1995 the government launched three major welfare schemes: a national social assistance scheme for persons over age 65, a school meal plan to benefit 110 million children, and a group insurance scheme. The prime minister also announced a plan to build 10 million rural houses.

Despite a booming national economy, the Congress (I) polled poorly in the 1996 general election, falling from 260 seats in the *Lok Sabha* to only 140 (an all-time low). In part, this drop in support stemmed from accusations of political corruption, but it also signalled a rise in Hindu nationalism in the form of the BJP. Though it gained the overall largest party representation, no party had sufficient seats to form a government. The BJP, led by Atal Bihari Vajpayee, was unable to form a stable coalition, and Vajpayee held the premiership for scarcely a week. A hastily contrived coalition, the United Front (UF), under Janata Dal politician H.D. Deve Gowda, soon was able to seat a government.

The UF announced a programme emphasizing its commitment to secularism and promising the continuation of economic reforms that had been initiated by Congress (I), as well as greater autonomy for states, increased assistance to farmers and lower-class workers, and reserved seats in legislatures for women. But the UF relied on the external support of the Congress (I) in exchange for continuing certain Congress policies. The coalition proved unstable, and Gowda was replaced as prime minister in April 1997 by Inder Kumar Gujral, also of the Janata Dal. Elevation to the prime ministership enabled Inder Kumar Gujral to seek with greater vigour better relations with India's immediate neighbours without demanding reciprocity. In addition, a 30-year agreement with Bangladesh to share the waters of the Ganges river came into effect on January 1.

However, an interim report on Rajiv Gandhi's assassination released in November stated that the Dravida Munnetra

Kazhagam (DMK) party, a member of the UF, shared responsibility in Gandhi's death (the claims were never substantiated). The Congress (I) removed its support and, after the collapse of the UF, new elections were slated for March 1998. The BJP increased its representatives at the election, while the Congress (I), now led by Sonia Gandhi, won five more seats. After much politicking the BJP formed a new governing coalition, again under Vajpayee, but the National Democratic Alliance crumbled in April 1999 and operated as a caretaker government until elections that autumn, when the BJP outpolled all other parties.

India had conducted its first nuclear-weapons test in 1974, but its programme for developing and fielding such weapons had been covert; and in 1995 the country had rejected a call to sign the Nuclear Non-proliferation Treaty (a conference in New York City in May had resolved to extend the treaty indefinitely). India, now under the BJP, publicly and proudly declared itself a member of those states possessing nuclear weapons, and in May 1998 – within months of the BJP coming to power – India tested a series of five nuclear weapons. This apparently was interpreted as sabre rattling by Pakistan, which responded by detonating its own nuclear devices. The international community harshly condemned both sides and urged the two new nuclear powers to begin a dialogue.

Despite several tentative steps toward rapprochement, armed conflict broke out between India and Pakistan in the high mountains of the Kargil region of Jammu and Kashmir state in May 1999. Eventually, intense international pressure induced the Pakistani government to withdraw its troops to its side of the line of control. Nonetheless, Kashmir continued to be a point of contention, and acts of terrorism conducted by extremists hoping to change Indian policy toward the region grew more common and severe.

On December 13 2001, five terrorists, armed with automatic weapons and explosives, made a bid to enter Parliament House in New Delhi. Security guards prevented their entrance, and in the exchange of fire all five raiders and nine other persons were killed. India held two Pakistan-based organizations, Jaish-e-Mohammad and Lashkar-e-Taiba, responsible. Vajpayee held discussions with General Pervez Musharraf of Pakistan in Agra, but these remained deadlocked.

The following February a train carrying Hindu pilgrims was attacked and set on fire by a Muslim mob in Godhra, Gujarat state, resulting in 58 deaths. This ignited a widespread counterattack on Muslims in Ahmedabad, Vadodara, and other towns and villages throughout the state. Hundreds were stabbed to death or burned alive; Muslim-owned shops and properties were looted; and houses were destroyed. More than 100,000 Muslims were forced to take shelter in relief camps. The forces of Hindu militancy received fresh impetus when Muslim terrorists attacked Aksharadham, a Hindu temple in Gandhinagar, in September and killed 28 worshippers.

Corruption continued to plague the government. In March 2001 a website, Tehelka.com, issued an extensively documented report that included videotapes of senior officials and prominent members of the ruling National Democratic Alliance (NDA) accepting money in exchange for defence contracts. Bangaru Laxman, president of the BJP, resigned from his post on March 13; Jaya Jaitly, president of the Samata Party, and George Fernandes, India's defence minister, followed suit two days later. Several other NDA officials were suspended.

Three new states came into being in India in 2000: Chhattisgarh (on November 1), Uttaranchal (on November 8), and Jharkhand (on November 15). They were carved out of three large states – Madhya Pradesh, Uttar Pradesh, and Bihar, respectively. Foreign relations in the period were marked by increased cooperation with foreign states. In 2000, US President Clinton and Vajpayee issued a statement in New Delhi outlining their "shared vision of a closer and qualitatively new relationship for shaping a future of peace, prosperity, democracy, pluralism and freedom." During a visit by Russian President Vladimir Putin that year, a declaration of strategic partnership for the new century and a series of agreements to provide for cooperation in defence production, nuclear energy, and information technology were signed. One of the pacts provided for Russia to supply India with 310 T-90 tanks, to enable licensed production in India of 140 Sukhoy fighter aircraft, to lease four TU-22 bombers, and to give an aircraft carrier that would be refitted at India's cost.

India also sought to improve bilateral relations with China. During the prime minister's visit to Beijing in 2003, it was agreed that border trade via Sikkim would resume. This was considered a major diplomatic win for India because China had not yet officially accepted Sikkim's accession to India. Bilateral trade with China grew at close to 90 per cent in 2003, and China emerged as a major destination for Indian exports. That same year Tamil Nadu's automobile industry acquired new lustre when South Korea's Hyundai began exporting cars to Europe from its Chennai (Madras) plant.

The economy continued to grow during this period, as the government moved toward a less bureaucratic business environment and began to sell publicly owned industries. In 2000 the government announced its intention to divest up to 60 per cent of its holdings in Air-India; the move was seen as a first step toward eventual privatization of the country's state-owned airline. The government also announced that it would reduce its holdings to 26 per cent in three key public-sector enterprises: Indo-Burmah Petroleum, the State Trading Corporation, and the Minerals and Metals Trading Corporation. Exports continued to grow – especially of software products – and in 2003 New Delhi announced that India would stop accepting official development assistance from all but five countries – the United States, the UK, Germany, Russia, and Japan.

Perhaps the most significant growth industry was that of information technology. In May 2000 the *Lok Sabha* passed the Information Technology Bill to boost e-commerce and internet-related business in the country. The bill was a milestone in India's journey toward becoming a key player in the knowledge economy. At the nucleus of the computer revolution were the major metropolitan cities, notably Mumbai (Bombay) and Chennai (Madras), and the silicon triangle of Bangalore (Bengaluru), Pune, and Hyderabad. With the help of these cities, India exported an estimated $4 billion worth of software to the West. Wipro Ltd., a conglomerate based in Bangalore, was identified as India's third largest information technology (IT) company and Wipro's chairman, Azim H. Premji, was listed as one of the world's richest men.

Unlike the Industrial Revolution, which benefited only India's urban elite, the knowledge revolution by 2000 had permeated all sections of Indian society. In a clutch of villages in Madhya Pradesh, an intranet connected rural cyber cafes, allowing villagers access to computerized land records. Project Gyandoot ("Messenger of Knowledge") helped farmers get the best prices for their produce from nearby markets such as Indore and Mumbai. Another wired village, Nayla, Rajasthan, used the internet in social development schemes.

What powered the computer revolution was India's intellectual capital – a technically trained workforce fluent in English more than four million strong – and a 10–12 hour time difference that ensured round-the-clock productivity for

North American and European countries outsourcing their software requirements. The low cost of labour and high quality of software capabilities in India spawned such IT-enabled services as call centres, medical transcription, animation, back-office operations, and revenue accounting.

The watershed year of this revolution was 1998, when such Indian companies as Infosys and Satyam Infoway emerged as world players as fears over computer problems on January 1 2000, plus preparations for the European Union's new currency unit, the euro, increased demand for Indian software programmers. The Hyderabad Information Technology Engineering Consultancy (Hi-Tec City) in Hyderabad powered the growth of this computer mecca, nicknamed Cyberabad. Companies from the United States such as Texas Instruments, Microsoft, IBM, Oracle, Motorola, and GE Capital established operations in India, including software development centres.

In 2004 the country faced national elections again. The BJP espoused a broad Hindu nativism, and during its years of government, Hindu products had been favoured over imports, names of cities changed – either to reflect the precolonial name (Chennai for Madras) or to bring the name more in line with local pronunciation (Kolkata for Calcutta) – and the party openly opposed what it considered non-Hindu values. Given India's tradition of secular politics, many Indians were uncomfortable with this. The Congress (I) regained ground lost in previous general elections, raising its representation in the *Lok Sabha* to 145 seats; the BJP's membership fell to 138 seats. Again, no party had an overall majority, so the Congress (I) formed a coalition known as the United Progressive Alliance (UPA). Congress leader Sonia Gandhi opted not to take the premiership, however, and instead recommended Manmohan Singh, a Sikh, for the post.

Singh had been minister of finance under Narasimha Rao until 1996, and he was the man most credited with restructuring the Indian economy during the 1990s. The election was seen by many as a turn away from the pro-urban policies adopted by the BJP. The economy had boomed since the early 1990s, driven especially by the high-technology and technical-services sector; and after 2000 India registered upwards of 8 per cent annual growth in national income for an unprecedented string of successive years. In addition, foreign direct investment in the country's infrastructure remained high.

The economy in many rural areas, however, had stagnated. Farming remained largely dependent on the monsoon, and many formerly remote areas were opened up merely so that their natural resources might be exploited with little benefit to local inhabitants. Low agricultural growth, at less than 2 per cent per annum, was an area of concern and at the root of rural distress. The new government aimed to revitalize the agrarian economy, step up investment in agriculture, provide access to credit (including lower interest rates on farm loans) and other financial support for farmers, and improve the quality of rural infrastructure. Employment generation and social equity were also important features of its agenda. Kocheril Raman Narayanan, a Dalit ("Oppressed"; the term now commonly used by those traditionally referred to as "untouchable"), had served as president (1997–2002) during the BJP era, and in 2007 Pratibha Patil became the country's first woman president.

In 2005, the government launched new initiatives to step up investment in roads, railways, airports, sea ports, and power. A rural infrastructure programme was launched to focus public expenditure on rural housing, power, telecommunications, and irrigation. The government continued to push for trade liberalization, entering into a range of new free-trade agreements, including ones with ASEAN (Association of South-east Asian Nations) member states. In July of that year, Prime Minister Singh and US President George W. Bush signed an agreement to cooperate in defence matters and in civil nuclear-energy development. India also signed bilateral strategic partnership agreements with the EU, Japan, and Russia and agreed to pursue strategic cooperation with China. In sectors such as railways, ports, and civil aviation, public-private partnerships (PPPs) proved beneficial. The PPP model was an important policy initiative of the UPA government, enabling private enterprise to build on public support.

The growth of industry and India's determination to develop all the infrastructure of a modern state has not been without its consequences, however, and pollution has become a vast problem. In 1993 conservationists campaigned against the Sardar Sarovar Dam project in western India across the Narmada river. Increasing concern regarding pollution around the Taj Mahal in Agra led the Supreme Court, in December 1996, to order the closing of nearly 300 factories in the area. In 1997 the court directed that the felling of trees in forests be stopped. However, the court, in a major judgement delivered in October 2000, rejected the petition of environmentalists and permitted the Sardar Sarovar Dam to be raised to a height of 295 feet (90 metres) initially and 453 feet (138 metres) eventually. Nevertheless, the environmental lobby continued to grow in strength and to have an increasing voice and impact on government.

Singh's government also sought to build diplomatic bridges to Pakistan and to combat terrorism both at home and abroad. In 2005, during Pakistani President Pervez Musharraf's visit to India, Singh and Musharraf spoke about the need to convert the line of control in the Kashmir region into a "soft" border, across which there could be freer and increased trade and movement of people. A first, but important, step toward that end was the resumption of bus services between Srinagar on the Indian side and Muzaffarabad on the Pakistani side.

Along with the growth of terror by Muslim extremists, India experienced a rise in violence among communist (mostly Maoist) groups known as Naxalites. First formed in the 1960s, Naxalite groups experienced a revival in the early twenty-first century, espousing a doctrine of liberation and emancipation. They generally operated in the fringes of society in the most economically backward regions and were highly attractive to marginalized tribal peoples, poor rural residents, and others with grievances, either real or imagined. The union government soon acknowledged that Naxalism, along with terrorism, was a significant threat to internal security in India.

India has also suffered a number of natural disasters since 1990, bringing international attention and aid. In September 1993 the districts of Latur and Osmanabad in Maharashtra were devastated by an earthquake, killing some 10,000 people and leaving 140,000 homeless. On the morning of January 26 2001, the western state of Gujarat suffered an earthquake of magnitude 7.9. Over 14,000 people died, more than 166,000 were injured, and some 370,000 houses were totally destroyed. The government set aside 2 per cent of the nation's income tax revenue to meet the expenditures for relief. Another devastating earthquake, in October 2005 in the Kashmir region, mainly affected the Pakistani-administered area, although hundreds died in Jammu and Kashmir state. An even greater tragedy occurred on December 26 2004, when coastal areas in the Indian Ocean were hit by a massive tsunami, triggered by an undersea earthquake off Sumatra. In India more than 16,000 people died or were missing and presumed dead – including more than 5,000 on the remote and low-lying Andaman and Nicobar Islands, where criticism of the Indian government's slow response to the disaster was especially vocal.

In the early twenty-first century India continued to increase its presence in international affairs and to enter trade agreements with other nations. At the UN in 2004 Singh joined the heads of government of Brazil, Germany, and Japan to launch an initiative by these four countries to be granted permanent-member status in the UN Security Council. At The Hague the same year he participated in the India–European Union Summit meeting, at which India and the EU signed a strategic partnership agreement. In 2006 a visit to India by US President George W. Bush concluded with an agreement on cooperation in the development of India's civilian nuclear-energy capability. The accord allowed sales (the first since 1974) of civilian nuclear fuel and technology to India.

In 2007 India celebrated the 60th anniversary of its foundation as a republic. In that time it had become a modern secular state, and its government's policies had worked to give equality to its more than one billion citizens regardless of ethnicity, religious affiliation, or caste status.

Perhaps the most significant political event of 2007, however, was the surprise win in the provincial legislative elections in northern Uttar Pradesh state by the Bahujan Samaj Party (BSP), led by 51-year-old Mayawati Kumari. The BSP's stunning victory brought into national focus the new political influence wielded by the Dalits, India's lowest social caste. With the BSP's electoral triumph, Mayawati, the first Dalit woman to head an Indian state government, regained the chief ministership of Uttar Pradesh – a post she had held three previous times – and raised interest in her for possible national leadership.

PART THREE

RELIGION, THE ARTS, AND PHILOSOPHY

5

RELIGION

Religion forms a crucial aspect of identity for most Indians. Hinduism is followed by about three-quarters of India's population. Muslims are the largest single minority faith (more than one-ninth of the total population), with large concentrations in many areas of the country, including Jammu and Kashmir, western Uttar Pradesh, West Bengal, Kerala, and many cities.

Other important religious minorities include Christians, most heavily concentrated in the north-east, Mumbai (Bombay), and the far south; Sikhs, mostly in Punjab and some adjacent areas; Buddhists, especially in Maharashtra, Sikkim, Arunachal Pradesh, and Jammu and Kashmir; and Jains, most prominent in Maharashtra, Gujarat, and Rajasthan. Those practising the Bahā'ī faith, formerly too few to be treated by the census, have dramatically increased in number as a result of active proselytization. Zoroastrians (the Parsis), largely concentrated in Mumbai and in coastal Gujarat, wield influence out of all proportion to their small numbers because of their prominence during the colonial period. Several tiny

communities of Jews are located along the western coast.
India's tribal peoples live mostly in the north-east; they practise various forms of animism, which is perhaps the country's
oldest religious tradition.

Hinduism

More strikingly than any other major religious community,
Hindus accept – and indeed celebrate – the organic, multi-
levelled, and sometimes internally inconsistent nature of their
tradition, a perspective expressed in the Hindu prayer "May
good thoughts come to us from all sides." Tolerance is therefore an important aspect of their religion.

For many, Hinduism is not a religion but a way of life.
Hindus speak of their religious identity as *sanatana dharma*,
emphasizing its continuous, seemingly eternal (*sanatana*) existence and the fact that it describes a web of customs,
obligations, traditions, and ideals (*dharma*). Religious atti-
tudes and acts permeate ordinary places, times, and activities;
bathing, dressing, cooking, eating, disposing of leftovers, and
washing the dishes may all be subject to ritual prescriptions.

The origins of Hinduism in India lie in Brahmanism or
Vedism, which developed in India among Indo-European-
speaking peoples who had come from southern Russia and
Central Asia in about 1500 BCE. The indigenous inhabitants of
the subcontinent then began to adapt their religious and social
life to Brahmanic norms, while also introducing their own
cults and gods into Hinduism. In 550–450 BCE breakaway
sects of ascetics arose, leading to the foundation of Buddhism
and Jainism.

At about 500 BCE asceticism became widespread. The
orthodox Brahmanical teachers reacted to this by devising

the doctrine of the four *ashrama*s, which divided life into four stages: the *brahmacharin* (celibate religious student); the *grihastha* (married householder); the *vanaprastha* (forest dweller); and the *sannyasin* (wandering ascetic). The *varnashrama dharma*, or the duties of the four classes (*varna*s) and the four *ashrama*s, constituted the ideal that Hindus were encouraged to follow.

The centuries immediately preceding and following the dawn of the Common Era were marked by the recension of the two great Sanskrit epics, the *Ramayana* and the *Mahabharata* (the latter incorporating into it the *Bhagavadgita*, the "Song of the Lord"). The worship of Vishnu, incarnate as Krishna in the *Mahabharata* and as Rama in the *Ramayana*, developed significantly, as did the cult of Shiva, who plays an active role in the *Mahabharata*. By the time of the Gupta emperors (fourth–sixth century), who took the title *paramabhagavata* ("supreme devotee of Vishnu"), two of the main branches of Hinduism – Vaishnavism and Shaivism – were fully recognized.

The medieval period was characterized by the growth of new devotional religious movements who taught in the popular languages of the time. The beginnings of *bhakti* ("sharing," or "devotion") in northern India probably had its origins in the ideas of two groups of poets – the Nayanars, worshippers of Shiva, and the Alvars, devotees of Vishnu. From time to time during this period Hindus took aggressive action against Buddhism. Buddhism in eastern India, however, was well on the way to being reabsorbed into Hinduism when the Muslims invaded the Ganges valley in the twelfth century. The great Buddhist shrine of Bodh Gaya, the site of the Buddha's enlightenment, became a Hindu temple and remained as such until contemporary times.

Buddhism was at the end of its existence in India, but among the Buddhist Tantrists appeared a new school of preachers, often known as Siddhas ("Those Who Have Achieved"). This was the Sahajayana ("Vehicle of the Natural" or "Easy Vehicle"), which taught that giving up the world was not necessary for release from transmigration and that one could achieve the highest state by living a life of simplicity in one's own home. Sahajayana influenced both Bengali devotional Vaishnavism, which produced a sect called Vaisnava-Sahajiya with similar doctrines, and the Natha yogis, whose teachings influenced Kabir and other later *bhakti* masters.

The advent of Islam in the Ganges basin at the end of the twelfth century resulted in the withdrawal of royal patronage from Hinduism in much of the area. The attitude of the Muslim rulers toward Hinduism varied, with some like Akbar (reigned 1556–1605) being well-disposed toward their Hindu subjects, but many temples were destroyed by the more fanatical rulers. By then, Hinduism was centred in the southern, Dravidian-speaking areas. The system of class and caste had become more rigid, and while large-scale Vedic sacrifices had practically vanished, simple domestic Vedic sacrifices continued, and new forms of animal, and sometimes vegetable, sacrifice had appeared. By that time, too, the main divinities of later Hinduism were worshipped: Rama, the hero of the epic poem, *Ramayana*; Rama's monkey helper, Hanuman, now one of the most popular divinities of India; and Krishna with his adulterous consort, Radha.

From the Gupta period onward, Hindu temples had become larger and more prominent, and their architecture developed in distinctive regional styles. In keeping with their wealth, the great walled temple complexes of south India were (and still are) small cities, containing the central and numerous lesser shrines, bathing tanks, administrative offices, homes of the temple employees, workshops, bazaars, and public buildings of many kinds. As some of the largest employers and greatest landowners in their areas, the temples played an important part in the economy. They also performed valuable social functions, serving as schools, dispensaries, poorhouses, banks, and concert halls.

New forms of south Indian *bhakti* also emerged. Among these was that of Ramanuja, a Tamil Brahman of the eleventh century who was for a time chief priest of the Vaishnava temple of Srirangam, near Tiruchchirappalli (Trichinopoly); and Vallabha (Vallabhacarya; 1479–1531), who emphasized the erotic imagery of the Vaishnava doctrine of grace and established a sect that stressed absolute obedience to the *guru* (teacher). The sect was to decline in the nineteenth century. In south India there emerged the school of Shaiva-siddhanta, still one of the most significant religious forces in that region. An important sect, founded in the twelfth century in the Kannada-speaking area of the Deccan, was that of the Lingayats, or Virashaivas ("Heroes of the Shaiva Religion"), which rejected the *Vedas*, the Brahman priesthood, and all caste distinctions.

Hinduism endured during the Mughal period, despite the widespread destruction of temples. Shaivism underwent significant growth in northern India. In the thirteenth century Gorakhnath (also known as Gorakshanatha), who became leader of a sect of Shaivite ascetics known as Nathas ("Lords") from the title of their chief teachers, introduced new ideas and practices to Shaivism. The Gorakhnathis were particularly important as propagators of Hatha Yoga. The poets and saints (highly respected ascetics who were at times believed to be incarnations of a deity) of medieval *bhakti* appeared throughout India.

After the fall of the Mughal Empire, the English East India Company, conscious of the disadvantages of unnecessarily antagonizing its Indian subjects, continued the patronage accorded by indigenous rulers to many Hindu temples. In the nineteenth and twentieth centuries, there were a number of reform movements that took on aspects of Hinduism. The most important were those of Ram Mohun Roy – outwardly a Hindu, but with an intense belief in strict monotheism and in the evils of image worship – who founded the Brahmo Samaj ("Society of God") in 1828, and of Dayanand Sarasvati, who founded the Arya Samaj in 1875. Dayanand rejected image worship, sacrifice, and polytheism and claimed to base his doctrines on the four *Vedas* as the eternal word of God.

Ramakrishna, a devotee at Daksineshvar, a temple of Kali north of Kolkata (Calcutta), attracted a band of educated lay followers who spread his doctrines. As a result of his studies and visions, he came to the conclusion that "all religions are true" but that the religion of a person's own time and place was for that person the best expression of the truth. Ramakrishna thus gave educated Hindus a basis on which they could justify the less rational aspects of their religion to a consciousness increasingly influenced by western values.

Among the followers of Ramakrishna was Narendranath Datta, who became an ascetic after his master's death and assumed the religious name Vivekananda. After lecturing in the United States and England, he returned to India in 1897 with a small band of western disciples and founded the Ramakrishna Mission, the most important modern organization of reformed Hinduism. Vivekananda, more than any earlier Hindu reformer, encouraged social service and, influenced by progressive western political ideas, set himself firmly against all forms of caste distinction and fostered a spirit of self-reliance in his followers. With branches in many parts of the world, the Ramakrishna Mission has done much to spread knowledge of its version of Hinduism outside India.

Other important figures included Shri Aurobindo, who established an *ashram* and achieved a high reputation as a sage; the great Bengali poet Rabindranath Tagore, who did much to disseminate Hindu religious thought in the West; Ramana Maharshi, a Tamil mystic who maintained almost complete silence and attracted a large band of devotees, especially in the Dravidian south; and Swami Shivananda, who established an *ashram* and an organization called the Divine Life Society near the sacred site of Rishikesh in the Himalayas and who based his teaching on more or less orthodox Vedanta (one of the six systems of Indian philosophy), combined with both Yoga and *bhakti*, but rejected caste and stressed social service.

During the fight for independence, Hindu religious concepts were enlisted in the nationalist cause. Bal Gangadhar Tilak, an orthodox Maharashtrian Brahman, used the annual festival of the god Ganesha for nationalist propaganda. His interpretation of the *Bhagavadgita* as a call to action was also a reflection of his nationalism, and through his mediation the scripture inspired later leaders, including Mohandas (Mahatma) Gandhi. The Bengali writer Bankim Chandra Chatterjee, in his novel *Anandamath*, 1882, described a band of martial ascetics who pledged to free India from Muslim domination under the Mughal Empire and who took as their anthem a stirring devotional song "Bande Mataram" ("I Revere the Mother") – whose title referred both to the fierce demon-destroying goddess Kali and to India itself. This song was soon adopted by other nationalists. Vivekananda emphasized the need to turn the emotion of *bhakti* toward the suffering poor of India. During his short career as a revolutionary, Shri Aurobindo made much use of "Bande Mataram," and he called on his countrymen to strive for the freedom of India in a spirit of devotion.

Mahatma Gandhi was much influenced by the *bhakti* of his native Gujarat, and in many ways was a Hindu traditionalist. He adopted an austere celibate life and followed a doctrine of nonviolence that can be found in many Hindu sources, although his beliefs were much strengthened by Christian ethical literature. His insistence on strict vegetarianism and celibacy among his disciples, in keeping with the traditions of Vaishnava asceticism, caused difficulty among some of his followers. Still, Gandhi's success represented a political culmination of the movement of popular *bhakti* begun in south India early in the Common Era.

Increasing nationalism, especially after the division of British India into India and Pakistan in 1947, led to a widening of the gulf between Hindus and Muslims. Many leaders of the Indian National Congress movement, such as Jawaharlal Nehru, carried their Hinduism lightly and favoured a secular approach to politics; the majority, however, followed the lead of Gandhi. Although to the right of the Congress politically, the Hindu Mahasabha, a nationalist group formed to give Hindus a stronger voice in politics, did not oppose nonviolence in its drive to establish a Hindu state in India. The transfer of power in 1947 was accompanied by slaughter and pillage of huge proportions and by mass migration. The tension culminated in the assassination of Gandhi by a Hindu fanatic in January 1948.

The policy of the new Indian government was to establish a secular state, and the successive governments have broadly kept to this policy. Discrimination against "untouchables" – now officially called Scheduled Castes and often referred to by euphemisms such as Harijans ("People of God") or the self-describing Dalits ("Oppressed") – has been forbidden, and legislation in 1955 and 1956 gave full rights of inheritance to widows and daughters, enforced monogamy, and permitted divorce on quite easy terms. The 1961 law forbidding dowries further undermined traditional Hinduism.

The social structure of traditional Hinduism is today slowly crumbling in the cities. Intercaste and interreligious marriages are becoming more frequent among the educated, although some aspects of the caste system show remarkable vitality, especially in the matter of appointments and elections. The bonds of the tightly knit Hindu joint family are also weakening, a process helped by legislation and the emancipation of women. The professional priests, who perform rituals for laypeople in homes or at temples and sacred sites, complain of the lack of custom, and their numbers are diminishing.

Nevertheless, Hinduism is far from dying. Films with mythological themes are enjoying a renaissance. Organizations such as the Ramakrishna Mission flourish and expand their activities. New teachers appear from time to time and attract considerable followings. Militant fundamentalist Hindu organizations such as the Society for the Self-Service of the Nation (Rashtriya Svayamsevak Sangh; RSS) are steadily growing.

The adaptability of Hinduism to changing conditions is illustrated by the appearance in the Hindu pantheon of a new divinity, the goddess Santosi Mata, who is of special utility in an acquisitive society. Santosi, who has no basis in any Puranic myth, is now worshipped throughout India, especially by women – largely as the result of a popular mythological film about her. Santosi, it is believed, grants practical and obvious blessings, such as a promotion for an overworked husband or a new household appliance. On both the intellectual and the popular level, Hinduism is thus in the process of adapting itself to new values and new conditions brought about by mass education and industrialization.

Five elements have given shape to the Hindu religious tradition: doctrine, practice, society, story, and devotion.

Doctrine is expressed in a vast textual tradition anchored to the *Veda*s (*Veda* means "Knowledge"), the oldest core of Hindu religious utterance, and organized through the centuries primarily by members of the learned Brahman class. Parts of the *Veda*s are quoted in essential Hindu rituals (such as the wedding cer-emony), and it is the source of many enduring patterns of Hindu thought.

Belief in the importance of the search for a One that is the All is characteristic. Most Hindus believe in brahman, an un-created, eternal, infinite, transcendent, and all-embracing principle that is the ultimate cause, foundation, source, and goal of all existence. Hindus differ, however, as to whether this ultimate reality is best conceived as lacking attributes and qualities – the impersonal brahman – or as a personal god, especially Vishnu, Shiva, or Shakti. Hindus generally accept the doctrine of transmigration and rebirth and the comp-lementary belief in karma – the influence of past actions on future lives. Actions generated by desire and appetite bind one's spirit (*jiva*) to an endless series of births and deaths. Desire motivates any social interaction, resulting in the mutual exchange of good and bad karma. In one prevalent view, the very meaning of salvation is emancipation (*moksha*) from this. In this view the only goal is the one permanent and eternal principle: the One, God, brahman.

The *Bhagavadgita* ("Song of the Lord"; *c*.100 CE), an extremely influential Hindu text, presents three paths to salvation: the *karma-marga* ("path of duties"), the disinter-ested discharge of ritual and social obligations; the *jnana-marga* ("path of knowledge"), the use of meditative concen-tration preceded by long and systematic ethical and contem-plative training (Yoga) to gain a supraintellectual insight into one's identity with brahman; and the *bhakti-marga* ("path of devotion"), love for a personal god. The *Bhagavadgita* states that because action is inescapable, the three paths are better thought of as simultaneously achieving the goals of world maintenance (*dharma*) and world release (*moksha*). Through the suspension of desire and ambition and through a taste for the fruits (*phala*) of one's actions, one is enabled to float free of life while engaging it fully. This matches the actual goals of most Hindus, which include executing properly one's social and ritual duties; supporting one's caste, family, and profession; and working to achieve a broader stability in the cosmos, nature, and society.

Because no one person can occupy all the social, occupational, and age-defined roles that are requisite to maintaining the health of the life-organism as a whole, universal maxims (such as *ahimsa,* the desire not to harm) are qualified by the more particular *dharma*s that are appropriate to each of the four major *varna*s (classes). These in turn are superseded by the *dharma*s appropriate to each caste (*jati*), and by obligations appropriate to one's gender and stage of life (*ashrama*).

For many centuries the relative value of an active life and the performance of meritorious works (*pravritti*), as opposed to the renunciation of all worldly interests and activity (*nivriti*), has been a much-debated issue. While philosophical works such as the mystically oriented and esoteric Upanishads emphasized renunciation, the *dharma* texts argued that the householder who maintains his sacred fire, begets children, and performs his ritual duties well also earns religious merit. Nearly 2,000 years ago these *dharma* texts elaborated the social doctrine of the four *ashramas* (literally, "abodes"). This held that a male member of any of the three higher classes should first become a chaste student (*brahmacharin*); then become a married householder (*grihastha*), discharging his debts to his ancestors by begetting sons and to the gods by sacrificing; then retire (as a *vanaprastha*), with or without his wife, to the forest to devote himself to spiritual contemplation; and finally, but not mandatorily, become a homeless wandering ascetic (*sannyasin*).

The texts describing such life stages were written by men for men; they paid scant attention to stages appropriate for women. Most women thus focused their religious lives on realizing a state of blessedness that was understood to be at once this-worldly and expressive of a larger cosmic well-being. Women have often directed the cultivation of the auspicious life-giving force (*shakti*) they possess to the benefit of their husbands and families but, as an ideal, this force has independent status.

Practice is the second strand in Hindu tradition and concerns common rituals, including various surviving elements of Vedic ritual and the worship of icons or images. Broadly, this is called *puja* ("honouring [the deity]"). The purpose of many rituals is to promote auspiciousness – a pervasive Hindu concept indicating all kinds of good fortune or well-being. One key element in all worship is *prasad*, translated simply as "blessing" or "grace" and sometimes more literally as "blessed leftovers." This term refers to the returned portion of a worshipper's or pilgrim's offering, which is understood as having value added by the intangible process of a deity's consumption.

Another important element of temple worship is seeing the deity, *darshan*; as the worshipper's gaze engages the deity's awareness of him or her, a channel of grace is formed. Ringing bells, blowing conch shells, singing or playing instrumental music, burning incense, and pouring clarified butter on to smouldering coals alert the deity to the devotee's presence. Worshippers commonly prostrate themselves, or circumambulate the deity's altar. Worship may also be performed at a home altar or a wayside shrine, and south Indian housewives traditionally turn their thresholds into auspicious altars for the goddess each morning as they draw ritual designs, which are almost instantly trampled back into dust.

Many of the Vedic rituals, such as the Vedic fire rituals, have now been replaced by image worship and other forms of devotionalism or have fallen into disuse. Those that survive tend to be domestic (*grihya*) rituals and include the remaining *samskara*s – transitional rites intended to prepare a person for a certain event or for the next stage in life by removing *taints* (sins) or by generating fresh qualities. Practised since antiquity, in later times 16 *samskara*s were recognized but today only those of impregnation, initiation, and marriage are regularly held.

The impregnation rite, consecrating the intended time of conception, consists of a ritual meal of pounded rice, an offering of rice boiled in milk, the sprinkling of the woman with water, and sexual intercourse; all acts are also accompanied by *mantras* (sacred utterances). In the third month of pregnancy the rite called *punsavana* (begetting of a son) follows. The birth is itself the subject of elaborate ceremonies, the main features of which are an oblation of *ghee* (clarified butter) cast into the fire; the introduction of a pellet of honey and *ghee* into the newborn child's mouth, an act intended to produce mental and physical strength; the murmuring of *mantras* for a long life; and rites to counteract inauspicious influences.

A hallmark of childhood *samskara*s is a general male bias, but there are also life-cycle rites that focus upon the lives of girls and women. In south India, for instance, one finds an initiation rite (*vilakkitu kalyanam*) that corresponds roughly to *upanayana*, the male initiation, and that gives girls the authority to light oil lamps and thereby to become full participants in proper domestic worship. The important *upanayana* initiation is held when a boy is between the ages of 8 and 12, and marks his entry into the community of the three higher classes of society.

Wedding ceremonies are the most important of all. The bridegroom is conducted to the home of his future parents-in-law, who receive him as an honoured guest; there are offerings of roasted grain into the fire; the bridegroom has to take hold of the bride's hand; he conducts her around the sacrificial fire; seven steps are taken by bride and bridegroom to solemnize the irrevocability of the union; both are, in procession, conducted to their new home, which the bride enters without touching the threshold. Of eight forms of marriage recognized by the ancient authorities, two have remained in vogue: the simple gift of a bride, and the legalization of the alliance by means of a marriage gift paid to the bride's family.

Many people also still perform the *sraddha* ceremony, in which food is offered to Brahmans for the benefit of the deceased, at least once a year. There are Shaiva and Vaishnava variants to rites and rituals.

There are also five obligatory offerings, made on a daily basis: (i) offerings to the gods (food taken from the meal), (ii) a cursory offering (*bali*) made to "all beings," (iii) a libation of water mixed with sesame offered to the spirits of the deceased, (iv) hospitality, and (v) recitation of the *Vedas*. As well as the important duties of morning and evening adorations (*sandhya*), Hindus observe *seva* (service), the regular, respectful attentions to the needs of enshrined deities or icons (*murti*). This may involve bathing an icon, changing its ornaments, ringing bells, and waving lights before it (*arati*).

The third strand that has served to organize Hindu life is society, most notably the caste system, which draws its authority from the *Rigveda*'s four-part cosmos and its human counterpart, a four-part social order comprising Brahmans (priests), Kshatriyas (nobles), Vaishyas (commoners), and Sudras (servants). Another dimension drawing Hindus into a single community of discourse is narrative, the stories of major figures in the Hindu pantheon. Often such narratives illustrate the interpenetration of the divine and human spheres, with deities such as Krishna and Rama entering entirely into the human drama.

Bhakti ("sharing," or "devotion"), a broad tradition of a loving god that is especially associated with the lives and words of vernacular poet saints throughout India, is the fifth strand of Hinduism. Devotional poems attributed to these inspired figures, called *bhakti* verse, have elaborated a store of images and moods to which access can be had in a score of languages. Devotion in ordinary life is usually embedded in the worship of a chosen deity, vows, and pilgrimage.

Hindu festivals take place throughout the year, some lasting for many days. The most important are Holi (formerly celebrating Kama, the god of sexual desire); a saturnalia connected with the spring equinox; and Diwali, which features worship and ceremonial lights in honour of Lakshmi (the goddess of wealth and good fortune), fireworks to chase away the spirits of the deceased, and gambling (an old ritual custom intended to secure luck for the coming year).

Islam

The Muslim faith was promulgated by the Prophet Muhammad in Arabia in the seventh century CE, entering India a century later. The Arabic term *islām*, literally "surrender," illuminates the fundamental religious idea of Islam – that the believer accepts "surrender to the will of Allah (Arabic: God)," the creator, sustainer, and restorer of the world. Islamic doctrine, law, and thinking in general are based upon four sources, or fundamental principles: (i) the Qur'an (literally, "Reading" or "Recitation"), regarded as the verbatim word, or speech, of God delivered to Muhammad by the angel Gabriel, (ii) the *sunnah* ("traditions"), the example of the Prophet – i.e. his words and deeds as recorded in compilations known as Hadith (literally, "Report"; a collection of sayings attributed to the Prophet), (iii) *ijmā'* ("consensus"), a principle of stability in thinking; points on which consensus was reached in practice were considered closed and further substantial questioning of them prohibited, and (iv) *ijtihād* ("individual thought"), required to find the legal or doctrinal solution to a new problem.

The doctrine about God in the Qur'an is rigorously monotheistic. The Qur'an describes human nature as frail and faltering, and prone to rebelliousness and pride. True faith (*iman*) thus consists of belief in the immaculate Divine Unity and Islam in one's submission to the Divine Will. The doctrine of social service, in terms of alleviating suffering and helping the needy, constitutes an integral part of Islamic teaching. With this socioeconomic doctrine, there emerges the idea of a closely knit community of the faithful who are declared to be "brothers unto each other." Opponents from within the community are to be fought and reduced with armed force, if issues cannot be settled by persuasion and arbitration.

Besides a measure of economic justice and the creation of a strong idea of community, the Prophet Muhammad effected a general reform of Arab society, in particular protecting its weaker segments – the poor, orphans, women, and slaves. Distinction and privileges based on tribal rank or race were repudiated in the Qur'an. During the earliest decades after the death of the Prophet, certain basic features of the religio-social organization of Islam were singled out to serve as anchoring points of the community's life and formulated as the "Pillars of Islam". These were the profession of faith: "There is no deity but God, and Muhammad is the messenger of God," upon which depends membership in the community; five daily canonical prayers; the tax called *zakat* ("purification," indicating that such a payment makes the rest of one's wealth religiously and legally pure), used primarily for the poor and now optional; fasting during the month of Ramadan; and the annual pilgrimage (*hajj*) to Mecca prescribed for every Muslim once in a lifetime – "provided one can afford it", and provided a person has enough provisions to leave for his family in his absence.

Muhammad ibn 'Abd Allah ibn 'Abd al-Muttalib (570–632 CE) was a member of a high-status tribe. He belonged to one of its less well-placed clans, but his marriage brought him wealth and status. He began to absent himself in the hills outside Mecca and it was while on retreat, at the age of 40, that he saw a figure whom he later identified as the angel Gabriel, who forced him to repeat these words: "Recite: In the name of God, the Merciful and Compassionate. Recite: And your Lord is Most Generous. He teaches by the pen, teaches man what he knew not." Muhammad had other visions and began to preach and attract followers. In 622 CE, when the Prophet migrated to Medina, his preaching was accepted and the community-state of Islam emerged.

By the time of the emigration, a new label had begun to appear in Muhammad's recitations to describe his followers; in addition to being described in terms of their faithfulness (*iman*) to God and his messenger, they were also described in terms of their undivided attention, that is, as muslims – individuals who assumed the right relationship to God by surrendering (*islām*) to his will.

During this early period, Islam acquired its characteristic ethos as a religion uniting in itself both the spiritual and temporal aspects of life and seeking to regulate not only the individual's relationship to God (through his conscience) but human relationships in a social setting as well. Thus, there is not only an Islamic religious institution but also an Islamic law, state, and other institutions governing society.

This dual religious and social character of Islam, expressing itself in one way as a religious community commissioned by God to bring its own value system to the world through the *jihad* (literally, "struggle" or "battle"; often translated as "holy war"), explains the astonishing success of the early Muslims. Within a century after the Prophet's death in 632 CE, they had brought a large part of the globe – from Spain across Central Asia to India – under a new Arab Muslim empire. Within another century Muslim conquerors surpassed the achievement of Alexander the Great, not only in the durability of their accomplishment but in its scope as well, reaching from the Iberian Peninsula to Central Asia. Islam's essential egalitarianism within the community of the faithful and its official discrimination against the followers of other religions won rapid converts among Jews and Christians.

Around 750, a schism developed between the more traditional Sunnī and their main opponents, the more radical Shi'ītes. While both groups followed the *sunnah* ("traditions") of Muhammad, for the Sunnī (more properly called the Jama'i-Sunnī) the principle of solidarity was essential. The Shi'ītes argued that the fundamental element of the *sunnah*, and one wilfully overlooked by the Jama'i-Sunnī, was Muhammad's devotion to his family and his wish that they succeed him through 'Ali, the cousin and son-in-law of Muhammad.

During and just after the lifetime of the Shi'ītes' leader Ja'far ibn Muhammad (Ja'far as-Sādiq), further splits occurred.

These gave rise to the Zaydiyyah (Zaydis), or Fivers (for their allegiance to the fifth imam); the Imaiis or Ithnā ʿAshariyah (Twelvers; followers of Jaʿfar's son Musa al-Kazim and imams in his line through to the 12th imam, who disappeared in 873); and the Ismaʿiliyah (Ismaʿilis) or Sabʿiyah (Seveners), who remained loyal to Ismaʿil, Jaʿfar's eldest son.

In the middle of the "Shiʿite century" (mid-tenth to mid-eleventh century) a major Sunnī revival occurred in the eastern part of the Islamic world, in connection with the emergence of the second major language of Islamicate high culture, New Persian. At this time, the Iranian dynasty, the Ghaznavids, entered India. Sebüktigin (ruled 977–997), a Samanid Turkic slave governor in Ghazna (now Ghazni), in the Afghan mountains, had made himself independent of his masters as their central power declined. His eldest son, Mahmud, expanded into Buyid territory in western Iran, identifying himself staunchly with Sunnī Islam. Presenting himself as a frontier warrior against the pagans, Mahmud then invaded and plundered north-western India, establishing a permanent rule in the Punjab. Later his power declined, and at the Battle of Dandanqan (1040), Mahmud's son, Masʿud I, lost control of Khorasan to the Seljuq Turks and withdrew to Lahore, from which his successors ruled until overtaken by the Ghurids in 1186.

The first Mongol invasions into the Islamic Empire occurred in 1220 under Genghis Khan. The Chagatai dominated the Syr Darya (Jaxartes) and Amu Darya (Oxus) basins, the Kabul mountain ranges, and eventually the Punjab. But in 1295 a Buddhist named Mahmud Ghazan became Khan and declared himself Muslim, compelling other Mongol notables to follow suit. By the 1330s, however, their rule had begun to be fragmented among numerous local leaders.

To the east the Delhi Sultanate of Turkic slave-soldiers (Mamluks) had withstood Mongol pressure, and it now began to extend Muslim control south into India, a feat that was virtually accomplished under Muhammad ibn Tughluq. Not possessing the kind of dynastic legitimacy the pastoralist Mongols had asserted, Muhammad ibn Tughluq tied his legitimacy to his support for the Shari'ah (Islamic law). He even sought to have himself invested by the titular 'Abbasid caliph whose line the Mamluks earlier had taken to and installed at Cairo. His concern with the Shari'ah coincided with the growing popularity of Sufism (Muslim mystics) in India.

After the twelfth century, it was the Sufis who were mainly responsible for the spread of Islam in India, though it was the far-ranging influence of Muslim traders that introduced Islam to the Indian east coast and to south India.

In the sixteenth century, Babur inaugurated the Mughal Empire in India. It flourished especially under his grandson Akbar (ruled 1556–1605) and his successors, who promoted a tolerant regime. With the accession of Aurangzeb (ruled 1659–1707), a stricter communalism emerged that imposed penalties on protected non-Muslims and stressed the shah's role as leader of the Muslim community, by virtue of his enforcing the Shari'ah. But by the beginning of the eighteenth century, the Empire had begun to disintegrate.

With the loss of political power during the period of western colonialism in the nineteenth and twentieth centuries, the concept of the Islamic community (*ummah*), instead of weakening, became stronger. In the twentieth century Islamic nationalism increased, alongside other nationalist expression. Partition in 1947 saw the mass emigration of Muslims into Pakistan.

Today, India's Muslim population is greater than that found in any country of the Middle East, and is only exceeded by that of Indonesia and, by a slight margin, by that of Pakistan or

Bangladesh. Sunnī Muslims are the majority sect in India almost everywhere. There are, however, influential Shiʻite minorities in Gujarat, especially among such Muslim trading communities as the Khojas and Bohras, and in large cities such as Lucknow and Hyderabad that were former capitals of preindependence Muslim states, in which much of the gentry was of Persian origin.

Sikhism

Sikhism was founded in the Punjab in the late fifteenth century. The Sikhs call their faith Gurmat (Punjabi: "the Way of the Guru"). According to Sikh tradition (its history relies on the traditional Sikh account, most elements of which are derived from hagiographic legend and lore), Sikhism was established by Guru Nanak (1469–1539) and subsequently led by a succession of nine other Gurus.

All ten human Gurus, Sikhs believe, were inhabited by a single spirit. Upon the death of the tenth, Guru Gobind Singh (1666–1708), the spirit of the eternal Guru transferred itself to the sacred scripture of Sikhism, Guru Granth Sahib ("The Granth as the Guru"), also known as the *Adi Granth* ("First Volume"), which thereafter was regarded as the sole Guru. In the early twenty-first century there were nearly 25 million Sikhs worldwide, the great majority of them living in the Indian state of Punjab.

In its earliest stage Sikhism was clearly a movement within the Hindu tradition. Nanak was raised a Hindu and eventually belonged to the Sant tradition of northern India, a movement associated with the great poet and mystic Kabir (1440–1518). The Sants composed hymns of great beauty expressing their experience of the divine, which they saw in all things. Like the followers of *bhakti*, the Sants believed that devotion to God is essential to liberation from the cycle of rebirth in which all human beings are trapped; unlike the followers of *bhakti*, however, the Sants maintained that God is *nirgun* ("without form") and not *sagun* ("with form"). They also promoted the meditation techniques of Hatha Yoga as the means of spiritual liberation.

The story of Nanak's life has been the imagined product of the legendary *janam-sakhi*s ("life stories") – which were composed between 50 and 80 years after the Guru's death in 1539, and only a tiny fraction of the material found in them can be affirmed as factual – and can also be gleaned from other variously reliable sources. A member of the Khatri (trading) caste, Nanak was not a typical Sant, yet he experienced the same spirit of God in everything outside him and everything within him as did others in the movement he founded.

Nanak was born in 1469 in the village of Rai Bhoi di Talvandi, in the Punjab, which has been the home of the Sikh faith ever since. For several years Nanak worked in a granary until his religious vocation drew him away from both family and employment. Nanak made five trips, one in each of the four cardinal directions of the compass, followed by one within the Punjab. He debated with Nath masters known as Siddhs, who were believed to have attained immortality through the practice of yoga, and he visited Baghdad, Mecca, and Medina. By 1520, however, he seems to have returned to the Punjab.

The remaining years of his life were spent in Kartarpur, central Punjab. By this time it must be assumed that Nanak was recognized as a Guru and that disciples who accepted him as their Guru gathered around him there. The actual year of Nanak's death is disputed, but it was most probably 1539. One of his disciples, Angad, was chosen by Nanak as his spiritual successor, and following Nanak's death he assumed the leadership of the young Sikh community as Guru Angad.

Nanak composed many hymns, which were collected in the *Adi Granth* by Guru Arjan, the fifth Sikh Guru, in 1604. He taught that all people are subject to the transmigration of souls and that the sole and sufficient means of liberation from the cycle of rebirth is meditation on the divine *nam* (Persian: "name"). According to Nanak, the *nam* encompasses the whole of creation – everything outside the believer and everything within him. Having heard the divine word (*shabad*) through a grace bestowed by God, or Akal Purakh (one of Nanak's names for God), and having chosen to accept the word, the believer undertakes *nam simaran* (meditation on the name). Through this discipline, he gradually begins to perceive manifold signs of the *nam*, and the means of liberation are progressively revealed. Ascending to ever-higher levels of mystical experience, the believer is blessed with a mounting sense of peace and joy. Eventually the *sach khand* ("abode of truth") is reached, and the believer passes into a condition of perfect and absolute union with Akal Purakh.

Sikhs believe that the "voice" with which the word is uttered within the believer's being is that of the spirit of the eternal Guru. Because Nanak performed the discipline of *nam simaran*, the eternal Guru took flesh and dwelt within him. Upon Nanak's death the eternal Guru was embodied, in turn, in each of Nanak's successors until, with the death of Guru Gobind Singh, it was enshrined in the holy scripture of the Sikhs, the Guru Granth Sahib.

The fourth Guru, Ram Das, made two significant changes to Sikh practice: he introduced the appointment of *masands* (vicars), charged with the care of defined congregations (*sangats*), and he founded the important centre of Amritsar, the capital of the Sikh religion and the location of the *Harimandir* (later known as the Golden Temple), the chief house of worship in Sikhism. Arjan, the fifth Guru, compiled the Goindval Pothis, a scripture of sacred hymns, which had been prepared at the instructions of Amar Das, the third Guru. Under the sixth Guru the doctrine of *miri/piri* emerged. Like his predecessors, the Guru still engaged in *piri*, spiritual leadership, but to it he now added *miri*, the rule of a worldly leader. The Panth ("Path"; the Sikh community) was thus no longer an exclusively religious community but was also a military one that was commonly involved in open warfare. All Sikhs were expected to accept the new dual authority of the Gurus.

The final contribution of the Gurus came with Gobind Singh (1666–1708). Guru Gobind Singh believed that the forces of good and evil fell out of balance on occasion, and at times the latter increased enormously. Akal Purakh then intervened in human history to correct the balance, choosing as his agents particular individuals who fought the forces of evil that had acquired excessive power. Gobind Singh believed that the Mughals, through Emperor Aurangzeb, had tipped the scale too far toward evil and that he had been divinely appointed to restore the balance between good and evil. He also believed that drawing the sword was justified to rein in evil.

Soon after the creation of the Khalsa ("Pure"; the purified and reconstituted Sikh community), Guru Gobind Singh was attacked by other chieftans from the Shiwalik Hills in league with the Mughal governor of the town of Sirhind. In 1704 he was compelled to withdraw from Anandpur. He escaped to southern Punjab, where he inflicted a defeat on his pursuers at Muktsar. He then moved on to Damdama, remaining there until 1706. When Aurangzeb died in 1707, Gobind Singh agreed to accompany Aurangzeb's successor, Bahadur Shah, to southern India. Arriving at Nanded on the banks of the Godavari river in 1708, he was assassinated. Guru Gobind

Singh is without doubt the beau ideal of the Sikhs, regarded as the supreme exemplar of all that a Sikh of the Khalsa should be. The duty of every Khalsa member, therefore, is to follow his path and to perform works that would be worthy of him.

The most significant figure in eighteenth-century Sikh history is Lacchman Dev, who was converted to the Sikh faith by Guru Gobind Singh and on whom was conferred the title of Bahadur ("the Brave"). He mounted a successful campaign in the Punjab against the governor of Sirhind, but after further fighting against the Mughals he was forced to surrender and was executed. He introduced changes to the Khalsa, and required his followers to be vegetarians and to wear red garments instead of the traditional blue. Those who accepted these changes were called Bandai Sikhs, while those opposed to them – led by Mata Sundari, one of Guru Gobind Singh's widows – called themselves the Tat Khalsa (the "True" Khalsa or "Pure" Khalsa).

With the fall of Mughal power in the mid-eighteenth century, the Sikhs formed groups later known as *misls* or *misals*. Beginning as warrior bands, the emergent *misls* and their *sardar*s (chieftains) gradually established their authority over quite extensive areas. The *misls* eventually faced the Afghan army of Ahmad Shah, several miles from Amritsar, and in the ensuing battle Dip Singh, the Sikh *misl* leader, was beheaded.

By the end of Ahmad Shah's invasions in 1769, the Punjab was largely in the hands of 12 *misls* and, with the external threat removed, the *misls* turned to fighting between themselves. Eventually, one *misldar* (commander), Ranjit Singh (the leader of the Sukerchakia *misl*, named after the town of Sukkarchak in what is now north-eastern Punjab province, Pakistan), won almost complete control of the Punjab. By 1799 he had entered Lahore, and in 1801 he proclaimed himself *maharaja* (ruler) of the Punjab. He sheathed the two upper storeys of the *Harimandir* in gold leaf, thereby converting it into what became known as the Golden Temple. He also created an entirely new army on a western model, and added the city of Multan, the Vale of Kashmir, and the citadel of Peshawar to the kingdom of the Punjab.

After his death, the Punjab quickly descended into chaos and, following two wars with the British, the state was annexed in 1849 to become a part of British India. For their loyalty to the British administration during the unsuccessful Indian Mutiny of 1857–58, the Sikhs were rewarded with grants of land and other privileges. Peace and prosperity within the Punjab made possible the founding of the first Singh Sabha, a religious and educational reform movement, in Amritsar in 1873. Its purpose was to demonstrate that Sikhs were not involved in the Indian Mutiny and to respond to signs of decay within the Panth, such as haircutting and tobacco smoking. A more radical branch of the Singh Sabha was established in Lahore in 1879. The Amritsar group came to be known as the Sanatan ("Traditional") Sikhs, whereas the radical Lahore branch was known as the Tat Khalsa.

The differences between the two groups were considerable. The Sanatan Sikhs regarded themselves as part of the wider Hindu community (then the dominant view within the Panth), and they tolerated such things as idols in the Golden Temple. The Tat Khalsa, on the other hand, insisted that Sikhism was a distinct and independent faith. Other radical adherents, influenced by western standards of scholarship, set out to revise and rationalize the *rahit-namas* (the manuals containing the Rahit, the Sikh code of belief and conduct), removing parts that were erroneous, inconsistent, or antiquated. Their work eventually resulted in a clear statement of the Five Ks – *kes* or *kesh* (uncut hair), *kangha* (comb), *kacch* (short trousers), *kara* (steel bracelet), and *kirpan* (double-edged dagger) – which has since been adopted by all orthodox Sikhs.

The controversy between the Sanatan Sikhs and the Tat Khalsa Sikhs continued for some time but, by the twentieth century, the Tat Khalsa interpretation was accepted as dominant.

After a dispute with the British in the Punjab during the early 1920s over control of the larger *gurdwara*s (Punjabi: "doorways to the Guru"; the Sikh houses of worship), the Legislative Council of the Punjab adopted the Sikh Gurdwaras Act of 1925, whereby the principal *gurdwara*s were entrusted to Sikh control. The *gurdwara*s have been governed ever since by the Shiromani Gurdwara Prabandhak Committee, an elected body that is regarded by many Sikhs as the supreme authority within the Panth.

During India's struggle for independence the Sikhs were on both sides of the conflict, with many continuing to serve in the British military and others opposing the colonial government. The partition between India and Pakistan in 1947 produced deep dissatisfaction among the Sikhs, who saw the Punjab divided between the two new states. Almost all Sikhs in the western Punjab migrated to the portion retained by India. Having settled there, however, they soon felt that the government of the Indian National Congress lacked sympathy for them, a situation that was put right by the creation in 1966 of the Punjabi *suba*, or the Punjabi state, within the union of India. Because the boundaries of the Punjab were redrawn to embrace those whose first language was Punjabi, the Sikhs constituted a majority in the new state.

For four decades following partition, the Sikhs enjoyed growing prosperity, including greater educational opportunities. The growth of the Punjab was interrupted in the mid-1980s by conflict between the central government and Sikh fundamentalists, who were demanding a separate Sikh nation-state. In an effort to rein in the principal Sikh political party – the Shiromani Akali Dal ("Leading Akali Party"; generally called Akali Dal) – the government enlisted the support of a young Sikh fundamentalist, Jarnail Singh Bhindranwale.

In 1984 Bhindranwale and his armed followers occupied the Akal Takht in the Golden Temple complex in Amritsar. In response, Indian Prime Minister Indira Gandhi ordered a military assault on the complex. Later that year Gandhi was assassinated by two of her Sikh bodyguards in retaliation. This in turn prompted widespread violence by Hindus against the Sikhs, particularly in the Delhi area, and led to guerrilla warfare against the central government in the Punjab that lasted until 1992. At the start of the twenty-first century, the demands of the fundamentalists still had not been met, but at least the Punjab was quiet. Meanwhile the appointment of the Sikh Manmohan Singh, as prime minister in 2004, was a source of great pride in the Sikh community.

Buddhism

Buddhism arose in north-eastern India sometime between the late sixth century and the early fourth century BCE, developing from the teachings of Siddhartha Gautama (Siddhartha, from the Sanskrit term, meaning "he who achieves his aim"), called the Buddha. Many modern scholars believe that the historical Buddha lived from about 563 to about 483 BCE. Others believe that he lived about 100 years later (from about 448 to 368 BCE). At this time in India, there was much discontent with Brahmanic (Hindu high-caste) sacrifice and ritual. In north-western India there were ascetics who tried to create a more personal and spiritual religious experience than that found in the *Vedas* (the Hindu sacred scriptures). In the literature that grew out of this movement, the Upanishads, a new emphasis on renunciation and transcendental knowledge can be found.

Buddhism, like many of the sects that developed in northeastern India at the time, was constituted by the presence of a charismatic teacher, by the teachings this leader promulgated, and by a community of adherents that was often made up of renunciant members and lay supporters. In the case of Buddhism, this pattern is reflected in the Triratna, the "Three Jewels" – Buddha (the teacher), *dharma* (the teaching), and *sangha* (the community).

The historical figure referred to as the Buddha was born on the northern edge of the Ganges river basin. The Buddha based his entire teaching on the fact of human suffering and the ultimately dissatisfying character of human life, and he offered a way beyond the transitoriness of human existence and desire – in short, enlightenment. The Buddha departed from traditional Indian thought in not asserting an essential or ultimate reality in things. Life is a stream of becoming, a series of manifestations and extinctions. The concept of the individual ego is a popular delusion and, if only the permanent deserved to be called the self (*atman*), then nothing is self.

To make clear the concept of no-self (*anatman*), Buddhists set forth the theory of the five aggregates or constituents (*khandhas*) of human existence: (i) corporeality or physical forms (*rupa*), (ii) feelings or sensations (*vedana*), (iii) ideations (*sanna*), (iv) mental formations or dispositions (*sankhara*), and (v) consciousness (*vinnana*). Human existence is only a composite of the five aggregates, none of which is the self or soul. A person is in a process of continuous change, and there is no fixed underlying entity.

The belief in rebirth (*samsara*) as a potentially endless series of worldly existences, in which every being is caught up, was already associated with the doctrine of karma (Sanskrit: *karman*; "act" or "deed") in pre-Buddhist India, and it was accepted by virtually all Buddhist traditions. According to the doctrine, good conduct brings a pleasant and happy result and creates a tendency toward similar good acts, while bad conduct brings an evil result and creates a tendency toward similar evil acts. Some karmic acts bear fruit in the same life in which they are committed, others in the immediately succeeding one, and others in future lives that are more remote. This furnishes the basic context for the moral life.

Awareness of these fundamental realities led the Buddha to formulate the Four Noble Truths: the truth of misery (*dukkha*), the truth that misery originates within us from the craving for pleasure and for being or nonbeing (*samudaya*), the truth that this craving can be eliminated (*nirodhu*), and the truth that this elimination is the result of following a methodical way or path (*magga*). The Buddha, according to the early texts, also discovered the law of dependent origination (*paticca-samuppada*), whereby one condition arises out of another, which in turn arises out of prior conditions.

The way to escape this cycle of birth, suffering, and death is found in the Eightfold Path, which is constituted by right views, right aspirations, right speech, right conduct, right livelihood, right effort, right mindfulness, and right meditational attainment. The aim of Buddhist practice is to be rid of the delusion of ego and thus free oneself from the fetters of this mundane world. One who is successful in doing so is said to have overcome the round of rebirths and to have achieved enlightenment. The state of such an enlightened human being is described in the West as *nirvana*.

In the centuries following the Buddha's death, the story of his life was remembered and embellished, his teachings were preserved and developed, and the community that he had established became a significant religious force. During its first century of existence, Buddhism spread from its place of origin in Magadha and Kosala throughout much of northern India. By the middle of the third century BCE, Buddhism had gained the favour of a Mauryan king, Asoka, who had established an empire that extended from the Himalayas in the north to almost as far as Sri Lanka in the south. To the rulers of the republics and kingdoms arising in north-eastern India, the patronage of newly emerging sects such as Buddhism was one way of counterbalancing the political power exercised by Brahmans (high-caste Hindus). According to contemporary inscriptions, Asoka attempted to establish in his realm a "true *dharma*" based on the virtues of self-control, impartiality, cheerfulness, truthfulness, and goodness.

After the fall of the Mauryan dynasty, during the Shunga-Kanva period (185–28 BCE), Buddhism in India suffered persecution. However, Buddhists persevered, and by the emergence of the Gupta dynasty (fourth century CE) Buddhism had become a leading if not dominant religious tradition in India. Stories about the Buddha's many previous lives, accounts of important events in his life as Gautama, stories of his "extended life" in his relics, and other aspects of his sacred biography were collected. Magnificent Buddhist monuments such as the great stupas (commemorative monuments, often reliquaries) at Bharhut and Sanchi were built, as well as many monasteries.

About the beginning of the Common Era, Buddhism split into two different groups. One was called the Hinayana (Sanskrit: "Lesser Vehicle"), a term given to it by its Buddhist opponents. This more conservative group, which included what is now called the Theravada (Pali: "Way of the Elders") community, compiled versions of the Buddha's teachings that had been preserved in collections called the *Sutta Pitaka*

("Basket of Discourse"), which contains the Buddha's sermons, and the *Vinaya Pitaka* ("Basket of Discipline"), which contains the rule governing the monastic order, and retained them as normative. The other branch, Mahayana ("Greater Vehicle"), by contrast, recognized the authority of other teachings that, from the group's point of view, made salvation available to a greater number of people. These supposedly more advanced teachings were expressed in *sutras* (scriptures) that the Buddha purportedly made available only to his more advanced disciples. In some Mahayana communities, for example, the strict law of karma was modified to accommodate new emphases on the efficacy of ritual actions and devotional practices.

Despite these vicissitudes Buddhism did not abandon its basic principles, but reinterpreted, rethought, and reformulated them in a process that led to the creation of a great body of literature. This literature includes the *Pali Tipitaka* ("Three Baskets") – the *Sutta Pitaka*; the *Vinaya Pitaka*; and the *Abhidhamma Pitaka* ("Basket of Special [Further] Doctrine"), which contains doctrinal systematizations and summaries.

By the time of the Gupta dynasty (*c.*320–*c.*600 CE), the Mahayana had become the most dynamic and creative Buddhist tradition in India. Their continued cultivation of various aspects of Buddhist teaching led to the emergence of the Yogacara school. A third major Buddhist tradition, the Vajrayana (Sanskrit: "Diamond Vehicle") or Esoteric tradition, developed out of the Mahayana school and became a powerful and dynamic religious force. Influenced by gnostic and magical currents pervasive at that time, its aim was to obtain spiritual liberation and purity more speedily. The new form of text associated with this tradition, the tantras, appeared during the Gupta period, and there are indications that distinctively Tantric rituals began to be employed at this time as well. It was during the Pala period (eighth–twelfth centuries), however, that the Vajrayana/Esoteric tradition emerged as the most dynamic component of Indian Buddhist life.

Also during the Gupta period, there emerged the Mahaviharas ("Great Monastery"), which often functioned as a university and which were to exert a profound religious and cultural influence not only in India but throughout many other parts of Asia as well. The most famous of these, at Nalanda, became a major centre for the study of Buddhist texts and the refinement of Buddhist thought.

Between 400 and 700 CE there was a decline in the Buddhist community (Faxian, a Chinese pilgrim who left China in 399, found "millions of monasteries" reduced to ruins), and the beginning of the absorption of Indian Buddhism by Hinduism. After the destruction of numerous Buddhist monasteries in the sixth century CE by the Huns, Buddhism revived, especially in the north-east, where it flourished for many more centuries under the kings of the Pala dynasty. The kings protected the Mahaviharas, built new centres at Odantapuri, near Nalanda, and established a system of supervision for all such institutions. Under the Palas the Vajrayana/Esoteric form of Buddhism became a major intellectual and religious force.

With the collapse of the Pala dynasty in the twelfth century, Indian Buddhism suffered yet another setback, and the Buddhist presence in India became negligible. While some scholars have maintained that Buddhism was so tolerant of other faiths that it was simply reabsorbed by a revitalized Hindu tradition, probably more important was the fact that Indian Buddhism, having become primarily a monastic movement, seems to have lost touch with its lay supporters.

At the end of the nineteenth century, a very small number of Indian intellectuals had become interested in Buddhism through western scholarship or through the activities of the

Theosophical Society. The Sinhalese reformer Anagarika Dharmapala also exerted some influence, particularly through his work as one of the founders of the Mahabodhi Society, which focused its initial efforts on restoring Buddhist control of the pilgrimage site at Bodh Gaya. Beginning in the early twentieth century, a few Indian intellectuals became increasingly interested in Buddhism as a more rational and egalitarian alternative to Hinduism, and a small Buddhist movement developed in south India. Even as late as 1950, however, an official government census identified fewer than 200,000 Buddhists in the country, most of them residing in eastern Bengal and Assam.

Since 1950 the number of Buddhists in India has increased dramatically. One small factor in this increase was the flood of Buddhist refugees from Tibet following the Chinese invasion of that country in 1959 to Dharmsala and elsewhere. Another very small factor was the incorporation of the predominantly Buddhist Sikkim into the Republic of India in 1975. The most important cause of the revival, however, was the mass conversion in 1956 of hundreds of thousands of Hindus, living primarily in Maharashtra state, who had previously been members of the so-called Scheduled Castes (formerly called "untouchables"). This had been initiated by Bhimrao Ramji Ambedkar, a leader of the Scheduled Castes who also had been a major figure in the Indian independence movement. In 1935 he had decided to lead his people away from Hinduism in favour of a religion that did not recognize caste distinctions, determined that Buddhism was the appropriate choice. The mass conversion occurred after a delay of more than 20 years. Since 1956 more than three million persons (a very conservative estimate) have joined the new Buddhist community.

The Buddhism of Ambedkar's community is based on the teachings found in the ancient Pali texts but also relies on

Ambedkar's own interpretations: the community's emphasis on a mythology concerning the Buddhist and aristocratic character of the Mahar (the largest of the scheduled castes); and its recognition of Ambedkar himself as a saviour figure who is often considered to be a *bodhisattva* (future buddha). The absence of a strong monastic community has allowed laypersons to assume the primary leadership roles.

Jainism

Jainism was founded in about the sixth century BCE by Vardhamana Mahavira, the 24th in a succession of religious leaders known as Jinas (Conquerors). It rejects the idea of God as the creator of the world but teaches the perfectibility of man, to be accomplished through the strictly moral and ascetic life. Largely confined to India, where it is estimated that there are roughly four million Jains, its mode of life is based on the tradition of *ahimsa* (nonviolence to all living creatures). The name Jainism, from the Sanskrit verb *ji*, "to conquer," refers to the ascetic battle that it is believed Jain renunciants must fight against the passions and bodily senses to gain omniscience and purity of soul or enlightenment.

Typical Jain life is characterized by strict vegetarianism, disciplined business or professional activity, and responsible conduct of family affairs, all intended to establish a sound social reputation. Lay Jains believe that pious activity – including fasting and almsgiving, and especially the practice of nonviolence – enables an individual not only to advance a little farther along the path to final liberation but to improve his or her current material situation.

Mahavira (599–527 BCE) was the son of a chieftain of the Kshatriya (warrior) class, but at 30 he renounced his princely status to take up the ascetic life. Mahavira spent the next $12^1/_2$ years following a path of solitary and intense asceticism. He then converted 11 disciples (called *ganadharas*) – two of these disciples, Indrabhuti Gautama and Sudharman, are regarded as the founders of the historical Jain monastic community. According to Jain tradition, the community numbered 14,000 monks and 36,000 nuns at the time of Mahavira's death.

A lasting schism over proper monastic practice occurred at this time, with the Shvetambara ("White-robed") sect arguing that monks and nuns should wear white robes and the Digambaras ("Sky-clad," i.e. naked) claiming that a true monk should be naked.

The consolidation of the Shvetambara-Digambara division was probably the result of a series of councils held to codify and preserve the Jain scriptures. The last one, held at Valabhi in Saurashtra (in modern Gujarat) in either 453 or 456 CE, without Digambara participation, codified the Shvetambara canon that is still in use.

During this early period Jainism spread westward to Ujjain, where it apparently enjoyed royal patronage. Later, in the first century BCE, according to tradition a monk named Kalakacarya apparently overthrew King Gardabhilla of Ujjain and orchestrated his replacement with the Shahi kings. During the reign of the Gupta dynasty (320–*c*.600 CE), a time of Hindu self-assertion, the bulk of the Jain community migrated to central and western India, becoming stronger there than it had been in its original home in the Ganges basin.

The early medieval period was the time of Digambara Jainism's greatest flowering, when it gained the patronage of prominent monarchs of three major dynasties – the Gangas in Karnataka (third–eleventh century); the Rashtrakutas, whose kingdom was just north of the Ganga realm (eighth–twelfth century); and the Hoysalas in Karnataka (eleventh–

fourteenth century). Many political and aristocratic figures had Jain monks as spiritual teachers and advisers. During this period Digambara writers produced numerous philosophical treatises, commentaries, and poems. Jainism also developed a formalized caste system.

In the period of their greatest influence (sixth–late twelfth century), Jain monks of both sects turned from living as wandering ascetics to permanent residence in temples or monasteries. A legacy of this transformation is the contemporary Digambara practice of the *bhattaraka*, through which a cleric takes monastic initiation and becomes an orange-robed administrator and guardian of holy places and temples. Some medieval Jain writers saw this compromise with ancient scriptural requirements as both a cause of and evidence for the religion's inexorable decline. However, Jainism's marginalization in India can best be ascribed to sociopolitical factors.

The invasion of India by Muslim forces in the twelfth century led to the loss of direct access to sources of power. While some Jain laymen and monks served Muslim rulers as political advisers or teachers – including Hiravijaya, who taught the Mughal emperor Akbar – the Shvetambara community was gradually compelled to redefine itself and today thrives as a mercantile group. At roughly the same time, various Shvetambara monastic subsects (*gaccha*) appeared. According to tradition, their leading teachers sought to reform lax monastic practice and participated in the conversion of Hindu Rajput clans in western India that subsequently became Shvetambara Jain caste groups.

Although most *gaccha*s accepted the practice of image worship, the Lumpaka (or Lonka Gaccha) did not. Founded by the mid-fifteenth-century layman Lonka Shah, the Lonka Gaccha denied the scriptural warranty of image worship and in the seventeenth century emerged as the non-image-worship-ing Sthanakavasi sect. At the end of the eighteenth century, the Sthanakavasi underwent a schism when Acarya Bhikshu founded the Terapanthi ("Following the 13 Tenets") sect.

In the south Digambara Jainism was attacked by Hindu devotional movements, such as that of the Virashaivas in the twelfth century in northern Karnataka (a stronghold of Digambara Jainism). With the advent of the Vijayanagar Empire in the fourteenth century, the Digambara Jains lost much of their royal support and survived only in peripheral areas of the south-west and in pockets of the north. The most significant Digambara reform movement occurred in the early seventeenth century, led by the layman and poet Banarsidas. This movement stressed the mystical elements of the Jain path and attacked what it saw as the emptiness of Digambara temple ritual and the profligacy of the community's clerical leaders.

By the middle of the nineteenth century image-worshipping Shvetambara monks had virtually disappeared, and control of temples and ritual passed into the hands of quasi-monastic clerics known as yati. Monastic life, however, experienced a revival under the auspices of charismatic monks such as Atmaramji (1837–96), and the number of Shvetambara image-worshipping renunciants grew to approximately 1,500 monks and 4,500 nuns in the twentieth century. The Digambara monastic community also experienced a revival of its ideals in the early twentieth century with the ascendence of the great monk Acarya Shantisagar, from whom virtually all the 120 or so contemporary Digambara monks claim lineal descent. In modern times the Shvetambara and Digambara communities in India have devoted much energy to preserving temples and publishing their religious texts, as well as to general welfare work.

The principal ingredients of Jain metaphysics are: an ultimate distinction between "living substance" or "soul" (jiva) and "nonliving substance" (ajiva); the doctrine of anekantavaha, or nonabsolutism (the thesis that things have infinite aspects that no determination can exhaust); the doctrine of naya (the thesis that there are many partial perspectives from which reality can be determined, none of which is, taken by itself, wholly true, but each of which is partially so); and the doctrine of karman, anglicized as karma (the matter that produces the chain of cause and effect and of birth and death).

The Jain religious goal is the complete perfection and purification of the soul. Liberation of the soul is impeded by the accumulation of *karman*s, bits of material, generated by a person's actions, that attach themselves to the soul and consequently bind it to physical bodies through many births. This has the effect of thwarting the full self-realization and freedom of the soul. As a result, Jain renunciants do not seek immediate enlightenment; instead, through disciplined and meritorious practice of nonviolence, they pursue a human rebirth that will bring them nearer to that state. Karmic particles are acquired as the result of intentional "passionate" action, and can be annihilated through a process called nirjara ("wearing away"), which includes fasting, restricting diet, controlling taste, and retreating to lonely places, along with mortifications of the body, atonement and expiation for sins, modesty, service, study, meditation, and renunciation of the ego.

Jain practice is based on the Three Jewels (Ratnatraya) of right knowledge, right faith, and right practice (respectively, samyagjnana, samyagdarshana, and samyakcaritra) and on yoga – the ascetic physical and meditative discipline of the monk, through which is cultivated true knowledge of reality, faith in the teachings of the Tirthankaras (literally, "Ford-makers"; i.e., one who leads the way across the stream of rebirths to salvation), and pure conduct, and which is the means to attain omniscience and thus moksha, or liberation. Right faith leads to calmness or tranquillity, detachment, kindness, and the renunciation of pride of birth, beauty of form, wealth, scholarship, prowess, and fame. But it leads to perfection only when followed by right practice. Yet, there can be no virtuous conduct without right knowledge, the clear distinction between the self and the nonself. In addition there is a requirement to perform the six "obligatory actions" at regular intervals, especially the *samayika*, a meditative and renunciatory ritual intended to strengthen the resolve to pursue the spiritual discipline of Jain *dharma* (moral virtue). The most significant time of the Jain ritual year is the four-month period when monks and nuns abandon the wandering life and live in the midst of lay communities.

The most famous of all Jain festivals, Mastakabhisheka ("Head Anointment"), is performed every 12 years at the Digambara sacred complex at Shravana Belgola ("White Lake of the Ascetics") in Karnataka state. In this ceremony, the (57 feet; 17 metres) high statue of Bahubali is anointed from above with a variety of substances (water, milk, flowers, etc.) in the presence of an audience that can approach one million.

Pilgrimage also has a role in Jainism. Places of pilgrimage were created during the medieval period at sites marking the principal events in the lives of Tirthankaras, and include Parasnath Hill and Rajgir in Bihar state and Shatrunjaya and Girnar Hills on the Kathiawar Peninsula.

Parsiism

The Parsis of India (whose name means "Persians") are followers of the Iranian prophet Zoroaster. They are descended from Persian Zoroastrians who emigrated to India to avoid religious persecution by the Muslims. The Parsis live chiefly in Mumbai (formerly Bombay) and in a few towns and villages mostly to the north of Mumbai but also in Bangalore (Bengaluru; in Karnataka state) and Karachi (Pakistan).

The exact date of the Parsi migration is unknown. According to tradition, the Parsis initially settled at Hormuz on the Persian Gulf, but finding themselves still persecuted they set sail for India, arriving in the eighth century. The migration may in fact have taken place as late as the tenth century, or at both times. They settled first at Diu in Kathiawar but soon moved to Gujarat, where they remained for about 800 years as a small agricultural community.

With the establishment of British trading posts at Surat and elsewhere in the early seventeenth century, the Parsis' circumstances altered radically. Mumbai came under the control of the East India Company in 1668 and, since complete religious toleration was decreed soon afterward, the Parsis from Gujarat began to settle there. The expansion of the city in the eighteenth century was largely owing to their industry and ability as merchants. By the nineteenth century they were manifestly a wealthy community, and from about 1850 onward they had considerable success in heavy industries, particularly those connected with railways and shipbuilding.

Contact of the Parsis with their fellow Iranian compatriots appears to have been almost completely severed until the end of the fifteenth century when, in 1477, they sent an official mission to the remaining Zoroastrians in Iran, a small sect called "Gabars" by the Muslim overlords. Until 1768 letters were exchanged on matters of ritual and law. As a result of these deliberations, in which the Parsis' traditions were in conflict with the purer traditions of the Gabars, the Parsis, in the eighteenth century, split into two sects on questions of ritual and calendar.

Though Zoroastrianism was never as aggressively mono-theistic as, for instance, Judaism or Islam – even in the thinking of its founder – it does represent an original attempt at unifying under the worship of one supreme god a polytheistic religion comparable to those of the ancient Greeks, Latins, South Asians, and other early peoples. Its other salient feature is dualism. Good and evil fight an unequal battle in which the former is assured of triumph. In this struggle humans must enlist because of their capacity of free choice. Fasting and celibacy are proscribed, except as part of the purificatory ritual. Humanity's fight has a negative aspect, nonetheless: adherents must keep themselves pure, by such practices as avoiding defilement by the forces of death or contact with dead matter.

Its principal texts are the Avesta and the *Bundahishn* ("Primal Creation"), a cosmology. The Avesta includes the *Videvdat*, or *Vendidad* ("Law Rejecting the Daevas"), with two introductory sections recounting how the law was given to man, and eighteen sections of rules; the *Siroza*, which enumer-ates the deities presiding over the 30 days of the month; and *Yashts* (hymns) addressed to one of 21 deities such as Mithra, Anahita, or Verethraghna.

In India all young Parsis must be initiated when they reach the age of seven. They receive the shirt (*sadre*) and the girdle (*kusti*), which they are to wear their whole life. Other ceremonies include purification. Penance entails reciting the *patet*, the firm resolve not to sin again, and the confession of sins to a *dastur* (a kind of bishop who oversees one or more temples) or to an ordinary priest if a *dastur* is not obtainable. The sacred fire must be kept burning continually and has to be fed at least five times a day. Prayers also are recited five times a day. The founding of a new fire involves a very elaborate ceremony.

Christianity

Indian Christian society is divided into groups geographically and according to denomination, but the overriding factor is one of caste. Caste groups may dine together and worship together but, as a rule, they do not intermarry. Roman Catholics form the largest single Christian group, especially on the western coast and in southern India. The many divisions among Protestants have been substantially reduced since independence as a result of mergers, creating the Church of North India and the Church of South India. Many small fundamentalist sects, however, have maintained their independence.

The Syrian Christians, found in the state of Kerala along the Malabar coast, trace their origin to the legendary visit of St Thomas the Apostle, early in the first century CE. The origins of the Christians of St Thomas are uncertain, though they seem to have been in existence before the sixth century and probably derive from the missionary activity of the East Syrian (Nestorian) Church centred at Ctesiphon. Despite their geographic isolation they retained the Chaldean liturgy and Syriac language, and maintained fraternal ties with the Babylonian (Baghdad) patriarchate; their devotional practices also included Hindu religious symbolism, vestiges of their early religion. Several mass migrations of Syrian Christians to the Malabar Coast (ninth century) also strengthened their ties with the Middle East.

With the arrival of Europeans from the sixteenth century onward, a second group of Christian converts emerged. Saint Francis Xavier, the greatest Roman Catholic missionary of modern times, was instrumental in the establishment of Christianity in India. Sent there by King John III of Portugal, to minister to the Christians and to evangelize the peoples in his new Asian dominions, Francis disembarked in Goa in May 1542. He spent much of the next three years on the south-eastern coast of India among the simple, poor pearl fishers, the Paravas. About 20,000 of them had accepted Baptism seven years before, chiefly to secure Portuguese support against their enemies; using a small catechism he had translated into the native Tamil with the help of interpreters, Francis now travelled tirelessly from village to village instructing and confirming them in their faith. In 1544 he baptized 10,000 of the Macuans on the south-western coast who had indicated their desire for Baptism.

Francis left the subcontinent for the Malay Archipelago (Indonesia) in 1545, but returned to India three years later, where more Jesuits had since arrived to join him. In Goa the College of Holy Faith, founded several years previously, was turned over to the Jesuits, and Francis began to develop it into a centre for the education of native priests and catechists for the diocese of Goa, which stretched from the Cape of Good Hope, at the southern tip of Africa, to China.

After the arrival of the Portuguese missionaries, the Portuguese set out to subject the Syrian Christians in Malabar to Rome. By 1662, most had come under Roman rule (the Syro-Malabar); the rest joined the Syrian Jacobite (Monophysite) Church, brought to Malabar in 1665 by Bishop Gregorios from Jerusalem. At the close of the eighteenth century, some of the Jacobites fell under the influence of Anglican missionaries and established the Mar Thomite Church. In 1930 the Syro-Malankara Church came into being as an eastern rite of the Catholic Church.

Judaism

The Bene Israel ("Sons of Israel"), descendants of Jewish settlers in the Bombay region of India, are the largest and

Gateway of India monument near the entrance to Mumbai (Bombay) Harbour, western India, on the east coast of the Arabian Sea. Originally commemorating the 1911 visit to Bombay of King George V and Queen Mary, the gate is now symbolically linked to the departure of the last British troops from India in 1948.

Hindu pilgrims gathering at Pushkar in the Great Indian Desert (Thar Desert), Rajasthan. The five temples and lake at Pushkar are dedicated to the god Brahma.

Ghats (steps) along the Ganges River, Varanasi, Uttar Pradesh.

(*above*) Picking tea leaves near Darjeeling (Darjiling), West Bengal, India. Some of the finest tea plantations of India are situated in this region.

(*left*) Rabindranath Tagore (1861–1941), the Bengali poet, short-story writer, song composer, playwright, essayist, and painter who was awarded the Nobel Prize for Literature in 1913.

(*top*) Mohandas K. Gandhi (1869–1948) in 1946. Leader of the Indian nationalist movement against British rule, Gandhi is considered to be the father of his country. He is internationally esteemed for his doctrine of nonviolent protest to achieve political and social progress.

(*middle*) Ravi Shankar (1920–). Indian musician, player of the sitar, composer, and founder of the National Orchestra of India.

(*bottom*) Indian classical *kathakali* dancers. Indigenous to southwestern India (Kerala), *kathakali* is a dance-drama which is traditionally enacted outdoors in performances that can last all night. During the action, voices chant the story as mimed by dancers; incidental dances, accompanied by ear-splitting drumbeats, enrich the performance.

Humāyūn's tomb, Delhi. Also called Nāṣin-ud-dīn-Muḥammad, Humāyūn was the son and successor of Bābur, who founded the Mughal dynasty. Humāyūn ruled from 1530 to 1540 and again from 1555 to 1556.

The Taj Mahal, in Agra, Uttar Pradesh. Built by the Mughal emperor Shah Jahan (reigned 1628–58) to immortalize his favourite wife, Mumtaz Mahal, the Taj Mahal is distinguished as the finest example of Mughal architecture, a blending of Indian, Persian, and Islamic styles. The Taj was designated a UNESCO World Heritage site in 1983.

(*top*) The Golden Temple (Harimandir). The chief *gurdwara*, or house of worship, of the Sikhs of India and their most important pilgrimage site; it is located in the city of Amritsar, in Punjab state. The Harimandir was built in 1604 by Guru Arjun, who symbolically had it placed on a lower level so that even the humblest had to step down to enter it.

(*bottom*) Boat traffic on the coastal waterways of Kerala.

oldest of several groups of Jews of India. Believed by tradition to have been shipwrecked on the Konkan coast of western India more than 2,100 years ago, they were absorbed into Indian society, maintaining many Jewish observances while operating within the caste system. Of some 67,000 Bene Israel at the turn of the twenty-first century, less than 5,000 remain in India as the great majority has emigrated to Israel.

Their presence in India is and may remain a mystery, and Bene Israel tradition itself varies. Some claim descent from the Ten Lost Tribes of Israel, who disappeared from history after the northern Kingdom of Israel was overrun by the Assyrians in 721 BCE; others that their ancestors fled by sea the persecution of Antiochus Epiphanes. Whatever the case, the survivors – by tradition seven men and seven women – settled in Konkan villages, adopted Hindu names, and took up the profession of oil production.

The existence of a Jewish community in India first attracted public attention from David Rahabi, who according to Bene Israel tradition may have arrived as early as 1000 CE, but who may have been David Ezekiel Rahabi (1694–1772) of Cochin (now Kochi), on the Malabar Coast, south of Konkan. Rahabi was instrumental in reviving Judaism among the Bene Israel. The Cochin Jews acted as cantors, ritual slaughterers, and teachers for the Bene Israel. Many Bene Israel migrated toward Bombay (now Mumbai) during this period. The first of numerous Bene Israel synagogues, all following the Sefardic (Spanish) liturgy, was built in Bombay in 1796.

In the early nineteenth century, Christian missionaries introduced Marathi-language versions of the Hebrew Bible (their Old Testament) to the inhabitants of the Konkan coast and set up English-language schools. This revelation, together with the model of normative Judaism provided by contact in the last half of the nineteenth century with Arabic-speaking

Jews of Baghdad (late eighteenth-century migrants to India), broke their isolation from the rest of the Jewish world. In 1948, when the state of Israel was established, many Bene Israel began to emigrate.

6

MUSIC AND DANCE

Indian music and dance are not just forms of entertainment but are essential elements in many of the activities of daily life, and play a prominent part in many rituals such as weddings, funerals, and religious processions. Music varies from the relatively simple two- or three-tone melodies of some of the hill tribes in central India to the highly refined art music heard in concert halls in the large cities. Some virtuosos, most notably Ravi Shankar (composer and sitar player) and Ali Akbar Khan (composer and sarod player), have gained world renown. The most popular dramatic classical performances relate to the great Hindu epics, the *Ramayana* and the *Mahabharata*. Regional variations of classical and folk music abound. Western classical music is represented by such institutions as the Symphony Orchestra of India, based in Mumbai, while some individuals (notably conductor Zubin Mehta) have achieved international renown.

In a musical tradition in which improvisation predominates, and written notation, when used, is skeletal and more a tool of the theorist than of the practising musician, the music of past generations is irrevocably lost. Thus, little is known of the musical culture of the Indus Valley civilization, though they seem to have used an arched, or bow-shaped, harp and more than one variety of drum.

After the arrival of the Aryans, in the first half of the second millennium BCE, came the oral tradition of the *Vedas* – first the collection of the hymns that comprises the *Rigveda*, by about 1000 BCE; then the Yajurveda, a kind of manual for the priest officiating at the sacrifices; the Samaveda, created for liturgical purposes; and later, the Atharvaveda, comprising mostly magic spells and incantations. Songs, instrumental music, and dance played an integral part in some of the sacrificial ceremonies. Unaltered for 3,000 years, the changes brought by the twentieth century weakened the traditional prominent position of the Vedic chant, and south India is now its main stronghold.

Before the advent of the Common Era, the epic poems *Ramayana* and *Mahabharata*, including the famous *Bhaga-vadgita*, as well as the collections of legends called the Puranas (depicting the lives of the various incarnations of the Hindu deities), began to be sung or recited by wandering minstrels and bards in much the same way as they still are. The stories were also enacted on the stage, particularly at the time of the religious festivals.

Theatrical music of the period apparently included songs sung on stage by the actors, as well as background music provided by an orchestra (which included singers) located offstage, in what was very like an orchestra pit. Melodies were composed on a system of modes (*jatis*), each of which was thought to evoke one or more particular sentiments (*rasa*) by its emphasis on specific notes. The *jatis* were similar to the modern concept of *raga* (i.e., they provided the melodic basis for composition and, presumably, improvisation).

In the next significant text on Indian music – the Brhaddesi, written by the theorist Matanga in about the tenth century CE – the *grama-raga*s are said to derive from the *jati*s. It is clear that *raga* was only one of several kinds of musical entities in this period, and is described as having "varied and graceful ornaments, with emphasis on clear, even, and deep tones and having a charming elegance." The *raga*s of this period seem to have been named after the different peoples living in the various parts of the country, suggesting that their origin might lie in folk music.

The mammoth thirteenth century text *Sangitaratnakara* ("Ocean of Music and Dance"), composed by the theorist Sarngadeva, is often said to be one of the most important landmarks in Indian music history. It was composed in the Deccan shortly before the conquest of this region by the Muslim invaders. A large part of this work is devoted to *marga* – that is, the ancient music that includes the system of *jati*s and *grama-raga*s – but Sarngadeva mentions a total of 264 *raga*s.

Muslim writers such as al-Jahiz and al-Mas'udi had already commented favourably on Indian music in the ninth and tenth centuries, and the Muslims in India seem to have been very much attracted by it. After the Muslim conquest of the Deccan (*c*.1310), a large number of Hindu musicians were taken with the royal armies and settled in the north. Although orthodox Islam considered music illegal, the acceptance of the Sufi doctrines, in which music was an accepted means to the realization of God, enabled Muslim rulers and noblemen to extend their patronage to this art.

At the courts of the Mughal emperors Akbar, Jahangir, and Shah Jahan, music flourished on a grand scale. Famous Indian musicians, such as Svami Haridas and Tansen, were legendary performers and innovators of this period. After the example set by Amir Khosrow, Muslim musicians took an active interest in the performance of Indian music and added to the repertoire by inventing new *raga*s, *tala*s, and musical forms, as well as new instruments.

The Muslim patronage of music was largely effective in the north of India and has had a profound influence on music there. Perhaps the main result of this was to de-emphasize the importance of the words of the songs. In addition, Sanskrit songs were gradually replaced by compositions in the various dialects of Hindi, Braj Bhasa, Bhojpuri, and Dakhani, as well as in Urdu and Persian. The growth of the Islamic Sufi movement and the increasing emphasis on devotion (*bhakti*) encouraged a new form of mystic-devotional poetry, composed by wandering mendicants who had dedicated their lives to the realization of God. Their poems were invariably set to music.

From the middle of the sixteenth century, a new method of describing *raga*s is found in musical literature. It was also at about this time that the distinction between north and south Indian music became clearly evident. In the literature, *raga*s are described in terms of scales having a common ground note. These scales were called *mela* in the south and *mela* or *thata* in the north. It was in the south that a complete theoretical system of *mela*s was introduced, in the *Caturdandiprakasika* ("The Illuminator of the Four Pillars of Music"), a text written in the middle of the seventeenth century. Although north Indian texts also describe *raga*s in terms of *mela*s or *thata*s, there is no attempt to arrange them systematically.

Musically, there has been a continuous evolution from the Islamic period to the present, and both north and south Indian classical music have continued to expand. The 72-*mela* system continues to be the basis of classifying the *raga*s in south India, and many new *raga*s have been composed. As a result, there are now *raga*s in all of the 72 *mela*s. In the twentieth century

Vishnu Narayana Bhatkande, one of the leading Indian musicologists, contributed a great deal toward diminishing the gap between performance and theory in north Indian music, through collecting and notating representative versions of a number of *raga*s from musicians belonging to different family traditions (*gharana*s), and then grouping them. New *raga*s are constantly being created, and some north Indian musicians are using the vast potential of the south Indian *mela* system as their source of inspiration.

Classical music

The best known in the West are the classical music of north India (sometimes called Hindustani music) and that of south India (Karnatic music). Both classical systems are supported by an extensive body of literature and elaborate musical theory. Until modern times classical music was patronized by the princely courts, but since independence the emphasis has shifted to the milieu of large concert halls. In the larger cities there are performances of western chamber music and occasionally symphony concerts.

Classical music is based on two main elements, *raga* and *tala*. The word *raga* is derived from a Sanskrit root meaning "to colour," the underlying idea being that certain melodic shapes, involving specific intervals of the scale, produce a continuity of emotional experience and "colour" the mind. Since neither the melodic shapes nor their sequence are fixed precisely, a *raga* serves as a basis for composition and improvisation. Indian music has neither modulation (change of key) nor changing harmonies; instead, the music is invariably accompanied by a drone that establishes the tonic, or ground note, of the *raga* and usually its fifth (five notes above). These are chosen to suit the convenience of the main performer, as there is no concept of fixed pitch. While a *raga* is primarily a musical concept, specific *raga*s have acquired, particularly in north Indian music, a number of extramusical elements and are associated with particular periods of the day, seasons of the year, colours, deities, and specific moods.

The second element of Indian music, *tala*, is best described as time measure and has two main constituents – the duration of the time measure in terms of time units that vary according to the tempo chosen, and the distribution of stress within the time measure. *Tala*, like *raga*, serves as a basis for composition and improvisation.

Much of the south Indian repertoire of compositions stems from three composers, Tyagaraja, Muthuswami Dikshitar, and Syama Sastri – contemporaries who lived in the second half of the eighteenth and the beginning of the nineteenth centuries. The devotional songs that they composed, called *krti*, are a delicate blend of text, melody, and rhythm, and are the most popular items of a south Indian concert. Other forms used in south Indian classical music derive largely from the musical repertoire of *bharata-natyam*, the classical south Indian dance.

The most common vocal form in north Indian classical music is the *khyal*, a Muslim word meaning "imagination." The *khyal* is contrasted with the *dhruvapada* (now known as *dhrupad*), which means "fixed words." The *thumri* is another north Indian vocal form and is based on the romantic-devotional literature inspired by the *bhakti* movement. The text is usually derived from the theme of Krishna and his mistress Radha.

Instrumental music has gained considerable prominence in north India in recent times. The most common instrumental form is the *gat*, which seems to have derived its elements from both *dhrupad* and *khyal*. Other forms are the *thumri*, basically an instrumental rendering of a vocal *thumri*, and *dhun*, which is derived from a folk tune and does not usually follow a conventional *raga*. One may also hear a piece called *raga-mala* (literally, "a garland of *raga*s"), in which the musician modulates from one *raga* to another, finally concluding with a return to the original *raga*. In recent times, instrumental duets, in which the musicians improvise alternately, have grown in popularity.

Indian classical music is generally performed by small ensembles of not more than five or six musicians. The ensemble used in present-day south Indian classical music consists of a singer or a main melody instrument, a secondary melody instrument, one or more rhythmic percussion instruments, and one or more drone instruments. The most commonly heard main melody instruments are the *vina*, a long-necked, fretted, plucked lute; the *venu*, a side-blown bamboo flute; the *nagaswaram*, a long, oboe-like, double-reed instrument with finger holes; the violin, imported from the West about 200 years ago; and the *gottuvadyam*, a long-necked lute without frets. The violin is by far the most common secondary melody instrument. Of the rhythm instruments, the *mridanga*, a double-conical, two-headed drum, is the most common. The most prominent drone instrument is the four-stringed *tamboura*, a long-necked lute without frets.

In north India the most prominent melody instruments are the *sitar*, a long-necked fretted lute; the *surbahar*, a larger version of the *sitar*; the *sarod*, a plucked lute without frets; the *sarangi*, a short-necked bowed lute; the *bansuri*, a side-blown bamboo flute; the *sheh'nai*, a double-reed wind instrument similar to the oboe, but without keys; and the violin. Secondary melody instruments are used only in vocal music, the two most common being the *sarangi* and the keyboard harmonium, an import from the West. The drone is usually provided by a *tamboura* (Bengali: *tanpura*) or a hand-pumped reed drone called *sur-peti* in north India. The *sheh'nai* is usually accompanied by one or more drone *sheh'nai*s, called *sur*. The rhythmic accompaniment is usually provided on the *tabla*, a pair of small drums played with the fingers. The *sheh'nai* in classical music is usually accompanied by a small pair of kettledrums, called *dukar-tikar*.

Popular music

Since about the 1930s a new genre of music, associated with the cinema, has achieved extraordinary popularity in India. Film music derives its inspiration from a number of sources, both Indian and Western; classical, folk, and devotional music are the main Indian sources, while western influence is seen most obviously in the use of large orchestras that employ both western and Indian instruments. In spite of the eclectic nature of Indian film music, most of the songs maintain an Indian feeling that arises largely from the vocal technique of the singers and the ornamentation of the melody line. This music is an experimental and developing form, and there have been attempts to add harmony and counterpoint.

The music of bands of oboes and drums announcing a wedding or a funeral, street musicians, religious mendicants, snake charmers, storytellers, and magicians also plays a prominent part in Indian musical life. In private homes still other forms of music are performed, ranging from religious chanting to traditional folk and devotional songs. In public places of entertainment, the listener may encounter modern theatrical music while courtesans still sing and dance in traditional fashion. Popular dance music, rock, and jazz in nightclubs are regularly performed in the larger cities.

In rural areas music, often sung, accompanies life-cycle events, such as birth, initiation, marriage, and death; events of the agricultural cycle, such as planting, transplanting, harvesting, and threshing; and work. Songs usually take the form of leader and chorus, and the musical accompaniment, if any, is generally provided by drone instruments, usually of the lute family, or percussion instruments such as drums, clappers, and pairs of cymbals. Occasionally, a fiddle or flute might also accompany the singers, who often dance while they sing. Songs are passed on from one generation to another, and in most cases the composers are unknown.

Apart from folk songs, one also hears outdoor instrumental music in villages. The music is provided by an ensemble of varying size, which consists basically of an oboe type of instrument (usually a *sheh'nai* in north India and *nagaswaram* in the south) and a variety of drums. Sometimes straight, curved, or S-shaped horns may be added.

Most areas are visited by religious mendicants, many of whom travel around the countryside singing devotional songs. Itinerant magicians, snake charmers, acrobats, and storytellers who travel in the rural areas often use music in their acts, and the storyteller generally sings his tales, which may be taken from the *Mahabharata* and the *Ramayana*, or from the Puranas. Sometimes the narrative songs are concerned with historical characters and describe the wars and the heroic deeds of the regional rulers. Some storytellers specialize in generally tragic stories of romance and of lovers.

Dance

Dance in India can be organized into three categories: classical, folk, and modern. Classical dance forms are among the best preserved and oldest practised in the twentieth century. The royal courts, the temples, and the guru-to-pupil teaching tradition have kept this art alive and unchanged. Folk dancing has remained in rural areas as an expression of the daily work and rituals of village communities. Modern Indian dance, a product of the twentieth century, is a creative mixture of the first two forms, with freely improvised movements and rhythms to express the new themes and impulses of contemporary India.

The popularity of dance in twentieth-century India can be judged from the fact that there is hardly any Indian motion picture that does not have half a dozen dances in it; a film company may not have a scriptwriter, but it must have a dance director. Folk dancing has also become more common as a contemporary cultural event in the cities. Most colleges have their folk-dance troupes, and even the police of the Punjab have their folk-dance groups to perform the *bhangra*. Religious festivals, however, remain the most important occasions for dance and theatrical activity.

India has evolved a type of dance drama that is a form of total theatre, using a complex gesture language that is universal in its appeal. Some of the classical dance-drama forms enact well-known stories derived from Hindu mythology. The twentieth-century dancers Uday Shankar and Shanti Bardhan created ballets that were inspired by such traditional dance-dramas.

Four distinct schools of classical Indian dance – *bharatanatya*; *kathakali*; *kathak*; and *manipuri* – exist in contemporary times, along with two types of temperament – *tandava*, representing the fearful male energy of Siva, and *lasya*, representing the lyrical grace of Siva's wife Parvati. *Bharatanatya*, which has the *lasya* character and whose home is Tamil Nadu state, expresses Hindu religious themes that date at least to the fourth century CE. According to the *Natya-sastra* (a comprehensive treatise on the dramatic arts), the dancer-actor communicates the meaning of a play through four kinds of *abhinaya* (histrionic representations): *angika*, transmitting emotion through the stylized movements of parts of the body; *vacika*, speech, song, pitch of vowels, and intonation; *aharya*, costumes and make-up; and *sattvika*, the entire psychological resources of the dancer-actor.

Kathakali, a pantomimic dance-drama in the *tandava* mood with towering headgear and elaborate facial make-up, originated in Kerala. Kathak is a mixture of *lasya* and *tandava* characterized by intricate footwork and mathematical precision of rhythmic patterns; it flourishes in the north. *Manipuri*, with its swaying and gliding movements, is *lasya*, and it has been preserved in Manipur state in the Assam Hills. In 1958 the Sangeet Natak Akademi (National Academy of Music, Dance and Drama) in New Delhi bestowed classical status on two other schools of dance – *kuchipudi*, from Andhra Pradesh, and *orissi*, from Orissa. These two styles overlap the *bharatanatya* school and therefore are not as distinctly different in temperament and style as other forms.

In addition, there are numerous regional folk dance traditions with an inexhaustible variety of forms and rhythms. The Adivasi tribal people of central and eastern India (Murias, Bhils, Gonds, Juangs, and Santals) are the most uninhibited in their dancing. It is difficult to categorize Indian folk dances, but generally they fall into four groups: social (concerned with such labours as tilling, sowing, fishing, and hunting); religious; ritualistic (to propitiate an angry goddess or demon with magical rites); or masked (a type that appears in all the above categories).

The *kolyacha*, a fisherman's dance indigenous to the Konkan coast of west-central India which enacts the rowing of a boat, is among the better known examples of social folk dance.

The national social folk dance of Rajasthan is the *ghoomar*, danced by women in long full skirts and colourful *chuneri*s (squares of cloth draping head and shoulders and tucked in front at the waist). In the Punjab, the most electrifying social folk dance is the male harvest dance, *bhangra*. Some major examples of religious folk dances are the *dindi* and *kala* dances of Maharashtra, which are expressions of religious ecstasy. *Garaba*, meaning a votive pot, is the best known religious dance of Gujarat; it is danced by a group of 50 to 100 women for nine nights in honour of the goddess Amba Mata.

Of the endless variety of ritualistic folk dances, many have magical significance and are connected with ancient cults. The *karakam* dance of Tamil Nadu state, mainly performed on the annual festival in front of the image of Mariyammai (goddess of pestilence), is to deter her from unleashing an epidemic. The greatest number of masked folk dances are found in Arunachal Pradesh, where the influence of Tibetan dance may be seen. The yak dance is performed in the Ladakh section of Jammu and Kashmir state and in the southern fringes of the Himalayas near Assam. The dancer impersonating a yak dances with a man mounted on his back.

More recently, dance in the form of ballet with complex choreography in the western sense has emerged as a distinct form. Modern Indian ballet started with Uday Shankar, who was chosen by the Russian ballerina Anna Pavlova to be her partner in the ballet *Radha and Krishna*. Young Shankar returned to India fired with enthusiasm. After studying the essentials of the four major styles of classical dance, he created new ballets with complex choreography and music, mixing the sounds from wooden clappers and metal cymbals with those of traditional instruments. He established a culture centre at Almora in 1939 and during its four years' existence created a whole generation of modern dancers.

Shanti Bardhan, a junior colleague of Uday Shankar, produced some of the most imaginative dance-dramas of the modern period. After founding the Little Ballet Troupe in Andheri, Bombay, in 1952 he produced *Ramayana*, in which the actors moved and danced like puppets. Narendra Sharma and Sachin Shankar, both pupils of Uday Shankar, have continued his tradition. Other important figures who have shaped modern Indian dance include Menaka, Ram Gopal, and Mrinalini Sarabhai, who has experimented with conveying modern themes through the *bharata-natya* and *kathakali* styles.

7

LITERATURE

Indian literature has a vast and rich heritage that dates back more than 3,000 years to the time of the *Vedas*, composed in Sanskrit but not written down until many centuries later, and continuing in several languages up to the present day. Forms range from sacred and devotional writings to poetry, plays, and folktales. There is also an important dramatic tradition associated with mythological tales and stories of the gods.

Bankim Chandra Chatterjee, who established the novel as a literary genre in India, wrote in Bengali, and most of his literary successors also preferred to write in Indian languages; many others, including Rabindranath Tagore, wrote in English. Today, the works of some Indian authors – such as the poet and novelist Vikram Seth and Booker Prize winners Salman Rushdie (1981), Arundhati Roy (1997), and Kiran Desai (2006) – are exclusively or almost exclusively in English, and such names have an international following.

Sanskrit and Indo-Aryan literature
to the eighteenth century

The earliest Indian literature is of a sacred character and dates from about 1400 BCE in the form of the *Rigveda*. The language of the *Rigveda*, a compilation of hymns to the high gods of the Aryan religion, is complex and archaic. It was simplified and codified in the course of the centuries from 1000 to 500 BCE, which saw the development of prose commentaries called the Brahmanas, Aranyakas, and Upanishads, and was finally established by Panini (grammarian of the fifth or sixth century BCE). His grammar has remained normative for the correct language, Sanskrit ("Tongue Perfected"), ever since.

The production of Sanskrit literature reached its height in the first to seventh centuries CE. In addition to sacred and philosophical writings, such genres as erotic and devotional lyrics, court poetry, plays, and narrative folktales emerged. Because Sanskrit was identified with the Brahminical religion of the *Vedas*, reform movements such as Buddhism and Jainism adopted other literary languages, for example, Pali and Ardhamagadhi respectively. Out of these and other derivative languages there evolved the modern languages of northern India.

The literature of those languages depended largely on the ancient Indian background, which includes the Sanskrit epics, the *Mahabharata* and *Ramayana*, the Krishna story as told in the *Bhagavata-Purana*, the other Puranic legends, and the fable anthologies, as well as philosophical writings. Tamil is an exception to this pattern of Sanskrit influence because it has a classical tradition of its own. Urdu and Sindhi are other exceptions, having arisen out of an Islamic background.

Side by side with the ritual texts there flourished a more secular literature carried on by bards. Originally charioteers to noblemen, they chronicled the martial history of the families to which they were attached. From these beginnings developed the epic style. The most famous of these is the *Mahabharata*, the longest poem in history which, like most Sanskrit poetry, consists of couplets. Composed around 400 BCE it underwent continuous elaboration, until by around 400 CE it had become a storehouse of Hindu lore.

The main narrative of the *Mahabharata* recounts the growing up of two sets of cousins, both of whom aspire to a throne. The protagonists, the Pandavas, stake their possessions in a dice game with the antagonists, the Kauravas, who are in effective control of the realm; they lose, and must live for 13 years in exile. Upon their return from exile they are refused their promised share of the kingdom. All of the Indian dynasties and tribes take sides in a war that lasts for 18 days, which only seven warriors, among them the Pandavas, survive.

This summary does no justice to an extremely complex story with hundreds of participants, but it sketches the general outline of epic events. Alongside the main story are unrelated secondary episodes, which greatly influenced succeeding literature, including the celebrated *Bhagavadgita* ("Song of the Lord"). Though its poetic style is simple and direct, the poem often reaches the height of expressiveness, as in its evocation of the theophany of Krishna as Vishnu.

The second great epic of Indian literature is the *Ramayana* – composed perhaps as early as 300 CE – which recounts the story of prince Rama and his wife Sita. It has made an indelible impression on Indian culture, morally as well as literarily: Rama is the perfect, just king; Sita, the model of an Indian wife; Laksmana (the brother), the paragon of fraternal love; and the monkey Hanuman, the epitome of a servitor's loyalty. It was translated into and adapted in many modern Indian languages, and its writer Valmiki was hailed by later classical poets as the first true poet (*kavi*).

The role of the *Mahabharata* as the storehouse of Hindu lore was supplemented by the *Harivamsa* ("Genealogy of Hari" – that is, the god Vishnu), which deals with the ancestry and exploits of Krishna, the Pandavas' friend and adviser in the epic but now wholly deified and identified with the great god Vishnu. Then, from perhaps the fourth century, the literature of the Puranas – which deal with the mythology of time and space and of deities, with sagas of great heroic dynasties, legends of saints and ascetics – took over.

The most important of them is the *Bhagavata-Purana* (ninth or tenth century), which celebrates the blessed lord (*bhagavat*), Vishnu. The influence of the *Bhagavata-Purana*, particularly the tenth book, on Indian religion, art, and literature has been monumental. In the opinion of one scholar, this book constitutes the greatest poem ever written; and so it is in the popular estimation of the Hindus. It was adapted in many Indian languages and provided themes and scenes for the flourishing miniature styles of the Middle Ages.

The literatures of early Buddhism, written in Pali, and Jainism, written in an adapted and stabilized literary dialect called Ardhamagadhi, were also largely scriptural. Incorporated into the Buddhist canon though are more general works of literature, such as the *Dharmapada* ("Words of Doctrine" or "Way of Truth") and the *Suttanipata* collection of 55 narrative and didactic poems. Of great importance is a huge volume called *Jataka*s ("Birth Stories"), recounting some 500 episodes supposedly having occurred in the Buddha's earlier lives and consisting of fairy tales, animal stories and fables (the future Buddha may be incarnate in an animal), ballads, and anecdotes. These mostly short tales abound in moving, delicate, often rustic touches that have made them the delight of the Buddhist world.

In the first centuries CE, a Sanskrit literary style, *kavya*, emerged, which governed canons of taste for a millennium and remained influential far later through modern Indian languages and their literatures. The style finds its classical expression in the so-called *mahakavya* ("great poem"), a form that consists of a variable number of comparatively short cantos and generally displays such set pieces as descriptions of cities, oceans, mountains, the seasons, the rising of the sun and moon, games, festivals, weddings, embassies, councils, war, and triumph.

The earliest surviving *kavya* was written by a Buddhist, the poet and philosopher Asvaghosa, probably in the late first or early second century CE – the *Buddhacarita* ("Life of the Buddha") and the *Saundarananda* ("Of Sundari and Nanda"). Unique in Sanskrit love poetry is Kalidasa's *Meghaduta* – the lament of an exiled *yaksa* (a mischievous elflike creature) who is pining for his beloved on a lonely mountain peak – in which the poet tries to go beyond the strophic unity of the short lyric, which normally characterizes love poems, by stringing the stanzas into a narrative. It is considered among the finest poems written in Sanskrit.

It is in the short, one-stanza lyric that Sanskrit poetry is revealed most intimately in its real aims. It may be an observation of anything: a fish glintingly jumping from a pond, aboriginal tribesmen engaged in a bloody rite, love in all its manifestations, a glimpse of God perceived or remembered. Some are especially famous: the *Suryastaka* ("Eight Strophes for the Sun"), by Mayura; the collections attributed to the philosopher Sankara (Shankara), the *Saundaryalahari* ("The Wavy River of the Beautiful Sky"); and the *Krsnakarnamrta* ("The Elixir of Hearing of Krishna"), by Bilvamangala.

Authors of these *subhasita*s ("well-turned" couplets) often collected them themselves, the favourite form being that of the *shataka* ("century" of verses), in which 100 short lyrics on a common theme were strung together. Well known are Hala's *Sattasai* ("The Seven Hundred," consisting of lyrics in the Maharastri dialect); the Sanskrit collections, of the seventh century; the famous "century" of Amaru, king of Kashmir; and the three "centuries" by the poet Bhartrhari.

It is difficult to pinpoint when the Indo-Aryan dialects first became identifiable as languages. From the turn of the eleventh century, there began to appear, at different times during the subsequent two or three centuries, the languages now known as the regional languages of the subcontinent: Hindi, Bengali, Kashmiri, Punjabi, Rajasthani, Marathi, Gujarati, Oriya, Sindhi (which did not develop an appreciable literature), and Assamese. Urdu did not develop until much later.

In all of the early literatures, writing was lyrical, narrative, or didactic; entirely in verse; and all in some way related to religion or love or both. In the sixteenth century, prose texts, such as the Assamese histories known as the *buranji* texts, began to appear. The narratives in the early stages are most often mythological tales drawn from the epics and Puranas of classical Hindu tradition, though in the seventeenth and eighteenth centuries secular romances and heroic tales were also treated in narrative poems. In addition to themes, regional literatures frequently borrowed poetic forms from the Sanskrit. The latter include the *barah-masa* ("twelve months"), in which 12 beauties of a girl or 12 attributes of a deity might be extolled by relating them to the characteristics of each month of the year; and the *cautis* ("thirty-four"), in which the 34 consonants of the northern Indian Devanagari alphabet are used as the initial letters of a poem of 34 lines or stanzas, describing 34 joys of love, 34 attributes, and so on.

The literatures of the different languages share stories and texts, such as those of Gopi-candra (the cult hero of the Natha Yogi sect, a school of mendicant *sannyasins*), which were known from Bengal to the Punjab even in the early period. From the late thirteenth to the seventeenth century, *bhakti* (devotional) poetry took hold in one region after another in northern and eastern India. Because of the *bhakti* movement, beautiful lyric poetry and passionate devotional song were created; and in some cases, as in Bengal, serious philosophical works and biographies were written for the first time in a regional language rather than in Sanskrit.

The first major work in Hindi evolved from the bardic tradition maintained at the courts of the Rajputs. The twelfth-century epic poem *Prthviraj Rasau*, by Chand Bardai of Lahore, recounts the feats of Prthviraj, the last Hindu king of Delhi before the Islamic invasions.

The most celebrated author in Hindi is Tulsidas of Rajapur (died 1623), a Brahmin whose most important work is the *Ramcaritmanas* ("Sacred Lake of the Acts of Rama"). More than any other work it has become a Hindu sacred text.

While developments in Bengali literature began somewhat earlier, they followed the same general course as those in Hindi. The oldest documents are Buddhist didactic texts, called *carya-pada*s ("lines on proper practice"), which have been dated to the tenth and eleventh centuries and are the oldest testimony to literature in any Indo-Aryan language. Well before the fifteenth century there existed texts in a typically Bengali genre called *mangal-kavya* ("poetry of an auspicious happening"), which consists of eulogies of gods and goddesses. It remained a favourite genre well into the eighteenth century, when Bharat-candra wrote the *Annada-mangal* ("Mangal of the Goddess Annada [the Giver of Food]"). Despite this popularity, it is the devotional lyrics to the divine pair Krishna and Radha that are still known and sung today in Bengal, and these lyrics are the gems of medieval Bengali literature.

The great flowering of *padavali* ("string of verse") songs, which describe and glorify all phases of Krishna's love for the cowherds' wives and established Bengali as a significant literary language, occurred in the sixteenth and seventeenth centuries. Religious biography (more like hagiography) and philosophy were also produced, one of the most important being the *Caitanya-caritamrta* ("Elixir of the Life of Caitanya") by the sixteenth-century author Krsnadas. One of the outstanding secular Bengali Muslim poets is Alaol, author of the Padmavati (*c*.1648).

The first great Assamese poet was Kaviraja Madhava Kandali (fourteenth century), who translated the Sanskrit *Ramayana* and wrote *Devajit*, a narrative on the god Krishna. The most famous poet of the period was the saint-poet Sankaradeva (1449–1568). Both his works and the medieval Oriya poet Jagannatha Das's *Bhagavata-Purana* are alive today. Peculiar to Assamese literature, and dating from the sixteenth century, are the *buranjis* chronicles.

The great names of early Marathi literature came out of the Varakari Panth sect and its association with *bhakti*, but its unique contribution is the tradition of *povada*s – heroic stories popular among a martial people, which flourished in the seventeenth century. By far the most famous of the Gujarati *bhakti* poets is the woman saint Mira Bal, who lived in the first half of the sixteenth century. Mira, though married, thought of Krishna as her true husband, and the lyrics telling of her relationship with her god and lover are among the warmest and most movingly personal in any Indian literature.

Punjabi developed a literature later than most of the other regional languages of the subcontinent; the first work identifi-

able as Punjabi is the *Janam-sakhi*, a sixteenth-century biography of the Sikh Guru Nanak by Bala. Writing that is not
merely incidentally Punjabi began in the seventeenth century
and is almost entirely by Muslims. Between 1616 and 1666, a
writer named 'Abdullah, for example, composed a major work
called *Bara Anva* ("Twelve Topics"), a treatise on Islam in
9,000 couplets. There are also many romances in the language.

As with Gujarati, the most famous poets of Kashmiri in the
medieval period are women. Lalla (fourteenth century) wrote
poems about the god Shiva; and Hubb Khatun (sixteenth
century) and especially Arani-mal (eighteenth century) are
famous for their hauntingly beautiful love lyrics. Despite these
outstanding poets in Kashmiri the great literary language of
Kashmir in the medieval period was Persian, which was
encouraged by many rulers of the region, such as Zayn-ul-
'Abidin, in whose fifteenth-century court were many scholars
and poets writing in both the Kashmiri and Persian languages.

In many of these regions, particularly Kashmir and the
Punjab, Muslims were the most influential contributors; Muslim chieftains gave impetus to the growth of Bengali literature
through their patronage of writers and through their efforts to
have Sanskrit classics translated into Bengali. It was, however,
in Persian and Urdu that Muslim men of letters made the
greatest contributions – which eventually led in the former case
to the establishment of an "Indian" school of Persian poetry
and, in the latter case, led to the emergence of a unique pan-
Indian language and literature in Urdu.

Mahmud of Ghazna, with whom the chain of Muslim
conquests in northern India began, was also the patron of
Ferdowsi, one of the greatest of Persian poets. The later
conquerors admired literature no less. The first truly great
poet of Indian origin was Amir Khosrow, who wrote in the
thirteenth and fourteenth centuries and who was connected

with royal courts all his life. He wrote five books of poems (*divans*) – altogether some 200,000 couplets. Khosrow's distinction lies not so much in the fact that he is an innovator, however, as in the fact that he is equally superb in narrative poetry, panegyrics, and lyrics.

In the centuries that followed Khosrow, until the end of the Islamic period, India contributed to Persian literature in two ways: first, through the production of dictionaries that helped to standardize the language; second, through the development of the so-called Indian style of Persian poetry, *sabk-e hindi*. The latter is characterized by keen observation of daily life, and in style (in the words of one modern critic) by emphasis on

> parallel statement . . . ; on complex conceit . . . arising out of economy of expression and telescoping into a single image a variety of emotional states; on "cerebral" artifice in pushing familiar images to unfamiliar and unexpected lengths; and on the creation of a synthetic poetic diction in which a whole phrase constitutes a single image.

The century (1556–1657) of the reigns of Akbar, Jahangir, and Shah Jahan was the most glorious period for Persian poetry in India – though (except for the India-born Fayzi), all of the important poets were immigrants from Persia. The greatest poet of the Indian style, however, was 'Abdul Qadir Bedil, born in 1644 in Patna. He came early under the influence of the Sufis, refused to be attached to any court, and travelled widely throughout India during his long life. Bedil's 16 books of poetry contain nearly 147,000 verses and include several *masnawi*s (couplets in rhymed pairs). A poet of great virtuosity and philosophic bent, his anti-feudal views and his critical and sceptical attitude toward all kinds of dogma make his poetry relevant even today.

Urdu literature began to develop in the sixteenth century, influenced by Sufi practices – Urdu poets generally chose an *ustad* (master), just as a Sufi novice chose a *murshid* (preceptor). They read poetry in private or semiprivate gatherings, called *musha'irah* – in and around the courts of the Qutb Shahi and 'Adil Shahi, kings of Golconda and Bijapur in the Deccan. During the next two centuries, centres of Urdu poetry were established first in Aurangabad and then in Delhi and Lucknow. Urdu prose truly began only in the nineteenth century, with translations of Persian *dastan*s (stories), books prepared at the Delhi College and the Fort William College at Calcutta, and later with the writers of the Aligarh movement.

There are many poetical forms, but for the most part the history of Urdu poetry in India is the story of Urdu *ghazal*. Favourite themes of these short lyrics are erotic love, Sufi love, and metaphysics. The two greatest *ghazal* writers are Mir Taqi Mir in the eighteenth century, and Mirza Asadullah Khan Ghalib in the nineteenth. They are in some ways diametrical opposites. The first prefers either very long metres or very short, employs a simple, non-Persianized language, and restricts himself to affairs of the heart. The other writes in metres of moderate length, uses a highly Persianized vocabulary, and ranges wide in ideas.

Unlike his fellow poets, Nazir Akbarabadi (who wrote in the late eighteenth and early nineteenth centuries) eschewed classical Perso-Arabic traditions in his short poems and wrote in both the language of popular speech and of literature. Nevertheless, though generally ignored in his time, Nazir – whose poems are on topics as diverse as popular festivals, the seasons, the vanities of life, erotic pleasures and pursuits, dancing bears, and miserly merchants – has gained increasing respect and recognition as the first and best poet of the people.

Non-Sanskrit literature
to the eighteenth century

Of the literatures produced in the Dravidian languages, Tamil
is the earliest. From the first three centuries of the Common
Era come eight anthologies of lyrics (love poems, heroic poems
on war, death, personal virtues, the ferocity and glory of kings,
and the poverty of poets), ten long poems, and a grammar
called the *Tolkappiyam* ("Old Composition"). Later came the
Patiren-kirkkanakku ("Eighteen Ethical Works"), usually
dated as post-Sangam (fourth–seventh century) – the most
celebrated of these is the *Tirukkural* ("Sacred Couplets"), which
deals with virtue (Sanskrit: *dharma*); *porul*, government and
society (Sanskrit: *artha*); and *kamam*, love (Sanskrit: *kama*).

The age of the Pallavas (300?–900) is known for its epics,
beginning with *Cilappatikaram* ("The Jewelled Anklet") by
Ilanko Atikal. One of the great achievements of Tamil genius,
the *Cilappatikaram* is a detailed poetic witness to Tamil
culture, its varied religions, town plans and city types, the
commingling of Greek, Arab, and Tamil peoples, and the arts
of dance and music. The *Perunkatai* ("The Great Story"), the
Civakacintamani ("The Amulet of Civakan") by Tiruttakka-
tevar, and *Culamani* ("The Crest Jewel") by Tolamolittevar
depict Jaina kings and their ideals of the good life, nonviolence, and the attainment of salvation through self-sacrifice. In
their episodic methods of narration and set descriptions of
erotic, heroic, and religious themes, these Jaina epics became
both models and sources for later epic works.

From the sixth century onward came *bhakti* poets, the
earliest of whom were the Nayanars (Shiva devotees) and
the Alvars ("Immersed Ones"; devoted to Vishnu). The most
important Nayanars were Appar and Campantar, in the
seventh century, and Cuntarar, in the eighth, who with his

vision of 63 Tamil saints – rich, poor, male, female, of every caste and trade, unified even with bird and beast in the love of God – epitomizes *bhakti*. Their songs have become part of temple ritual.

The Tamil Cola Empire (tenth–thirteenth centuries) saw an awakening of neighbouring literatures: Kannada, Telugu, and Malayalam. The first extant Kannada work is the ninth-century *Kavirajamarga* ("The Royal Road of Poets"), a rhetoric work containing the first descriptions of the Kannada country, people, and dialects. From the tenth century on, *campu* narratives (part prose, part verse) became popular both in Kannada and in Telugu, as did renderings of the Sanskrit epics *Ramayana* and *Mahabharata* and Jaina legends and biography.

Pre-fifteenth-century Tamil influence on early Malayalam, the language of Kerala, was strong and led to the literature of *pattu* ("song"), the best known of which is *Ramacaritam* (*c.* twelfth–thirteenth century; "Deeds of Rama"). The predominant influence on Malayalam was, however, Sanskrit, and the mixture of this language with Malayalam resulted in a literary dialect called *manipravala* (meaning, "necklace of diamonds and coral"). Many kinds of poems were composed in Malayalam: *kudyattam*s (dramatic); didactic works such as the eleventh-century *Vaisikatantram* ("Advice to a Courtesan by Her Mother"); thirteenth- and fourteenth-century *campu*s on dancers; and several short poems in praise of women and kings. At the same time a live *pacca* ("pure, fresh") Malayalam tradition produced folk songs and ballads such as *Vadukkan Pattukal* (hero ballads of the northern Malabar Coast).

By the fifteenth century the three styles – the indigenous folk style, the Tamil, and the Sanskrit – had begun to converge in works such as *Krsna Pattu* ("Song of Krishna"). Such grafting reached its full flowering in the sixteenth-century poet Eluttaccan (Father [or Leader] of Letters), who popularized the *kilippattu* ("parrot song"), a genre in which the narrator is a parrot, a bee, a swan, and so on.

During this same period, collections of many scriptural works were made. The hymns of the Nayanars in Tamil were arranged and anthologized, as was Cekkilar's twelfth-century *Tontar Puranam*, or *Periyapuranam*, narrating in epic style the lives of the 63 great Shaiva saints. By the twelfth century the Virashaiva poet-saints had a new Kannada genre, the *vacana* ("saying" or "prose poem"), in which in the language of the people and in intense and searing expressions of *bhakti*, they expressed their radical views on religion and society. Harihara, in the late twelfth century, and his disciple and nephew Raghavanka, in the thirteenth century, wrote of the lives of saints. The Virashaiva saints' lives and the *vacana* literature were codified in a masterpiece called *Sunya Sampadane* ("The Achievement of Nothing"). Telugu Shaiva poets such as Palkuriki Somanatha – whose *Panditaradhya Caritra* is a life of the Shaiva devotee Panditaradhya as well as a book of general knowledge including social customs, arts, crafts, and particularly music – were similarly active at this time.

From the fourteenth to the sixteenth century, during the Vijayanagar Empire, Kannada and Telugu were under the aegis of one dynasty and also came under the influence of neighbouring Muslim Bahmani kingdoms. Among the works of Shrinatha, a fifteenth-century poet honoured in many courts, are Sanskrit poems, *Haravilasam* ("Four Shaiva Tales"), and *Palanati Vira Caritra*, a popular ballad on a fratricidal war. Bammera Potana is widely known for his *Bhagavatam*, a masterpiece that is said to excel the original Sanskrit *Bhagavata-Purana*. Tallapaka Annamacarya fathered an exciting new genre of devotional song, all addressed to the god Shri Venkateshvara of Tirupati (a form of Vishnu).

The sixteenth century was an age of patronage by Vijaya-nagar kings, beginning with Krishna Deva Raya, himself a poet versed in Sanskrit, Kannada, and Telugu. Among the most famous court poets were Pingali Suranna, whose verse novel, *Kalapurnodayam* (1550) – a story full of surprises, magic, and changes of identity – is justly celebrated; and Tenali Ramakrishna, known for his clownish pranks and humour, whose writings are the centre of a very popular cycle of tales in all four Dravidian languages.

During the sixteenth century, and for the next few centuries, Telugu poets also flourished outside Telugu country, especially in Tanjore (Thanjavur) and Madurai in Tamil country, and Pudukkotta and Mysore in Kannada country. Their most important contribution was Kannada and Telugu dance dramas on mythological themes, called *yaksagana*. The fifteenth and sixteenth centuries also produced some of the most popular classics in Kannada. Of these the greatest is Gadugu's *Kumara Vyasa*, and Naranappa's ten cantos of the *Mahabharata*.

The folk *tripadi* ("three-line verse") of Sarvajna (1700?) is a household word for wit and wisdom, and the proverb-like aphorisms of Vemana and Sarvajna are widely quoted by pundit and layman alike. Equally popular in the Malayalam region is the eighteenth-century folk poet of *tullal*s (a song-dance form), Kuncan Nampiyar, unparalleled for his wit and exuberance and his humorous renderings even of mythic characters.

The seventeenth and eighteenth centuries was a period of many schisms and the founding of monasteries, which led to many sectarian and polemic works. Muslims and Christians also wrote epics in the Hindu Purana style – for example, Umark-p-pulavar's seventeenth-century Cira-p-puranam, on the life of the Prophet Muhammad. Probably the most impressive Tamil poetry of this period is that of Arunakiriv's learned and melodious *Tiruppukal* (a praise of Munikan) and of the Cittars, eclectic mystics known for their radical, fierce folk songs and common-speech style.

The seventeenth and eighteenth centuries are also periods of folk expression, which include many *tiruvilaiyatal* ("stories of God's sport") Puranas; temple tales (about miracles that took place in the temple); *kuravanci* ("gypsy," a kind of musical dance drama); *pallu*s (plays about village agricultural life); realistic *nonti-natakam*s ("dramas of the lame"), in which a Hindu temple god cures lameness; *kummi* (songs sung by young girls); and *ammanai* (ballads). Noteworthy historical ballads are *Katta Pomman*, about a chieftain who revolted against the British, and *Tecinku-racan Katai*, about the prince of Gingi and his Muslim friend.

Modern Indian literature

Literature languished during much of the period of British rule, but beginning in the nineteenth century British and western literary models had a great impact on Indian literature, leading to the so-called Hindu Renaissance, centred in Bengal. The most striking result was the introduction of the use of vernacular prose on a major scale. Such previously unknown forms as the novel and short story began to be adopted by Indian writers, as did realism and a new interest in social questions and psychological description.

Perhaps first among novelists of the late nineteenth and early twentieth centuries is Saratchandra Chatterjee, whose social concerns with the family and other homely issues made his work popular. But the early twentieth century is best known for the poet Rabindranath Tagore. Poet, playwright, novelist, painter, essayist, musician, and social reformer, Rabindra-nath's little book of songs called *Gitanjali* was much praised by Ezra Pound and William Butler Yeats. He was the last of an era, looking back as he did to the religious and political history of Bengal for his inspiration. Those who followed him were more concerned with introspection and dramatic imagery.

If Tagore was the last poet in the Bengali tradition, Jiba-nananda Das, known for vivid and unusual imagery, was the first of a new breed and has had much influence on younger writers. Other important poets are Sudhindranath Datta, a poet much like Pound in careful and etymological use of language, and prose writer Buddhadeva Bose, leader of the Kallol school and editor of an influential literary magazine, *Kavita*. Unjustifiably called obscene, his writing was experi-mental, probing into social and psychological realities of Bengali life.

Among writers in other languages in the subcontinent, one of the most outstanding early modern writers was the Assa-mese Lakshminath Bezbaruwa, who founded a literary monthly, *Jonaki* ("Moonlight"), in 1889, and was responsible for infusing Assamese letters with nineteenth-century Roman-ticism. The short story has also flourished; notable practi-tioners in Assamese are Mahichandra Bora and Holiram Deka, and in Kannada are Panje Mangesh Rao and B.M. Srikantiah.

Modern Rajasthani literature began with the works of Suryamal Misrama. His most important works are the *Vamsa Bhaskara*, accounts of the Rajput princes who ruled in what was then Rajputana (the present-day state of Rajasthan) during the lifetime of the poet (1872–1952), and the *Vira satsai*, a collection of couplets dealing with historical heroes.

Marathi poetry of the period started with Kesavasut, who declared a revolt against traditional Marathi poetry and started a school, lasting until 1920, that emphasized home and nature, the glorious past, and pure lyricism. After that, the period was dominated by the Ravikiran Mandal poets, who proclaimed that poetry was not for the erudite and sensitive but was instead a part of everyday life. Contemporary poetry, after 1945, has sought to explore people and their lives in all its variety; it has been subjective and personal, and has tried to speak colloquially.

Nationalism has been an influence in many forms. The nationalism and social reform movements of the Arya Samaj led to the composition of long narrative poems in Hindi, exemplified by those of Maithili Sharan Gupta. In Gujarat, the year 1886 saw the *Kusumamala* ("Garland of Flowers"), a collection of lyrics by Narsingh Rao. Nanalal, who experimented in free verse, was the first poet to eulogize Mohandas Gandhi.

Among Punjabi poets who wrote nationalist poetry in a humorous or satiric mood were Bhai Vir Singh in the nineteenth century, and Purana Singh, Amrita Pritam, and Baba Balwanta in the twentieth century. The fathers of modern Urdu poetry were Hali and Muhammad Husayn Azad, the latter particularly characterized by a fine sensitivity for the past, but the great modern Urdu poet was Iqbal. Writing in the early twentieth century, he was influenced by the general sense of national purpose and the freedom movement, and his poetic imagery, the power of his expression, and his philosophical outlook won the admiration of his fellow Muslims. In Rajasthan poets were inspired to write verse that was both nationalistic and in the traditional heroic vein; among them are Hiralala Sastri, Manikyalala Varma, and Jayanarayana Vyasa. Progressive social ideals inspired such poets there as Ganeshilala Vyasa, Murlidhara Vyasa, and Satyaprakasha Jodhi.

In Urdu literature the modern period coincides with the mid-nineteenth-century emergence of a middle class that saw in western thought and science a means to much-needed social reform. Nazir Ahmad's novels are about the conflicts of Muslim middle-class people. The more famous novelists of the later period are Ratan-Nath Sharshar, 'Abd-ul-Halim Sharar, and Mirza Ruswa.

The growth of the novel was one of the most significant developments in the twentieth century. Two trends, represented by the work of Prem Chand and Jainendra Kumar, led Hindi fiction in different directions: while social realists like Yashpal, Upendranath Ashk, Amritlal Nagar, Mohan Rakesh, Rajendra Yadav, Kamleshwar, Nagarjuna, and Renu faithfully analysed the changing patterns of Indian society, writers such as Ila Chandra Joshi, "Agyeya," Dharm Vir Bharati, and Shrikant Varma explored the psychology of the individual – and not necessarily within the Indian context. The Gujarati Govardhanram also stands out; his *Sarasvatichandra* is a classic, the first social novel.

A high place is held in Marathi literature by V.M. Joshi, who in his novels explored the education and evolution of a woman (*Susila-cha Diva*, 1930) and the relation between art and morals (*Indu Kale va Sarala Bhole*, 1935). Important after 1925 were N.S. Phadke, who advocated art for art's sake, and V.S. Khandehar, who countered the former with an idealistic art for life's sake. Noteworthy contemporary novelists are S.N. Pendse, V.V. Shirwadkar, G.N. Dandekar, and Ranjit Desai.

Tamil literary works in modern times have been divided between the scholastic traditional prose style of the *Patinenkilkkanakku* and a more popular vernacular language. The scholastic and formalist character predominated until the advent, in the early twentieth century, of the poet and prose writer Subrahmanya Bharati. He sought to synthesize the popular and the scholastic traditions of Tamil literature, and created thereby a Tamil that was amenable to all literary expression.

The first novel in Tamil appeared in 1879, the *Piratapamutaliyar Carittiram* by Vetanayakam Pillai, who was inspired by English and French novels. In important respects Pillai's work is typical of all early modern Tamil fiction: his subject matter is Tamil life as he observed it, the language is scholastic, and the inspiration comes from foreign sources. Quite different is the *Kamalampal Carittiram* ("The Fatal Rumor") by Rajam Aiyar, whom many judge to be the most important prose writer of nineteenth-century Tamil literature. The story is a romance, yet life in rural Tamil country is treated very realistically, with humour, irony, and social satire. In language Aiyar follows the classical style, which he intermixes with informal conversation – a style that has been imitated by modern authors.

In the first half of the twentieth century R. Krishnamurthy, under the pseudonym Kalki, wrote immensely popular historical romances. In the 1930s Putumaippittan wrote realistically, critically, and even bitterly about the failings of society. L.S. Ramatirthan, who started by writing in English, is probably the finest contemporary stylist at work in Tamil.

There has been Indian literary activity in English for the last 200 years. It began with the insistence of the reformist Rammohan Ray and other like-minded Hindus that, for India to take its rightful place among nations, a knowledge of and education in English were essential. English literary activity took on a new aspect with the independence movement, whose leaders and followers found in English the one language that united them.

Among the first poets were Henry Derozio, Kashiprasad Ghose, and Michael Madhusudan Datta, all of whom wrote narrative verse. Sarojini Naidu is judged by many the greatest of women poets; among her writings are *The Golden Threshold* (1905), *The Bird of Time* (1912), and *The Broken Wing* (1917). Sri Aurobindo, who started out as an ardent nationalist and was jailed by the British, but later established a hermitage in Pondicherry (now Puducherry), left behind a rich oeuvre of verse that has inspired a contemporary school of mystic poets.

The independence movement gave strong impetus to expository prose, including the work of Bal Gangadhar Tilak, who edited the English journal *Mahratta*. Mohandas Gandhi's autobiography *My Experiments with Truth* (originally published in Gujarati, 1927–29) is now an Indian classic. In this he was followed by Jawaharlal Nehru, whose *Discovery of India* is justly popular.

Prose fiction in English began in 1902 with the novel *The Lake of Palms*, by Romesh Chunder Dutt. The next important novelist is Mulk Raj Anand, who fulminated against class and caste distinction in a series of novels, *The Coolie* (1936), *Untouchable* (1935), *Two Leaves and a Bud* (1937), and *The Big Heart* (1945). Less fierce, though a better craftsman, is R.K. Narayan, who during his long career published nearly three dozen novels (as well as several collections of short stories), among them *The Guide* (1958), *The Man-Eater of Malgudi* (1961), and *The Vendor of Sweets* (1967); his work has a wider circle of readers outside India than within. The most popular is Raja Rao, whose novels *Kanthapura* (1938), The *Cow of the Barricades* (1947), and *The Serpent and the Rope* (1960) attracted a wide following.

Drama

Classical Sanskrit theatre flourished during the first nine centuries of the Common Era. Classical structure, form, and style of acting and production with aesthetic rules were consolidated in Bharata Muni's treatise on dramaturgy, *Natyasastra*, which classified drama into ten types. The two most important are *nataka* ("heroic"), which deals with the exalted themes of gods and kings and draws from history or mythology (Kalidasa's *Sakuntala* and Bhavabhuti's *Uttararamacarita* fall into this category), and *prakarana* ("social"), in which the dramatist invents a plot dealing with ordinary human beings, such as a courtesan or a woman of low morals (Sudraka's *Mrcchakatika*, "The Little Clay Cart," belongs to this type). The only surviving Sanskrit drama is *kudiyattam*, still performed by the Cakkayars of Kerala.

After the decline of Sanskrit drama, folk theatre developed in various regional languages from the fourteenth to the nineteenth centuries. Some conventions and stock characters of classical drama (stage preliminaries, the opening prayer song, the *sutra-dhara* [stage manager], and the *vidusaka* [clown]) were adopted into folk theatre, which lavishly employs music, dance, drumming, exaggerated make-up, masks, and a singing chorus. Thematically it deals with mythological heroes, medieval romances, and social and political events, and it is a rich store of customs, beliefs, legends, and rituals.

The most crystallized forms are the *jatra* of Bengal; the *nautanki*, *ramlila*, and *raslila* of north India; the *bhavai* of Gujarat; the *tamasha* of Maharashtra; the *terukkuttu* of Tamil Nadu; and the *yaksagana* of Kanara. Of the nonreligious forms, the *jatra* and the *tamasha* are the most important. The *jatra* performance consists of action-packed dialogue with only about six songs. The *tamasha* (a Persian word meaning "fun," "play," or "spectacle") originated at the beginning of the eighteenth century in Maharashtra as an entertainment for the camping Mughal armies. Flourishing in the courts of Maratha rulers of the eighteenth and nineteenth centuries, it attained its artistic apogee during the reign of Baji Rao II (1796–1818). In contemporary times, over 700 *tamasha* troupes with 2,000 dancer-actresses tour the rural areas, providing a living for about 40,000 people. But the *jatra* is the most successful commercially. Its star actors draw more than any other professional actor in the theatrical centre of Kolkata (formerly Calcutta).

Popular in north India are the *putliwala*s ("puppeteers") of Rajasthan. The puppet plays deal with kings, lovers, bandits, and princesses of the Mughal period. In the absence of a powerful Indian city theatre (with the exception of a few in Kolkata, Mumbai, and Tamil Nadu state), folk theatre has kept the rural audiences entertained for centuries and has played an important part in the growth of modern theatres in different languages.

Modern Indian theatre first developed in Bengal at the end of the eighteenth century as a result of western influence, and other regional theatres followed. With the help of local linguist Golak Nath Dass, a Russian bandmaster in a British military unit named Gerasim Lebedev produced the first Bengali play, *Chhadmabes*, "The Disguise", in 1795 on a western-style stage with Bengali players of both sexes. Subsequently, Bengali playwrights began synthesizing western styles with their own folk and Sanskrit heritage. With growing national consciousness, theatre became a platform for social reform and propaganda against British rule. Among the most important playwrights were Michael Madhu Sudan (1824–73), Dina Bandhu Mitra (1843–87), Girish Chandra Ghosh (1844–1912), and D.L. Roy (1863–1913).

The success of Dina Bandhu Mitra's *Nildarpan*, "Mirror of the Indigo", dealing with the tyranny of the British indigo planters over the rural Bengali farm labourers, paved the way for professional theatre. The actor-director-writer Girish Chandra Ghosh founded in 1872 the National Theatre. To overcome censorship difficulties, playwrights turned to historical and mythological themes with veiled symbolism that was clearly understood by Indian audiences. Girish's historical tragedies *Mir Qasim*, 1906; *Chhatrapati*, 1907; and *Sirajud-daulah*, 1909 bring out the tragic grandeur of heroes who fail because of some inner weakness or betrayal of their colleagues. D.L. Roy emphasized the same aspect of nationalism in his historical dramas *Mebarapatan*, *Shahjahan*, 1910; and *Chandragupta*, 1911.

Rabindranath Tagore (1861–1941), steeped in Hindu classics and indigenous folk forms but responsive to European techniques of production, evolved a dramatic form quite different from those of his contemporaries. He used music and dance as essential elements in his latter years and created the novel opera-dance form in which a chorus sat on the stage and sang while the players acted out their roles in dance and stylized movements.

Urdu and Hindi drama began with the production of *Indrasabha* by Wajid Ali Shah in 1855, and was developed by the Parsi theatrical companies until the 1930s. Parsi theatre was an amalgam of European techniques and local classical forms, folk dramas, farces, and pageants. The star film actor Prithvi Raj Kapoor founded Prithvi Theatres in Bombay in 1944, and brought robust realism to Hindi drama. Out of Prithvi's eight productions the best was *Pathan*, 1946, which deals with the friendship between a tribal Muslim *khan* and a Hindu *dewan*. Hindi language dramas in contemporary times include those of Jayashankar Prasad. Realism in Marathi was first brought to the stage in the twentieth century by Mama Varerkar, who tried to interpret many social problems.

8

ARCHITECTURE

Early Buildings

The favoured materials of early Indian architecture appear to have been wood or baked or sun-dried brick, but little has survived from before the fifth century CE. Stone buildings followed in the sixth century and soon became popular, becoming the material of preference in Islamic monuments. The principles of wooden construction played an important part in determining the shape of Indian architecture and its various elements and components. Among the earliest remains of brick buildings are those of the urban centres of the Indus Valley civilization (c.2500–1800 CE), notably Mohenjo-daro, Harappa, and Kalibangan.

Most surviving examples of Indian architecture before the Islamic period are of a religious nature, consisting mainly of Buddhist shrines, stupas, and temples. The stupa, the most typical monument of the Buddhist faith, consists essentially of a domical mound in which sacred relics are enshrined. Stupas appear to have had a regular architectural form during the

Mauryan dynasty (*c*.321-185 BCE): the mound was sometimes provided with a parasol surrounded by a miniature railing on the top, raised on a terrace, and the whole surrounded by a large railing consisting of posts, crossbars, and a coping (the capping on the top course). A famous stupa of the period (later enlarged) is at Sanchi in Madhya Pradesh.

Along with stupas were erected roofless shrines enclosing a sacred object such as a tree or an altar. Temples of brick and timber with vaulted or domical roofs were also constructed; these have not survived, but the rock-cut caves in the Barabar Hills near Gaya preserve their form. The interiors of most caves consist of two chambers: a shrine, elliptical or circular in plan with a domed roof (such as Sudama cave in the hills near Gaya) and an adjacent antechamber, roughly rectangular and provided with a barrel vault.

Over the next 500 years, up to the third century CE, stupas become progressively larger and more elaborate. The railings were often profusely carved, as at Bharhut, Sanchi II, and Amaravati in Madhya Pradesh, and they also had elaborate gateways. An attempt was made to increase their height by multiplying the terraces that supported the dome and by increasing the number of parasols on top. In Gandhara and south-eastern India, particularly, sculptured decoration was extended to the stupa proper, so that terraces, drums, and domes – as well as railings – were decorated with figural and ornamental sculpture in bas-relief.

In the cave temples of western India, cut into the scarp of the Western Ghats and stretching from Gujarat to southern Maharashtra, two main types of buildings can be distinguished: the temple proper (*caitya*) and the monastery (*vihara*, *sangharama*). The former is generally an apsidal hall with a central nave flanked by aisles. The apse is covered by a half dome, while two rows of pillars, which demarcate the nave, support a barrel-vault roof that covers the rest of the building. In the apsidal end is placed the object to be worshipped, generally a stupa, the hall being meant for the gathered congregation. In front of the hall is a porch, separated from it by a screen wall. The pillars are generally octagonal with a pot-shaped base and a capital of addorsed animals placed on a bell-shaped, or campaniform, lotus in the Maurya tradition. The most significent example is at Karli, dating approximately to the closing years of the first century BCE. Toward the end of the period a quadrilateral plan appears more and more frequently, as, for example, at Kuda and Sailarwadi.

In addition to the *caitya*, or temple proper, numerous one-storey monasteries (*viharas*) are also cut into the rock. These are generally provided with a pillared porch and a screen wall pierced with doorways leading into the interior, which consists of a "courtyard" or congregation hall in the three walls of which are the monks' cells. At Uparkot in Junagadh, Gujarat, is a remarkable series of rock-cut structures dating from the third–fourth century CE, which appear to be secular in character and in all probability served as royal pleasure houses.

The large number of representations of buildings found on relief sculpture from sites such as Bharhut, Sanchi, Mathura, and Amaravati are a rich source of information about early Indian architecture. They depict walled and moated cities with massive gates, elaborate multi-storey residences, pavilions with a variety of domes, together with the simple, thatched-roofed huts that remained the basis of most Indian architectural forms. A striking feature of this early Indian architecture is the consistent and profuse use of arched windows and doors, which are extremely important elements of the architectural decor.

Dating toward the close of the fourth and the beginning of the fifth century CE is a series of temples that marks the opening phase of a new architectural style, ultimately leading to the great and elaborate temples of the eighth century onward. Two main temple types have been distinguished in the Gupta period. The first consists of a square, dark sanctum with a small, pillared porch in front, both covered with flat roofs. This type of temple answers the simplest needs of worship, a chamber to house the deity and a roof to shelter the devotee. Temple No. 17 at Sanchi in Madhya Pradesh is a classic example. It is the second type of temple that points the way to future developments. It also has a square sanctum, or *cella*, but instead of a flat roof there is a pyramidal superstructure, or spire (*shikhara*). Among the most interesting examples are a brick temple at Bhitargaon in Uttar Pradesh and the Vishnu temple at Deogarh in Bihar, built entirely of stone. The sanctums of both temples are square in plan, with three sides provided with central offsets (vertical buttress-like projections) that go up to the top of the *shikhara*, with a niche in which is placed an image.

Stupas continued to be built during the Gupta period, increasing in height by multiplying and heightening the supporting terraces and elongating the drum and dome. A good example of this new form is the Dhamekh stupa at Sarnath in Uttar Pradesh. The rock-cut temple and monastery tradition also continued, notably in western India, where excavations, especially at the Ajantata Caves, display extreme richness and magnificence. The monasteries are characterized by the introduction of images into some of the cells, so that they partake of the nature of temples instead of being simple residences.

Medieval temples

Architectural styles initiated during the fifth and sixth centuries found their fullest expression in the medieval period (particularly from the ninth to the eleventh centuries), when great stone temples were built. Two main types can be broadly distinguished, one found generally in northern India, the other in southern India. To these can be added a third type, sharing features of both and found in Karnataka and the Deccan.

North Indian temples generally consist of a sanctum enshrining the main image, usually square in plan and shaped like a hollow cube, and one or more halls (called *mandapa*s). The sanctum may or may not have an ambulatory, but it is invariably dark, the only opening being the entrance door. The doorway surrounds are richly decorated with bands of figural, floral, and geometrical ornament and with river-goddess groups at the base. A vestibule (*antarala*) connects the sanctum to the halls, which are of two broad types: the *gudhamandapas*, which are enclosed by walls, light and air let in through windows or doors; and open halls, which are provided with balustrades rather than walls and are consequently lighter and airier. The sanctum almost invariably, and the *mandapa*s generally, have *shikhara*s; those on the sanctum, appropriately, are the most dominant in any grouping. Internally, the sanctum has a flat ceiling, while those of the halls, supported by carved pillars, are coffered and of extremely rich design.

The sanctum is often set on a raised base or plinth (*pitha*), above which is a foundation block or socle (*vedibandha*), decorated with a distinct series of mouldings; above the *vedibandha* rise the walls proper (*jangha*), which are capped by a cornice or a series of cornice mouldings (*varandika*), above which rises the *shikhara*. The entire temple complex may be raised on a terrace (*jagati*), which is sometimes of considerable height and size. The attendant shrines – generally four – are placed at the corners of the terrace, forming a quincunx arrangement (*pancayatana*) that is fairly widespread. The temple complex may be surrounded by a wall with an arched doorway (*torana*).

The *shikhara* is the most distinctive part of the north Indian temple and is of two basic types – the curvilenear *latina*, which is covered in creeper-like tracery and is surmounted by a pot and crowning finial (*kalasa*); and the rectilinear and shorter *phamsana*, which is capped by a bell-shaped member called the *ghanta*. From the tenth century onward the *shekhari* type of spire, an elaboration of the *latina* type, became increasingly popular. In its developed form it consisted of a central *latina* spire (*mulasrnga*) with one or more rows of half spires added on the sides (*urah-srnga*) and the base strung with miniature spires (*srngas*). The corners, too, are sometimes filled with quarter spires, the whole mass of carved masonry recalling a mountain with a cluster of subsidiary peaks. The *latina* and *shekhari* spires are generally found on the sanctum, while the *phamsana* and its variants are usually confined to the *mandapa*s. The sanctum spires also have a large and prominent projection in front (*shukanasa*), generally rising above the vestibule (*antarala*). These projections are essentially large ogee arches of complex form, which often contain the image of the presiding deity.

Although basically reflecting a homogeneous architectural style, temple architecture in northern India developed a number of distinct regional variations. Among the most important are the styles of Orissa, central India, Rajasthan, and Gujarat.

The greatest centre of the Orissa school, which usually favours a *latina shikhara* over the sanctum and has plain interiors, is the ancient city of Bhuvaneshvara, in which are concentrated almost 100 examples of the style, ranging in date from the seventh to the thirteenth century. The most famous example, however, is the colossal building at Konarak, dedicated to Surya, the sun god. The temple and its accompanying hall are conceived in the form of a great chariot drawn by horses. All that survives are the ruins of the sanctum and the *gudhamandapa*, with gigantic *phamsana shikhara* rising in three stages and adorned with colossal figures of musicians and dancers, and a separate dancing hall.

The area roughly covered by the modern state of Madhya Pradesh in central India gave rise to several schools of architecture, centred on Gwalior and adjacent areas (ancient Gopadri); modern Bundelkhand, known in ancient times as Jejakabhukti; the ancient country of Dahala, of which Tripuri, near modern Jabalpur, was the capital; and Malava (Malwa).

In the Gwalior area in the ninth century a series of magnificent temples was built, including the Mala-de at Dyaraspur, the Shiva temples at Mahka and Indore, and a temple dedicated to an unidentified mother goddess at Barwa-Sagar. The period appears to have been one of experimentation, a variety of plans and spires having been tried: the *shekhari* type in its formative stages; a star-shaped plan; and a twin *latina* spire over a rectangular sanctum. The largest and perhaps the finest temple is the Teli-ka-Mandir on Gwalior Fort, rectangular in plan and capped by a pointed barrel vault. The walls are decorated with niches (empty at present), topped by tall pediments (triangular gable ornament).

The style of this region became increasingly elaborate from the tenth century, during the supremacy of the Kacchapaghata dynasty. The many examples from this period are distinguished by a low plinth and rich sculptural decoration on the walls. Outstanding among them are the Kakan-madh at Suhania (1015–35) and the Sas-Bahu temple (completed 1093) in Gwalior Fort.

The earliest temples of the Dahala area, dating from the eighth and ninth centuries, are the simple shrines at Bandhogarh, which consist of a sanctum with *latina* spire and porch.

To the tenth century, when the local Kalacuri dynasty was rapidly gaining power, belong the remarkable Siva temples at Chandrehe and Masaun, the former being circular in plan, with a *latina* spire covered with rich *candrasala* tracery. The Gola Math at Maihar has the more conventional square sanctum, with a very elegant *latina shikhara*, the walls of which are adorned with two rows of figural sculpture.

The Malava region appears to have been the first to develop the *bhumija* type of *shikhara* (tenth century). The finest and most representative group of these structures is at Un. The best preserved and easily the finest *bhumija* temple is the Udayes-vara (1059–82), situated at Udaipur. The *shikhara*, based on a stellate plan, is divided into quadrants by four *lata*s (offsets), each one of which has five rows of aediculae (niches for statues). The large hall has three entrance porches, one to the front and two to the sides, and walls that are richly carved. The whole complex, including seven subsidiary shrines, is placed on a broad, tall platform. Structures in the *bhumija* manner continued to be made in Malava up to the fifteenth century, and also spread into Rajasthan, Gujarat, and later (up to the sixteenth century) to north Deccan and Berar.

A group of temples at Osian, dating to about the eighth century, represents the opening phases of medieval temple architecture in Rajasthan. They stand on high terraces and consist of a sanctum, a hall, and a porch. The sanctum is generally square and has a *latina* spire. Richness of sculpture and architectural elaboration are characteristic, and the door-way surrounds and pillars are elaborately decorated. The walls are embellished with sculpture, often placed in niches with tall pediments. Some of the finest temples of the style date from the tenth century, the most important of which are the Ghatesvara temple at Badoli and the Ambika Mata temple at Jagat. The Ambika-Mata temple, of the mid-tenth century, is exceptionally fine. It consists of a sanctum, a *gudhamandapa* and a parapeted porch with projecting eaves. The walls of the sanctum and the hall are covered with fine sculpture, the superstructures being of the *shekhari* and the *phamsana* types.

From the tenth century onward, the styles of Rajasthan and neighbouring Gujarat grew closer and closer together until the differences between them were gradually obliterated. The temples at Kiradu in Rajasthan, dating from the late tenth and eleventh centuries, are early examples of this shared style. The Somesvara temple (*c.*1020) is the most important, and clearly shows the movement toward increasing elaboration and ornamentation. The mouldings of the plinth, for example, are multiplied to include bands of elephants, horses, and soldiers. The walls are covered with sculpture, and the spire is of the rich *shekhari* type. Traditional architecture continued even after the Islamic invasions, particularly during the reign of Rana Kumbha of Mewar (*c.*1430–69). During this period, the tall nine-storey Kirttistambha and other temples at Chitor and also the great Chaumukha temple at Ranakpur (1438) were built.

Gujarat was the home of one of the richest regional styles of northern India. Its distinctive features are clear in an interesting group of temples from Roda (*c.* eighth century). The sanctum is square in plan and has *latina* spires that are weighty and majestic. The walls are relatively plain, with niches (housing images) provided only on the central projection. The masonry work is exceptionally good, a characteristic of Gujarat architecture throughout its history. The great Sun Temple at Modhera, datable to the early years of the eleventh century, represents a fully developed Gujarat style of great magnificence. The temple consists of a sanctum (now in ruins), a *gudhamandapa* of extraordinary richness, and an arched entrance in front of which was the great tank. The Rudramala at Siddhapur, the most magnificent temple of the twelfth century, is now in a much-ruined condition, with only the *torana* (gateway) and some subsidiary structures remaining. With the Islamic conquest, the Gujarat architects adapted their considerable skills to meet the needs of a patron of different religion and quickly produced a totally successful Indian version of Islamic architecture.

The north Indian style was largely confined to India above the Vindhyas, though for a short period it also flourished in Karnataka. Here, temples of the northern and the southern styles are found next to each other, notably at Aihole and Pattadkal. The northern style was also cultivated at Pattadkal, where the most important examples are the Kasivisvanatha, the Galaganatha, and the Papanatha. Alampur, now in Andhra Pradesh, has eight temples of the northern style with *latina* spires. These belong to the late seventh and early eighth centuries and are the finest, and among the last, examples of the northern style in southern India.

The architectural style of the Kashmir region, which continued from the eighth to the twelfth century, is quite distinct. Unlike other northern Indian regions, the roof of the Kashmir sanctum is of the *phamsana* type, with eaves raised in two stages. The greatest example to survive is the ruined Sun Temple at Martand (mid-eighth century), though its *shikhara* is missing. The temple is placed in a rectangular court enclosed by a series of columns. Access to the court is through an imposing entrance hall, the walls of which have doorways with gabled pediments and a trefoil (shaped like a trifoliate leaf) recess.

The home of the south Indian style, sometimes called the *dravida* style, appears to be Tamil Nadu. Examples, however, are found all over southern India, particularly in Karnataka and Andhradesa, now largely covered by the states of Karnataka and Andhra Pradesh. Both Andhradesa and Karnataka developed variants.

A typical south Indian temple consists of a hall and a square sanctum that has a superstructure of the *kutina* type. Pyramidal in form, the *kutina* spire consists of stepped storeys, each of which simulates the main storey and is conceived as having its own "wall" enclosed by a parapet. The parapet itself is composed of miniature shrines strung together – square ones (*kuta*s) at the corners, and rectangular ones with barrel-vault roofs (*sala*s) in the centre; the space between them connected by miniature wall elements called *harantaras*. (Conspicuous in the early temples, these stepped storeys of the superstructure with their parapets became more and more ornamental, so that in the course of time they evolved into more or less decorative bands around the pyramidal superstructure.) On top of the stepped structure is a necking that supports a solid dome or cupola (instead of the north Indian grooved disc), which in turn is crowned by a pot and finial. The walls of the sanctum rise above a series of mouldings, and the surface of the walls does not have the prominent offsets seen in north Indian temples but is instead divided by pilasters. In the Karnatic version, particularly from the late tenth century onward (sometimes called the *vesara* style), this arrangement of the superstructure is loaded with decoration, thus considerably obscuring the component elements. At the same time, these elements are so manipulated that they tend to form distinct vertical bands, in this respect closely recalling the *shikhara*s of northern India.

The design of the hall-temple roofed by a barrel vault, popular in the centuries before and after Christ, was adopted in southern India for the great entrance buildings (*gopura*s) that give access to the sacred enclosures in which the temples stand. Relatively small and inconspicuous in early examples, by the mid-twelfth century they had outstripped the main temple in size.

The early phase of Tamil Nadu architecture – which, broadly speaking, coincided with the political supremacy of the Pallava dynasty (c.650–893) – is best represented by the important monuments at Mahabalipuram. The finest temple at this site and of this period is an elegant complex of three shrines called the Shore Temple (c.700). The capital city of Kanchipuram also possesses some fine temples – for example, the Kailasanatha (dating a little later than the Shore Temple), with its stately superstructure and subsidiary shrines attached to the walls. The enclosure wall has a series of small shrines on all sides and a small *gopura*.

The ninth century marked a fresh movement in the south Indian style, revealed in several small, simple, but most elegant temples set up during the ascendancy of the Cola and other dynasties. One of the most important is the Vijayalaya Colisvara temple at Narttamalai (mid-ninth century), with its circular sanctum, spherical cupola, and massive, plain walls. These simple beginnings led rapidly (in about a century) to the mightiest of all temples in the south Indian style, the Brhadishvara or Rajarajeshvara temple, built at the Cola capital of Thanjavur. A royal dedication of Rajaraja I, the temple was begun around 1003 and completed about seven years later. The main walls are raised in two storeys, above which the superstructure rises to a height of 190 feet (60 metres). It has 16 storeys, each of which consists of a wall with a parapet of shrines carved in relatively low relief. The style continued to the thirteenth century, ending with Kampaharesvara (1178–1223) temple at Tribhuvanam.

From the middle of the twelfth century onward, the *gopura*s became extremely large and were elaborately decorated with sculpture, dominating the architectural ensemble. Their construction is similar to that of the main temple, except that they are rectangular in plan and capped by a barrel vault rather than a cupola. Among the finest examples are the Sundara Pandya *gopura* (thirteenth century) of the Jambukesvara temple at Tiruchchirappalli, and the *gopura*s of a great Siva temple at Chidambaram, built largely in the twelfth–thirteenth century. Even larger *gopura*s, if not of such fine quality, continued to be built up to the seventeenth century.

*Gopura*s were often given enclosure walls and over the course of time several walls and *gopura*s were successively built, each enclosing the other so that at the present day one often has to pass through a succession of walls with their *gopura*s before reaching the main shrine. A particularly interesting example is the Ranganatha temple at Shrirangam, which has seven enclosure walls and numerous *gopura*s, halls, and temples. In addition to the *gopura*s, temples also continued to be built. The Subrahmanya temple of the seventeenth century, built in the compound of the Brhadisvara temple at Thanjavur, indicates the vitality of architectural traditions even at this late date.

In Karnataka, the early phase, as in Tamil Nadu, opens with the rock-cut cave temples. Because the Karnataka region was more receptive to southern influences, a large number of structural temples are basically south Indian with only a few north Indian elements. The Virupaksa at Pattadkal (*c*.733–746) is the most imposing and elaborate temple in the south Indian manner. It is placed within an enclosure, with access through a *gopura*. The superstructure, consisting of four storeys, has a projection in the front, a feature inspired by the prominent projections, or *sukanasa*, of north Indian temples.

With the tenth century, the Karnatic idiom begins to show an increasing individuality. The Kallesvara temple at Kukkanur (late tenth century) and a large Jaina temple at Lakkundi (*c*.1050–1100) clearly demonstrate the transition. The super-structures, though basically of the south Indian type, have offsets and recesses that tend to emphasize a vertical, upward movement. The Lakkundi temple is also the first to be built of chloritic schist, which is the favoured material of the later period and which lends itself easily to elaborate sculptural ornamentation. With the Mahadeva temple at Ittagi (*c*.1112) the transition is complete, the extremely rich and profuse decoration characteristic of this shrine being found in all work that follows. Dating from the reign of the Hoysala dynasty (*c*.1141) is a twin Hoysalesvara temple at Halebid, the capital city. The sanctums are stellate in form but lack their original superstructures. The pillars of the interior are lathe-turned in a variety of fanciful shapes, and the exterior is almost totally covered with sculpture.

The Karnatic version of the south Indian style extended northward into Maharashtra, where the Kailasa temple at Ellora, erected in the reign of the Rastrakuta Krishna I (eighth century), is its most stupendous achievement. The entire temple is carved out of rock and is over 100 feet (30 metres) high. It is placed in a courtyard, the three sides of which are carved with cells filled with images; the front wall has an entrance *gopura*. The tall base, or plinth, is decorated with groups of large elephants and griffins, and the superstructure rises in four storeys.

Islamic mosques and tombs

The earliest examples of Islamic architecture to survive date from the closing years of the twelfth century and are located at Delhi, the main seat of Muslim power. The Quwat-ul-Islam mosque (completed 1196), consisting of cloisters around a courtyard with the sanctuary to the west, was built from the remains of demolished temples. In 1198 an arched facade (*maqsurah*) was built in front to give the building an Islamic aspect, but its rich floral decoration and corbelled arches are Indian in character. The Qutb Minar, a tall (288 feet; 88 metres high), fluted tower provided with balconies, stood outside this mosque.

The earliest Islamic tomb to survive is the Sultan Ghari, built in 1231, but the finest is the tomb of Iltutmish (who ruled from 1211 to 1236). The interior, covered with Arabic inscriptions, in its richness displays a strong Indian quality. The first use of the true arch in India is found in the ruined tomb of Balban (died 1287).

In contrast to this early phase, the style of the fourteenth century at Delhi, ushered in by the Tughluq dynasty, is impoverished and austere. The buildings, with a few exceptions, are made of coarse rubble masonry and overlaid with plaster. The tomb of Ghiyas-ud-Din Tughluq (*c*.1320–25), placed in a little fortress, has sloping walls faced with panels of stone and marble. The most notable mosques of this period and of the fifteenth century are the Begampur and Khirki. In the early sixteenth century, Sher Shah Sur refined this style – the Qal'ah-e Kuhnah Masjid and his tomb at Sasaram (*c*.1540) being the finest of a series of distinguished works that were created during his reign.

The provinces, which gradually became independent sultanates, did not lag behind. The sultanate of Gujarat, in particular, is notable for its great contribution to Islamic architecture in India. The style, which is basically indigenous, reinterprets foreign influences, producing works notable for their integrity and unity. The Jami' Masjid (*c*.1424), for example, in Ahmadabad (Ahmedabad) is a masterly exposition of the style.

The Deccan was another great centre, but in contrast to Gujarat it took little from the indigenous building traditions. Among the earliest works is the Jami' Masjid at Gulbarga (1367), with its extraordinary cloisters consisting of wide arches on low piers. Bidar possesses a remarkable series of 12 tombs, the most elaborate of which is that of 'Ala-ud-Din Ahmad Bahmani (died 1457), which has extremely fine decorations in coloured tile. Some of the finest examples of Islamic architecture in the Deccan, however, are in Bijapur. The most important buildings of this city are the great Jami' Masjid (begun in 1558) with its superb arched cloisters; the ornate Ibrahim Rawza; and the Dol Gunbad (built by Muhammad 'Adil Shah), a tomb of exceptional size and grandeur, with one of the largest domes in existence.

The advent of the Mughal dynasty marks a striking revival of Islamic architecture in northern India. Persian, Indian, and the various provincial styles were successfully fused to produce works of unusual refinement and quality. The tomb of Humayun, begun in 1564, inaugurates the new style; Akbar's great fort at Agra (1565–74) is also noteworthy. The most important achievements, however, are to be found at Fatehpur Sikri (see Part 5 for details). The Jami' Masjid (1571), with the colossal gateway known as the Buland Darwaza, for example, is one of the finest mosques of the Mughal period. Most of the buildings are of post and lintel construction, arches being used very sparingly.

The tomb of the emperor Akbar at Sikandara, near Agra, is of unique design, being in the shape of a truncated square pyramid 340 feet (103 metres) on each side. It consists of five terraces, four of red sandstone and the uppermost of white marble. Begun about 1602, it was completed in 1613 during the reign of Akbar's son Jahangir.

The reign of Shah Jahan (1628–58) is as remarkable for its architectural achievements as was that of Akbar. He built the great Red Fort at Delhi (1639–48), with its dazzling hall of public audience, the flat roof of which rests on rows of columns and pointed, or cusped, arches; and the Jami' Masjid (1650–56), which is among the finest mosques in India. But it is the Taj Mahal (c.1632–49), built as a tomb for Queen Mumtaz Mahal, that is the greatest masterpiece of his reign (see Part 5 for details). All the resources of the Mughal Empire were put into its construction. Other notable buildings of Shah Jahan's reign include the Moti Masjid (c.1648–55) and the Jami' Masjid at Agra (1548–55).

Architectural monuments of the reign of Aurangzeb represent a distinct decline. The royal mosque at Lahore (1673–74), however, retains the grandeur and dignity of earlier work; and the Moti Masjid at Delhi (1659–60) possesses much of the early refinement and delicacy. The tomb of Safdar Jang at Delhi (c.1754) was among the last important works to be produced under the Mughal dynasty, and had already lost the coherence and balance characteristic of mature Mughal architecture.

European traditions and modern architecture

Buildings imitating contemporary styles of European architecture, often mixed with a strong provincial flavour, were known in India from at least the sixteenth century. Among the most famous of the baroque architecture of the Portuguese colony of Goa to survive is the church of Bom Jesus, which was begun in 1594 and completed in 1605.

The eighteenth and nineteenth centuries witnessed the erection of several buildings deeply indebted to neo-classical styles; these buildings were imitated by Indian patrons, particularly in areas under European rule or influence. Subsequently attempts were made by the British, with varying degrees of success, to engraft the neo-Gothic and also the neo-Saracenic styles on to Indian architectural tradition. At the same time, buildings in the great Indian metropolises came under increasing European influence; the resulting hybrid styles gradually found their way into cities in the interior. In Kolkata (Calcutta), the Raj Bhavan (the state governor's residence) is an imitation of Kedleston Hall in Derbyshire. The British architect Edwin Lutyens (1869–1944) designed the planning of New Delhi and some of its most notable buildings in the early twentieth century.

More recently, an attempt has been made to grapple with the problems of climate and function, particularly in connection with urban development. The influence of the Swiss architect Le Corbusier, who worked on the great Chandigarh project involving the construction of a new capital for Punjab in the early 1950s, and that of other US and European masters, has brought about a modern architectural movement of great vitality which is in the process of adapting itself to local requirements and traditions.

Of particular importance is the work of the Indian architect and urban planner Charles Correa. Complementing the Indian landscape, he designed on an organic and topographic scale in early commissions such as the Handloom Pavilion (1958) in Delhi. In the late 1960s he created New Bombay (now Navi Mumbai). Considerations of the Indian climate also drove many of Correa's decisions: he developed the "tube house," a narrow house form designed to conserve energy, which was realized in the Ramkrishna House (1962–64) and the Parekh House (1966–68), both in Ahmedabad, which has a hot and arid climate. Also in response to climate, Correa often employed a large oversailing shade roof or parasol, an element first seen in the Engineering Consultant India Limited complex (1965–68) in Hyderabad. He also designed the Bhopal State Assembly building.

9

VISUAL ARTS

Indian sculpture

On the Indian subcontinent, sculpture seems to have been the favoured medium of visual artistic expression. The subject matter is almost invariably religious. The Buddha image formulated around the first century CE is presented as an energetic, earthy being, radiating strength and power. In Hindu imagery images with several arms, and sometimes heads, represent the Indian mind's attempt to define visually the infiniteness of divinity. Folk beliefs and fertility cults also played an important part in the development of Indian art. Among the perennial motifs, those expressing life and abundance – such as the lotus, the pot overflowing with vegetation, water, or the like, the tree, the amorous couple, and above all the male *yaksa* divinities and their female counterpart, the *yaksi*s – are most significant. The maternal as the ideal of female beauty can be traced to the same beliefs.

The story of Indian sculpture begins with the Indus civilization, and small carved objects, such as terracotta figurines, soapstone or steatite seals carved for the most part with animals, and a few statuettes of stone and bronze. The terracotta sculpture and the seals show two clear and distinct stylistic trends: one plastic and sensuous, the other linear and abstract. Among a group of stone and bronze sculptures in the National Museum, New Delhi, is a fragmentary torso from Harappa, barely four inches (10 centimetres) high but of imposing monumentality; and a jaunty bronze dancing girl with head tilted upward (about $4^1/_2$ inches; 11 centimetres high), from Mohenjo-daro, clearly demonstrates, in the attenuated and wiry tension, the second component of Indus Valley art.

Little is known of Indian art in the period between the Indus Valley civilization and the reign of the Maurya emperor Asoka. When sculpture again began to be found, it was remarkable for its maturity. The most famous examples are great circular stone pillars, products of Asoka's imperial workshop, found over an area stretching from Delhi to Bihar. The best, such as the lion capital at Sarnath, are capped by campaniform lotus capitals supporting an animal emblem. The Rampurva lion, with his smooth, muscled contours, wiry sinews, rippling, flamboyant mane, and alert stance, reveals the work of a superior artist.

The lion was the animal most often represented, but figures of elephants and bulls are also known. At Dhauli in Orissa, the fore part of an elephant is carved out of rock. The modelling is soft and gentle, and the plump, fleshy qualities of the young animal's body are suffused with warmth and natural vitality. The assimilation of foreign influences (here Persian) and their drastic reinterpretation by Indian artists is typical of Indian art.

Some human figures, more or less life size, and terracotta figurines can also be assigned to the Mauryan period. The

Didarganj *yaksi* female divinity (Patna Museum), a master-piece, displays the Indian ideal of female beauty, the heavy hips and full breasts strongly emphasizing the maternal aspect. Small stone discs (also called ring stones because several of them are perforated in the centre), executed in bas-relief, found from Taxila to Patna, are clearly connected with the cult of a nude mother goddess.

The sculpture that is found throughout India from the middle of the second century BCE is startlingly different, and favoured low relief. Among the most important, and perhaps the earliest, remains in northern India are reliefs from the great stupa at Bharhut, dating approximately to the middle of the second century BCE. The work is characterized by essentially cubical forms and very elaborate and precisely detailed ornamentation of surfaces. The decoration of the supporting posts includes large images of *yaksas* and *yaksis*, amorous couples, the overflowing pot, the goddess Sri standing on lotuses while being ceremonially bathed by elephants and other symbols of abundance; still others contain the earliest illustrations of events in the Buddha's life and of narratives of his former incarnations as related in the Jataka tales. Continuous narrative, in which events succeeding in time are shown in the same space, is often resorted to – the first occurrence of what was to become a favourite narrative technique. The top part (the coping) of the stone rail is also carved on both faces; on one of them is a continuous creeper bearing lotus flowers, leaves, and buds; on the other, again the winding stem of a creeper, but bearing other good things of life – such as clothes, jewellery, and fruits – and also scenes illustrating Jataka stories.

Bharhut states for the first time themes and motifs that would henceforth remain a part of Indian sculpture. The style spread over a large part of northern India, reaching its height in the sculpture of the four gateways (*torana*s) of the Great Stupa (Stupa I) at Sanchi in eastern Malava with a sensuous beauty unparalleled in Indian art. Among the finest representations are those carved on the architraves of the *torana*s: the wars for the relics, the defeat of Mara, the Visvantara Jataka, and the Saddanta Jataka. Particularly striking is the masterly handling of animals, and the ornamental trees, waterfalls, pools, mountains, and rivers of the Indian landscape. Entire cities, with surrounding walls, elaborate gatehouses, and palatial mansions, are depicted.

A very accomplished style also existed in south-east India; the most important sites are Jaggayyapeta and Amaravati. One of the greatest achievements of the Indian sculptor, however, are the large panels, depicting amorous couples, located in the entrance porch of the Karli *caitya*. These possess a massiveness and monumentality that is a characteristic of the distinct western Indian idiom. Sculpture decorating the monasteries cut into the twin hills of Udayagiri and Khandagiri in Orissa represents yet another early Indian local idiom. Most remarkable is a long frieze and reliefs on the guard rooms of Rani Gumpha monastery, depicting forested landscapes filled with rocks from which waterfalls flow into lakes that are the sporting grounds of wild elephants.

The most important sculptures in the round in the first and second centuries BCE are the life-size images of *yaksa*s and *yaksi*s, the most famous of which is a colossal figure recovered from the village of Parkham, near Mathura (Archaeological Museum). The widespread nature of the cult is evidenced by the occurrence of *yaksa* images throughout India. At Pitalkhora there is an exceptionally fine image of a *yaksa* conceived as a potbellied dwarf carrying a shallow bowl on his head. Similar *yaksa*s, employed as atlantes (male figures used as supporting elements), are also found on the western gateway of the Great Stupa at Sanchi and at other sites, notably Sarnath. The terracotta sculpture of the period consists mainly of relief plaques made from moulds, and generally depicts popular divinities or scenes from daily life.

The first to the fourth century CE is characterized by the dominance in northern India of the ancient school of Mathura. Other schools, such as those that flourished at Sarnath and Sanchi in the first two centuries before Christ, were markedly restricted in their artistic output. The narrative bas-relief tradition was on the wane, and the emphasis was on carving individual figures, either in high relief or in the round. For the first time, images appear of the Buddha, bodhisattvas, and various other divinities including specifically Hindu images representing the gods Vishnu, Shiva, Varaha, and Devi slaying the buffalo demon; some of these figures begin to feature several arms, a characteristic of later iconography.

The development of the Buddha image can be seen in a famous sculpture (discovered at Sarnath and now in the Sarnath Museum) of Mathura, manufactured and dedicated by the monk Bala. Carved in the round, the image is shown in a pose of strict frontality, the left hand held at the waist and the right arm, now damaged, originally raised to the shoulder. The body is clothed in simple monastic garments. This standing Buddha image, as seen in the Bala statue, is the standard Mathura type, several examples of which are known.

There are also many images of *yaksi*s, often engaged in playful and enticing activities such as plucking blossoms from trees or leaning on its branches, dancing, bathing under a waterfall, and adorning themselves. Their enticing bodies are now presented as unified organic entities, lacking all traces of the stiff, puppet-like aspect that had not been entirely overcome even at the Great Stupa of Sanchi. Among the most beautiful is a group that was recovered from Kankali Tila and now in the State Museum at Lucknow.

During this period, also, a fresh incursion of foreign influence by way of western Asia was received, quickly assimilated, and transformed in the characteristic manner of Indian art. Typical is a group of portrait sculptures of the Mathura's Kushan (Kusana) rulers (Archaeological Museum).

Contemporary with the school of Mathura, and extending almost into the sixth century, is the Gandhara school, with Taxila in Pakistan as its centre and stretching into eastern Afghanistan. Its style is unlike anything else in Indian art, stressing a relatively naturalistic rendering of form. The school evolved a distinct type of Buddha image, an adaptation of an Apollo figure, suggesting foreign influence, with rather sweet and sentimental features, and was also rich in relief sculptures depicting Buddhist myth and legend.

The ancient Indian relief style found its fullest expression at Andhradesa, notably at the great sites of Amaravati and Nagarjunikonda. Railing pillars and other parts of stupas decorated with Jataka tales and scenes from the Buddha's life are found in great number and are of the most exquisite quality. Free-standing images of the Buddha, on the other hand, are relatively rare, being found only toward the close of the period. Here he is shown clad in a rather thick garment with stylized folds, and in less formal pose than with Mathura images.

During the fourth and the fifth centuries, when much of northern India was ruled by the Gupta dynasty, Indian sculpture entered its classic phase. The more or less sensuous and earthy rendering of form was drastically transformed, so that artistic expression closely conformed to the religious vision. The edificatory, didactic intent of early relief sculpture is abandoned. Instead, the works produced are pronouncedly meditative; and the repose and calm that settles on the images of the Buddha, the master of the inner contemplative life, is also seen on images of other divinities throughout India.

The impetus for the new schools seems to have come from Mathura. The transformation into the new idiom is best illustrated by a splendid image of the Buddha dated AD 384 (Indian Museum, Kolkata) and in a series of fifth-century Buddhas (now in museums around the world). The Mathura images established an iconographical type that became the norm for the Buddha image and show him wearing a diaphanous robe, the hand gestures delicate and varied, the hair usually rendered by rows of small curls. Sarnath, a famous centre of Indian art, developed a sweeter and more elegant version of the Buddha image in the late fifth century, one of the masterpieces of Indian art being the seated Buddha preaching (Sarnath Museum). Here the weight of the body is thrown more on one leg, and the hips, shoulders, and head are turned, giving the figure movement.

Images of other divinities come from throughout India: the famous image of Vishnu from Katra Kesavadeva in Mathura is one of the finest (National Museum, New Delhi). The god is conceived as a royal figure, wearing a crown and jewellery, his features imbued with a dignified calm that is suitable to his function as the preserver and is also characteristic of most Gupta art. One of the masterpieces of the rock-cut caves at Udayagiri, near Vidisa in central India, is a great relief panel depicting the boar incarnation of Vishnu lifting the earth goddess from the watery deeps into which she had been dragged by a demon.

Indian sculpture from the seventh century onward developed, broadly speaking, into two styles that flourished in northern and southern India, respectively. In each of these regions there also developed additional local idioms, so that there was a wide variety of schools. All, however, evolved in a consistent manner, the earlier phase marked by relatively plastic forms, the later by a style that emphasizes a more linear rendering. The sculpture was used mainly as a part of the architectural decor, and often entailed a mechanical production, with the result that works of quality are few.

The north Indian style was marked by the decline and disintegration of classical forms and the emergence of new styles emphasizing breadth but with a pronounced feeling for rhythm. In the ninth century, a new elegance, a richer decorativeness, and a staccato rhythm so characteristic of the medieval styles of the tenth and eleventh centuries begin to be clearly seen and felt. An idea of the style can be formed from an important group of sculptures at Abaneri, the Shiva temple at Indore, and the Teli-ka-Mandir temple at Gwalior.

With the tenth century, the style has become harder and more angular, the figures covered with a profusion of jewellery that tends to obscure the forms it decorates; examples are Khajuraho (dated 941) and the Harasnath temple at Mt Harsha (c. mid-tenth century), in Rajasthan. These features are further accentuated in the eleventh century, when many temples of great size, adorned with prodigious amounts of sculpture, were erected all over northern India. This phase of artistic activity is represented at important centres from Gujarat to Orissa; one of them is Khajuraho.

The medieval phase in southern India opened with elegant seventh-century sculptures at Mahabalipuram, by far the most impressive of which is a large relief depicting the penance of Arjuna (previously identified as an illustration of the mythical descent of the Ganges). It is carved on the face of a granite boulder, with a deep cleft in the centre, representing a river, down which water actually flowed from a reservoir situated above. On both sides are carved numerous figures of divinities, human beings, and animals that crowd the hermitage where Arjuna, practising penance, is visited by Shiva.

The light, aerial forms gained stability and strength in subsequent centuries, culminating in superb sculptures adorning small, elegant shrines built during the late ninth century when the Cola dynasty was consolidating its power – the temples at Tiruvalisvaram, Kodumbalur, Kilaiyur, Shrinivasanalur, Kumbakonam are examples of this period. With the tenth and eleventh centuries sculpture was carved in flatter planes and more angular forms, and the fresh, blooming life of earlier work is gradually lost. This can be seen in the sculpture of the numerous temples of Thanjavur and Gangaikondacolapuram. The subsequent phase, extending up to the thirteenth century, is represented by work at Darasuram and Tribhuvanam; although the forms become increasingly congealed, brittle works of fine quality continue to be produced.

Besides the two main idioms, the local schools of Maharashtra and Karnataka are of particular interest. In Maharashtra, the Mathura style was adapted to figures on a massive scale, most notably in the magnificent cave temple at Elephanta which shows Shiva in his cosmic aspect. A series of large, splendid panels (sixth century CE) depicting incidents from Hindu mythology in high relief are to be found in the Ramesvara cave temple at Ellora; notable among them is a fearsome representation of the dancing Kali, goddess of death. Toward the thirteenth and fourteenth centuries a very distinctive style developed in Karnataka, its unrestrained extravaganza unique even for Indian art. The sculpture is in very high relief and literally covered with the most elaborate ornaments and jewellery from top to toe.

In south Indian bronze sculpture the ninth and tenth centuries were periods of high achievement. In the early stages the forms were smooth and flowing, with a fine balance maintained between the body and the complex jewellery, the lines of which follow and reinforce every movement of the plastic surface. The bronzes of the later period lose this cohesiveness, and the modelling also became flatter and sharper. Most bronze images are representations of Hindu divinities. A striking southern contribution to Indian iconography is a four-armed Shiva as Lord of the Dance (Nataraja), shown within a flaming halo (aureole), one hand holding the double-headed drum symbolizing sound, or creation, and the other holding the fire that puts an end to all that is created. The palm of the third hand faces the devotee, assuring him of freedom from fear, while the fourth hand points to the raised foot, the place of refuge from ignorance and delusion, which are symbolized by the dwarf demon crushed beneath the other foot. Several splendid images are known, the finest being, perhaps, the great image still worshipped in the Brhadisvara temple at Thanjavur.

Under Islam representation of living beings is prohibited, and the centre of the Islamic artistic tradition lies in calligraphy, in which the word is the medium of divine revelation. The twelfth century thus marks the end of traditional sculpture all over northern India, except for a few pockets not yet penetrated by the Islamic invasions. A brief revival took place in parts of Gujarat and Rajasthan in the fifteenth century, but the sculpture merely imitated the work of the late medieval phase. In southern India sculpture continued beyond the Islamic invasions into the seventeenth century, but became progressively lifeless.

Indian painting

Climate has taken a devastating toll on early Indian visual art, leaving behind only a few tantalizing examples. The earliest

Indian paintings, found in rock shelters over almost all India and chiefly comprising scenes of hunting and war, date from the eighth century BCE. The earliest substantial remains, however, are those found in rock-cut cave temples at Ajanta, in western India. They belong to the second or first century BCE and are in a style reminiscent of the relief sculpture at Sanchi. Also found at Ajanta are the most substantial remains of Indian painting of about the fifth century CE and a little later, when ancient Indian civilization was in full flower. These tempura paintings decorate the walls and ceilings of the numerous cave temples and monasteries at the site. The themes illustrate the major events of the Buddha's life as told in the Jataka tales, and the various divinities of the expanding Buddhist pantheon. The ceilings are covered with rich motifs, based generally upon the lotus stem and the world of animals and birds. The style is unlike anything seen in later Indian art – expansive, free, and dynamic.

Hardly any other work of this great period survives. Cave temples at Badami, in the Karnataka country, and Sittanavasal, in Tamil Nadu, probably of the late sixth and seventh centuries CE are already but echoes of the style of the fifth century, which appears to have died out around this time. Small illustrations on palm leaf, chiefly painted at the great Buddhist establishments of eastern India in the eleventh and twelfth centuries, appear to have conserved some elements of this ancient style; but they have lost its dramatic impact, which is replaced by a studied preciosity and an inhibited meticulousness. With the destruction of these Buddhist centres by the Islamic invader, the east Indian style seems to have come to an end.

The style of Ajanta is succeeded in western India by what has been named the western Indian style. The style is heavily dependent on line, the contours of the figures are sharp and angular, the forms dry and abstract; and the fluent, stately rhythms of Ajanta have become laboured and halting. Among the earliest examples are a few surviving wall paintings of the Kailasa temple (mid-eighth century) at Ellora, but the most copious examples of this style survive in illustrated manuscripts commissioned by members of the Jaina community around the eleventh and twelfth centuries. Painted on palm leaf, the style, as at Ellora, relies for its effect on line, and progressively becomes more angular and wiry until all naturalism has been erased. The figures are almost always shown in profile, the full-face view generally reserved for representations of the *tirthankaras* (the Jaina saviours).

A convention that appears unfailingly for the duration of the western Indian style is the eye projecting beyond the face shown in profile, meant to represent the second eye, which would not be visible in this posture. In the beginning, the illustrations are simple icons in small panels; but gradually they become more elaborate, with scenes from the lives of the various Jaina saviours as told in the *Kalpa-sutra* and from the adventures of the monk Kalaka as related in the Kalakaharyakatha, the most favoured.

Even greater elaboration was possible with the increasing availability of paper from the late fourteenth century; with larger surfaces to paint on, by the middle of the fifteenth century artists were producing opulent manuscripts, such as the *Kalpa-sutra* in the Devasanopada library, Ahmadabad. The text is written in gold on coloured ground, the margins gorgeously illuminated with rich decorative and figural patterns, and the main paintings often occupying the entire page. Blue and gold, in addition to red, are used with increasing lavishness, testifying to the prosperity of the patron. With some variations the style endured throughout the sixteenth century and even extended into the seventeenth. It even became a national style, and painting at other centres in India interpreted and elaborated its forms in their own individual manner.

The taste of the Islamic rulers in India in the sixteenth century turned away from western Indian style to the flourishing traditions of Islamic painting abroad, notably Iran. As a result there appears to have developed what can only be called an Indo-Persian style, based essentially on the schools of Iran but also affected by the individual tastes of the Indian rulers and by the local styles. The earliest known examples are paintings dating from the fifteenth century onward. The most important are the *Khamseh* ("Quintet") of Amir Khosrow of Delhi (Freer Gallery of Art, Washington, DC), a *Bostan* painted in Mandu (National Museum, New Delhi), and, most interesting of all, a manuscript of the *Ne'mat-nameh* (India Office Library, London), painted for a sultan of Malwa in the opening years of the sixteenth century. Its illustrations are derived from the Turkmen style of Shiraz but show clear Indian features adapted from the local version of the western Indian style.

By the opening years of the sixteenth century, a new and vigorous style had come into being. The earliest dated example is an Aranyaka Parva of the *Mahabharata* (1516, The Asiatic Society of Mumbai), and among the finest are series illustrating the *Bhagavata-Purana* and the *Caurapancasika* of Bilhana. A technically more refined variant of this style, preferring the pale, cool colours of Persian derivation, a fine line, and meticulous ornamentation, exists contemporaneously and is best illustrated by a manuscript of the ballad *Candamyana* by Mulla Daud (*c*. first half of the sixteenth century, Prince of Wales Museum of Western India, Mumbai). The early sixteenth century thus appears to have been a period of inventiveness and set the stage for the development of the Mughal and Rajput schools, which thrived from the sixteenth to the nineteenth century.

Although the Mughal dynasty came to power in India with Babur's great victory at Panipat in 1526, the Mughal style was almost exclusively the creation of Akbar. Trained in painting at an early age by a Persian master, Khwaja 'Abd-us-Samad, Akbar created a large atelier which he staffed with artists recruited from all parts of India. The atelier, at least initially, was under the superintendence of Akbar's teacher and another great Persian master, Mir Sayyid 'Ali; but the distinctive style that evolved owed not a little to the highly individual tastes of Akbar himself.

The work of the Mughal atelier covered a wide variety of subjects: histories, romances, poetic works, myths, legends, and fables, of both Indian and Persian origin. The manuscripts were first written by calligraphers, with blank spaces left for the illustrations. These were executed largely by groups of painters, including a colourist who did most of the actual painting, and specialists in portraiture and in the mixing of colours. Chief of the group was the designer, who formulated the composition and sketched in the rough outline. A thin wash of white, through which the initial drawing was visible, was then applied and the colours filled in. The colour was applied in several thin layers and frequently rubbed down with an agate burnisher, a process that resulted in the glowing, enamel-like finish.

The earliest paintings (*c.*1560–70) of the school of Akbar are illustrations of *Tuti-nameh* ("Parrot Book," Cleveland Museum of Art) and the stupendous illustrations of the *Dastan-e Amir Hamzeh* ("Stories of Amir Hamzeh," Österreichisches Museum für Angewandte Kunst, Vienna). The *Tuti-nameh* shows the Mughal style in the process of formation – the hand of artists belonging to the various non-Mughal traditions is clearly recognizable, but the style also reveals an intense effort to cope with the demands of a new patron. The transition is achieved in the *Dastan-e Amir Hamzeh*, quite unlike Persian work in its leaning toward naturalism and filled with swift, vigorous movement and bold colour. The forms are individually modelled, except for the geometrical ornament used as architectural decor; the figures are superbly interrelated in closely unified compositions, in which depth is indicated by a preference for diagonals; and much attention is paid to the expression of emotion.

Immediately following were some very important historical manuscripts, including the *Tarikh-e Khandan-e Timuriyeh* ("History of the House of Timur," *c.*1580–85, Khuda Baksh Library, Patna) and other works concerned with the affairs of the Timurid dynasty, to which the Mughals belonged. Each of these contains several hundred illustrations, and the painter provides a fairly detailed picture of contemporary life and of the rich fauna and flora of India. It was in the illustrations to Persian translations of the Hindu epics, the *Mahabharata* and the *Ramayana*, that the Mughal painter revealed to the full the richness of his imagination and his unending resourcefulness, and the *Razm-nameh* (City Palace Museum, Jaipur), as the *Mahabharata* is known in Persian, is one of the outstanding masterpieces of the age.

In addition to such large manuscripts, books, generally poetic works, with a smaller number of illustrations done by a single master artist were produced. In style the works tend to be finely detailed and exquisitely coloured. *A Divan ("Anthology") of Anwari* (Fogg Art Museum, Cambridge, Massachusetts), dated 1589, is a relatively early example. The paintings are very small, none larger than 5 inches by $2^1/_2$ inches (12 by 6 centimetres) and most delicately executed. On a larger scale are the manuscripts that represent the most delicate and refined works of the reign of Akbar: the Bahari-stan of Jami (1595, Bodleian Library, Oxford); a Khamseh of Nezami (1593, British Museum, London); a Khamseh of Amir Khosrow (1598, Walters Art Gallery, Baltimore and Metro-politan Museum of Art, New York); and an Anwar-e Suhayli (1595–96, Bharat Kala Bhavan, Varanasi).

Although the emperor Jahangir showed a keen interest in painting and maintained an atelier of his own, the tradition of illustrating books began to die out, for he much preferred portraiture. Among the most elaborate works are the great court scenes showing Jahangir surrounded by his numerous courtiers. The compositions have lost the bustle and movement so evident in the works of Akbar's reign; the figures are more formally ordered, their comportment in keeping with the strict rules of etiquette of the Mughal court. Though many have magnificent borders decorated with a wide variety of floral and geometrical designs, the colours are subdued and har-monious, the bright glowing palette of the Akbari artist having been quickly abandoned.

Many of the paintings produced at the imperial atelier are preserved in the albums assembled for Jahangir and his son Shah Jahan, the most spectacular of which is the *Muraqqah-e Gulshan* (most surviving folios are in the Gulistan Library in Tehran and the Staatliche Museen Preussischer Kultur-besitz, Berlin). Jahangir honoured his painters, designating his favourite Abu al-Hasan Nadir-uz-Zaman ("Wonder of the Age"). Several pictures by the master are known, among them a perceptive study of Jahangir looking at a portrait of his father. Also much admired was Ustad Mansur, desig-nated Nadir-ul-'Asr ("Wonder of the Time"), whose studies of birds and animals are unparalleled. Bishandas was singled out by the emperor as unique in the art of por-traiture.

Under Shah Jahan painting in the tradition of Jahangir continued, but the style becomes noticeably rigid. The best work is found in the *Shahjahannameh* ("History of Shah Jahan") of the Windsor Castle Library and in several albums assembled for the emperor. Genre scenes, showing gatherings of ascetics and holy men, lovers in a garden or on a terrace, musical parties, carousals, and the like, became quite abundant. They sometimes show touches of genuine quality, particularly in the reign of Muhammad Shah (1719–48) who was passionately devoted to the arts, but generally from the reign of Aurangzeb (1659–1707) the standard declined, and Mughal painting essentially came to an end during the reign of Shah 'Alam II (1759–1806).

Elsewhere, three schools of painting developed from the sixteenth century: the Deccani, the Rajasthani and the Pahari. Deccani painting, which flourished over much of the Deccan Plateau from at least the last quarter of the sixteenth century, is reminiscent of the contemporary Mughal school but with a distinct local flavour. The style patronized by the sultans of Bijapur, notably the tolerant and art-loving Ibrahim 'Adil Shah II of Bijapur, is particularly distinguished. Some splendid portraits of him, and a wonderful series depicting symbolically the musical modes (*ragamala*), survive.

The Rajasthani style appears to have come into being in the sixteenth century. Up to the end of the seventeenth century it retained its essentially hieratic and abstract character, as opposed to the naturalistic tendencies cultivated by the Mughal atelier. The subject matter of this style is essentially Hindu, devoted mainly to the illustration of myths and legends, the epics, and above all the life of Krishna. Related popular themes were pictorial representations of the *ragamala* modes and illustrations of poetical works such as the *Rasikapriya* of *Kesavadasa*, which dealt with the sentiment of love. Portraits, seldom found in the early phase, became increasingly common in the eighteenth century, as did court scenes, scenes of sporting and hunting events, and other scenes concerned with the courtly life of the great chiefs and feudal lords of Rajasthan.

The Rajasthani style developed various distinct schools at Mewar, Bundi, Kotah, Markar, Bikaner, Kishangarh, and Jaipur (Amber), and beyond present-day Rajasthan, notably Gujarat, Malwa, and Bundel Khand. Of these, the Mewar school is among the most important and came to influence the development of painting throughout Rajasthan. The earliest is a *ragamala* series painted at Chawand in 1605 (Gopi Krishna Kanoria Collection, Patna); the style grew more elaborate over time, and ambitious and extensive illustrations of the *Bhagavata*, the *Ramayana*, the poems of Surdas, and the *Gitagovinda* were completed, all full of strength and vitality. From the close of the seventeenth century the works begin to decline, increasingly coming under Mughal influence.

As important as that of Mewar was the school that developed at Bundi and later at Kotah. The earliest examples are a *ragamala* series of extraordinarily rich quality, probably dating from the end of the sixteenth century. The Bundi style seems to have found Mughal painting an inspiring source, but artists of this school always displayed a pronounced preference for vivid movement, which is unique in all of Rajasthan. Toward the second half of the seventeenth century work at Bundi came unmistakably under the influence of Mewar; many miniatures, including several series illustrating the *Rasikapriya*, were produced. Kotah also appears to have become an important centre of painting at this time, developing a great fondness for hunting and sport scenes, work which continued well into the nineteenth century.

Closely allied to the Rajasthani schools both in subject matter and technique is the Pahari style, so named because of its prevalence in the erstwhile hill states of the Himalayas. It can be divided into two main schools – the Basohli and the Kangra. The Basohli style flourished toward the close of the seventeenth century and features bold colour, vigorous drawing, and primitive intensity of feeling, quite surpassing the work of the plains. The earliest dated paintings are illustrations to the *Rasamanjari* of Bhanudatta (a Sanskrit work on poetics), executed for a ruler of Basohli (1690, Boston Museum of Fine Arts); other paintings include illustrations of Hindu works and idealized portraits. The Basohli style began to fade by the mid-eighteenth century, being gradually re placed by the Kangra style, which continued almost to the end of the nineteenth century. Influenced by the Mughal styles of Delhi and Lucknow, a curvilinear line, easy flowing rhythms, calmer colours, and a mood of sweet lyricism distinguish it. Among the greatest works are large series illustrating the *Bhagavata-Purana* (National Museum, New Delhi); the *Gita-govinda*; and the *Satsai* of Bihari (both in the collection of the maharaja of Tehri-Garhwal), all painted in 1775–80.

Rising British power, which assumed political supremacy in the nineteenth century, resulted in a radical change of taste through the influence of western ideas. Rooted at Delhi and the erstwhile provincial Mughal capitals of Murshidabad, Lucknow, and Patna, it ultimately spread throughout India. Most of the works produced were singularly impoverished, but occasionally there were some fine studies of natural life.

A reaction set in during the early twentieth century, symbolized by what is called the Bengal school. The glories of Indian art were rediscovered, and the school consciously tried to produce what it considered a truly Indian art inspired by the creations of the past. Its leading artist was Rabindranath Tagore and its theoretician was E.B. Havell, the principal of the Calcutta School of Art. Nostalgic in mood, the work was mainly sentimental though often of considerable charm. To-day, Indian painting is very much a part of the international scene, the artists painting in a variety of idioms, often attempt-ing to come to terms with their heritage and with the emer-gence of India as a modern culture.

Decorative arts

Fragmentary ivory furniture (*c*. first century CE) excavated at Begram, in eastern Afghanistan, though of Indian origin, is one of the few indications of the existence in ancient India of a secular art concerned with the production of luxurious and richly decorated objects meant for daily use. The ivory caskets, chairs, and footstools are profusely decorated and confirm the wide reputation for superb ivories that India had in ancient times. Nothing as spectacular has come down from the suc-ceeding periods, but stray examples such as the so-called Charlemagne chessman (*c*. eighth century, Cabinet des Me-dailles, Paris) indicate that ivory craftsmanship was always vital. Relatively unaffected by Islamic influence, ivory produc-tion continued in southern India up to modern times; an exquisitely carved box from Vijayanagar (sixteenth century, Prince of Wales Museum of Western India, Bombay) is rep-resentative.

Decorative work in metal also flourished. A hoard at Kolhapur, consisting of plates, various kinds of vessels, lamps and *objets d'art*, including a superb bronze elephant with riders, constitutes the most important surviving group of metal objects and is datable to about the second century CE. Ritual utensils, notably elaborate incense burners, of the eighth–ninth century have been excavated at Nalanda; and a large number of fourteenth-century ceremonial vessels, apparently belonging to the local temple, were discovered at Kollur, in Mysore state. Gold played an extremely important role in the manufacture of jewellery, and small amounts of jewellery have been excavated at Mohenjo-daro and Harappa (third millennium BCE); and a very important group, of delicate workmanship, has been excavated at Taxila (c. second century CE).

From earliest times India has been famous for the variety and magnificence of its textiles, but virtually nothing has survived the heat and moisture; only a few fragments of printed textiles, dating from the fourteenth century, are preserved – at Fustat in Egypt, where they had been exported.

Objects that can be clearly designated as works of decorative art become much more extensive for the later periods, during which Islamic traditions were having a profound effect on Indian artistic traditions. Traditions of craftsmanship established during the Islamic period came to full flower during the reign of the Mughal dynasty, the finest objects being made in the imperial workshops. Well-organized, these shops specialized in particular items such as textiles, carpets, jewellery, ornamental arms and armour, metalware, and jade.

An important contribution to carpet weaving was the landscape carpet that reproduced pictorial themes inspired by miniature painting, the sixteenth and seventeenth centuries in particular producing works of the most outstanding quality. In response to growing European trade, a considerable amount of furniture was produced, mostly wood inlaid with ivory (only the ornamental and figural work was Indian, the form was European). Also in a hybrid Indo-European style were the Christian objects produced by a local school of ivory carvers at Goa.

Metal objects of sumptuous quality were also made, a unique example of which is a splendid, elaborately chiselled sixteenth-century cup in the Prince of Wales Museum of

Western India in Bombay. This tradition was continued in the seventeenth and particularly the eighteenth century, when vessels made of a variety of metals and adorned with engraved, chiselled, inlaid, and enamelled designs were very popular. Arms and armour, in particular, were decorated with the skill of a jeweller. Particularly striking are the carved hilts, often done in animal shapes.

Jade or jadeite was used together with crystal to make precious vessels as well as sword and dagger hilts. The greatest period for jade carving seems to have been the seventeenth century; a few outstanding examples associated with the emperors Jahangir and Shah Jahan are of singular delicacy and perfection. The practice of inlaying jade, and also stone, with precious or semiprecious stones became more popular with the reign of Shah Jahan and increasingly characteristic of Indian jade craftsmanship from that time on.

Architectural decoration provides a clear idea of the range of ornamental patterns used by the Mughal artist. They consisted mainly of arabesques (intricate interlaced patterns made up of flower, foliage, fruit, and sometimes animal and figural outlines) and infinitely varied geometric patterns together with floral scrolls and other designs adapted from Indian traditions. From the seventeenth century, a type of floral spray became the most favoured motif and was found on almost every decorated object. The motif, symmetrical but relatively naturalistic at the beginning, became progressively stiff and stylized, but never lost its importance in the ornamental vocabulary.

After the fall of the Mughal Empire and the rise of British power, economic conditions (including competition with machine-made goods imported from English factories) and a change in taste from increasing European influence had disastrous consequences for traditional craftsmanship, especially in the late nineteenth and twentieth centuries.

10

PHILOSOPHY

Indian philosophy includes orthodox – *astika*, one who believes in a transcendent world (*asti paralokah*) and accepts the authority of the *Vedas* – systems, namely the Nyaya, Vaisesika, Samkhya, Yoga, Purva-mimamsa, and Vedanta schools of philosophy; and unorthodox – *nastika*, one who does not believe in a transcendent world (*nasti paralokah*) and does not accept the authority of the *Vedas* – systems, such as Buddhism and Jainism (see Chapter 5 for these religious philosophies) and Carvaka (radical materialism). Three basic concepts form the cornerstone of Indian philosophical thought: the self or soul (*atman*), works (karma, or *karman*), and salvation (*moksa*). Of these, the concept of karma, signifying moral efficacy of human actions, seems to be the most typically Indian.

Vedic hymns from the second millennium BCE are the oldest extant record from India of the process by which the human mind makes its gods and of the deep psychological processes of mythmaking leading to profound cosmological concepts. The Upanishads (Hindu philosophical treatises) contain one of the first conceptions of a universal, all-pervading, spiritual reality leading to a radical monism (absolute nondualism, or the essential unity of matter and spirit). The Upanishads also contain early speculations by Indian philosophers about nature, life, mind, and the human body, not to speak of ethics and social philosophy. The classical, orthodox, systems (*darsanas*) debate such matters as the status of the finite individual; the distinction as well as the relation between the body, mind, and the self; the nature of knowledge and the types of valid knowledge; the nature and origin of truth; the types of entities that may be said to exist; the relation of realism to idealism; the problem of whether universals or relations are basic; and the very important problem of salvation (*moksa*) – its nature, and the paths leading up to it.

There is, in relation to western thought, a striking difference in the manner in which Indian philosophical thinking is presented as well as in the mode in which it historically develops. Out of the presystematic age of the Vedic hymns and the Upanishads and many diverse philosophical ideas current in the pre-Buddhistic era, there emerged with the rise of the age of the *sutras* (aphoristic summaries of the main points of a system) a neat classification of systems (*darsanas*), a classification that was never to be contradicted and to which no further systems are added. To offer new innovations, or original insights therefore and to be counted as a great master (*acarya*), one has to write a commentary (*bhasya*) on the *sutras* of the *darsana* concerned, or one must comment on one of the *bhasyas* and write a *tika* (subcommentary). At any stage, a person may introduce a new and original point of view, but at no stage can he claim originality for himself. The development of Indian philosophical thought has thus been able to combine, in an almost unique manner, conformity to tradition and adventure in thinking.

All "orthodox" philosophies can trace their basic principles back to some statement or other in the *Vedas*, whose authority rests on the Hindu tradition that they were not composed by any person but are, in fact, created by Brahma, the supreme creator. Furthermore, the *Vedas* give knowledge about things – whether *dharma* (what ought to be done) or Brahman (the absolute reality) – which cannot be known by any other empirical means of knowledge. The Vedic hymns (*mantras*) seem to be addressed to gods and goddesses (*deva*, one who gives knowledge or light), and show an awareness of the unity of the deities, of the fact that it is one God who is called by different names. In general, they show interest in the full enjoyment of life here and hereafter rather than an anxiety to escape from it. The idea of transmigration and the conception of the different paths and worlds traversed by good men and those who are not good – i.e. the world of Vishnu and the realm of Yama – are found in the *Vedas*. The chain of rebirth as a product of ignorance and the conception of release from this chain as the greatest good of the spiritual life are markedly absent.

The Upanishads answer the question "Who is that one Being?" by establishing the equation Brahman equals *atman*. Brahman – meaning now that which is the greatest, than which there is nothing greater, and also that which bursts forth into the manifested world, the one Being of which the hymn of creation spoke – is viewed as nothing but *atman*, identifiable as the innermost self in man but also, in reality, the innermost self in all beings.

Buddhism, Jainism, and the Ajivikas rejected the sacrificial polytheism of the Brahmanas and the monistic mysticism of the Upanishads. All three recognized the rule of natural law in the universe. Buddhism, however, retained the Vedic notions of karma and *moksa*, though rejecting the other fundamental concept of *atman* (see Buddhism, Chapter 5). The great epic *Mahabharata* represents the attempt of Vedic Brahmanism to adjust itself to the new circumstances reflected in the process of the aryanization (integration of Aryan beliefs, practices, and institutions) of the various non-Aryan communities and especially in the *Bhagavadgita* ("Divine Song" or "Song of the Lord") incorporates many trends of religious and philosophical thought (see Hinduism, Chapter 5). In its practical teaching, it accommodates all the three major "paths" to *moksa*: the paths of action (karma), devotion (*bhakti*), and knowledge (*jnana*).

The *sutra*s

A unique feature of the development of Indian thought was the systematization of each school of thought in the form of *sutra*s, or extremely concise expressions, intended to reduce the doctrines of a science or of a philosophy into a number of memorable aphorisms, formulas, or rules. The word *sutra*, originally meaning "thread," came to mean such concise expressions. Later philosophical composition took the form of commentaries and subcommentaries upon these *sutra*s.

The *Purva-mimamsa* ("First Reflection"), or *Karmamimamsa* ("Study of [Ritual] Action"), is the system that investigates the nature of Vedic injunctions and scriptural interpretation and meaning. For both Jaimini (fourth century BCE) and Sabara (third century BCE, Jaimini's chief commentator), performance of the Vedic sacrifices is conducive to the attainment of heaven; both emphasize that nothing is a duty unless it is instrumental to happiness in the long run.

Discussing the nature of ways of knowing, Jaimini reasons that only the injunctions contained in the scriptures – which, according to Mimamsa and the Hindu tradition, are not composed by any finite individual (*apauruseya*) – are the sources of valid knowledge of *dharma* (defined as the desired object – *artha*). The commentary of Sabara sought to establish the intrinsic validity of experiences, and traced the possibility of error to the presence of defects in the ways of knowing. He also critically examined Buddhist subjective idealism and the theory of utter emptiness of things, and proved the existence of soul as a separate entity that enjoys the results of one's actions in this or the next life.

Badarayana, a contemporary of Jaimini, was the other major interpreter of Vedic thought. His *sutra*s laid the basis for the development of Vedanta philosophy. The central theme of Badarayana's investigations is the path of knowledge and Brahman – i.e. the absolute reality. Badarayana's *sutra*s have four books (*adhyaya*s). The first is concerned with the theme of *samanvaya* ("reconciliation"), that the many conflicting statements of the scriptures agree on the concept of Brahman, the one absolute being from whom all beings arise, in whom they are maintained, and into whom they return. The second book establishes *avirodha* ("consistency") by showing (i) that dualism and Vaisesika atomism are neither sustainable interpretations of the scriptures nor defensible rationally, (ii) that though consciousness cannot conceivably arise out of a non-conscious nature, the material world could arise out of spirit, (iii) that the effect in its essence is not different from the cause, and (iv) that though Brahman is all-perfect and has no want, creation is an entirely unmotivated free act of delight (*lila*). The Buddhist (Vijnanavada) view that there are no external objects but only minds and their conceptions is refuted, as also the Buddhist doctrine of the momentariness of all that is. The third book concerns the spiritual discipline and the various stages by which the finite individual (*jiva*) may realize his essential identity with Brahman. The fourth book distinguishes between the results achieved by worshipping a personal Godhead and those achieved by knowing the one Brahman. The goal is liberation and consequent escape from the chain of rebirth.

The most important later commentators on the *Mimamsa* were Kumarila and Prabhakara, the author of the commentary *Brhati* ("The Large Commentary"). Kumarila, like Jaimini and Sabara, restricted *Mimamsa* to an investigation into *dharma*, whereas Prabhakara assigned to it the wider task of enquiring into the meaning of the Vedic texts. In their principles of interpretation of the scriptures the two schools differ radically. For Prabhakara words mean a course of action or things connected with action; the Vedic texts are the sole authoritative testimony for knowing what ought to be done. Under Kumarila's theory words convey their own meanings, not relatedness to something else.

Kumarila supported the thesis that all moral injunctions are meant to bring about a desired benefit and that knowledge of such benefit and of the efficacy of the recommended course of action to bring it about is necessary for instigating a person to act. Prabhakara defended the ethical theory of duty for its own sake. The Bhattas (the name for Kumarila's school) recognize *apurva* (supersensible efficacy of actions to produce remote effects) as a supersensible link connecting the moral action performed in this life and the supersensible effect (such as going to heaven) to be realized afterward. Prabhakara understood by *apurva* only the action that ought to be done.

Both the Bhatta and the Prabhakara schools, in their metaphysics, were realists; both undertook to refute Buddhist idealism and nihilism. The Bhatta ontology recognized five types of entities: substance (*dravya*), quality (*guna*), action (karma), universals (*samanya*), and negation (*abhava*). The Prabhakara ontology recognized eight types of entities; from the Bhatta list, negation was rejected, and four more were added: power (*sakti*), resemblance (*sadrsa*), inherence-relation (*samavaya*), and number (*samkhya*). Though both the schools admitted the reality of the universals, the Prabhakaras insisted that true universals must be perceivable, and rejected abstract universals such as "existence."

As ways of valid knowing, the Bhattas recognized perception, inference, verbal testimony (*sabda*), comparison (*upamana*), postulation (*arthapatti*), and nonperception (*anupalabdhi*). The last is regarded as the way men apprehend an absence: this was in conformity with Sabara's statement that *abhava* (nonexistence) itself is a *pramana* (way of true knowledge). Postulation, rather than inference, is viewed as the sort of process by which one may come to know for certain the truth of a certain proposition. "Comparison" is the name given to the perception of resemblance with a perceived thing of another thing that is not present at that moment. The Prabhakaras rejected nonperception as a way of knowing and were left with a list of five concerning definitions of perception.

The consequence of their arguments was the Mimamsa view of the universe as being eternal, with no creator. It also does not admit the need of admitting a being who is to distribute moral rewards and inflict punishments, this function being taken over by the notion of *apurva*. Theoretically not requiring a God, the system, however, posits a number of deities as entailed by various ritualistic procedures, with no ontological status assigned to the gods.

The *Samkhya-karika*s

In the *Samkhya-karika* (or "Verses on Samkhya," *c.* second century CE), Isvarakrsna describes himself as laying down the essential teachings of Kapila. The *karika*s are atheistic, and the traditional expositions of the Samkhya are based on this work.

According to the *karika*s, there are many selves, each being of the nature of pure consciousness. The self is neither the original matter (*prakrti*) nor an evolute of it. Though matter is composed of the three *gunas* (qualities), the self is not; though matter, being nonintelligent, cannot discriminate, the self is discriminating; though matter is object (*visaya*), the self is not; though matter is common, the self is an individual (*asamanya*); unlike matter, the self is not creative (*aprasavadharmin*). The existence of selves is proved on the ground that nature exhibits an ordered arrangement, the like of which is known to be meant for another (*pararthatva*). This other must be a conscious spirit. That there are many such selves is proved on the grounds that different persons are born and die at different times, that they do not always act simultaneously, and that they show different qualities, aptitudes, and propensities. All selves are, however, passive witnesses (*saksin*), essentially alone (*kevala*), neutral (*madhyastha*), and not agents (*akarta*).

Phenomenal nature, with its distinctions of things and persons, is regarded as an evolution out of a primitive state of matter. The original *prakrti* (primeval stuff) is uncaused, eternal, all-pervading, one, independent, self-complete, and has no distinguishable parts; the things that emerge out of this primitive matrix are, on the other hand, caused, noneternal, limited, many, dependent, wholes composed of parts, and manifested. But Matter, whether in its original unmanifested state or in its manifested forms, is composed of three *gunas* – originally in a state of equilibrium and subsequently in varying states of mutual preponderance – nondiscriminating (*avivekin*); object (*visaya*); general, nonconscious, and yet creative. Of the three *gunas*, harmony or tension (*sattva*) is light (*laghu*), pleasing, and capable of manifesting others. Activity (*rajas*) is dynamic, exciting, and capable of hurting. Inertia (*tamas*) is characterized by heaviness, conceals, is static, and causes sadness.

The *Samkhya-karika* delineates three ways of knowing (*pramana*): perception (via the senses), inference, and verbal testimony (the word of one who has authoritative knowledge). There is, in addition to the three ways of knowing, consideration of the modes of functioning of the sense organs. The outer senses apprehend only the present objects, while the inner senses (*manas*, *antahkarana*, and *buddhi*) have the ability to apprehend all objects – past, present, and future. The sense organs, on apprehending their objects, are said to offer them to *buddhi* (intelligence), which both makes judgements and enjoys the objects of the senses. *Buddhi* is also credited with the ability to perceive the distinction between the self and the natural components of the person.

In its ethics, the *karika*s manifest an intellectualism that is characteristic of the Samkhya system. Suffering is due to ignorance of the true nature of the self, and freedom, the highest good, can be reached through knowledge of the distinction between the self and nature. In this state of freedom, the self becomes indifferent to nature and becomes what it in fact is – a pure witness consciousness.

The *Yoga-sutra*s

The *Yoga-sutra*s of Patanjali (second century BCE) are the earliest extant textbook on Yoga. They stand in close relation to the Samkhya system, so much so that tradition regards the two systems as one. Yoga adds a 26th principle to the Samkhya list of 25 – i.e. the supreme lord, or Isvara – and has thus earned the name of Sesvara-Samkhya, or theistic Samkhya. But whereas Samkhya is intellectualistic and emphasizes metaphysical knowledge as the means to liberation, Yoga is voluntaristic and emphasizes the need of going through severe self-control as the means of realizing intuitively the same principles.

In the *Yoga-sutra*s, God is defined as a distinct self (*purusa*), untouched by sufferings, actions, and their effects; his existence is proved on the ground that the degrees of knowledge found in finite beings, in an ascending order, has an upper limit – i.e. omniscience, which is what characterizes God. He is said to be the source of all secular and scriptural traditions. Surrender of the effects of action to God is regarded as a recommended observance.

As in Samkhya, the self is distinguished from the mind (*citta*). The mental state is only known in introspection. The mind cannot know both itself and its object; rather, it is known by the self, whose essence is pure, undefiled consciousness and is unchangeable. To say that the self knows means that the self is reflected in the mental state and makes the latter manifested. The aim of Yoga is to arrest mental modifications (*citta-vrtti*) so that the self remains in its true, undefiled essence and is thus not subject to suffering.

Much of the discipline laid down in the *Yoga-sutra*s concerns perfection of the body, with the intent to make it a fit instrument for spiritual perfection. Steadiness in bodily posture and control of the breathing process are accorded a high place. Patanjali lays down an eightfold path consisting of aids to Yoga: restraint (*yama*), observance (*niyama*), posture (*asana*), regulation of breathing (*pranayama*), abstraction of the senses (*pratyahara*), concentration (*dharana*), meditation (*dhyana*), and trance (*samadhi*). In the final stage of *samadhi*, all mental modifications cease to be and the self is left in its pure, undefiled state of utter isolation. This is freedom (*kaivalya*), or absolute independence.

Samkhya and Yoga

In the later Samkhya, Yoga is an emphasis on austere asceticism and a turning away from the ritualistic elements of Hinduism deriving from the Brahmanical sources. Though they continue to remain as an integral part of the Hindu faith, no major religious order thrived on the basis of these philosophies.

In general, the *Samkhya-sutra*s show a greater Brahmanical influence, and the author of the *sutra*s tried to show that the Samkhya doctrines are consistent with theism or even with the Upanishadic conception of Brahman. Later commentators such as Vijnanabhiksu (sixteenth century), in his *Samkhya-pravacana-bhasya* ("Commentary on the Samkhya Doctrine"), made use of such contexts to emphasize that the atheism of Samkhya is taught only to discourage men to try to be God, that originally the Samkhya was theistic, and that the original Vedanta also was theistic.

Vacaspati (ninth century), in his *Tattva-kaumudi*, also introduced into the Samkhya theory of knowledge a distinction between two stages of perceptual knowledge. In the first, a stage of nonconceptualized (*nirvikalpaka*) perception, the object of perception is apprehended vaguely and in a most general manner. In the second stage, this vague knowledge (*alocanamatram*) is then interpreted and conceptualized by the mind. Vijnanabhiksu's *Yogavarttika*, however, ascribed to the senses the ability to apprehend determinate properties, even independently of the aid of *manas*.

These later commentators also argued that because the self is not truly an agent acting in the world, neither merit nor demerit, arising from one's actions, attaches to the self. In the long run, what really matters is knowledge. Nonattached performance of one's duties is an aid toward purifying intelli-

gence so that it may be conducive to the attainment of knowledge: hence the importance of the restraints and observances
laid down in the *Yoga-sutra*s. The greatest good is freedom –
i.e. aloofness (*kaivalya*) from matter.

Alongside Patanjali's Yoga (known as Raja Yoga), Hatha
Yoga came to be practised (*hatha* means "violence," or
"violent effort"; *ha* means "sun," *tha* means "moon;" *hatha*
therefore means "sun and moon," indicating breaths, or
breaths travelling through the right and left nostrils). Hatha
Yoga emphasizes bodily postures, regulation of breathing, and
cleansing processes as a means to spiritual perfection; its basic
text is the *Hatha-yoga-pradipika* ("Light on the Hatha Yoga",
c. fifteenth century).

The *Vaishesika-sutra*s

The *Vaishesika-sutra*s were written by Kanada, a philosopher
who flourished *c*. second–fourth century, and they are pluralistic. The ten chapters begin by explaining *dharma*, defined
as that which confers prosperity and ultimate good on humanity, and then enumerates the categories of being and how the
world is perceived. They advocate an atomistic cosmology
(theory of order) and a pluralistic ontology (theory of being).
There also are the eternal substances: ether, in which sound
inheres as a quality; space, which accounts for man's sense of
direction and distinctions between far and near; and time,
which accounts for the notions of simultaneity and nonsimul-
taneity and which, like space, is eternal and is the general cause
of all that has origin.

The overall naturalism of the *Vaishesika-sutra*s, their great
interest in physics, and their atomism are counterbalanced by
the appeal to *adrsta* (a supersensible force), to account for

whatever the other recognized entities cannot explain – such things as the movements of needles toward a magnet or the circulation of water in plants and movements of the soul after death.

Knowledge belongs to the self; it appears or disappears with the contact of the self with the senses and of the senses with the objects. Perception of the self results from the conjunction of the self with the mind. Perception of objects results from proximity of the self, the senses, and the objects. Error exists because of defects of the senses. *Moksa* is a state in which there is no body and no rebirth. It is achieved by knowledge. The performance of Vedic injunctions generates *adrsta* and the merits and demerits accumulated lead to *moksa*.

The *Nyaya-sutra*s

The *Nyaya-sutra*s, composed by Gautama or Aksapada in about the second century BCE, are concerned with salvation – i.e. complete freedom from pain – which is attained by knowledge of the 16 categories: means of valid knowledge (*pramana*) – perception, inference, comparison, and verbal testimony; objects of valid knowledge (*prameya*); doubt (*samsaya*); purpose (*prayojana*); example (*drstanta*); conclusion (*siddhanta*); the constituents of a syllogism (*avayava*); argumentation (*tarka*); ascertainment (*nirnaya*); debate (*vada*); disputations (*jalpa*); destructive criticism (*vitanda*); fallacy (*hetvabhasa*); quibble (*chala*); refutations (*jati*); and points of the opponent's defeat (*nigrahasthana*).

Although the *sutra*s do not explicitly develop a detailed theory of causation, the later Nyaya theory is sufficiently delineated; no event is uncaused, and no positive entity could arise out of mere absence. There are two kinds of entities:

eternal and noneternal. God is viewed as the efficient cause of the universe, rather than its material cause, and human deeds produce their results under the control and cooperation of God.

Nyaya-Vaishesika schools

Although the authors of the Nyaya-Vaishesika schools used each other's doctrines and the fusion of the two schools was well on its way as early as the commentators Prashastapaha (fifth century CE) and Uddyotakara (seventh century CE), the two schools continued to have different authors and lines of commentators until the tenth century.

Both the Nyaya-Vaishesika schools are realistic with regard to things, properties, relations, and universals. Both schools are pluralistic (also with regard to individual selves) and theistic. Both schools admit external relations (the relation of inherence being only partly internal), atomistic cosmology, new production, and the concept of existence (*satta*) as the most comprehensive universal. Both schools regard knowledge as a quality of the self, and they subscribe to a correspondence theory regarding the nature of truth and a theory of pragmatism-cum-coherence regarding the test of truth.

Uddyotakara's *Varttika* (*c.* 635) introduced, for the first time, the doctrine of six modes of contact (*samnikarsa*) of the senses with their objects, which has remained a part of Nyaya-Vaishesika epistemology. Prashastapaha's *Vaishesika* commentary (*c.* fifth century) does not closely follow the *sutra*s but is rather an independent explanation. Prashastapada added seven more qualities to Kanada's categories of being and made the *Vaishesika* fully theistic by introducing doctrines of creation and dissolution.

The Nyaya-Vaishesika general metaphysical standpoint allows for both particulars and universals, both change and permanence. There are ultimate differences as well as a hierarchy of universals, the highest universal being existence. Universal is defined as that which is eternal and inheres in many. Ultimate particularities belong to eternal substances, such as atoms and souls, and these account for all differences among particulars that cannot be accounted for otherwise. Inherence (*samavaya*) is the relation that is maintained between a universal and its instances, a substance and its qualities or actions, a whole and its parts, and an eternal substance and its particularity.

Knowledge is regarded as a distinguishing but not essential property of a self. Consciousness is defined as a manifestation of object but is not itself self-manifesting; it is known by an act of inner perception (*anuvyavasaya*). Knowledge either is memory or is not; knowledge other than memory is either true or false; and knowledge that is not true is either doubt or error. In its theory of error, these philosophers maintained an uncompromising realism by holding that the object of error is still real but is only not here and now. True knowledge (*prama*) apprehends its object as it is; false knowledge apprehends the object as what it is not. True knowledge is either perception, inference, or knowledge derived from verbal testimony or comparison.

The founder of the school of Navya-Nyaya (*navya* meaning "new"), with an exclusive emphasis on the *pramana*s, was Gangesa Upadhyaya (thirteenth century), whose *Tattvacintamani* ("The Jewel of Thought on the Nature of Things") is the basic text for all later developments.

By means of a new technique of analysing knowledge, judgemental knowledge can now be analysed into three kinds of epistemological entities in their interrelations: "qualifiers" (*prakara*); "qualificandum," or that which must be qualified (*visesya*); and "relatedness" (*samsarga*). There also are corresponding abstract entities: qualifierness, qualificandumness, and relatedness. The knowledge expressed by the judgement "This is a blue pot" may then be analysed into the following form: "The knowledge that has a qualificandumness in what is denoted by 'this' is conditioned by a qualifierness in blue and also conditioned by another qualifierness in potness."

A central concept in the Navya-Nyaya logical apparatus is that of "limiterness" (*avacchedakata*). If a mountain possesses fire in one region and not in another, it can be said, in the Navya-Nyaya language, "The mountain, as limited by the region *r*, possesses fire, but as limited by the region *r'* possesses the absence of fire." The same mode of speech may be extended to limitations of time, property, and relation. The logicians developed the notion of negation to a great degree of sophistication.

The Carvakas

A pre-Buddhistic system of philosophy, the Carvaka (or the Lokayata) is one of the earliest materialistic schools of philosophy. In their epistemology, they viewed sense perception alone as a means of valid knowledge. The validity of inferential knowledge was challenged on the ground that all inference requires a universal major premise ("All that possesses smoke possesses fire"), whereas there is no means of arriving at a certainty about such a proposition. Since inference is not a means of valid knowledge, all such supersensible objects as "afterlife," "destiny," or "soul", do not exist. The authority of the scriptures also is denied.

On the basis of such a theory of knowledge, the Carvakas defended a complete reductive materialism according to which the four elements of earth, water, fire, and air are the only original components of being and all other forms are products of their composition. Consciousness thus is viewed as a product of the material structure of the body and characterizes the body itself – rather than a soul – and perishes with the body. In their ethics, the Carvakas upheld a hedonistic theory according to which enjoyment of the maximum amount of sensual pleasure here in this life and avoidance of pain that is likely to accompany such enjoyment are the only two goals that people ought to pursue.

The linguistic philosophies: Bhartrhari and Mandana-Misra

The linguistic philosophers considered here are the grammarians led by Bhartrhari (seventh century CE) and Mandana-Mishra (eighth century). As his first principle, Bhartrhari rejects a doctrine on which the realism of Mimamsa and Nyaya had been built – the view that there is a kind of perception that is nonconceptualized and that places persons in direct contact with things as they are. For Bhartrhari this is not possible, for all knowledge is "penetrated" by words and "illuminated" by words. Thus, all knowledge is linguistic, and the distinctions of objects are traceable to distinctions among words.

Metaphysically, Bhartrhari comes close both to Shankara's *Advaita* ("Nondualism" or "Monism") and the work of the Buddhist philosophers, such as Dharmakirti. This metaphysical theory also uses the doctrine of *sphota* ("that from which the meaning bursts forth"). Most Indian philosophical schools were concerned with the problem of what precisely is the bearer of the meaning of a word or a sentence. The gram-

marians distinguished between the word and sound and made
the word itself the bearer of meaning. As bearer of meaning,
the word is the *sphota*. Furthermore, Bhartrhari held that a
word is an abstraction from a sentence; thus, the sentence-
sphota is the primary unit of meaning. A word is also grasped
as a unity by an instantaneous flash of insight (*pratibha*). This
theory of *sphota* was employed by the grammarians to support
their theory of word monism.

   Mandana-Misra, in his *Vidhiviveka*, referred to three varieties of this monism. According to the first two (*sabdapratya-
savada* and *sabda-parinamavada*), the phenomenal world is
still real, though either falsely superimposed on words or a
genuine transformation of the word essence. The last (*sabda-
vivartavada*) doctrine holds that the phenomenal distinctions
are unreal appearances of an immutable word essence.

Vedanta

No commentary on the *Vedanta-sutra*s survives from the
period before Shankara, who was influenced by one written
earlier by Gaudapada, though he modified his views. For
Shankara the distinction between the empirical and the illusory – both being opposed to the transcendental – is central to
his way of thinking.

   Though Vedanta is frequently referred to as one *darshana*
(viewpoint), there are, in fact, radically different schools of
Vedanta; what binds them together is common adherence to
the Upanishads, the *Vedanta-sutra*s, and the *Bhagavadgita* –
known as the three prasthanas (the basic scriptures, or texts) of
the Vedanta. From the religious point of view, Shankara
extolled metaphysical knowledge as the sole means to liberation and regarded even the concept of God as false; Ramanuja

recommended the path of *bhakti* combined with knowledge and showed a more tolerant attitude toward the tradition of Vedic ritualism; and Madhva, Nimbarka, and Vallabha all propounded a personalistic theism in which love and devotion to a personal God are rated highest. Although Shankara's influence on Indian philosophy could not be matched by these other schools of Vedanta, in actual religious life the theistic Vedanta schools have exercised a much greater influence than the abstract metaphysics of Shankara.

Shankara's thesis is that the one, universal, eternal, and self-illuminating self whose essence is pure consciousness without a subject (*asraya*) and without an object (*visaya*) from a transcendental point of view alone is real. Shankara's metaphysics is based on a criterion of reality, which may be briefly formulated as follows: the real is that whose negation is not possible. It is then argued that the only thing that satisfies this criterion is consciousness.

Shankara distinguished between three senses of being: the merely illusory (*pratibhasika*); the empirical (*vyavaharika*, which has unperceived existence and pragmatic efficacy); and the transcendental being of one, indeterminate Brahman. In his epistemology, Shankara's followers, like Kumarila, accepted six ways of knowing: perception, inference, verbal testimony, comparison, nonperception, and postulation. In general, cognitions are regarded as modifications of the inner sense in which the pure spirit is reflected or as the pure spirit limited by respective mental modifications.

Shankara regarded moral life as a necessary preliminary to metaphysical knowledge and thus laid down strict ethical conditions to be fulfilled by one who wants to study Vedanta. For him, however, the highest goal of life is to know the essential identity of his own self with Brahman, and though moral life may indirectly help in purifying the mind and intellect, over an extended period of time knowledge comes from following the long and arduous process whose three major stages are study of the scriptures under appropriate conditions, reflection aimed at removing all possible intellectual doubts about the nondualistic thesis, and meditation on the identity of atman and Brahman. *Moksa* is not, according to Shankara, a perfection to be achieved; it is rather the essential reality of one's own self to be realized through destruction of the ignorance that conceals it. God is how Brahman appears to an ignorant mind that regards the world as real and looks for its creator and ruler. Religious life is sustained by dualistic concepts: the dualism between man and God, between virtue and vice, and between this life and the next. In the state of *moksa*, these dualisms are transcended. An important part of Shankara's faith was that *moksa* was possible in bodily existence. Because what brings this supreme state is the destruction of ignorance, nothing need happen to the body; it is merely seen for what it really is – an illusory limitation on the spirit.

Shankara's early pupils raised and settled issues that were not systematically discussed by Shankara himself – issues that later divided his followers into two large groups: those who followed the *Vivarana* (a work written on Padmapada's *Pancapadika* by one Prakasatman in the twelfth century) and those who followed Vacaspati's commentary (known as Bhamati) on Shankara's *bhasya*.

Among the chief issues that divided Shankara's followers was the question about the locus and object of ignorance. The Bhamati school regarded the individual self as the locus of ignorance and sought to avoid the consequent circularity (arising from the fact that the individual self is itself a product of ignorance) by postulating a beginningless series of such selves and their ignorances. The Vivarana school regarded both the locus and the object of ignorance to be Brahman and sought to avoid the contradiction (arising from the fact that Brahman is said to be of the nature of knowledge) by distinguishing between pure consciousness and valid knowledge (*pramajnana*). The latter, a mental modification, destroys ignorance, and the former, far from being opposed to ignorance, manifests ignorance itself, as evidenced by the judgement "I am ignorant." The two schools also differed in their explanations of the finite individual. The Bhamati school regarded the individual as a limitation of Brahman just as the space within the four walls of a room is a limitation of the big space. The Vivarana school preferred to regard the finite individual as a reflection of Brahman in the inner sense. Later followers of Shankara, such as Shriharsa in his *Khandana-khandakhadya* and his commentator Citsukha, used a destructive, negative dialectic in the manner of Nagarjuna to criticize man's basic concepts about the world.

Others, such as Ramanuja (eleventh century) and Madhva (born 1199?), refuted Shankara's position. Ramanuja sought to synthesize a long tradition of theistic religion with the absolutistic monism of the Upanishads. A most striking feature of his epistemology is his uncompromising realism. Whatever is known is real, and only the real can be known. This led him to reject Shankara's conception of Brahman as an indeterminate, qualityless, and differenceless reality on the ground that such a reality cannot be perceived, known, thought of, or even spoken about. Also rejecting Shankara's conception of reality, Ramanuja defended the thesis that Brahman is a being with infinitely perfect excellent virtues, a being whose perfection cannot be exceeded.

The state of *moksa* is not a state in which the individuality is negated. What is destroyed is egoism, the false sense of independence. The means thereto is *bhakti*, leading to God's grace. But by *bhakti* Ramanuja means *dhyana*, or intense meditation with love. Obligation to perform one's scriptural duties is never transcended. Liberation is a state of blessedness in the company of God. A path emphasized by Ramanuja for all persons is complete self-surrender (*prapatti*) to God's will and making oneself worthy of his grace. In his social outlook, Ramanuja believed that *bhakti* does not recognize barriers of caste and classes.

Madhva belonged to the tradition of Vaisnava religious faith and showed a great polemical spirit in refuting Shankara's philosophy and in converting people to his own fold. An uncompromising dualist, he identified five types of differences: difference between soul and God, between soul and soul, between soul and matter, between God and matter, and that between matter and matter. Brahman is the fullness of qualities, and by his own intrinsic nature, Brahman produces the world. The individual, otherwise free, is dependent only upon God. In his epistemology, Madhva admitted three ways of knowing: perception, inference, and verbal testimony. In Madhva's system the existence of God cannot be proved; it can be learned only from the scriptures. Both bondage and release are real and devotion is the only way to release, but ultimately it is God's grace that saves. Scriptural duties, when performed without any ulterior motive, purify the mind and help one to receive God's grace.

Among the other theistic schools of Vedanta, brief mention may be made of the schools of Nimbarka (*c.* twelfth century), Vallabha (fifteenth century), and Caitanya (sixteenth century).

Nimbarka's philosophy is known as Bhedabheda, because he emphasized both identity and difference of the world and finite souls with Brahman. His religious sect is known as the Shanaka-sampradaya of Vaisnavism. Of the three realities admitted – God, souls, and matter – God is the independent reality, self-conscious, controller of the other two, free from all defects, abode of all good qualities, and both the material and efficient cause of the world. Both souls and matter are pervaded by God. Liberation is because of a knowledge that makes God's grace possible. There is no need for Vedic duties after knowledge is attained, nor is performance of such duties necessary for acquiring knowledge.

Vallabha's philosophy is called pure nondualism – "pure" meaning "undefiled by *maya*." His religious sect is known as the Rudra-sampradaya of Vaisnavism and also Pustimarga, or the path of grace. Brahman, or Shri Krishna, is viewed as the only independent reality; in his essence he is existence, consciousness, and bliss, and souls and matter are his real manifestations. From his aspect of "existence" spring life, senses, and body. From "consciousness" spring the finite, atomic souls. From "bliss" spring the presiding deities, or *antaryamin*s. This threefold nature of God pervades all beings. World is real, but *samsara* (the cycle of birth and death) is unreal, and time is regarded as God's power of action. The means to liberation is *bhakti*, which is defined as firm affection for God and also loving service (*seva*). *Bhakti* does not lead to knowledge, but knowledge is regarded as a part of *bhakti*. The notion of "grace" plays an important role in Vallabha's religious thought. He is also opposed to renunciation.

Caitanya (1485–1533) was one of the most influential and remarkable of the medieval saints of India. His life is characterized by almost unique emotional fervour, hovering on the pathological, which was directed toward Shri Krishna (the incarnation of Vishnu). The discourses recorded by contemporaries give an idea of his philosophical thought that was later developed by his followers, particularly by Rupa Gosvamin and Jiva Gosvamin, and these became the main sources of the philosophy of Bengal Vaisnavism. Caitanya rejected the conception of an intermediate Brahman. Brahman, according to him, has three powers: the transcendent power that is threefold (the power of bliss, the power of being, and the power of consciousness) and the two immanent powers, namely the powers of creating souls and the material world. The relation between God and his powers is neither identity nor difference, nor identity-with-difference. This relation, unthinkable and suprarational, is central to Caitanya's philosophy. *Bhakti* is the means to emancipation. *Bhakti* is conceived as a reciprocal relation between man and God, a manifestation of God's power in man.

PART FOUR

INDIA TODAY

11

GOVERNMENT AND SOCIETY

India's constitutional framework

The architects of India's constitution were heavily influenced by the British model of parliamentary democracy. A number of principles were also adopted from the Constitution of the United States of America, including the separation of powers among the major branches of government, the establishment of a supreme court, and the adoption, albeit in modified form, of a federal structure (a constitutional division of power between the union [central] and state governments). The mechanical details for running the central government, however, were largely carried over from the Government of India Act of 1935, passed by the British Parliament, which served as India's constitution in the waning days of British colonial rule.

The new constitution promulgated on January 26 1950 proclaimed India "a sovereign socialist secular democratic republic." One of the longest and most detailed constitutions in the world, it includes a detailed list of "fundamental rights," a lengthy list of "directive principles of state policy" (goals that the state is obligated to promote), and a much shorter list of "fundamental duties" of the citizen. The remainder of the constitution outlines in great detail the structure, powers, and manner of operation of the union (central) and state governments. It also includes provisions for protecting the rights and promoting the interests of certain classes of citizens (such as disadvantaged social groups, officially designated as "Scheduled Castes" and "Scheduled Tribes"), and the process for constitutional amendment. The extraordinary specificity of India's constitution is such that amendments, which average nearly two per year, have frequently been required to deal with issues that in other countries would be handled by routine legislation. With a few exceptions, the passage of an amendment requires only a simple majority of both houses of parliament, but this majority must form two-thirds of those present and voting.

The union government has exclusive authority in foreign policy, defence, communications, currency, taxation on corporations and nonagricultural income, and railways. State governments have the sole power to legislate on such subjects as law and order, public health and sanitation, local government, betting and gambling, and taxation on agricultural income, entertainment, and alcoholic beverages. Where both the union government and state governments may legislate – areas such as criminal law, marriage and divorce, contracts, economic and social planning, population control and family planning, trade unions, social security, and education – union law generally takes precedence. An exceedingly important power of the union government is that of creating new states, combining states, changing state boundaries, and terminating a state's existence. The union government may also create and dissolve any of the union territories, whose powers are more limited than those of the states.

There are three branches of the union government: the executive branch, which consists of the president (India's head of state), vice president, and a Council of Ministers (led by the prime minister); the legislative branch, within which are the two houses of parliament – the lower house, *Lok Sabha* (House of the People), and the upper house, *Rajya Sabha* (Council of States) – and the president of India (who is also considered part of parliament); and the judicial branch, at the apex of which is the Supreme Court whose decisions are binding on the higher and lower courts of the state governments.

India's president is elected to a five-year renewable term by an electoral college consisting of the elected members of both houses of parliament and the elected members of the legislative assemblies of all the states. The vice president presides over the *Rajya Sabha*. The powers of the president are largely nominal and ceremonial. The president normally acts on the advice of the prime minister, though he or she may proclaim a state of emergency or impose direct presidential rule at the state level when it is thought that a particular state legislative assembly has become incapable of functioning effectively. The president may also dissolve the *Lok Sabha* and call for new parliamentary elections after a prime minister loses a vote of confidence.

Effective executive power rests with the Council of Ministers, headed by the prime minister, who is chosen by the majority party or coalition in the *Lok Sabha* and is formally appointed by the president. The Council of Ministers, also formally appointed by the president, is selected by the prime minister. The most important group within the council is the cabinet. Of the two houses of parliament, the more powerful is the *Lok Sabha*, in which the prime minister leads the ruling party or coalition. The constitution limits the number of elected members of the *Lok Sabha* to 530 from the states and 20 from the union territories, allotted roughly in proportion to their population. The president may also nominate two members of the Anglo-Indian community if it appears that this community is not being adequately represented. Members of the *Lok Sabha* serve for terms of five years, unless the house is dissolved before that.

Membership in the *Rajya Sabha* is not to exceed 250. Of these members, 12 are nominated by the president to represent literature, science, art, and social service, and the balance is proportionally elected by the state legislative assemblies. The *Rajya Sabha* is not subject to dissolution, but one-third of its members retire at the end of every second year. Legislative bills may originate in either house – except for financial bills, which may originate only in the *Lok Sabha* – and require passage by simple majorities in both houses in order to become law. The day-to-day functioning of the government is performed by permanent ministries of the Indian Administrative Service and other public service agencies.

India's foreign policy has been officially one of nonalignment with any of the world's major power blocs. The country was a founding member of the Nonaligned Movement during the Cold War. India has also been a major player among the group of more than 100 low-income countries, loosely described as the "Global South," that have sought to deal collectively in economic matters with the industrialized states of the "Global North."

It has maintained its membership in the Commonwealth. It was a charter member, even though not yet independent, of the United Nations (as it was of the earlier League of Nations). In 1985 India joined six neighbouring countries in launching the South Asian Association for Regional Cooperation.

The government structure of the states, defined by the constitution, closely resembles that of the union. The executive branch is composed of a governor and a council of ministers, led by the chief minister. All states have a *Vidhan Sabha* (Legislative Assembly), popularly elected for terms of up to five years, while a small (and declining) number of states also have an upper house, the *Vidhan Parishad* (Legislative Council), roughly comparable to the *Rajya Sabha*. State governors are also regarded as members of the legislative assemblies, which they may suspend or dissolve when no party is able to muster a working majority.

Each Indian state is organized into a number of districts, which are divided for certain administrative purposes into units variously known as *tahsils*, *taluqs*, or subdivisions. These are further divided into community development blocks, each typically consisting of about 100 villages. Superimposed on these units is a three-tiered system of local government. At the lowest level, each village elects its own governing council (*gram pancayat*). The chairman of a *gram pancayat* is also the village representative on the council of the community development block (*pancayat samiti*). Each *pancayat samiti*, in turn, selects a representative to the district-level council (*zila parishad*). Separate from this system are the municipalities, which generally are governed by their own elected councils. From the state down to the village, government appointees administer the various government departments and agencies. Grants from higher levels facilitate particular projects, but the approval or withholding of these has often served as a lever for the accumulation of personal power and as a vehicle of corruption.

The tradition of an independent judiciary has taken strong root in India. The Supreme Court determines the constitutional validity of union government legislation, adjudicates disputes between the union and the states (as well as disputes between two or more states), and handles appeals from lower-level courts. Each state has a high court and a number of lower courts. The high courts may rule on the constitutionality of state laws, issue a variety of writs, and serve as courts of appeal from the lower courts, over which they exercise general oversight.

Oversight of the electoral process is vested in the Election Commission. There is universal adult suffrage, and the age of eligibility is 18. Seats are allocated from constituencies of roughly equal population. A certain number of constituencies in each state are reserved for members of Scheduled Castes and Scheduled Tribes, based on their proportion of the total state population. Those reserved constituencies shift from one election to the next. As candidates do not have to be and frequently are not residents of the areas they seek to represent, none runs the risk of losing a seat solely by virtue of the allocation procedure.

The Indian party system is complex. Based on performance in past elections, some parties are recognized as national parties and others as state parties. Parties are allocated symbols (for example, a cow or a hammer and sickle), and ballots are printed with these symbols to help illiterate voters. The only party that has enjoyed a nationwide following continuously from the time of independence (in fact, since its founding in 1885) is the Indian National Congress. There have been several party schisms, however, and the Indian National Congress–Indira, or simply the Congress (I) – created in 1978 by the former prime minister Indira Gandhi and her supporters – has been by far the most successful of its derivative entities. Parties to the left of the Congress have included not only the Communist Party of India (which generally followed the lead of the Soviet Union), and the subsequently formed Communist Party of India (Marxist) (more inclined toward policies espoused by China), but also an assortment of small, mainly short-lived Marxist and socialist groups. Parties to the right of the Congress have largely appealed either to Hindu sentiments (such as the Bharatiya Janata ["Indian People's"] Party, the BJP) or those of other communally defined groups, and some have sought to further the interests of landed constituencies (the preindependence princely families or the more recently affluent peasant factions). Over time there has been a steady increase in the number and power of parties promoting the parochial interests of individual states.

Police and the armed forces

Most police functions in India are handled through the states. There are, however, a number of centrally controlled police forces, including the Central Bureau of Investigation (to deal with certain breaches of union laws), the Border Security Force, the volunteer auxiliary force of Home Guards (to help in times of emergency, such as riots or natural disasters), the Central Reserve Police Force, and the Central Industrial Security Force. There are also several paramilitary forces deployed to provide internal security and border defence.

The combined Indian armed forces – comprising the army, navy, coast guard, and air force – are among the largest in the world and are well equipped. The army is the largest of these, with more than four-fifths of military personnel. Much of the military's equipment was obtained from the former Soviet Union. The country's nuclear arsenal – thought to consist of several dozen relatively small devices – is controlled by Strategic Forces Command; the military also deploys short- and medium-range ballistic missiles.

Health and welfare

India's medical and public health services have improved dramatically since independence. As a result, average life expectancy at birth has risen by more than 25 years since the Second World War. While death from starvation has become rare, malnutrition has remained widespread. Much of the population lacks access to safe drinking water, and dysentery and other waterborne diseases are major killers, especially of children. Poorly treated and improperly disposed sewage pose serious health problems.

Great strides have been made in combating certain diseases, including smallpox (declared eradicated in 1977) and malaria. But AIDS and HIV infection have increased – although the overall proportion of the population affected is quite tiny, the number of people infected is one of the highest for any country in the world. There has been considerable expansion in the number of hospitals and rural primary health centres. Supplementing these government services are private medical practitioners, a great many of whom follow a variety of traditional medical systems. Of these, the ancient Ayurvedic system is by far the most widespread.

Welfare services have proliferated since independence. Many programmes target specific sections of the population, such as Scheduled Castes, Scheduled Tribes, nomadic populations, women, children, and the disabled. The resources for such services, however, are inadequate. Pensions exist only for government workers and a portion of the organized sector of the economy.

Housing stock does not meet current needs and is continually challenged by the growing population. Homelessness is common, particularly in major urban centres such as Delhi, Kolkata, and Mumbai, where accommodation prices are among the highest in the world and beyond the reach of many residents. Large numbers of city dwellers reside in unregistered and makeshift slums. Relatively few government housing projects have been undertaken. Rural housing is somewhat less pressed.

Piped water is mainly limited to large towns and cities, but even there it seldom reaches all neighbourhoods and cannot be depended on in all seasons. Sewage facilities are even more limited. Professional scavengers, publicly and privately employed, fill the need for waste disposal in most urban areas and, along with pigs, in many villages as well. Those who cook with gas generally rely on purchased gas cylinders. An increasing number of villages, however, have installed simple cow-dung gas plants, which enable them to generate methane and still utilize the fermented dung for fertilizer.

Education

The provision of free and compulsory education for all children up to age 14 is among the directive principles of the Indian constitution. The overall rate of literacy has increased markedly since the late twentieth century, but a noticeable disparity has remained between males and females (roughly three-quarters and about half, respectively). There is also a considerable disparity in literacy rates between the states. The state of Kerala has the highest rate, where nearly all are literate, in contrast to Bihar, where the proportion is about half.

The great majority of all children of primary-school age are enrolled, though many, especially girls, may not attend regularly. Enrolment thereafter falls off precipitously, to about half of all children aged 11 to 14. The union government has tried to promote the education of girls and other socially disadvantaged groups, through grants for the support of particular programmes and a variety of progressive educational initiatives. In addition to publicly financed schools, there are at all levels private and church-run schools (largely by Christian missions).

The number of universities and equivalent institutions increased more than sevenfold in the first four decades after independence, and has continued to grow. At the same time, funding for libraries, laboratories, and other facilities has been a constant and serious problem. In the past, virtually all higher instruction was in English but, as new universities and their thousands of affiliated colleges have spread out to smaller cities and towns, state languages increasingly have been used. Reserved quotas in universities and lower admission standards for members of Scheduled Castes and Scheduled Tribes – whose prior education often has been less than adequate – have put additional stress on the system.

12

THE ECONOMY

India has one of the largest, most highly diversified economies in the world but, because of its enormous population, it is – in terms of income and gross national product (GNP) per capita – one of the poorest countries on Earth. Since independence, India has promoted a mixed economic system in which the government, constitutionally defined as "socialist," plays a major role as central planner, regulator, investor, manager, and producer. Starting in 1951, the government based its economic planning on a series of five-year plans influenced by the Soviet model. Initially, the attempt was to boost the domestic savings rate, which more than doubled in the half century following the First Five-Year Plan (1951–55). With the Second Five-Year Plan (1956–61), the focus began to shift to import-substituting industrialization, with an emphasis on capital goods. A broad and diversified industrial base developed. However, with the collapse of the Soviet system in the early 1990s, India adopted a series of free-market reforms that fuelled the growth of its middle class, and its highly educated and well-trained workforce made India one of the global centres of the high-technology boom that began in the late twentieth century and produced significant annual growth rates. The agricultural sector remains the country's main employer (about half of the workforce), though, with about one-fifth of the gross domestic product (GDP), it is no longer the largest contributor to the GDP. Manufacturing remains another solid component of the GDP. However, the major growth has been in trade, finance, and other services which, collectively, are by far the largest component of the GDP.

Large corporate undertakings dominate many spheres of modern economic activity, while tens of millions of generally small agricultural holdings and petty commercial, service, and craft enterprises account for the great bulk of employment. There are few things that India cannot produce, though much of what it does manufacture would not be economically competitive without the protection offered by tariffs on imported goods, which have remained high despite liberalization. Foreign trade traditionally has been low.

Most large-scale building activities – such as the construction of railways, national and state highways, harbours, hydroelectric and irrigation projects, and government-owned factories and hotels – have been built by government-managed construction agencies, the largest of which is the Central Department of Public Works. Beginning in the 1990s, the private sector contributed greatly to the growth of services with the establishment of a robust computer software and services industry, located largely in the urban areas of Bengaluru (Bangalore) and Hyderabad. With a large number of English speakers, India has also emerged as a low-cost alternative for US telecommunications companies and other enterprises to establish telephone call centres.

Probably no more than one-fifth of India's vast labour force is employed in the so-called "organized" sector of the economy (e.g. mining, plantation agriculture, factory industry, utilities, and modern transportation, commercial, and service enterprises), but that small fraction generates a disproportionate share of the GDP, supports most of the middle- and upper-class population, and generates most of the economic growth. It is the organized sector to which most government regulatory activity applies and in which trade unions, chambers of commerce, professional associations, and other institutions of modern capitalist economies play a significant role. Apart from rank-and-file labourers, the organized sector engages most of India's professionals and virtually all of its vast pool of scientists and technicians.

Much of the organized sector is unionized, and strikes are frequent and often protracted. Many of the unions are affiliated with one of a number of government-recognized and regulated all-India "central" trade union organizations, several of which have membership in the millions. The more important of these are affiliated with national political parties.

Taxes are levied in India at the federal, state, and local levels. At the national level, the union government collects income tax, customs duties, and tariffs, and assesses value-added taxes such as sales tax. The states raise much of their revenue through the collection of stamp taxes (for the issuance of various licences) and through the collection of agricultural tax. Local governments collect income in the form of property taxes and fees for services.

Agriculture, forestry, and fishing

Roughly half of all Indians derive their livelihood directly from agriculture. The area cultivated has risen steadily and now encompasses considerably more than half of the country's total area, a proportion matched by few other countries in the world. In the more fertile regions, such as the Indo-Gangetic Plain or the deltas of the eastern coast, the proportion of cultivated to total land often exceeds nine-tenths.

In all but a small part of the country, the supply of water for agriculture is highly seasonal and depends on the often fickle south-west monsoon. As a result, farmers are able to raise only one crop per year in areas that lack irrigation, and the risk of crop failure is fairly high. The prospects and actual development of irrigation also vary greatly from one part of the country to another – being particularly favourable on the Indo-Gangetic Plain, which benefits from relatively even flow of the rivers from the Himalayas and vast reserves of groundwater; but severely curtailed in peninsular India, where rainfall is highly seasonal and hard rock formations make it difficult to sink wells.

Although India does possess extensive areas of fertile alluvial soils, less than half of the cultivable land is of high quality. More than half of all farms are less than 3 acres (1.2 hectares) in size, while much of the remainder is controlled by a small number of relatively affluent peasants and landlords. Most cultivators own farms that provide little more than a bare subsistence for their families. Further, nearly one-third of all agricultural households own no land at all and must work for the larger landholders or must supplement their earnings from some subsidiary occupation.

Agricultural technology has undergone rapid change. Government-sponsored large-scale irrigation canal projects, begun by the British in the mid-nineteenth century, were greatly extended after independence. Since then, deep wells (called tube wells in India) from which water is raised either by electric or diesel pumps, and tank irrigation, a method by which water is drawn from small reservoirs created along the courses of minor streams, have been used in several parts of India.

The demand for chemical fertilizers also has been steadily increasing, although since the late 1960s the introduction of new, high-yielding hybrid varieties of seeds (HYVs), mainly for wheat and secondarily for rice, has brought about the most dramatic increases in production, especially in Punjab (where their adoption is virtually universal), Haryana, western Uttar Pradesh, and Gujarat. So great has been the success of the so-called Green Revolution that India was able to build up buffer stocks of grain sufficient for the country to weather several years of disastrously bad monsoons with virtually no imports or starvation and even to become, in some years, a modest net food exporter. During the same period, the production of coarse grains and pulses, which were less in demand than rice and wheat, either did not increase significantly or decreased. Hence, the total per capita grain production has been notably less than that suggested by many protagonists of the Green Revolution, and the threat of major food scarcity has not been eliminated.

Most Indian farms grow little besides food crops, especially cereal grains, and these account for more than three-fifths of the area under cultivation. The most popular grains, in terms of both area sown and total yield, are rice and wheat. Other important cereals, in descending order of sown acreage, are sorghum (called *jowar* in India), pearl millet (*bajra*), corn (maize), and finger millet (*ragi*), all typically grown on relatively infertile soils unsuitable for rice or wheat. After cereals, pulses are the most important category of food crop.

Nonstaple food crops, eaten in only small amounts by most Indians, include potatoes, onions, various greens, eggplants, okra, squashes, and other vegetables, as well as such fruits as mangoes, bananas, mandarin oranges, papayas, and melons. Sugarcane is widely cultivated, especially in areas near processing mills. A wide variety of crops – mainly peanuts (groundnuts), coconuts, mustard, cottonseed, and rapeseed – are grown as sources of cooking oil. Others, such as the ubiquitous chilies, turmeric, and ginger, are raised to provide condiments or, in the case of betel leaf (of the pan plant) and betel (areca nut), as digestives. Tea is grown, largely for export, on plantations in Assam, West Bengal, Kerala, and Tamil Nadu, while coffee is grown almost exclusively in southern India, mainly in Karnataka. Tobacco is cultivated chiefly in Gujarat and Andhra Pradesh.

Foremost among the commercial industrial crops is cotton. Maharashtra, Gujarat, and Punjab are the principal cotton-growing states. Jute, mainly from West Bengal, Assam, and Bihar, is the second leading natural fibre. Much of it is exported in processed form, largely as burlap. An even coarser fibre is derived from coir, the outer husk of the coconut, the processing of which forms the basis for an important cottage industry in Kerala. Coconuts and oilseeds are also important for the extraction of industrial oils.

Despite the fact that Indians eat little meat, livestock-raising plays an important role in the agricultural economy. India has by far the largest bovine population of any country in the world. Cattle and buffalo are used mainly as draught animals but also serve many other purposes – to provide milk, as sources of meat (for those, including Muslims, Christians, and Scheduled Castes, for whom beef eating is not taboo), and as sources of fertilizer, cooking fuel (from dried cow-dung cakes), and leather. Milk yields from Indian cattle and buffaloes are quite low. While many orthodox Indians are vegetarians, others will eat goat, mutton, poultry, eggs, and fish, all of which are produced in modest quantities. Sheep are raised for both wool and meat. Pigs, which serve as village scavengers, are raised and freely eaten by several Scheduled Castes.

Commercial forestry is not highly developed in India. Nevertheless, the annual cutting of hardwoods is among the highest of any country in the world. Species that are sources of timber, pulp, plywoods, veneers, and matchwood include teak, deodar (a type of cedar), sal (*Shorea robusta*), sissoo (*Dalbergia sissoo*), and chir pine (*Pinus roxburghii*). Substantial amounts are used for making charcoal. Minor forest products include bamboo, cane, gum, resins, dyes, tanning agents, lac, and medicinal plants.

The principal areas for commercial forestry are the Western Ghats, the western Himalayas, and the hill regions of central India. Most of India's formerly forested area has been converted to agricultural use (though some of that land is no longer productive), and other large areas have been effectively turned into wasteland from either overgrazing or overexploitation for timber and firewood. In an effort to counteract forest depletion, the central and state governments have vigorously supported small-scale afforestation projects; these have met with mixed success, both economically and ecologically.

Fishing is practised along the entire length of India's coastline and on virtually all of its many rivers. Production from marine and freshwater fisheries has become roughly equivalent. Because few fishing craft are mechanized, total catches are low, and annual per capita fish consumption is modest. The shift to mechanization and modern processing, however, has been inexorable. Thus, an increasingly large part of the catch now comes from fishing grounds that the small craft of coastal fishing families are unable to reach. The problem is most severe in Kerala, the leading fishing state. Major marine catches include sardine and mackerel; freshwater catches are dominated by carp. Intensive inland aquaculture, for both fish and prawns (the latter of which has become an important export), has increased significantly.

Resources and power

Although India possesses a wide range of minerals and other natural resources, its per capita endowment of such critical resources as cultivable land, water, timber, and known petroleum reserves is relatively low. Nevertheless, the diversity of resources, especially of minerals, exceeds that of all but a few countries and gives India a distinct advantage in its industrial development.

Domestically supplied minerals form an important underpinning for India's manufacturing industry, as well as a source of modest export revenues. Nationalizing many foreign and domestic enterprises, and government initiation and management of others, gave the Indian government a predominant role in the mining industry. However, government involvement has been gradually reduced as private investment has grown.

Among mineral resources, iron ore (generally of high quality) and ferroalloys are particularly abundant, and all are widely distributed over peninsular India. Of the many metals produced, iron – mined principally in Madhya Pradesh, Bihar, Goa, Karnataka, and Orissa – ranks first in value. Copper, derived mainly from Rajasthan and Bihar, is a distant second. Gold, zinc and lead (often mined together), the ferroalloys (chiefly manganese and chromite), and bauxite also are important. Noteworthy nonmetallic minerals include limestone, dolomite, rock phosphate, gypsum, building stone, and ceramic clays.

In terms of the value of production, fuel minerals far exceed all others combined. Petroleum ranks first in value, followed by coal (including lignite). India produces only a portion of its petroleum needs but produces a slight exportable surplus of coal. Virtually all of India's petroleum comes from the offshore Bombay High Field and from Gujarat and Assam, while coal comes from some 500 mines, both surface and deep-pit, distributed over a number of states. By far the most important coal-producing region is along the Damodar river, including the Jharia and Raniganj fields in Bihar and West Bengal, which account for about half the nation's output and virtually all the coal of coking quality. Natural gas is of little importance. Uranium is produced in modest quantities in Bihar.

The country's utilities, overwhelmingly in government hands, are barely able to keep pace with the rapidly rising demand for various types of service. The bulk of all electricity generated is from widely dispersed coal-powered thermal plants; most of the remainder is from hydroelectric plants; and only a tiny amount comes from a few nuclear installations. Power outages and rationing are frequently necessary in periods of peak demand. More than half of all electricity is industrially used. Agricultural use, largely for raising irrigation water from deep wells, exceeds domestic consumption. Rural electrification is increasing rapidly, and the great bulk of all villages are now tied into some distribution grid.

Manufacturing, finance, and trade

India's manufacturing industry is highly diversified. A substantial majority of all industrial workers are employed in the millions of small-scale handicraft enterprises which largely serve the local needs of the villages where they are situated. In terms of total output and value added, however, mechanized factory production predominates. Many factories, especially those manufacturing producers' goods (such as basic metals, machinery, fertilizers, and other heavy chemicals), are publicly owned and operated by either the central or the state governments.

There also are thousands of private producers, including a number of large and diversified industrial conglomerates. The privately owned Tata Iron and Steel Company (Tata Steel), for instance, is one of the largest and most successful steel producers. In the Middle East, East Africa, and South-east Asia, some Indian corporations have established "turnkey operations," which are turned over to local management after a stipulated period. Foreign corporations, however, have been slow to invest in Indian industry because of excessive regulation (subsequently relaxed) and rules limiting foreign ownership of controlling shares. The Chota Nagpur Plateau, where abundant coal supplies are in close proximity to high-grade iron ore, has become India's principal area for heavy industry – including many interconnected chemical and engineering enterprises. Production of heavy transport equipment, such as locomotives and trucks, is also concentrated there.

The long-established textile industries – especially cotton, but also jute, wool, silk, and synthetic fibres – account for the greatest share of manufacturing employment. Few large cities are without at least one cotton mill. Jute milling is highly concentrated in "Hugliside," the string of cities along the Hugli (Hooghly) river, just north of Kolkata. Even more widespread than textile mills are small processing plants for agricultural and mining products, such as cotton ginning (processing), oil pressing and crushing, and initial smelting of ores. Consumer goods industries are largely concentrated in large cities. State governments have sponsored numerous industrial parks, for which entrepreneurs are offered various concessions, including cheap land and reduced taxes.

India's government-regulated and largely government-owned banking system is well developed. Its principal institution is the Reserve Bank of India (founded 1935), which regulates the circulation of banknotes, manages the country's reserves of foreign exchange, and operates the currency and credit system. With the nationalization of the country's 14 largest commercial banks in 1969 and further nationalizations in 1980, most commercial banking passed into the public sector. In 1975 the government instituted a system of regional rural banks, the principal purpose of which was to meet the credit needs of small farmers and tenants. This has gone a long way toward lessening the strength of rapacious village money-lenders. Stock exchanges exist in most of the largest Indian cities.

The volume of India's foreign trade, given the diversity of its economic base, is low. There is, moreover, a chronic and large foreign trade deficit, which is aggravated by substantial imports of smuggled goods, mostly luxuries. In terms of value, gems and jewellery (particularly for the Middle Eastern market) long led the export market, followed by ready-made garments and leather and leather products. However, since the turn of the twenty-first century, engineering products have become the leading export, and chemicals and chemical products and food and agricultural products have slipped in behind gems and jewellery. Imports are highly diverse and include petroleum and petroleum products, precious metals, and chemicals and chemical products.

India's trade links are worldwide. The United States and the former Soviet Union were long the principal destinations for India's exports. The United States remains a major destination of Indian goods, while the countries of the European Union (EU), China (including Hong Kong), and the United Arab Emirates have also been important. The main import sources are China, the EU, and the United States.

Transportation and telecommunications

At independence, India had a transportation system superior to that of any other large postcolonial region. In the decades that followed, it built steadily on that base, and railways in particular formed the sinews that initially bound the new nation together. Although railways have continued to carry the bulk of goods traffic, there has been a steady increase in the relative dependence on roads and motorized transport.

With some 39,000 miles (62,800 kilometres) of track length, India's rail system, entirely government-owned, is one of the most extensive in the world, and also the world's most heavily used system. Railway administration is handled through nine regional subsystems. Routes are mainly broad-gauge (5.5 feet; 1.68 metres) single-track lines, though with increasing conversion to double-track lines, as well as a shift from steam locomotives to diesel-electric or electric power. Electrified lines have become especially important for urban commuter traffic. South Asia's first subway line began operation in Kolkata in 1989, and Delhi followed with a new system in the early twenty-first century.

Although relatively few new rail routes have been built since independence, the length and capacity of the road system and the volume of road traffic have undergone phenomenal expansion. The length of hard-surfaced roads, for example, has increased from only 66,000 to some 950,000 miles (106,000 to 1,530,000 kilometres) since 1947, but this still represented less than half of the national total of all roads. During the same period, the increased volume of road traffic for both passengers and goods was even more dramatic, increasing exponentially. A relatively small number of villages (almost entirely in tribal regions) are still situated more than a few hours' walk from the nearest bus transport. Bus service is largely owned and controlled by state governments, which also build and maintain most hard-surfaced routes.

A small number of major ports, led by Mumbai, Kolkata, and Chennai, are centrally managed by the Indian government, and these handle the bulk of maritime traffic; a much larger number of intermediate and minor ports are state-managed. Of the country's shipping companies engaged in either overseas or coastal trade, the largest is the publicly owned Shipping Corporation of India. Only about one-third of India's more than 3,100 miles (5,000 kilometres) of navigable inland waterways are commercially used, and those no longer carry a significant volume of traffic.

Civil aviation was nationalized in 1953 into two government-owned companies: Air India, for major international routes from airports at New Delhi, Mumbai, Kolkata, and Chennai; and Indian Airlines, for routes within India and neighbouring countries. The government has tightly restricted access to Indian air routes for foreign carriers, and several small domestic airlines have attempted to service short-haul, low-capacity routes. The networks and volume of traffic are expanding rapidly, and all large and most medium-size cities now have regular air service.

The telecommunications sector has traditionally been dominated by the state; even after the liberalization of the 1990s, the government – through several state-owned or operated companies and the Department of Telecommunications – has continued to control the industry. Although telephone service is quite dense in some urban areas, many rural towns and villages have no telephone service. Mobile telephone services are available in major urban centres through a number of private vendors. The state dominates television and radio broadcasting through the Ministry of Information and Broadcasting. The number of personal computers, though large in raw numbers, is relatively small given the country's population. Although many individuals have Internet service subscriptions, cybercafes located in most major urban areas provide access for a great proportion of users.

13

EVERYDAY LIFE IN MODERN INDIA

Family

In India the family is the most important social unit, and it is the family that dominates people's daily lives. There is a strong preference for extended families, consisting of two or more married couples (often of more than a single generation), who share finances and a common kitchen. Marriage is virtually universal, divorce rare, and virtually every marriage produces children. Almost all marriages are arranged by family elders on the basis of caste, degree of consanguinity, economic status, education (if any), and astrology. A bride traditionally moves to her husband's house. However, nonarranged "love marriages" are increasingly common in cities.

Within families, there is a clear order of social precedence and influence based on gender, age and, in the case of a woman, the number of her male children. The senior male of the household typically is the recognized family head, and his wife is the person who regulates the tasks assigned to female family members. Males enjoy higher status than females. This is reflected in significantly different rates of mortality and morbidity between the sexes, allegedly (though reliable statistics are lacking) in occasional female infanticide, and increasingly in the abortion of female fetuses following prenatal gender testing. This pattern of preference is largely connected to the institution of dowry, which can be a major financial liability for the bride's family. Traditionally, women were expected to treat their husbands as if they were gods, and obedience of wives to husbands has remained a strong social norm. This expectation of devotion may follow a husband to the grave; within some caste groups, widows are not allowed to remarry even if they are bereaved at a young age.

Hindu marriage has traditionally been viewed as the "gift of a maiden" (*kanyadan*) from the bride's father to the household of the groom. This gift is also accompanied by a dowry, which generally consists of items suitable to start a young couple in married life. In some cases, however, dowries demanded by grooms and their families have become quite extravagant, and some families appear to regard them as means of enrichment. There are instances when young brides have been treated abusively – even tortured and murdered – in an effort to extract more wealth from the bride's father; such "dowry deaths" have contributed to a reaction against the dowry in some modern urban families.

A Muslim marriage is considered to be a contractual relationship made by the bride's father or guardian and, though there are often dowries, there is formal reciprocity in which the groom promises a *mahr*, a commitment to provide his bride with wealth in her lifetime.

The population growth rate in India, though high, fell significantly during the 1990s. Like most non-Islamic Asian countries, India and Sri Lanka, aware of the adverse impact high rates of population growth have on economic growth and social progress, embarked on official birth-control and family planning programmes, which have met with considerable success.

In former colonies such as India the basic welfare services grew out of modified versions of the European poor laws, charitable and missionary activities, and the introduction of western juvenile justice procedures. Traditional networks of informal care remain, however, the main source of assistance in adversity and old age. High rates of migration and un-planned urban growth, however, have weakened these net-works in impoverished rural areas and overwhelmed the limited public services in new cities and towns.

Caste

Beyond the family, the most important unit is the caste. A caste, generally designated by the term *jati* ("birth"), refers to a strictly regulated social community into which one is born. Within a village all members of a caste recognize a fictive kinship relation and a sense of mutual obligation, but ideas of fictive kinship extend also to the village as a whole, continuing even when a woman marries and goes to another village. If she is then badly treated in her husband's village, it may become a matter of collective concern for her natal village, not merely for those of her own caste. In general, a person is expected to marry someone within the same *jati*, follow a particular set of rules for proper behaviour (in such matters as kinship, occu-pation, and diet), and interact with other *jati*s according to the group's position in the social hierarchy.

In India virtually all nontribal Hindus recognize their mem-bership in one of these hereditary social communities. *Jati*s are usually assigned to one of four large caste clusters, called *varna*s, after the divisions given in the *Rigveda*, each of which has a traditional social function: Brahmans (priests), at the top of the social hierarchy and, in descending prestige, Kshatriyas (warriors), Vaishyas (originally peasants but later merchants), and Sudras (artisans and labourers).

The particular *varna* in which a *jati* is ranked depends in part on its relative level of "impurity," determined by the group's traditional contact with any of a number of "pollutants," including blood, menstrual flow, saliva, dung, leather, dirt, and hair. Intercaste restrictions were established to prevent the relative purity of a particular *jati* from being corrupted by the pollution of a lower caste.

A fifth group, the Panchamas (from Sanskrit *panch*, "five"), theoretically were excluded from the system because their occupations and ways of life typically brought them in contact with such impurities. They were formerly called the "untouchables" (because their touch, believed by the upper castes to transmit pollution, was avoided), but the nationalist leader Mohandas K. Gandhi referred to them as Harijan ("Children of God"), a name that gained popular usage. More recently, members of this class have adopted the term Dalit ("Oppressed") to describe themselves. Officially such groups, which account for nearly one-sixth of India's population, are referred to as Scheduled Castes. Generally landless, they perform most of the agricultural labour, as well as a number of ritually polluting caste occupations (for example, leatherwork among the Chamars, the largest Scheduled Caste).

While inherently nonegalitarian, *jati*s provide Indians with social support and, at least in theory, a sense of having a secure and well-defined social and economic role. In most parts of India, there are one or more dominant castes that own the majority of land, are politically most powerful, and set a cultural tone for a particular region. A dominant *jati* typically forms anywhere from one-eighth to one-third of the total rural population but may in some areas account for a clear majority (such as Sikh Jats in central Punjab, Marathas in parts of Maharashtra, or Rajputs in north-western Uttar Pradesh). The second most numerous *jati* is usually from one of the Scheduled Castes. Depending on its size, a village typically will have between 5 and 25 *jati*s, each of which might be represented by anywhere from 1 to more than 100 households.

The caste system is also prevalent among Muslims, many of whom in South Asia were recruited from the Hindu population and who, despite the egalitarian tenets of Islam, persisted in their social habits. Hindus, in turn, accommodated the Muslim ruling class by giving it a status of its own. In South Asian Muslim society a distinction is made between the Ashraf (Arabic, plural of *sharif*, nobleman), who are supposedly descendants of Muslim Arab immigrants, and the non-Ashraf, who are Hindu converts. The Ashraf is further dived into four subgroups: (i) Sayyids, originally a designation of descendants of Muhammad through his daughter Fatimah and son-in-law, Ali, (ii) Sheikhs (Arabic: "Chiefs"), mainly descendants of Arab or Persian immigrants but also including some converted Rajputs, (iii) Pashtuns, members of Pashto-speaking tribes in Afghanistan and north-western Pakistan, and (iv) Mughals, persons of Turkish origin, who came into India with the Mughal armies.

The non-Ashraf Muslim castes are of three levels of status: at the top, converts from high Hindu castes, mainly Rajputs, insofar as they have not been absorbed into the Sheikh castes; next, the artisan caste groups, such as the Julahas, originally weavers; and lowest, the converted "untouchables," who have continued their old occupations. These converts of Hinduism observe endogamy in a manner close to that of their Hindu counterparts.

The caste system, contrary to the popular image of its changelessness, has always been characterized by the efforts of various *jati*s to raise themselves in the social order. Such efforts have been more successful among low, but ritually pure, castes than in the case of those living below the line of pollution.

Two routes have been available for improvement of caste status. The traditional route has comprised the adoption of certain critical elements of the way of life of clean (upper) castes. These include the ritual of initiation into the status of a clean *jati*; wearing of the holy thread symbolic of such status; vegetarianism; teetotalism; abstention from work that is considered polluting or demeaning; and the prohibition of widow remarriage. The process is gradual and not always successful. The critical test of success lies first in higher castes accepting cooked food from members of the upwardly mobile *jati* and, second, in equivalent-status castes providing services that are deemed "demeaning." Socially ambitious castes have also been known, when possible, to supplement the criterion of social purity with other secular criteria. These include numerical strength, economic well-being (notably in the form of land ownership) and the ability to mobilize physical force sufficient for these castes to emerge as the wielders of power in village affairs and local politics. One of the aspects of social change today relates to the dissociation of ritual status and secular (economic, political) power.

The rigidity of the caste system has also been challenged by opposing ideologies, and in particular by the development of *bhakti* devotionalism that originated in southern India in the third century and spread to the north and repudiated caste. The impact of the social egalitarianism of Islam was also considerable (although caste, as indicated above, is also found among Muslims as well as among Christians, Sikhs, Jains, and

Jews). The introduction of new occupations and professions, theoretically caste-neutral, in the nineteenth century under colonial rule weakened the system, and Gandhi's taking up of the cause of the Scheduled Castes, as part of the national movement, was also influential. The Constitution of 1950 provided that seats for the Scheduled Castes in the lower (directly elected) houses of state and central legislatures would be reserved in the same proportion as their share of the population as a whole. This was to have been a temporary measure, but it has since been extended from time to time, most recently in 1999, when it was extended for another ten years. The quota at present is about 15 per cent.

The mobilization of castes as individual communities or as associations comprising several castes with similar secular interests, to compete with rival castes, emerged in the 1950s as a significant feature in electoral politics. In the 1990s the Dalit movement began adopting a more aggressive approach to ending caste discrimination, and many converted to other religions, especially Buddhism, as a means of rejecting the social premises of Hindu society. One of the most important landmarks in the politics of caste was the extension of reservations in 1990 to "backward classes," defined by caste identity, and other than those already covered, namely the Scheduled Castes. This step raised the reserved quota in legislatures by about 27 per cent to make a total of almost half of the total seats (Scheduled Castes 15 per cent; Scheduled Tribes 7.5 per cent; other backward classes [OBCs] 27.5 per cent) – a limit that the Supreme Court has ruled must not be exceeded. The measure has been defended in the name of social justice and as compensation for age-old, caste-based deprivations. It has also been criticized for being based on arbitrary criteria for identifying backwardness, for eroding constitutional guarantee of equality of opportunity, and for placing a low value on talent and merit. The consequence of the act was to perpetuate caste status as a vested interest, and indeed from time to time, the names of more communities are added to the category of OBCs under the pressure from caste lobbies.

The processes of urbanization, industrialization and secularization have, however, gradually weakened the caste system through a dilution of the religious values underlying caste as well as a radical alteration of the nature of economic activity. Hierarchical ranking is being displaced by increasing internal differentiation of castes (in terms of educational levels, occupations, incomes, lifestyles) on the one hand, and the restatement of external (intercaste) relations in terms of difference on the other. Nevertheless, although there has been some relaxation of caste distinction among young urban dwellers and those living abroad – where notions of ritual purity and pollution have all but disappeared – in rural areas, where three-quarters of Indians live, caste identity remains.

Bollywood

The Indian motion-picture industry now ranks as the most popular form of mass entertainment in the country. In some years India – whose film industry is centred in Mumbai (Bombay), thus earning the entire movie-making industry the sobriquet "Bollywood" in honour of Hollywood, its US counterpart – makes more feature-length films than any other country in the world. While most films are formulaic escapist pastiches of drama, comedy, music, and dance, some of India's best cinematographers, such as Satyajit Ray, are internationally acclaimed. Others, such as filmmakers Ismail Merchant, M. Night Shyamalan (Manoj Shyamalan), and Mira Nair, gained their greatest success making films abroad.

India's moviemaking industry began in 1934 when, after early Indian experiments in silent film, Bombay Talkies, launched by Himansu Rai, spearheaded the growth of Indian cinema. With sound, there was a revival of the popular nineteenth-century folk-music drama based on centuries-old religious myths. Despite the fact that films had to be produced in as many as ten regional languages, the popularity of these "all-talking, all-singing, all-dancing" mythologicals or historicals played an enormous role in encouraging the growth of the Indian film industry. An average of 230 features were released per year throughout the 1930s, almost all for domestic consumption.

Over the years, several classic genres emerged from Bollywood: the historical epic, notably *Mughal-e-Azam* (1960); the curry western, such as *Sholay* (1975); the courtesan film, such as *Pakeezah* (1972), which highlights stunning cinematography and sensual dance choreography; and the mythological movie, represented by *Jai Santoshi Maa* (1975).

Stars, rather than plots, were often the driving force behind the films. Beginning in 1936, when Ashok Kumar and Devika Rani emerged as the first major star pair, the Indian public developed an insatiable appetite for news about their screen heroes. This interest continued with male actors such as Raj Kapoor, Dilip Kumar, and Dev Anand in the 1950s and 1960s, Rajesh Khanna in the 1970s, Amitabh Bachchan in the 1980s, and Shahrukh Khan in the 1990s. Popular female icons included Madhubala in the 1950s, Mumtaz in the 1960s, Zeenat Aman in the 1970s, Hema Malini in the 1980s, and Madhuri Dixit and Kajol in the 1990s.

Serious postwar Indian cinema was for years associated with the work of Satyajit Ray, a director of singular talent who produced the great Apu trilogy – *Pather panchali*, "The Song of the Road," 1955; *Aparajito*, "The Unvanquished," 1956;

Apur sansar, "The World of Apu," 1959 – under the influence of both Jean Renoir and Italian neo-realism. Ray continued to dominate the Indian cinema through the 1960s and 1970s with such artful Bengali films as *Devi*, "The Goddess," 1960; *Charulata*, "The Lonely Wife," 1964; *Aranyer din ratri*, "Days and Nights in the Forest," 1970; and *Ashanti sanket* "Distant Thunder," 1973. The Marxist intellectual Ritwik Ghatak received much less critical attention than his contemporary Ray, but through such films as *Ajantrik*, "Pathetic Fallacy," 1958, he created a body of alternative cinema that greatly influenced the rising generation.

In 1961 the Indian government established the Film Institute of India to train aspiring directors. It also formed the Film Finance Commission (FFC) to help fund independent production and, later, experimental films. The National Film Archive was founded in 1964. These organizations encouraged the production of such important first features as Mrinal Sen's *Bhuvan Shome*, "Mr Shome," 1969; Basu Chatterji's *Sara akaash*, "The Whole Sky," 1979; Mani Kaul's *Uski roti*, "Daily Bread," 1969; Kumar Shahani's *Maya darpan*, "Mirror of Illusion," 1972; Avtar Kaul's *27 Down*, 1973; and M.S. Sathyu's *Garam hawa*, "Scorching Wind," 1973, and promoted the development of a nonstar "parallel cinema" centred in Bombay. A more traditional path was followed by Shyam Benegal, whose films (*Ankur*, "The Seedling," 1974; *Nishant*, "Night's End," 1975; *Manthan*, "The Churning," 1976) are relatively realistic in form and deeply committed in sociopolitical terms.

During the 1970s the regional industries of the south-western states – especially those of Kerala and Karnataka – began to subsidize independent production, resulting in a "southern new wave" in the films of such diverse figures as G. Aravindan (*Kanchana sita*, "Golden Sita," 1977), Adoor Gopalakrishnan

(*Elipathayam*, "Rat-Trap," 1981), and Girish Karnad (*Kaadu*, "The Forest," 1973). Despite the international recognition of these films, the Indian government's efforts to raise the artistic level of the nation's cinema were largely unsuccessful.

At the turn of the twenty-first century, Bollywood was producing as many as 1,000 feature films annually in all of India's major languages and in a variety of cities, and international audiences began to develop among South Asians in the United Kingdom and in the United States. Standard features of Bollywood films continued to be formulaic story lines, expertly choreographed fight scenes, spectacular song-and-dance routines, emotion-charged melodrama, and larger-than-life heroes.

Changes in Bollywood in regard to financing and production, however, now saw the industry move to improve the artistic quality of its product and to expand its audience beyond South Asia, as well as extend its range of subject matter. The Bollywood movie broke significantly into the international market in 2001, thanks to Ashutosh Gowariker's remarkable *Lagaan*, "Land Tax". Using indigenous conventions, this skilfully related story of a group of Indian peasants challenged to compete at cricket with the arrogant British military establishment provided gripping and intelligent entertainment at any level. More limited international acceptance was earned by Santosh Sivan's Bollywood epic *Asoka*, "Ashoka the Great," the story of a historical hero of the third century BCE. Contemporary subjects were treated in Digvijay Singh's *Maya* (2001), a shocking tale of child abuse sanctified as religious ceremony and in Rituparno Ghosh's *Utsab*, "The Festival," 2000, which chronicled the family crises brought to a pitch in the course of an annual festive reunion. Mira Nair's *Monsoon Wedding* (2001) was a perceptive, witty, fast-moving ensemble work about the romantic problems of a large Punjab family assembled for a wedding.

In 2003 industry film producers extended the conventions of Indian commercial cinema to embrace new elements of thriller, science fiction (Rakesh Roshan's *Koi . . . mil gaya*, "I Found Someone"), and gangster movies (Ram Gopal Varma's *Company*, 2002). Outside this mainstream, Rituparno Ghosh adapted Rabindranath Tagore's 1902 novel of feminism and colonial resistance, *Chokher bali* ("Grain of Sand"; 2003). Vishal Bharadwaj's *Maqbool* (2003) transposed Shakespeare's *Macbeth* to the criminal areas of modern Mumbai. Mahesh Dattani's *Mango Soufflé* (2002), adapted from the director's own play *On a Muggy Night in Mumbai,* was a social breakthrough for India, a sympathetic portrayal of homosexuality in a well-heeled professional society.

While the Bollywood commercial cinema extended its range to include melodramas on contemporary subjects such as terrorism (Farah Khan's *Main hoon na,* "I Am Here") and an Indian-Pakistani Romeo and Juliet story (Yash Chopra's *Veer-Zaara*) in 2004, Shyam Benegal made *Bose: The Forgotten Hero,* the biography of the militant Bengali revolutionary Subhas Chandra Bose, a contemporary of Gandhi. On another level, Buddhadeb Dasgupta's *Swapner din* (*Chased by Dreams*) took as its central character a young man who tours with a mobile film projector and a repertory of government propaganda films, interweaving an often uncomfortable reality and his dream life.

The same year actress Aishwarya Rai was at the forefront of a revolution in Indian cinema. Rai starred in *Bride and Prejudice,* her first major English-language film, a music- and dance-filled Bollywood adaptation of Jane Austen's *Pride and Prejudice* that was directed by Gurinder Chadha, director of the 2002 hit *Bend It like Beckham.* Rai's acting career had begun with acclaimed performances in *Iruvar*, "The Duo," 1997 and . . . *Aur pyaar ho gaya* (1997; based on the 1994 movie *Only You*). Both were films that broke from the simplistic structure typical of Bollywood films at the time and helped to push Rai to the forefront of the "New Bollywood."

In 2006, popular Indian cinema's propensity for cannibalizing US films bore exuberant fruit in the Hindi-language sci-fi spectacular *Krrish*, directed by Rakesh Roshan and featuring Hrithik Roshan, his son, as the superhero tasked with saving the world from yet another megalomaniac scientist. More serious Hindi products once again pushed the boundaries of Bollywood cinema. These included *Omkara*, Vishal Bharadwaj's dark and powerful version of Shakespeare's *Othello*, updated to the milieu of gangsters in a village in Uttar Pradesh. *Rang de basanti*, "Paint It Saffron," directed by Rakeysh Omprakash Mehra, centred on young people making a documentary about freedom fighters opposing the British raj, and stretched Bollywood's boundaries with its fusion of politics and romance. In *Kabul Express*, Kabir Khan married breezy comedy with the devastated landscapes of war-torn Afghanistan.

Food and cuisine

Although there is considerable regional variation in Indian cuisine, the day-to-day diet of most Indians lacks variety. Depending on income, two or three meals generally are consumed. The bulk of almost all meals is whatever the regional staple might be: rice throughout most of the east and south, flat wheat bread (*chapati*) in the north and north-west, and bread made from pearl millet (*bajra*) in Maharashtra. This is usually supplemented with the puree of a pulse (*daal*), a few vegetables, and, for those who can afford it, a small bowl of yogurt. Chilies and other spices add zest to this simple fare. For most Indians, meat is a rarity, except on festive occasions. Fish, fresh milk, and fruits and vegetables, however, are more widely consumed. In general, tea is the preferred beverage in northern and eastern India, while coffee is more common in the south.

There has been a prohibition on animal slaughter from the beginning. The *Rigveda* lauded the cow as sinless, and disallowed eating of its flesh. Its hymn to *pilu* (nutrition) lists a large number of edible materials, all of which are vegetarian. A movement thus developed in favour of vegetarianism, which was adopted by the Hindu clergy and later by many sections of Hindus, especially followers of Vishnu. At present, about a quarter of the total population of India is vegetarian, but there are considerable variations from state to state.

In traditional Indian cookery, spice mixtures called *masala* are prepared in the home. Some *masala* are blended with a liquid, such as water or vinegar, to make a paste. The primarily vegetarian curries of southern India, seasoned with sambar podi and other traditional blends, are the most pungent, often containing hot chilies. By contrast classic, or Mughal, *garam masala* of northern India contains only raw cardamom seeds, cinnamon, cloves, and black pepper. Lamb and poultry are common features in the curries of the north.

From very early times a wide range of foods has been available in the Indian subcontinent, and the cultivation of wheat, barley and rice was widespread in early civilizations. By 1000 BCE rice had become a staple all over the fertile alluvial plains of India. Some pulses (legumes), such as chickpea and lentil, came to India from the Middle East, while others – green gram and black gram – were indigenous. The nuts of the

coconut palm floated across the southern seas from Papua
New Guinea to flourish in southern India and Sri Lanka. The
crossing of a Malaysian pulpy fruit with a native wild species
was to produce cultivars of the banana. Similarly, the so-called
noble cane came from Papua New Guinea and crossed with a
wild grass to evolve into a thin but sweet sugarcane. Radishes
and carrots were eaten in India long before they arrived in
Europe, and a wide range of other vegetables, including gourds
and pumpkins, as well as many fruits were part of the diet too.

Spices have long been associated with India, and many grew
wild. Pepper was exported from early times, turmeric and
ginger are probably indigenous, while onion and garlic came
from Afghanistan at an early date. Meat and fish were consumed in abundance by 1000 BCE – the Indian jungle fowl is
acknowledged as the predecessor of the world's domestic
chickens – as well as milk from cows, buffalo and goats. In
the sixteenth century came the all-important chili.

A variety of rice, wheat and barley dishes were consumed
over the centuries. In the third to sixth century rice was
combined with pulses and ground, fermented and shallow
pan-fried to make *adai* and *dosai*, common snacks and break-
fast foods still eaten today. The *mandaka* (a wheat dough
circle stuffed with a sweetened paste of green gram and then
shallow-fried) is mentioned in Buddhist literature *c.*500 BCE,
and there are records of the *samitah*, made the same way,
among medical writers. This delicacy still survives as the
mande and *poli* in central India. From 1000 CE onwards,
Muslim influence is evident in various kinds of wheat *roti*,
which are still in vogue: the *chapati* and the *phulka*; the
paratha; and the *puris* or thicker *lucchis*. Other varieties of
roti are the *naan*, tandoori *roti* and the *kulcha*.

Throughout the country, edible oils were extracted from
sesame seed and other oilseeds (such as coconut in Kerala, and

rapeseed and mustard seed in the Indo-Gangetic Plain) using pestle and mortar devices that employed animal traction. Although to the Aryans the only acceptable cooking fat was *ghee*, the rest of the population from the start have used local vegetable oils for cooking and frying. Meats, fish and fowl were prepared in a variety of ways. Meat cooked with fruit juices was popular in Vedic times, and cooked chicken and peacock could be further fried in *ghee* and simmered again with lentils, cloves and caraway seeds. Fish, tortoises and crab were roasted. From the earliest times, tandoori ovens were used for grilling and skewers for roasting. An important later influence on food was that of Muslims, especially during the Mughal Empire. Pig meat was banned, as was alcohol, and new spice combinations adopted, such as *pulaos*, and *biryanis* introduced.

The domestic hearth in an Indian home is an area of sanctity, frequently positioned next to the area of worship, and away from the sitting, sleeping, or visitor-receiving areas. In literal terms *kaccha* means essentially raw, partly done, or imperfect, and *pucca* means the opposite, that is ripe or well done, but the terms have a different connotation in ritual cooking practice. *Kaccha* foods – such as boiled rice, *daal* or *roti* – were prepared fresh for each meal, following elaborate rules. Before the cooks entered the kitchen they bathed, donned fresh, handwashed clothes, and removed any upper garments they may have been wearing. Once cooking started, they could not leave the kitchen until the food had been cooked, served, and eaten according to ritual. In contrast, *pucca* foods broadly speaking were fried foods made with a superior cooking fat, such as *ghee*. Such foods, once cooked, could be taken outside the house and shared with others.

The purpose of cooking was to conjoin the cultural proper-ties of the food with those of the eater, using methods that were ritually pure and auspicious. Five elements were involved, namely fire, water, *ghee*, *anna* (grains cultivated using a plough), and *phala* (uncultivated products [like fruits] that did not employ a plough). Milk and *ghee* were regarded as already cooked foods and therefore pure in themselves. Cooking without fire would include washing vegetables with water to render them pure before peeling, cutting, sifting or grinding. It could also mean sundrying fruit or vegetables so that they could be preserved, or pickling vegetables and semi-ripe fruit using oil and spices. Cooking with fire was divided into cooking *pucca* foods, where *ghee* was used, or *kaccha* foods, where it was not.

Food has long played a part in ritual celebrations and events marking the stages of life. At a wedding ceremony, grains played a prominent symbolic role. Turmeric-stained rice was tied at the top of the sacred pillar (*sth-ambha*) set up in the courtyard, and wheat grains were planted a few days earlier and watered so that new shoots would be visible during the ceremony. A ritual earthen pot (*kalash*) with a lighted lamp placed in it would be decorated with barley grains. The priest worshipped the sun with uncooked red *masoor dhal*, the silvery moon with yellow turmeric or the chickpea grains, and saturn with black sesame seeds. The bride threw parched grains (*lajah*) into the fire, and the couple was showered with rice grains as a symbol of fertility. During pregnancy, a bride avoided foods classified as "cold" or "pungent." For 12 days after childbirth the household was considered "polluted", and the new mother was given special food, often rich in garlic or fenugreek, to stimulate lactation. After a death in the family all cooking in the house stopped, and food was provided by other relatives. Auspicious foods, such as milk and its products, chickpea and its flour, and turmeric, were avoided until the final ceremony 11 days later. At subsequent rites of remembrance these foods were also spurned, in favour of such items as sweetcakes of rice and barley, boiled mung *daal*, and green bananas.

In many temples, especially in south India, an enormous amount of food is cooked every day for offering to the deity and then, when sanctified, for distribution to pilgrims who may be fed in huge dining halls. Each temple has its own foods. In the temple at Tirupati in Andhra Pradesh, 70,000 sweet *laddhu*s are made every day, besides 30,000 each of such savoury items as the *vada*, *dosai*, and *rava-appam*. At the great Jagannatha Temple at Puri, Orissa, 1,000 people at 750 fire-places prepare a hundred varieties of dishes daily. The food prepared in *gurdwara*s is called *langar*; sanctified Sikh food is termed *karha prasad* and takes the form of a wheat *halva*.

For centuries a strong connection has been acknowledged between food and health under the three pillars (*vriddhatrayi*) of *ayurveda* (*ayur*, "life" and *veda*, "knowledge"). Nature represented a harmonious blend of three qualities (*guna*), which comprised all that was good and noble (*sattva*), all that was energetic (*rajas*) and all that represented inertia (*tamas*). Humans also were composed of the three *guna*s and the universe was a macrocosm of the individual human body. All food had ten contrasting *guna*, the most important of which was *rasa* (taste), of which there were six basic kinds: sweet, acid, salt, pungent, bitter, astringent. In order to maintain an equilibrium in the body, every major meal was expected to include all six *rasa*, beginning with a sweet item, continuing with sour and salty preparations, and ending with pungent, astringent, and bitter items. Even today a formal wedding feast in south India would follow such a pattern, with a rigid place prescribed for each item on a banana-leaf plate, and a well-defined serving order.

Clothing, dyeing, and textiles

Clothing for most Indians is quite simple and typically un-tailored. Men (especially in rural areas) frequently wear little more than a broadcloth *dhoti*, worn as a loose skirtlike loin-cloth or, in parts of the south and east, the tighter wraparound *lungi*. In both cases the body remains bare above the waist, except in cooler weather, when a shawl also may be worn, or in hot weather, when the head may be protected by a turban. The more affluent and higher-caste men are likely to wear a tailored shirt, increasingly of western style. Muslims, Sikhs, and urban dwellers generally are more inclined to wear tailored clothing, including various types of trousers, jackets, and vests.

Although throughout most of India women wear saris and short blouses, the way in which a sari is wrapped varies greatly from one region to another. In Punjab, as well as among older female students and many city dwellers, the characteristic dress is the *shalwar-kamiz*, a combination of pyjama-like trousers and a long-tailed shirt (saris being reserved for special oc-casions). Billowing ankle-length skirts and blouses are the typical female dress of Rajasthan and parts of Gujarat. Most rural Indians, especially females, do not wear shoes and, when footwear is necessary, prefer sandals.

The modes of dress of tribal Indians are exceedingly varied and can be, as among certain Naga groups, quite ornate. Throughout India, however, western dress is increasingly in vogue, especially among urban and educated males, and western-style school uniforms are worn by both sexes in many schools, even in rural India.

Natural dyes are derived from plants, animals, insects and the earth. A wide range of climatic zones and terrains in India has resulted in a rich diversity of dye plants, about a hundred being found in the Himalayan region alone. Of these, the most commonly used are madder for dyeing shades of red and indigo for dyeing shades of blue and black. The famous blue indigo (*neel* in Sanskrit) is mainly obtained from plants of the *Indigofera* genus; there are about 40 species in India, of which 16 yield dye, but only 4 are commercially cultivated. An almost blackish blue colour is obtained by dyeing yarn 16 times in the traditional natural Indian indigo vat. Natural yellow, the most commonly used source of which is pomegranate, is also widely used in traditional Indian textiles. Natural yellow, orange, and pinks can be obtained from *kasumbo* and *latkan*. *Catechu*, an extract prepared from the wood of *Acacia catechu*, is an excellent brown dye.

The traditional way to design using natural indigo has been to print, paint, or tie the result, and then dye in the indigo vat. The dye does not penetrate wherever the resist is applied, and the design is secured. Though both mechanical and chemical resists exist, traditionally mechanical resists were the ones that were most commonly used. In India, wax and mud were painted or printed on the fabric and then the fabric was dyed several times. This practice continues even today, although chemical indigo is used. Wooden blocks are normally used for printing with natural resists.

Tying is another method used widely. There are two types: yarn and fabric. In yarn tie-dye, the yarn is tied and dyed a number of times to achieve each colour, and then is used to make fabric. The famous *patola* of India is designed using this method. In fabric tie-dye, the designs vary according to the way in which the fabric is held while tying and the thickness of the yarn used. The *bandhani* and *legheria* of India are based on this technique.

The simplest traditional method of producing fabric is to weave different designs using dyed yarns. In the north-eastern states of India this method is mostly used to create beautiful designs on loin looms. Yarns dyed dark-blue, red and black with natural dyes are used to weave the distinctive designs of each tribe. These colours and designs are symbolic, and convey the status of the user as well as the identity of his or her tribe and subtribe. Yellow is the next most frequently used colour. Shades of orange are used by the Meithei or Manipur.

In Madhya Pradesh and Orissa, pictorial motifs from the surrounding areas are woven into fabrics used by the Bastar and Oriya tribals. Maroon and brown yarn, dyed using *aal* roots, are used in these designs. In Andhra Pradesh, cotton saris for widows were woven using bluish-black yarn dyed with natural indigo – production of naturally dyed saris has now stopped.

Plaiting, weaving, and dyeing of textiles has been known on the subcontinent since ancient times. Cotton was first cultivated in India, and the weavers developed their skills from early times. There are records of exports of fine quality cotton textiles to the Romans. The movement of people from Central Asia introduced innumerable techniques of manufacturing woven carpets, gelims, decorative hangings, tents, and personal apparel. Weaving came to be practised by a highly professional weaving community. It was only in the northeastern part of India that it was practiced by all the women of the household. Knowledge of spinning and weaving very fine cotton spread throughout the area. The *jamdani* technique of weaving shadow-like patterns, indigenous to India, found its way to many parts of the world, though the finest were woven in Bengal.

A wide range of cloths was produced, and each region had its own distinctive styles. The finer cotton was used for turbans throughout India; women wore saris of varying lengths from about 17 to 25 feet (4 to 8 metres). The fine quality saris of woven cotton from Chanderi and Maheswari of Madhya Pradesh, as well as Sholapur and Pune of Maharashtra, were often embellished with gold thread. In Tamil Nadu brilliantly coloured and richly woven saris were a speciality of Kanchipuram, Madurai, Salem, and Coimbatore. Checkered cotton cloth dyed with indigo and woven in the eastern coastal area of Andhra Pradesh, and known in the eighteenth century as Real Madras Handkerchief (RMH), was exported widely, as was Indian printed cotton.

The *eri* silk worm is indigenous to Assam, but distinctive styles of silk weaving are found throughout India. Gujarat was one of the oldest centres of silk weaving, employing a range of techniques such as *brocading, meenakari, tanchoi, mashru, velvet, and gajji*. Surat was the centre for production of gold thread as well as gold-brocaded weaving. Varanasi later became an important silk centre, and the small town of Baluchar, in West Bengal, became the centre for producing distinctive pictorial saris, which appeared to be based on line drawings of miniatures. Naupatna wove silk and created silken *ikat*-inscribed patterns for offering by devotees to the Jagannath Temple at Puri. Thanjavur, Kumbakonam, and Madurai were the centres of the highly specialized silk and gold brocaded saris used for marriage as well as offering to the deities.

In wool, Kashmir weavers were known for weaving high quality pashmina shawls with intricately woven patterns, especially with tree of life patterns and intricate borders. Other patterns – garden designs, multicoloured flowers – were later introduced. Soft blankets known as *gudma* and *thulma* were woven in the mountain areas, as well as woven shawls made using tapestry techniques on the borders. Felting of wool to make *namda*s for floor coverings and caps was carried on in the desert areas of Rajasthan and Gujarat.

The use of embroidery, appliqué and other surface decoration to cloth has been widespread for centuries. In the seventeenth century Dutch and English factories were set up to produce embroidered goods, and the exports of embroidered cottons and silks to Europe continued until the nineteenth century. After industrialization, however, many handloom weavers' livelihoods were threatened, and a number of spinning mills were established in India. Since independence the Indian government has adopted special programmes for the protection and development of the handloom and handicrafts industry, establishing a number of cottage and small industry institutions as well as organizations to promote them, such as The All India Handloom Board and the Silk Board. The powerloom sector, however, has adversely affected its handloom competitor; in 1999–2000 the powerloom sector provided 57 per cent of cloth used in the country, the handloom sector 19 per cent, and the organized textile mill industry met just a small part of the industry's requirements. Nevertheless, the textile industry today remains one of India's most important industries and is responsible for a third of the country's export earnings.

Sports and games

The history of sports in India dates to thousands of years ago, and numerous games, including chess, wrestling, and archery, are thought to have originated there. Polo, boxing and chess are among the games that were played in ancient India. It is said that Akbar played the game in his harem by using slave girls as chess pieces and moving them on a chess court built in the palace of Fatehpur Sikri. Kite flying has always been popular, and also kite fights. Contemporary Indian sports are a diverse mix, with traditional games such as *kabaddi* and *kho-kho*, and those introduced by the British, especially cricket, football (soccer), and field hockey, enjoying great popularity.

Kabaddi, primarily an Indian game, is believed to be some 4,000 years old. Combining elements of wrestling and rugby, the team sport has been a regular part of the Asian Games since 1990. *Kho-kho*, a form of tag, ranks as one of the most popular traditional sports in India, and its first national championship was held in the early 1960s. It is now played across the country at various levels, including national level for various groups including schools, and at inter-university level.

Indian gymnastics does not figure on the Asian or world map, but there are some popular native forms such as *mallakhamb* (*malla*, "gymnast" and *khamb*, "pole"), most commonly played in Maharashtra. It is a form of gymnastics executed in relation to a pole fixed in the ground. The sport is over 800 years old. Today about 14 states participate in the *mallakhamb* national competitions. Another ancient game from Maharashtra is *atya-patya*. In this game the playing area is divided into nine trenches emerging from both sides of a long central trench. A point is awarded for every trench crossed which the members of the opposite team block.

There are a number of martial arts and contact sports that originated from tribal cultures. *Kalaripayattu* was the most popular in the sixteenth century during the reign of Tacholi Otheyanan, a chieftain of North Malabar. Today a *kalaripayattu* display includes physical training, mock duels, and combat, both armed and unarmed. *Silambam* is another form of martial arts and is prevalent in Tamil Nadu. The game in some ways resembles modern fencing. *Thang-ta*, *sarit-sarak* and *cheibei gad ga* are other forms of martial arts prevalent in Manipur. Various forms of wrestling also exist in India.

Mukna, which has been played since the fifteenth century in Manipur, is a form of wrestling in which the use of legs is permitted. *Inchai* and *inbuan* are variants of the game, both popular in Mizoram. Nagaland has an indigenous form of wrestling in which the players grasp each other's waist girdles.

Archery, traditionally a martial art practised by the Kshatriya princes, began to be enjoyed in India as a modern Olympic sport in 1975. India organized the first Asian Meet in Kolkata (Calcutta) in 1980, and first participated at an international level in the 1986 and 1988 Seoul Asian Games. Purnima Mahato of Bigar bagged seven gold medals at the Pune National Games in January 1994, the maximum ever won by an individual archer. In 2005, at the Madrid World Championship, Indian archer Tarundeep Rai won the men's silver.

The first national shooting championship – organized by the National Rifle Association of India – was held in Delhi in 1952. India has since been actively participating in all the major international championships, including the Olympic Games, and has won laurels. Jaspal Rana, India's ace pistol shooter, won eight medals at the Chennai (Madras) South Asian Federation Games (SAF) in 1995; 4 gold medals at the Commonwealth Games in 2002; and 7 gold medals at the 2004 SAF in Islamabad. He also won a gold medal in the men's 25-metre Centre Fire Pistol (Pairs) with Samaresh Jung at the 2006 Commonwealth Games. The first team gold medal for India was won at the Asian clay-shooting championships in 1995. The Indian team also did well at the 2002 Commonwealth Games, where it won 14 golds and 7 silvers; in the 2006 Commonwealth Games in Melbourne it gained 16 golds. The most distinguished breakthrough for the team came at the 2004 Athens Olympics, when Rajyavardhan Singh Rathore – a serving Indian army officer – finished second in the final of the men's double-trap shooting event, winning India the first-ever silver medal in shooting. With that win Rathore also became the first individual Olympic silver medallist of India since independence. Further honours followed for India: at the 2006 Commonwealth games, Samaresh Jung won 5 golds, 1 silver, and 1 bronze, and Gagan Narang won 4 golds.

Racquet sports have gained in popularity in recent decades, and India now competes at national and international levels in badminton, squash, and tennis. The Badminton Association of India was formed in 1934, but British army officers are known to have played the game in the 1860s. The first national championship was held in 1936; Prakash Padukone, the youngest to win the title – in Chennai in 1971 – went on to win the title for a record nine years. Leroy D'sa, one of the all-time finest doubles players, held a record in the later 1990s with 7 doubles titles in the senior doubles championships, as well as 14 appearances in final matches. Dpankar Bhattacharya, Vimal Kumar and Madhumita Bisht qualified for participation in badminton's debut as a full-medal event at the Barcelona Olympics in 1992; only Bhattacharya made it to the quarter-finals. Padukone and Kumar started the Prakash Padukone Badminton Academy in Behgaluur in October 1994. In 2006 Saina Nehwal became the first Indian woman to win a badminton Grand Prix event, claiming the singles title at the Philippines Open in Manila.

India has yet to produce a world champion squash player. However, Joshna Chinappa – an Indian squash prodigy who was also the youngest Indian women's national champion – became the first Indian to win the British Squash Championship title in 2003, won the British Open Junior and the Asian Junior in 2005, and the following year entered the league of the top 50 players in the world. The same year, 2006, Indian's top male squash player, Ritwik Bhattacharya, moved up to a career best of 49 in the world rankings. To Bbaneswari Kumari, however, goes India's most successful squash record in Indian squash history, having won the national title 16 times, equalling the world record for the number of national titles won, a feat that gained her a place in the *Guinness Book of World Records*.

India was one of the founder members of the International Table Tennis Federation in 1926, and the Table Tennis Federation of India was formed in 1938; the latter holds the national and inter-state championships and runs a Table Tennis Academy in Rajasthan. The current titles record holders, with eight national titles each, are Kamlesh Mehta (men) and Indu Puri (women). Chetan Baboor achieved the greatest success at an international level in men's table tennis in India when, in March 1999, he defeated the world number one, China's Liu Guo Liang, in the first Asian Top-12 championship.

Tennis, and especially the Wimbledon championship, is avidly followed by many Indians and is one of the few sports where Indians have consistently done well. Stars include the father and son duo of Ramathan and Ramesh Krishnan; the three Amritraj brothers, Vijay, Anand and Ashok; and the famous doubles partnership of Leander Paes and Mahesh Bhupathi. The country has reached the Davis Cup finals on three occasions, in 1966, in 1974 with the Amritraj brothers, and in 1987. The high point of India's record at Wimbledon was in 1999 when Leander Paes and Mahesh Bhupathi won their second consecutive Grand Slam men's doubles after the French Open, to record India's best ever performance in the event. The two have been among the most successful doubles pairs in tennis history, and Paes also won an Olympic bronze medal for singles in 1996 at the Atlanta Games.

Vijay Amritraj, who reached the US Open championship quarter-finals in 1973, remained in the top-50 men players for more than a decade thereafter and achieved a career-high 16 championships in 1980. A more recent tennis sensation is Sania Mirza, who became the first and only Indian woman to reach the fourth round of a Grand Slam tournament at the 2005 US Open, having won the women's doubles title at Wimbledon two years earlier. That year, 2005, she also became the highest-ranked female tennis player from India (42). India holds South Asia's only ATP tour event, the Gold Flake Open, at Chennai.

Indians are passionate about cricket, which probably appeared on the subcontinent in the early eighteenth century. The country competed in its first official Test in 1932, and its international showing has gone from strength to strength. One of the great highlights occurred in 1983, when – led by captain Kapil Dev, one of the most successful cricketers in history – India won the World Cup. In 1926 India joined the Imperial Cricket Conference (renamed the International Cricket Conference in 1965), which had been founded in 1909 by England, Australia, and South Africa. India has also taken part in one-day internationals, introduced in 1972. In 1987, the World Cup was held in India and Pakistan, the first time it had been played outside England.

On the national scene, the Ranji Trophy is a prestigious inter-state tournament played every year. At a higher zonal level, the Duleep Trophy is held annually and the season ends with the Irani Trophy match that pits the Ranji Trophy winners against a Rest of India XI.

One of the earliest notable players was K.S. Ranjitsinhji, the *nawab* of Pataudi, who played Test cricket for England and scored 154 not out against Australia at Old Trafford in 1896. He became the first Indian cricketer to be honoured by the Wisden Cricketers' Almanac. Lala Amarnath became the first Indian to score a Test century when he made 118 against a visiting English side at Bombay (now Mumbai) in 1933. In 1951–52 India recorded its first Test victory, beating England by an innings and 8 runs. And it was also against England that India won its first series, 1961–62.

With the advent of Sunil Gavaskar in 1971 and then Kapil Dev in 1979, India began to challenge the world's leading teams, and since the mid-1970s it has been regarded as one of the major cricketing nations. Both these men were world record-breakers: Gavaskar went on to play 125 Test matches for India and scored 34 centuries, a record that has stood for almost 30 years – he was also the first to achieve a score of 10,000 runs in Test cricket. Kapil Dev became the highest-scoring wicket taker in the world with 434 wickets. In the 1990s Tendulkar was the new sensation, breaking most existing batting records during the first decade of his career. Anil Kumble, in a Test match against Pakistan in 1999, took all 10 wickets in an innings, the first time the feat has been repeated since Englishman Jim Laker set that record four decades earlier.

In 1999 India became involved in a scandal regarding match fixing in Test matches. While many Test nations had banned betting on Test matches, in India and Pakistan betting on cricket was legal and cricketers playing international matches there reported being asked by bookmakers and betting syndicates to underperform in return for money. A number of players were eventually found to have fixed matches. Members of the Australian, South African, Indian, and Pakistani national teams were all tainted by this scandal – several players were banned from cricket for life, and the integrity of the game was called into question.

In the 2005–06 Test series India drew against England, but recorded its first victory in the West Indies in 35 years. At season's end Rahul Dravid was second in the world rankings.

There were two International Cricket Council (ICC) World Cups in 2007. While the original 50-over version was retained by Australia, the inaugural Twenty20 model was won by India, in a narrow 5-run victory over Pakistan. In the 2006–07 Test series India lost to South Africa, but recovered to claim its first series victory in England since 1986. Ably led by Rahul Dravid, India found a bowler of real penetration in Zaheer Khan, who took 18 wickets.

The first copy of the rules of football (soccer) arrived in Calcutta (now Kolkata) with a college professor in 1883, and by 1892 the first cup competition was held. At first mainly a colonial pastime, the All India Football Federation was formed in 1937. India began to take part in international competitions in 1951, when the national team entered the tournament of the Asian Games and won. They have since won once more and finished in the top four on three other occasions. They have done less well in the Asian Cup, only qualifying twice for the finals since 1956. The country's participation in the World Cup has been limited to three appearances. India has established itself as the leading power in South Asia and in the 1997 South Asian Football Federation was easily the best team.

Softball was introduced in 1961, and has since been growing in popularity. In 1997 India organized the Asian Youth Championship in Chennai, where teams from a number of Asian countries participated.

Golf is also played throughout India. The Royal Calcutta Golf Club, established in Kolkata in 1829, is the oldest golf club in India and was the first outside Britain; the Bombay Golf Club came 12 years later. The Royal Calcutta Golf Club initiated an amateur championship for India, and the two clubs paved the way for many in eastern and southern Asia. The nation, however, has struggled to find champions. Only in the late twentieth century was a PGA tournament brought to

India; about the same time, a few Indian golfers began to make their mark, among them Ali Sher, Basad Ali, Arjun Atwal, Jyoti Randhawa and Jeev Milkha Singh.

Another popular sport is volleyball, introduced to India in the first half of the twentieth century. The sport has a permanent place in the SAF Games, but while India has achieved some success in the men's game, the same cannot be said for the women's competition. In the first SAF championship, in 1987, India won a gold medal; it also won in 1991, and has won further medals in the Asian Games.

Weightlifting and wrestling are also enjoyed competitively. Karnam Malleswari won the world title for weightlifting twice in 1994. In 1995 Karnam Malleswari and Kunjurani Devi were classed as number one in the world by the International Weightlifting Federation. At the 1990 Commonwealth Games India won the team championship with 11 golds. In wrestling India achieved some early successes, including a bronze in the 1952 Olympics (won by K.D. Jadhav) and golds at the 1962 Asian Games, and later won four golds, four silvers, and a bronze at the 1982 Commonwealth Games. Women's championships have also been held, and Juliet Kumari has the distinction of being India's first professional woman wrestler. Mohammed Qamaruddin Khan and his ten sons, seven of whom have represented Andhra Pradesh in the nationals, have earned fame as Greco-Roman and freestyle wrestlers.

Water sports are common in Kerala, Manipur, and the Nicobar Islands. In Kerala, a *chundan vallom* or snake boat race is held during the festival of Onam. The boats used are huge and may have as many as 100 members on a team. *Hiyang tannaba* is a seasonal boat race held during the Lai Haraoba festival in Manipur. *Asol aap* is a boat race prevalent in the Nicobar Islands. The form is similar to modern canoeing.

Swimming is popular throughout India and is organized at national, university, and school level, as well as at clubs. In competitive swimming, India took some years to achieve success; Indian swimmers first entered the Olympics in 1928, but it was not until the Asian Games in 1951 that they won any medals. It was more than three decades before the next medal was won, at the Seoul Asiad in 1986 when Khazan Singh won a silver in the 200-metre butterfly event – and that was the last win of the twentieth century. Singh, however, holds the record of winning the maximum number of medals in an international meet, garnering eight golds at the first SAF Games in Kathmandu in 1984. In long-distance swimming, Arti Pradhan was the first woman in the world to swim the Strait of Gibraltar, on August 29 1988.

The first international championship medal in yachting to be won by an Indian was a bronze won by Surinder Mongia and Anil Bahl in 1981 in an Enterprise-class boat. In 1991 Farokh Tarapore and Kelly Rao won a gold in the Enterprise Regatta at Mumbai, and further medals have been won since. India has been consistently winning yachting medals in the Asian Games: in 1982 Tarapore and Sarir Karanjia won all seven of the races and achieved a gold.

India made its Olympic Games debut at the 1920 Games in Antwerp, though it did not form an Olympic association until 1927. The following year, in Amsterdam, India competed in field hockey, its national game, for the first time. The national team's victory that year – it conceded not a single goal in its five matches – was the first of six consecutive gold medals in the event between 1928 and 1956; they won again in 1964 and 1980. The game had been spread by the British in the early nineteenth century, flourishing particularly in cantonment towns and among the Punjabi. International competition began in 1895. The All India Hockey Federation was formed in 1925, and within three years the sport had become India's national game. Since 1956, when India beat Pakistan, the two countries have frequently been pitted against each other in one of modern sport's most passionate rivalries, but since the 1970s their hegemony has weakened; the more recent performances of Indian teams have been unpredictable, though India won a gold medal in the Asian Games in 1998. In an attempt to resuscitate its hockey fortunes, three hockey academies have been formed – the Air India Academy in Delhi, Special Area Games Academy at Ranchi in Jharkhand, and the Steel Authority of India Limited (SAIL) Academy of Rourkela in Orissa – all aimed at producing players of high calibre, while the Nehru Hockey Cup held in the capital every year encourages participation at school level.

PART FIVE

THE MAJOR SITES
TO VISIT

DELHI

Delhi is the country's second largest city and seat of the national government, surpassed in population only by Greater Mumbai (Bombay). New Delhi, the capital of India, lies immediately to the south. It has generally been presumed that the city was named for Raja Dhilu, a king who reigned in the first century BCE.

Delhi has been the capital city of a succession of mighty empires and powerful kingdoms, and numerous ruins mark the sites of the various cities. According to popular tradition, the city has changed its locality a total of seven times. All of these locations are confined to a triangular area of about 70 square miles (180 square kilometres) called the Delhi triangle. Two sides of this triangle are represented by the rocky hills of the Aravali Range in the west and south, and the third side by the shifting channel of the Yamuna river. The present site of Delhi is bounded to the west by a northern extension of the Aravali Range, known as the Delhi Ridge.

Many areas of the city have a specific character. In Old Delhi there is a strong feeling of *mohalla* ("neighbourhood"), partly induced by the peculiar housing layout. Gates or doorways open on to private residences and courtyards, or on to *katra* (one-room tenements facing a courtyard or other enclosure and having access to the street by only one opening or gate). The Civil Lines area consists of residences for upper income groups. The government housing areas also exhibit segregation by income groups. In some developed areas, "mixed neighbourhoods" have been created. Chanakyapuri (more commonly known as the Diplomatic Enclave), with its concentration of foreign embassies, represents a microcosm of international architecture. Cultural "islands" have formed in such areas as the Bengali Market area or Karol Bagh. Slums are inhabited mostly by construction workers, sweepers, factory labourers, and other low-income groups. There are also urban village enclaves, such as Kotla Mubarakpur, where houses and streets retain rural characteristics though residents have urban occupations.

Delhi's population has increased some 40-fold from the 240,000 inhabitants it had in 1911. At the time of independence there was a large influx of refugees into the city, and the population has since grown steadily. More than half of the residents come from outside the territory. Most of these immigrants are from other Indian states and adjacent countries, and only a small proportion consists of resident foreigners. The great majority of the population is Hindu; Muslims constitute the largest minority, followed by smaller numbers of Sikhs, Jains, Christians, and Buddhists.

History

The earliest reference to a settlement at Delhi is found in the epic *Mahabharata*, which mentions a city called Indraprastha, built about 1400 BCE under the direction of Yudhisthira, a Pandava king, on a huge mound somewhere between the sites where the historic Old Fort (Purana Qilah) and Humayun's Tomb were later to be located. Although nothing remains of Indraprastha, according to legend it was a thriving city. Then, in the first century BCE, Raja Dhilu built a city near the site of the future Qutb Minar. Thereafter Delhi faced many vicissitudes and did not reemerge into prominence until the twelfth century CE, when it became the capital of the Cauhan (Cahamana) ruler Prthviraja III. After the defeat of Prthviraja in the late twelfth century, the city passed into Muslim hands. Qutb al-Din Aybak, founder of the Mu'izzi (Slave) dynasty and builder of the famous tower Qutb Minar (completed in the early thirteenth century), also chose Delhi as his capital.

'Ala' al-Din Khalji (reigned 1296–1316) built the second city of Delhi at Siri, a short distance north-east of the Qutb Minar. The third city of Delhi was built by Ghiyath al-Din Tughluq (1320–25) at Tughlakabad, but it had to be abandoned in favour of the old site near the Qutb Minar because of a scarcity of water. His successor, Muhammad ibn Tughluq, extended the city farther north-east and built new fortifications around it. It then became the fourth city of Delhi, under the name Jahanpanah. These new settlements were located between the old cities near the Qutb Minar and Siri Fort. Muhammad ibn Tughluq's successor, Firuz Shah Tughluq, abandoned this site altogether and in 1354 moved his capital farther north near the ancient site of Indraprastha and founded the fifth city of Delhi, Firuzabad, which was situated in what is now the Firoz Shah Kotla area.

After the invasion and sack of Delhi by Timur (Tamerlane) at the end of the fourteenth century, the last of the sultan kings moved the capital to Agra. Babur, the first Mughal ruler, reestablished Delhi as the seat of his empire in 1526. His son

Humayun built a new city, Din Panah, on the site between Firoz Shah Kotla and the Purana Qila. Sher Shah, who overthrew Humayun in 1540, razed Din Panah to the ground and built his new capital, the Sher Shahi (Purana Qila), as the sixth city of Delhi.

Delhi later again lost importance when the Mughal emperors Akbar (1556–1605) and Jahangir (1605–27) moved their headquarters, respectively, to Fatehpur Sikri and Agra, but the city was restored to its former glory and prestige in 1638, when Shah Jahan laid the foundations of the seventh city of Delhi, Shahjahanabad, which has come to be known as Old Delhi. The greater part of the city is still confined within the space of Shah Jahan's walls, and several gates built during his rule – the Kashmiri Gate, the Delhi Gate, the Turkman Gate, and the Ajmeri Gate – still stand.

With the fall of the Mughal Empire during the mid-eighteenth century, Delhi again faced many vicissitudes – raids by the Maratha, the invasion by Nader Shah of Persia, and a brief spell of Maratha rule – before the British arrived in 1803. Under British rule the city flourished, except during the Indian Mutiny in 1857. In 1912 the British moved the capital of British India from Calcutta (now Kolkata) to the partially completed New Delhi, the construction of which was finished by 1931.

Since India's independence Delhi has grown far beyond its original boundaries, and into adjacent states as its population has increased. New Delhi, once adjacent to Delhi, is now part of the larger city, as are the sites of the former seats of empire. Between ancient mausoleums and forts have sprouted high-rise towers, commercial complexes, and other aspects of the modern city.

This rapid development has not been without cost. It has placed a colossal strain on the city's infrastructure and on the ability to provide utilities. Most problematic, in a city in which the population had more than doubled in the final two decades of the twentieth century, fully one-tenth of Delhi's residents lived in urban slums called *jhuggi-jhompri*s, lacking the most basic services. Further, traffic congestion in Delhi had become among the worst in the world, and the Indian capital has become among the most polluted cities in the world. Anti-pollution measures undertaken since the 1980s have improved Delhi's air quality considerably, but overcrowding, conges-tion, and an overburdened infrastructure have remained as major obstacles for the city to overcome.

Architecture

There is perhaps no city in India that can compare with Delhi in the number of its monuments. These edifices illustrate the types of Indian architecture from the time of the imperial Gupta dynasty 1,600 years ago to the period of British rule, when the style of such architects as Sir Edwin Lutyens and Sir Herbert Baker was in evidence in New Delhi. Delhi is parti-cularly rich in material for the study of Indo-Muslim archi-tecture.

The monuments of the early Pashtun style (1193–1320) – represented by the Quwat-ul-Islam mosque, the Qutb Minar, the tomb of Iltutmish (ruled 1211–36), and the Ala'i Gate – reveal the adoption and adaptation of Hindu materials and style to Islamic motifs and requirements. One of the earliest examples of Islamic architecture to survive in the subcontinent is the Quwat-ul-Islam mosque (completed 1196), consisting of cloisters around a courtyard with the sanctuary to the west. In 1198 an arched facade (*maqsurah*) was built in front to give the building an Islamic aspect, but its rich floral decoration and corbelled arches are Indian in character. The Qutb Minar, a tall (288 feet; 88 metres high), fluted tower with balconies, stood outside this mosque. Iltutmish's tomb is the finest early Islamic tomb to survive. Its interior, covered with Arabic inscriptions, in its richness displays a strong Indian quality.

The later Pashtun styles represented in Tughlakabad and in the tombs of the Sayyid kings (1414–51) and Lodi kings (1451–1526) are characterized by finer domes and decoration and the use of finer marbles and tiles. The Mughal building style flourished from the mid-sixteenth to the late seventeenth century: Persian, Indian, and the various provincial styles were successfully fused to produce works of unusual refinement and quality. The tomb of Humayun, begun in 1564, inaugurates the new style. Built of red sandstone and marble, it shows considerable Persian influence. The later Mughal architecture is found in the Red Fort (Lal Qila) and the Principal Mosque (Jama Masjid).

The Red Fort – so called because of its red sandstone walls – is one of the most important buildings of the city. It was built by Shah Jahan in the mid-seventeenth century. The massive walls, 75 feet (23 metres) in height, enclose a complex of palaces, gardens, military barracks, and other buildings. The two most famous of these are the Hall of Public Audience (*Diwan-i-Am*), with its 60 red sandstone pillars supporting a flat roof, and the smaller Hall of Private Audience (*Diwan-i-Khas*) with a pavilion of white marble, which housed the famous Peacock Throne.

The architectural styles in the British period – represented by the Central Secretariat; Parliament House (Sansad Bhavan); and the Presidential House (Rashtrapati Bhavan, formerly the British viceroy's house) – combine the best features of the modern English school of architecture with traditional Indian forms. Sir Edwin Lutyens was responsible for the planning of

New Delhi and the design of the Presidential House. The New Delhi plan was characterized by wide avenues with trees in double rows on either side, creating vistas and connecting various points of interest. Besides the diagonal road pattern the most prominent feature is the Central Vista Park, starting from the National Stadium in the east, continuing to the All India War Memorial Arch (popularly called the India Gate) and the Central Secretariat (*Kendriya Sachivalaya*), and culminating in the west at the Presidential House. In this, Lutyens' single most important building (built 1913–30), he combined aspects of classical architecture with features of Indian decoration.

Post independence, public buildings in Delhi began to show a utilitarian bias and a search for a synthesis of Indian and western styles. The Children's Building (a children's centre) and Rabindra Building (a fine arts centre) show a trend toward a new style, using modern materials. Along the Yamuna riverfront, memorials set in flowering gardens have been built for such twentieth-century national leaders as Mahatma Gandhi (*Raj Ghat*), Jawaharlal Nehru (*Shanti Vana*), and Lal Bahadur Shastri (*Vijay Ghat*).

Economy

In the economy of Delhi, the service sector comes first in importance and is the largest employer. The industrial sector is second, and the commercial sector third. Agriculture once contributed significantly to the economy but now is of little importance. A substantial proportion of Delhi's working population is engaged in various services, including public administration, the professions, the liberal arts, and various personal, domestic, and unskilled-labour services. As a trading and commercial centre, Delhi has held a dominant position in northern India for many centuries. In modern times it has also become a manufacturing centre and one of India's most important sources of export goods.

Traditionally Delhi has been renowned for its artistic work, such as ivory carving and painting, gold and silver embroidery, decorative ware, copperware, and brassware. In modern times industry has become diversified, and Delhi has become important for small-scale industries such as electronics and engineering goods, automobile parts, precision instruments, machinery, and electrical appliances. Clothing, sports and leather goods, handloom products, and handicrafts are also produced. A large and thriving tourist sector has also developed.

Delhi's position as the national capital and as a major industrial city has accentuated its function as a banking, wholesale-trade, and distribution centre. It is the headquarters of the Reserve Bank of India and of the regional offices of the State Bank and other banking institutions. It is also a divisional headquarters for the insurance business and an important stock-exchange centre. Delhi has long acted as a major distribution centre for much of northern India – much of the distributive trade carried on from within the Old Delhi area, where most of the markets are located. The city is also a focal point in India's transportation network, with the most important air terminus in northern India for both domestic and international air services.

Cultural life

Delhi's cultural life has been influenced considerably by the cosmopolitan character of its population. Much has been borrowed and adapted from western culture, a process accelerated since independence by the influence of the modern mass media. Television, however, has also facilitated a greater awareness of regional and national interests. Although the cultural activities of earlier days – such as dancing, music, and poetry forums – have been yielding place to the cinema, the cabaret, and clubs, there are also theatre groups and institutions that have fostered indigenous literature and fine arts. Many of India's major cultural institutions – including the national academies of music, dance, and drama; of art; and of letters – are located in Delhi, as are many libraries, archives, and museums. Delhi is home to numerous fairs and festivals, including religious festivals and celebrations, and an annual film festival.

Delhi is a city of gardens and fountains, notable examples being the Roshan Ara Gardens and the meticulously planned and laid out Mughal Gardens. Many park and garden areas have grown up around historical monuments, such as the Lodi Gardens (around the Lodi Tombs) and the Firoz Shah Kotla Grounds (around Ashoka's Pillar). Among the major recreation areas are the Delhi Ridge and the Yamuna riverfront.

AGRA

Lying about 125 miles (200 kilometres) south-east of Delhi and founded by Sultan Sikandar Lodi in the early sixteenth century, Agra was the Mughal capital during various periods of their Empire. In the late eighteenth century the city fell successively to the Jats, the Marathas, the Mughals, the ruler of Gwalior and, finally, the British in 1803. It was the capital of Agra (later North-Western) province from 1833 to 1868, and was one of the main centres of the Indian Mutiny (1857–58). Agra is a major road and rail junction, and a commercial and industrial centre known for its leather goods, cut stone, and hand-woven carpets. Tourism is a major factor in the city's economy.

Agra is best known as the site of the Taj Mahal (seventeenth century). It is also the site of the sixteenth-century Red Fort (1565–74), built by Akbar, which contains the seventeenth-century Pearl Mosque (*Moti Masjid*), constructed of white marble; a palace, the *Jahangiri Mahal*; the Great Mosque (*Jami' Masjid*), with its monumental Victory Gate (*Buland Darwaza*), one of the finest mosques of the Mughal period; and the elegant white marble Itimad al-Dawlah tomb (1628).

The beautiful Taj Mahal was the crowning architectural achievement of the emperor Shah Jahan (1628–58). In its harmonious proportions and its fluid incorporation of decorative elements, the Taj Mahal is distinguished as the finest example of Mughal architecture, a blending of Indian, Persian, and Islamic styles. It was built to immortalize Shah Jahan's favourite wife, Mumtaz Mahal ("Chosen One of the Palace"), who died in childbirth in 1631 after having been the emperor's inseparable companion since their marriage in 1612. The name Taj Mahal is a corruption of her title.

The plans for the complex have been attributed to various architects of the period, although the chief architect was probably Ustad Ahmad Lahawri, an Indian of Persian descent. The five principal elements of the complex – main gateway, garden, mosque, *jawab* (literally "answer", a building mirroring the mosque), and mausoleum (including its four minarets) – were conceived and designed as a unified entity according to the tenets of Mughal building practice, which allowed no subsequent addition or alteration. Building commenced about 1632. More than 20,000 workers were employed from India, Persia, the Ottoman Empire, and Europe to complete the mausoleum itself by about 1638–39; the adjunct buildings were finished by 1643, and decoration work continued until at least 1647. Construction of the 42-acre (17-hectare) complex spanned 22 years, at a cost between four and five million rupees.

Resting in the middle of a wide plinth 23 feet (7 metres) high, the mausoleum proper is of white marble that reflects various hues according to the intensity of sunlight or moonlight. It has four nearly identical facades, each with a wide central arch rising to 108 feet (33 metres) and chamfered (slanted) corners incorporating smaller arches. The majestic central dome, which reaches a height of 240 feet (73 metres) at the tip of its finial, is surrounded by four lesser domes. The acoustics inside the main dome cause the single note of a flute to reverberate five times. The interior of the mausoleum is organized around an octagonal marble chamber ornamented with low-relief carvings and *pietra dura* (stone mosaics); therein are the cenotaphs of Mumtaz Muhal and Shah Jahan. These false tombs are enclosed by a finely wrought filigree marble screen. Beneath the tombs, at garden level, lie the true sarcophagi. Standing gracefully apart from the central building, at each of the four corners of the square plinth, are elegant minarets.

Flanking the mausoleum near the north-western and north-eastern edges of the garden, respectively, are two symmetrically identical buildings – the mosque, which faces east, and its *jawab*, which faces west and provides aesthetic balance. Built of red Sikri sandstone with marble-necked domes and architraves, they contrast with the mausoleum's white marble.

The garden is set out along classical Mughal lines – a square quartered by long watercourses (pools) – with walking paths, fountains, and ornamental trees. The southern end of the complex is graced by a wide red sandstone gateway with a recessed central arch, two storeys high. White marble panelling around the arch is inlaid with black Qur'anic lettering and floral designs. The main arch is flanked by two pairs of smaller arches. Crowning the northern and southern facades of the gateway are matching rows of white cupola-like chattris (*chhattri*s), 11 to each facade, accompanied by thin ornamental minarets that rise to some 98 feet (30 metres). At the four corners of the structure are octagonal towers capped with larger chattris.

Two notable decorative features are repeated throughout the complex: *pietra dura* and Arabic calligraphy. As embodied in the Mughal craft, *pietra dura* incorporates the inlay of semiprecious stones of various colours, such as lapis lazuli, jade, crystal, turquoise, and amethyst, in highly formalized and intertwining geometric and floral designs. The colours serve to moderate the dazzling expanse of the white Makrana marble. Under the direction of Amanat Khan al-Shirazi, Qur'anic verses were inscribed across numerous sections of the Taj Mahal in calligraphy. One of the inscriptions in the gateway is known as Daybreak (Qur'an, 89: 28–30) and invites the faithful to enter paradise. Calligraphy also encircles the soaring arched entrances to the mausoleum proper. To ensure its uniform appearance from the vantage point of the terrace, the lettering increases in size according to its relative height and distance from the viewer.

FATEHPUR SIKRI

The deserted Mughal city of Fatehpur Sikri, one of the most notable achievements of Islamic architecture in India, is about 25 miles (40 kilometres) south-west of Agra. It was founded in 1569 by the great Mughal emperor Akbar. In that year Akbar had visited the Muslim hermit Chishti, who was residing in the village of Sikri. Chishti correctly foretold that Akbar's wish for an heir would be gratified with the birth of a son, who was born in Sikri that very year (he would later rule as the emperor Jahangir). The grateful Akbar decided that the site of Sikri was auspicious and made it his capital.

Deserted only a few years after it was built, when the Mughal capital was moved to Delhi in 1586 because of the inadequate water supply, Fatehpur Sikri is a great complex of palaces and lesser residences and religious and official buildings, all erected on top of a rocky ridge. Akbar personally directed the building of the *Jami' Masjid* (Great Mosque, 1571), which stretches some 540 feet (165 metres) in length and contains an ornate tomb for Chishti. One of the finest mosques of the period, it served as a model for later congregational mosques built by the Mughals. The mosque's southern entrance, the colossal gateway *Buland Darwaza* (Victory Gate, 1575), gives a feeling of immense strength and height and is one of India's greatest architectural works. Constructed out of red sandstone, it is attractively carved.

Fatehpur Sikri contains other early Mughal structures, exhibiting both Muslim and Hindu architectural influences, including the palace of Akbar's wife (*Jodha Bai*), the exquisitely carved Turkish Sultana's house (the *Panch-Mahal*), and the *Divan-e 'Amm*. The so-called *Divan-e Khass* (Hall of Private Audience) is arresting in its interior arrangement, which has a single massive column encircled by brackets supporting a stone throne platform, from which radiate four railed balconies.

VARANASI

Located on the left bank of the Ganges river, Varanasi is one of the seven sacred cities of the Hindus, and one of the oldest continuously inhabited cities in the world. Its early history is that of the first Aryan settlement in the middle Ganges valley. By the second millennium BCE, Varanasi was a seat of Aryan religion and philosophy and was also a commercial and industrial centre famous for its muslin and silk fabrics, perfumes, ivory works, and sculpture. Varanasi was the capital of the kingdom of Kasi during the time of Buddha (sixth century BCE), who gave his first sermon at nearby Sarnath. The city remained a centre of religious, educational, and artistic activities as attested by the celebrated Chinese traveller Hsüan-tsang, who visited it in c. 635 CE and said that the city extended for about 3 miles (5 kilometres) along the western bank of the Ganges.

Varanasi subsequently declined during three centuries of Muslim occupation, beginning in 1194. Many of the city's Hindu temples were destroyed. The Mughal emperor Akbar in the sixteenth century brought some relief to the city's religious and cultural activities. There was another setback during the reign of the Mughal emperor Aurangzeb in the late seventeenth century, but later the Marathas sponsored a new revival. Varanasi became an independent kingdom in the eighteenth century, and under subsequent British rule it remained a commercial and religious centre. In 1910 the British made Varanasi a new Indian state, with Ramnagar (on the opposite bank) as headquarters but with no jurisdiction over the city of Varanasi. In 1949, after Indian independence, the Varanasi state became part of the state of Uttar Pradesh.

Varanasi has the finest river frontage in India, with miles of *ghats* (steps) for religious bathing. An array of shrines, temples, and palaces rises tier-on-tier from the water's edge. The inner streets of the city are narrow, winding, and impassable for motor traffic; the newer, outer suburbs are more spacious and are laid out more systematically. The sacred city is bounded by a road known as Panchakosi; every devout Hindu hopes to walk this road and to visit the city once in a lifetime and, if possible, to die there in old age. More than 1,000,000 pilgrims visit the city each year.

Among the city's numerous temples the most venerated are that of Visvanatha, dedicated to Shiva; that of Sankatmochana, dedicated to the monkey-god Hanuman; and that of Durga. The Durga Temple is famous for the swarms of monkeys that inhabit the large trees near it. The Great Mosque of Aurangzeb is another prominent religious building. Two of the more important modern temples are those of Tulasi Manas and the Visvanatha on the campus of the Banaras Hindu University. At Sarnath, a few miles north of Varanasi, there are ruins of ancient Buddhist monasteries and temples as well as temples built by the Maha Bodhi Society and by Chinese, Burmese, and Tibetan Buddhists.

Varanasi has been a city of Hindu learning through the ages. There are innumerable schools and countless Brahman *pandits* (learned men), responsible for the continuation of traditional learning, as well as three universities. The city is also a centre of arts and crafts and of music and dance. It is famous for the production of silks and brocades, as well as for wooden toys, bangles made of glass, ivory work, and brassware.

MUMBAI (BOMBAY)

Mumbai is the country's financial and commercial centre and principal port on the Arabian Sea. Located on a site of ancient settlement, Mumbai took its name from the local goddess Mumba – a form of Parvati, the consort of Shiva – whose temple once stood in what is now the south-eastern section of the city.

The city occupies a peninsular site originally composed of seven islets lying off the Konkan Coast. Since the seventeenth century, drainage and reclamation projects, as well as the construction of causeways and breakwaters, have joined the islets to form a larger body known as Bombay Island. East of the island are the sheltered waters of Bombay Harbour. In 1950 Mumbai (then called Bombay) expanded northward with the inclusion of the large island of Salsette. By 1957 a number of suburban municipal boroughs and some neighbouring villages were incorporated into Greater Bombay. Since then the Mumbai metropolitan region has continued to expand. The largest of the harbour's islands is Elephanta, which is famous for its eighth- and ninth-century cave temples.

The older part of Mumbai is much built up and the city's history of burgeoning urbanization has created slums areas. The financial district is located in the southern part of the city (around old Fort Bombay). Farther south (around Colaba) and to the west along Netaji Subhas Road (Marine Drive) and on the affluent Malabar Hill are residential neighbourhoods. To the north of the fort area is the principal business district, which gradually merges into a commercial-residential area. Still farther north are residential areas, and beyond them are recently developed industrial areas as well as some shantytown districts.

A high rate of air and water pollution has been caused by the many factories still crowding the city, the growing volume of motor-vehicle traffic, and nearby oil refineries. City planners have sought, with mixed results, to persuade business enterprises to locate across Bombay Harbour in the developing "twin city" of New Mumbai, by banning the development of new industrial units and the expansion of existing ones inside the city.

Mumbai's growth since the 1940s has been steady if not phenomenal. At the turn of the twentieth century its population was 850,000; by 1981 it had grown to more than 8,200,000. The city has one of the highest population densities in the world: in 1981 Greater Bombay had an average of more than 35,000 persons per square mile; some parts of the inner city now have nearly one million persons per square mile, perhaps the world's highest density. The city is truly cosmopolitan, with representatives of almost every religion and region of the world. Almost half of the population is Hindu; but there are also important communities of Muslims, Christians, Buddhists, Jains, Sikhs, Zoroastrians, and Jews.

History

The Kolis, an aboriginal tribe of fishermen, were the earliest known inhabitants, though Paleolithic stone implements found at Kandivli, in Greater Mumbai, indicate human occupation during the Stone Age. The area was known as Heptanesia to the ancient Greek astronomer and geographer Ptolemy, and was a centre of maritime trade with Persia and Egypt in 1000 BCE. It was part of Asoka's empire in the third century BCE and was ruled in the sixth–eighth century CE by the Calukyas, who left their mark on Elephanta Island (Gharapuri). The Walkeswar Temple at Malabar Point was probably built during the rule of Silahara chiefs from the Konkan Coast (ninth–thirteenth century). Under the Yadavas of Devagiri (1187–1318), the settlement of Mahikavati (Mahim) on Bombay Island was founded in response to raids by the Khalji dynasty of Hindustan in 1294. In 1348 the city was conquered by invading Muslim forces and became part of the kingdom of Gujarat.

A Portuguese attempt to conquer Mahim failed in 1507, but in 1534 Sultan Bahadur Shah, the ruler of Gujarat, ceded the island to the Portuguese. In 1661 it came under British control as part of the marriage settlement between King Charles II and Catherine of Braganza, sister of the king of Portugal. The crown ceded it to the East India Company in 1668. In the beginning, Bombay merely gave the company a toehold on the west coast, but with the fall of the Mughal Empire and the destruction of Maratha power in the nineteenth century, trade and communications to the mainland were established and those to Europe were extended – Bombay's prosperity had begun. In 1857 the first spinning and weaving mill was established, and by 1860 Bombay had become the largest cotton market in India. The American Civil War (1861–65) and the resulting cutoff of cotton supplies to Britain caused a great trade boom in Bombay. But, with the end of the Civil War, cotton prices crashed and the bubble burst. By that time, however, Bombay had become a strong centre of import trade.

With the opening of the Suez Canal in 1869 Bombay prospered, though slums and unsanitary conditions steadily multiplied with its increasing population. Plague broke out in 1896, and a City Improvement Trust was established to open new localities for settlement and to erect dwellings for the artisan classes. An ambitious scheme for the construction of a seawall to enclose an area of 1,300 acres (525 hectares) was proposed in 1918, but it was not finished until the completion of what is now Netaji Subhas Road, from Nariman Point to Malabar Point, after the Second World War. In the postwar years the development of residential quarters in suburban areas was begun, and the administration of Bombay city through a municipal corporation was extended to the suburbs of Greater Bombay. The city had served as the former capital of Bombay presidency and Bombay state, and it was made the capital of Maharashtra state in 1960.

During the late nineteenth and early twentieth centuries, Bombay was a centre of both Indian nationalist and regional Maratha political activity. In 1885 the first session of the Indian National Congress was held in the city, and at its 1942 session the Congress passed the "Quit India" resolution, which demanded complete independence. From 1956 until 1960 Bombay was the scene of intense Maratha protests against the two-language (Marathi-Gujarati) make-up of Bombay state, a legacy of British imperialism, which led to the state's partition into the modern states of Gujarat and Maharashtra.

Architecture

Bombay's architecture is a mixture of florid Gothic styles, characteristic of the eighteenth and nineteenth centuries, and contemporary designs. The older administrative and commercial buildings are intermingled with skyscrapers and multistorey concrete-block buildings.

Perhaps Mumbai's most famous monuments are Elephanta's eighth- and ninth-century cave temples. Situated atop a large hill, they occupy some 54,800 square feet (5,000 square metres). The main temple is a long hall stretching 90 feet (27 metres); carved into the rock on the walls and ceiling of the cave are rows of columns and crossbeams. The plan of the temple is such that important points are laid out in the form of a mandala. A series of sculptured panels lining the walls of the cave portrays images from Indian mythology, the most celebrated of which is the 20 feet (6 metre) high Trimurti – a three-headed bust of Shiva in the roles of destroyer, preserver, and creator emerging from a mountain. Other sculptures depict Shiva crushing Ravana with his toe; the marriage of Shiva and Parvati; Shiva bringing the Ganges river to earth by letting her flow through his hair; and Shiva as the embodiment of cosmic energy, dancing to drums. A *linga* (phallic symbol) is housed in a sanctuary at the western end of the temple. When the island was ceded to the Portuguese in the sixteenth century, it ceased to be a place of worship.

Economy

Mumbai has long been the centre of India's cotton-textile industry, which has remained important but also has been in decline. New growth industries – metals, chemicals, automobiles, electronics, engineering, and a host of ancillary enterprises, as well as such industries as food processing, papermaking, printing, and publishing – have been at the core of expansion of manufacturing employment. The city also contains the Indian Atomic Energy Commission. However, housing is scarce for all but the very rich, and commercial and industrial enterprises find it increasingly difficult to attract middle-level professional, technical, or managerial staff. There is continuous in-migration of unskilled labour from the hinterland.

The city is the economic hub and commercial and financial centre of India. The Reserve Bank of India, the country's Central Bank, a number of other commercial banks, and the Life Insurance Corporation of India as well as other major long-term investment financial institutions, are located in Mumbai. The Bombay Stock Exchange is the country's leading stock and share market.

Cultural life

Mumbai's cultural life reflects its polyglot population. The city is the stronghold of the Indian film industry, and has an open-air theatre. Western and Indian music concerts, festivals and Indian dance shows are performed throughout the year. The Prince of Wales Museum of Western India, housed in a building of Indo-Saracenic architecture, contains three main sections of art, archaeology, and natural history. Nearby is the Jehangir Art Gallery. Mumbai is an important centre for the Indian printing industry and has a vigorous press. All-India Radio is centred in the city, and television services there began in 1972.

Krishnagiri Forest, a national park in the north of Greater Mumbai, is a pleasant vacation resort located near the Kanheri

Caves, site of an ancient Buddhist university; the more than 100 caves contain gigantic Buddhist sculptures dating from the second to ninth century CE. There are several public gardens, including the Jijamata Garden, which houses Mumbai's zoo, and the Baptista Garden, located on a water reservoir in Mazagaon.

KOLKATA (CALCUTTA)

Located on the east bank of the Hughli (Hooghly) river, up-stream from the head of the Bay of Bengal, Kolkata (formerly Calcutta) is India's largest city and one of its major ports. It is the cultural, artistic, literary, and intellectual centre of the country. Fashioned by the colonial British in the manner of a grand European capital, yet with a large number of its residents living in the meanest of slums, contemporary Kolkata is a city of sharp contrasts. No other Indian city has its intellectual vitality and political awareness, and a lively trading of polemics on walls has led to Kolkata being dubbed the "city of posters."

The most striking aspect of the layout of Kolkata is its rectangular, north-south orientation. With the exception of the central areas where Europeans formerly lived, the city has grown haphazardly. The bulk of the city's administrative and commercial activity is concentrated in the Barabazar district, a small area north of the Maidan. This has encouraged the development of a pattern of daily commuting that has over-burdened Kolkata's transportation system, utilities, and other municipal facilities.

The city also has an acute housing shortage. There are hundreds of *basti*s (slums), where about one-third of the city's population lives; and, following a high rate of population growth for more than a century, overcrowding has reached virtually intolerable proportions in many sections of the city. Large refugee colonies have sprung up in the northern and southern suburbs. More than four-fifths of the population is Hindu. Muslims and Christians constitute the largest minorities, but there are some Sikhs, Jains, and Buddhists. Kolkata was ethnically segregated under British rule, the Europeans living in the city centre and Indians living to the north and south. The pattern of segregation has continued in the contemporary city, although the distribution is now based on religious, linguistic, educational, and economic criteria.

History

The name Kalikata was mentioned in the rent-roll of the Mughal emperor Akbar (reigned 1556–1605) and also in the *Manasa-mangal* of the Bengali poet Bipradas (1495). The history of Kolkata as the British settlement of Calcutta dates to the time of the Mughal Empire, when Job Charnock, an agent of the English East India Company, established a trading post there in 1690. In 1696, when a rebellion broke out in the nearby district of Burdwan, the Mughal provincial administration permitted the company to fortify the trading post in order to defend themselves. The rebels were easily crushed by the Mughal government, but the settlers' defensive structure remained and in 1700 came to be known as Fort William. In 1698 the English were allowed to purchase the *zamindari* right (the right of revenue collection; in effect, the ownership) of three local villages which had been settled by Indian merchants.

In 1717 the Mughal emperor Farrukh-siyar granted the East India Company freedom of trade in return for a yearly payment of 3,000 rupees; this arrangement gave a great impetus to the growth of Calcutta. A large number of Indian merchants flocked to the city. The servants of the company, under the company's flag, carried on a duty-free private trade. When the Marathas from the south-west began incursions against the Mughals in the western districts of Bengal in 1742, the British obtained permission from the *nawab* (ruler) of Bengal to dig an entrenchment, later known as the Maratha Ditch; this came to mark the city's eastern boundary.

In 1756 the *nawab*'s successor, Siraj-ud-Dawlah, captured the fort and sacked the town. Calcutta was recaptured in January 1757 and the *nawab* defeated shortly afterward at Plassey (June 1757), after which British rule in Bengal was assured. Gobindapore was cleared of its forests, and the new Fort William was built on its present site, overlooking the Hooghly at Calcutta, where it became the symbol of British military ascendancy.

Calcutta did not become the capital of British India until 1772, when the first governor-general, Warren Hastings, transferred all important offices to the city from Murshidabad. In 1773 Bombay (now Mumbai) and Madras (Chennai) became subordinate to the government at Fort William.

In 1706 the population of Calcutta was about 10,000 to 12,000. It increased to nearly 120,000 by 1752 and to 180,000 by 1821. The White (British) Town was built on ground that had been raised and drained. Outside the British town were built the mansions of the newly rich, as well as clusters of huts. The names of different quarters of the city – such as Kumartuli (the potters' district) and Sankaripara (the

conch-shell workers' district) – still indicate the various occupational castes of the residents of the growing metropolis. Two
distinct areas, one British, one Indian, came to coexist in
Calcutta.

Public improvements to conditions in the city – having been
described as pestilential – took place between 1814 and 1836,
but cyclones in 1864, 1867, and 1870 devastated the poorer,
low-lying areas. By successive stages, as British power extended over the subcontinent, the whole of northern India
became a hinterland for the port of Calcutta. The construction
of railways (beginning in 1854) quickened the development of
business and industry. It was at this time that the Grand Trunk
Road from Calcutta to Peshawar (now in Pakistan) was
completed. British mercantile, banking, and insurance interests
flourished, and the Indian sector became a hub of commerce.
Calcutta became the intellectual centre of the subcontinent.

The twentieth century marked the beginning of Calcutta's
woes. Lord Curzon, viceroy of India, partitioned Bengal in
1905, and in 1912 the capital of British India was moved from
Calcutta to Delhi. As Calcutta's population grew larger, social
problems also grew, as did demands for home rule for India.
Communal riots occurred in 1926 and, when Mahatma
Gandhi called for noncompliance with unjust laws, riots
occurred in 1930. In the Second World War, Japanese air
raids on Calcutta's docks caused damage and loss of life. The
most serious communal riots of all took place in 1946, when
the partition of British India became imminent and tensions
between Muslims and Hindus reached their height.

In 1947 the partition of Bengal between India and Pakistan
left Calcutta the capital of West Bengal only, losing the trade of
a part of its former hinterland. At the same time, millions of
refugees from East Pakistan (now Bangladesh) flocked to
Calcutta, aggravating social problems and increasing over-

crowding, which had already assumed serious proportions. Today, although the city now known as Kolkata is not as economically dynamic as some Indian cities, it continues to be the cultural, artistic, literary, and intellectual centre of the country.

Architecture

The Kolkata cityscape has changed rapidly. The Chowringhee area in central Kolkata, once a row of palatial houses, has been given up to offices, hotels, and shops. Western influence is dominant in Kolkata's architectural monuments. The Raj Bhavan (the state governor's residence) is an imitation of Kedleston Hall in Derbyshire, UK; the High Court resembles the Cloth Hall at Ypres, Belgium; the Town Hall is in Grecian style with a Doric-Hellenic portico; St Paul's Cathedral is of Indo-Gothic-style architecture; the Writers' Building is of Gothic-style architecture with statuary on top; the Indian Museum is in an Italian style; and the General Post Office, with its majestic dome, has Corinthian columns. The beautiful column of the Sahid Minar (Ochterlony Monument) is 165 feet (50 metres) high. Its base is Egyptian, its column Syrian, and its cupola in the Turkish style. The Victoria Memorial represents an attempt to combine classical western influence with Mughal architecture; the Nakhoda Mosque is modelled on Akbar's Tomb at Sikandra; and the Birla Planetarium is based on the *stupa* (Buddhist reliquary) at Sanchi.

The West Bengal Legislative Council is a dignified building in the modern architectural style. The Ramakrishna Mission Institute of Culture, the most important example of post-independence construction, follows the style of ancient Hindu palace architecture in north-western India.

Economy

Kolkata's position as one of India's preeminent economic centres is rooted in its industries, financial and trade activities, and role as a major port. It is also a major centre for printing, publishing, and newspaper circulation, as well as for recreation and entertainment. In the 1980s large-scale public works programmes and centralized regional planning contributed to the improvement of economic and social conditions. Since the 1990s, large-scale manufacturing companies have been mostly replaced with small-scale assembly factories, as well as commercial and other service-sector economic firms. Militant trade unions have, however, slowed the introduction of new technology and deterred entrepreneurial activity and investment. Unemployment has been a continuing and growing problem since the 1950s.

Kolkata is the world's largest processor of jute, with mills on both banks of the Hooghly river. Engineering constitutes the city's other major industry. In addition, city factories produce and distribute a variety of consumer goods – notably foodstuffs, beverages, tobacco, and textiles – other light manufactures, and chemicals. The Calcutta Stock Exchange plays an important part in the organized financial market of the country. Foreign banks also have a significant business base in the city and the Indian Chamber of Commerce is based there.

Cultural life

Kolkata is the most important cultural centre of India. It is the birthplace of modern Indian literary and artistic thought, and the efforts of its citizens to preserve Indian culture and civilization have no parallel in the rest of the country. Numerous and diverse organizations that contribute to Kolkata's cultural life have been established there, including the Asiatic Society, the Bengal Literary Society (Bangiya Sahitya Parishad), the Ramakrishna Mission Institute of Culture, the Academy of Fine Arts, the Birla Academy of Art and Culture, and the Maha Bodhi Society.

Greater Kolkata's Indian Museum, founded in 1814, is the oldest in India and is the largest museum of its kind in the country; the archaeology and numismatic sections contain the most valuable collections. Other museums include Victoria Memorial, which traces Britain's relations with India; and the Asutosh Museum of Indian Art, which exhibits the folk art of Bengal. Valuable library collections are to be found in the Asiatic Society, Bengal Literary Society, and the University of Calcutta, while the National Library is the largest in India and contains a fine collection of rare books and manuscripts.

The literary movement spawned in Kolkata in the mid-nineteenth century, through exposure to western forms, sparked a cultural renaissance throughout India. The best exponent of this movement was Rabindranath Tagore, winner of the Nobel Prize for Literature of 1913. Kolkata is also a centre of traditional and contemporary music and dance. In 1937 Tagore inaugurated the first All-Bengal Music Conference in the city. Since then, a number of classical Indian music conferences have been held there every year. Uday Shankar's school of dance, music, and drama has been in the city since 1965. Kolkata's National Theatre was established in the 1870s, and the city is an important centre of professional and amateur theatre and of experimental drama. The city has also been a pioneering centre of motion-picture production in India.

There are more than 200 parks, squares, and open spaces. The Maidan, about 2 miles (3.2 kilometres) in length and a mile (1.6 kilometres) in width, is the best known; the major football (soccer), cricket, and hockey fields are located there. Adjacent to the Maidan is one of the oldest cricket fields in the world, Ranji Stadium, in the Eden Gardens.

DARJEELING (DARJILING)

Darjeeling (Darjiling) lies about 305 miles (490 kilometres) north of Kolkata (Calcutta) on a long, narrow mountain ridge of the Sikkim Himalayas. On a clear day the city affords a magnificent view of Kanchenjunga (28,169 feet; 8,586 metres), and Mount Everest can be seen from a nearby viewing point. Darjeeling is a noted hill resort, and the city's economy is based largely on tourism.

Darjeeling was ceded by the raja of Sikkim to the British in 1835 and was developed as a sanatorium for British troops. It was constituted a municipality in 1850. The Chaurastha ("Four Roads") district encompasses the Mall, where the roads converge; it is the city's main shopping centre and the most attractive promenade. Observatory Hill, Darjeeling's highest point, is crowned by Mahakal Temple, which is sacred to both Hindus and Buddhists.

Birch Hill contains a natural park and the Himalayan Mountaineering Institute. The Lloyd Botanic Gardens, well-known for their varieties of Himalayan flora, were laid out in 1865. Besides these attractions, the city has a zoo, a natural history museum, and a racecourse.

RAJASTHAN

Rajasthan, meaning "The Abode of the Rajas," lies in the north-west of India. It is one of the least densely populated states in India – there are only a few large towns, including Jaipur (the capital city), Ajmer, Jodhpur, Udaipur, Kota, Bikaner, and Alwar. The Rajputs, though representing only a small percentage of the population, are its most important section. They are proud of their warlike reputation and of their ancestry. In the north and west the Jats and Gujars are among the largest agricultural communities.

The principal religion is Hinduism, followed by Islam, and there are smaller communities of Christians and Sikhs. Jainism has followers among the trading class and the wealthy section of society, with pilgrimage centres at Mahavirji, Ranakpur, Dhulev, and Karera. Nathdwara is an important religious centre for the Vallabhacarya sect of Krishna followers.

History

Archaeological evidence indicates that early humans lived along the banks of the Banas river and its tributaries some 100,000 years ago. Arising between the seventh and eleventh centuries were several Rajput dynasties, including that of the Gurjara-Pratiharas, who kept the Arab invaders of Sindh at bay. By the eleventh century the Cauhans (Cahamanas) had emerged as the major power in eastern areas of the state. In the following centuries other clans, such as the Kachwahas, Bhattis, and Rathors, succeeded in establishing independent kingdoms in the region.

The second battle of Tarain, fought near Delhi in 1192, initiated a new period in Rajasthan's history. Muhammad Ghuri's victory over a Rajput army under Prthviraja III not only led to the destruction of Rajput power in the Gangetic Plain but also firmly established the Muslim presence in northern India. As Muslim forces pushed south and then west along the traditional routes to Gujarat, the Rajput kingdoms of Rajasthan were encircled. The next four centuries saw repeated, though unsuccessful, attempts by the central power based in Delhi to subdue the Rajput states of the region.

Rajput strength reached its zenith at the beginning of the sixteenth century under Rana Sangram Singh (Sanga) of Mewar, but he was defeated in a fierce battle by the Mughal invader Babur, and the brief splendour of a united Rajput polity waned rapidly. Toward the end of the sixteenth century the Mughal emperor Akbar destroyed Rajput strongholds; he also entered into a series of alliances with numerous Rajput ruling houses, as well as arranging marriages with Rajput princesses for himself and his heirs. Thus, many Rajput states of Rajasthan were brought into the imperial fold. Under Akbar, the Rajput states of the region were grouped together under the Suba of Ajmer, an administrative unit of the Mughal Empire.

After the death (1707) of the emperor Aurangzeb, the Rajput state of Bharatpur was developed by a Jat conqueror, but by 1803 most of the rest of Rajasthan paid tribute to the Maratha dynasties of west-central India. Later in the nineteenth century the British subdued the Marathas and organized the Rajput states into Rajputana province. During this period the idea of Indian nationalism was born. Maharishi Dayanand wrote at Udaipur his *Satyarath Prakash*, intended to restore Hinduism to its pristine purity, which created a ferment in Rajputana. Important movements of thought also occurred among the Jaina *sadhu*s (holy men) and scholars. Ajmer was the centre of political activity, and nationalist leaders included Arjun Lal Sethi, Manik Lal Varma, Gopal Singh, and Jai Narain Vyas.

After India became independent in 1947, the princely states and chiefships of Rajputana were integrated by stages into Greater Rajasthan, and the Rajput princes surrendered their political powers to the central government. In 1998 the state was the site of India's first nuclear weapons tests.

Economy

Rajasthan is a predominantly agricultural and pastoral state, and exports food grains and vegetables. Although most of its area is arid or semiarid, it is the country's largest wool-producing state. It has a monopoly in camels and in draught animals of various breeds.

There are industrial complexes at Jaipur, Kota, Udaipur, and Bhilwara. Rajasthan produces India's entire output of lead and zinc concentrates, emeralds, and garnets. More than 90 per cent of the country's gypsum and silver ore are also produced there. The main industries are based on textiles, vegetable oil, wool, minerals, and chemicals, while handicrafts, such as leather goods, marble work, jewellery, pottery, and embossed brass have earned much foreign exchange.

Cultural life

Hardly a month passes in Rajasthan without a religious festival. The most remarkable and typical is Gangor, when clay images of Mahadevi and Parvati (representing the benevolent aspects of the Hindu mother goddess) are worshipped by women of all castes for 15 days and are then taken out to be immersed in water. Their procession is joined by priests and officers and is led to the water by trumpeters and drummers. Another important festival is held at Pushkar near Ajmer, taking the form of a mixed religious festival and camel and cattle fair. The tomb of the Sufi mystic Khwajah Mu'in-ud-Din Chishti at Ajmer is one of the most sacred Muslim shrines in India. As many as 300,000 pilgrims, many from foreign countries, visit the shrine on the occasion of the saint's 'urs (death anniversary).

Rajasthan has made its contribution to Indian art, and there is a rich literary tradition, especially of bardic poetry. Chand Bardai's poem *Prithvi Raj Raso* or *Chand Raisa* – the earliest manuscript of which dates to the twelfth century – is particularly notable. A popular source of entertainment is the *khyal*, a dance drama composed in verse with festive, historical, or romantic themes.

Places of Rajasthan

Jaipur, the capital of Rajasthan, is a walled town surrounded (except to the south) by hills. Founded in 1727 by Maharaja Sawai Jai Singh to replace Amber as the capital of the princely state of Jaipur, and known for its beauty, it is sometimes called the "pink city" because its buildings are predominantly rose-coloured. The city is unique in its straight-line planning. Its chief buildings are the city palace; Jantar Mantar (an eighteenth-century open-air observatory); Hawa Mahal (Hall of Winds); Ram Bagh palace; and Nahargarh (Tiger Fort).

Ajmer is on the lower slopes of Taragarh Hill, on the summit of which stands a fortress. Probably founded about 1100 by the Rajput ruler Ajayadeva, it was annexed to the Delhi Slave dynasty in 1193. Upon payment of tribute it was returned to its Rajput rulers, but it was taken by Akbar I in 1556. In 1770 it was annexed by the Marathas, after which the area was a continual Rajput-Maratha battleground until it was ceded to the British in 1818. Architectural monuments include an ancient Jaina temple (converted *c.*1200 into a mosque); the white marble tomb complex of the Muslim saint Muʿin-ud-Din Chishti (d. 1236); and the palace of Akbar, now a museum. To the north lies Ana Sagar, a lake created in the eleventh century, on the shores of which stand marble pavilions built by Shah Jahan.

Jodhpur, founded in 1459 by Rao Jodha, a Rajput, served as the capital of the former princely state of Jodhpur. It reached the zenith of its power under the ruler Rao Maldeo (1532–69), and gave allegiance to the Mughals after the invasion of the Mughal emperor Akbar in 1561. The fort, which contains the palace and a historical museum, is built on an isolated rock eminence that dominates the city. The town's industries include the manufacture of cotton textiles, brass and iron utensils, bicycles, ink, and polo equipment. Jodhpur is also famous for its handicraft products, which include ivory goods, glass bangles, lacquerwork, marble stonework, and carpet weaving.

Udaipur, in the south of Rajasthan, lies in the hills of the Aravali Range. Established in the eighth century by Sisodia Rajputs, the dynasty was later to long resist the Muslim invasions. In the eighteenth century the state suffered from internal dissension and incursions by the Marathas, and came under British paramountcy in 1818. In 1948 it merged with the union of Rajasthan.

A walled city, Udaipur stands on a ridge crowned by the Maharana's palace, which was begun in 1570. To the west lies Lake Pichola with its two small islands and marble palaces, one of which served as a refuge for the Mughal emperor Shah Jahan when, before his accession, he revolted against his father, Jahangir. Udaipur is an agricultural distributing centre. Cloth, embroidery, ivory, and lacquerware handicrafts are also manufactured there.

Bikaner was built from 1488 by Bika, a Rajput chieftain, after he conquered the area. He died in 1504, and his successors gradually extended their possessions. The state adhered loyally to the Mughal emperors. Rai Singh, who succeeded as chieftain of Bikaner in 1571, became one of Akbar's most distinguished generals and was named the first raja of Bikaner. As Mughal dominance ebbed, wars between Bikaner and the princely state of Jodhpur raged intermittently in the eighteenth century. A treaty establishing British paramountcy was concluded in 1818, and the state was made subject to the Rajputana agency in 1883. The state's military force included the Bikaner Camel Corps, which gained renown in China during the Boxer Rebellion (1900) and in the Middle East during the First World War. In 1949 Bikaner became part of the Indian state of Rajasthan.

The old part of Bikaner city is surrounded by a stone wall that is 15–30 feet (5–9 metres) high and has five gates. Bikaner is now a trade centre for wool, hides, building stone, salt, and grain. Bikaneri woollen shawls, blankets, carpets, and sugar candy are famous, and there are also ivory and lacquerware handicrafts. The old part of the city is overlooked by a fort and has numerous buildings of bright red and yellow sandstone. Within the fort are several palaces of different periods, a museum housing Rajput miniature paintings, and a library of Sanskrit and Persian manuscripts.

PUNJAB AND AMRITSAR

Punjab state, in its present form, came into existence on November 1 1966, when most of the predominantly Hindi-speaking areas of the older unit were separated to form the new state of Haryana. Its major cities are Amritsar, Ludhiana, Jalandhar, and Patiala. The foundations of the present Punjab (historical Panjab) were laid by Banda Singh Bahadur, a hermit who became a military leader and, with his fighting band of Sikhs, temporarily liberated the eastern part of the province from Mughal rule in 1709–10. Banda Singh's defeat and execution in 1716 were followed by a prolonged struggle between the Sikhs on one side and the Mughals and Afghans on the other. By 1764–65 the Sikhs had established their dominance in the region. Ranjit Singh (1780–1839) built up the Punjab into a powerful kingdom and attached to it the adjacent provinces of Multan, Kashmir, and Peshawar.

In 1849 the Punjab fell to the troops of the English East India Company and subsequently became a province under British rule. By the late nineteenth century, however, the Indian nationalist movement took hold in this province.

One of the movement's most significant events, the massacre ordered by British general Reginald E.H. Dyer, took place at Amritsar in 1919. When India gained its independence in 1947, the British province of Punjab was split between the new sovereign states of India and Pakistan, and the smaller, eastern portion became part of India. Since independence, the history of the Indian sector of the Punjab has been dominated by Sikh agitation for a Punjabi-speaking state and thus, on November 1 1966, Punjab was divided into Haryana (with most of the Hindi-speaking areas) and a new, smaller state of Punjab. The northernmost districts were transferred to Hima chal Pradesh. Punjab's recently built capital, the city of Chandigarh, was retained as the joint administrative headquarters of Haryana and Punjab.

Although Sikhs had won the use of Punjabi within the state, by the 1980s factions of the Shiromani Akali Dal ("Leading Akali Party") and the All India Sikh Students' Federation were demanding the establishment of an autonomous Sikh homeland, or Khalistan ("Land of the Pure"). Militant groups began to use terrorism, including the indiscriminate killing of Punjabi Hindus and even those Sikhs who opposed the creation of Khalistan. In June 1984, in an effort to dislodge Sikh militants fortified in the Golden Temple (*Harimandir*), the Indian army carried out an attack. The Sikh leader Jarnail Singh Bhindranwale and most of his armed followers were killed, as were at least 100 Indian soldiers. In retaliation, Prime Minister Indira Gandhi was assassinated by two of her Sikh bodyguards. Despite numerous attempts at a negotiated settlement, a climate of violence and disorder has continued.

The economy of Punjab is characterized by a productive, increasingly commercial agriculture – largely the result of the Green Revolution, which brought modern agricultural technology to the state – a diversity of small- and medium-scale industries, and the highest per capita income in the nation. With less than 2 per cent of the total area of India, Punjab produces more than 10 per cent of India's food grain. It contributes almost half of the rice stock held by the Central Pool (national repository system of surplus food grain) and more wheat than all other states combined. The industries with the largest number of workers include cotton, woollen and silk textiles, metal products and machinery, food and beverages, and transport equipment and parts.

Folklore, ballads of love and war, fairs and festivals, dancing, music, and Punjabi literature are characteristic expressions of the state's cultural life. The origins of Punjabi literature are the mystical and religious verse of the thirteenth-century Muslim Sufi (mystic) Shaikh Farid, and of the fifteenth–sixteenth-century Guru Nanak, founder of the Sikh faith. Both used Punjabi extensively as a medium of poetic expression. Punjabi literature entered its modern phase at the beginning of the twentieth century with the writings of the poet and author Bhai Vir Singh and the poets Puran Singh and Dhani Ram Chatrik.

Punjab holds numerous religious and seasonal festivals, such as Dussehra, Diwali, and Baisakhi, as well as anniversary celebrations in honour of Gurus and saints.

The state's outstanding architectural monument is the Golden Temple at Amritsar, the largest and most important city in Punjab, and the centre of Sikhism. Amritsar was founded in 1577 by Ram Das, fourth Guru of the Sikhs, on a site granted by the Mughal emperor Akbar. Ram Das ordered the excavation of the sacred tank (pool) called *Amrita Saras* ("Pool of Nectar"), from which the city's name is derived. A temple was erected on an island in the tank's centre in 1604 by Arjun, the fifth Guru of the Sikhs, who symbolically had it placed on a lower level so that even the humblest had to step down to enter it. Entrances on all four sides signified that it was open to worshippers of all castes and creeds.

The temple was destroyed several times by Afghan invaders. During the reign (1801–39) of Maharaja Ranjit Singh it was rebuilt in marble, and the upper part of the temple was decorated with a gold foil-covered copper dome. The structure thus became known as the Golden Temple (*Harimandir*). Amritsar became the centre of the Sikh faith, and as the centre of growing Sikh power the city experienced a corresponding increase in trade.

The Temple blends Indian and Saracenic styles. Its chief motifs, such as the dome and the geometric design, are repeated in most of the Sikh places of worship. The Golden Temple is rich in gold filigree work, panels with floral designs, and marble facings inlaid with coloured stones. It is connected to land on its west by a marble causeway running across the water of the pool. Other important buildings in Amritsar include the Martyr's Memorial at Jallianwalla Bagh and the Hindu Temple of Durgiana.

TAMIL NADU, CHENNAI (MADRAS), AND MADURAI

Tamil Nadu, in the extreme south of the subcontinent, is the Tamil-speaking area of what was formerly the Madras Presidency. The state is divided naturally between the flat country along the eastern coast and the hilly regions in the north and west. The Tamils are proud of their Dravidian language and culture, and they have resisted attempts by the union government to make Hindi the national language.

While it has an industrial core in Chennai, the state capital, and the state is one of the most urbanized of India, Tamil Nadu is essentially agricultural. Most of the people live in more than 64,000 nucleated villages. The poorest low-caste villagers live in segregated areas called *ceri*. The Chennai metropolitan conurbation, covering the industrial areas, townships, and villages surrounding Chennai city, has the largest population, but there are other conurbations, of which those around Madurai, Coimbatore, and Tiruchchirappalli are the most important.

Cotton ginning, spinning, and weaving continue to be the major industries, followed by the production of automobiles, motorcycles, transformers, sugar, agricultural implements, fertilizers, cement, paper, chemicals, and electric motors. The railway-coach factory at Perambur is one of the largest in Asia. There is an oil refinery at Chennai and a larger thermal-power project at Neyveli; both are public-sector ventures. The state ranks second only to Kerala in the production of fish. Tamil Nadu is also rich in handicrafts, most notably handloomed silk, metal icons, leather work, *kalamkari* (hand-painted fabric, using natural dyes), brass, bronze, and copper-wares, and carved wood, palm leaf, and cane articles.

The history of Tamil Nadu begins with the establishment of a trinity of Tamil powers in the region – namely, the Cera, Cola, and Pandya kingdoms. By about 200 CE the influence of northern Aryan powers had progressed, there was extensive foreign trade and the Aryan sage Agastya had established himself as a cultural hero. From the mid-sixth century until the ninth century, the Calukyas of Badami, the Pallavas of Kanci, and the Pandyas of Madurai fought a long series of wars in the region. The period, nonetheless, was marked by a revival of Hinduism and the advance of the fine arts. From about 850, Tamil Nadu was dominated by the Colas. In the mid-fourteenth century the Hindu kingdom of Vijayanagar, which included all of Tamil Nadu, came into prominence – they ruled for 300 years.

In 1640 England's East India Company opened a trading post at the fishing village of Madraspatnam (now Chennai) with the permission of the local ruler. The history of Tamil Nadu from the mid-seventeenth century to 1946 is the story of the Madras Presidency in relationship to the rise and fall of British power in India. After 1946 the Madras Presidency was able to make steady progress, as it had a stable government. In 1953 the Telugu-speaking state of Andhra Pradesh was formed, and in 1956 the presidency was further divided into the states of Kerala, Mysore (now Karnataka), and Tamil Nadu.

Hinduism remains at the core of the culture. In most towns – particularly Chidambaram, Kanchipuram, Thanjavur (Tanjore), and Madurai – the *gopuram*s (gateway towers) of the temples are dominant. The car festivals, during which large chariots decorated with icons are taken in procession around the temple, attract large congregations of devotees. *Bharatanatya*, one of India's major classical dance forms, and Karnatic music are both widely practised. The Dakshina Bharat Hindi Prachar Sabha (1918) at Chennai is engaged in popularizing the Hindi language, and along with the Gandhigram Rural Institute (1956), which promotes Mahatma Gandhi's concept of rural higher education, is of national importance. A vigorous effort has been made to make Tamil instead of English the medium of instruction at university level.

Chennai (Madras)

Chennai (the government of Tamil Nadu officially changed the name of the city from Madras in 1996) lies on the Coromandel Coast. When the English East India Company built a fort and trading post there in 1639–40, the weaving of cotton fabrics was a local industry, and the English invited the weavers and native merchants to settle near the fort. By 1652 the factory of Fort St George was recognized as a presidency (an administrative unit governed by a president), and between 1668 and 1749 the company expanded its control. About 1801, by which time the last of the local rulers had been shorn of his powers, the British had become masters of southern India and Madras had become their administrative and commercial capital.

Madras developed without a plan from its seventeenth-century core, formed by the fort and the Indian quarters. To the north and north-west are the industrial areas; the main residential areas are to the west and south, and the old villages are in the centre. The most distinctive buildings in the city are the seven large temples in the Dravidian style, situated in the sections of George Town, Mylapore, and Triplicane. Of the buildings from the British period, the Chepauk Palace and the University Senate House (both in the Deccan Muslim style) and the Victoria Technical Institute and the High Court buildings (both in the Indo-Saracenic style) are generally considered to be the most attractive. In the Pallava site of Mahabalipuram, south of Chennai, a number of small temples were carved in the seventh century from outcroppings of rock; they represent some of the oldest religious buildings in the Tamil country.

Industries include vehicle factories, an electrical-engineering firm, rubber and fertilizer factories, and a refinery. The main commodities exported are leather, iron ore, and cotton textiles. Cultural institutions include the Music Academy, devoted to the encouragement of Carnatic music. The Kalakshetra is a centre of dance and music, and the Rasika Ranjini Sabha, in Mylapore, encourages the theatrical arts. The suburban town of Kodambakkam, with its numerous film studios, is described as the Hollywood of southern India. There is a small collection of East India Company antiquities in the Fort Museum and a collection of paintings in the National Art Gallery.

Madurai

Madurai is the second largest, and probably oldest, city in Tamil Nadu. Located on the Vaigai river and enclosed by the Anai, Naga, and Pasu (Elephant, Snake, and Cow) hills, the compact old city, site of the Pandya (fourth–eleventh century CE) capital, centres on Minaksi-Sundaresvara Temple. The temple, Tirumala Nayak palace, Teppakulam tank (an earthen embankment reservoir), and a 1,000-pillared hall were rebuilt in the Vijayanagar period (sixteenth–seventeenth century) after the total destruction of the city in 1310. The city walls were removed by the British in 1837 to enable the city to expand, and administrative and residential quarters formed north of the river.

Large-scale industry has developed in the suburbs, predominantly cotton spinning and weaving and the manufacture of transport equipment, tobacco, and sugar. Small-scale handloom weaving of silks and cottons, which have made Madurai famous throughout history, remains important.

KERALA AND KOCHI (COCHIN)

Kerala stretches for 360 miles (580 kilometres) along the Malabar Coast and is a region of great natural beauty. Anai Peak (8,842 feet; 2,695 metres), the highest peak of peninsular India, crowns the Western Ghats. Between the coastal plain and the rocky highlands is a sequence of plantation crops – rubber in the foothills and above that coffee and then tea. A linked chain of lagoons and backwaters along the coast, interspersed with vast coconut palm groves, forms the so-called Venice of India. The Periyar Tiger Reserve is the largest wildlife sanctuary, and there are two national parks (Eravikulam and Silent Valley) and several other wildlife sanctuaries.

Kerala is the most densely populated state in India. While only about one-fifth of the population is urban, the close proximity of scattered rural houses gives rise to tropical-rural equivalents of megalopolises, especially in the coastal plain. The major urban and industrial complexes are Cannanore, Kozhikode (Calicut), Alwaye, Kochi (Cochin)-Ernakulam, Alleppey, and Quilon. The capital is Trivandrum, where there is a large fort containing several palaces and a Vaishnava (Vishnuite) temple, which is a noted pilgrimage centre.

Kerala is a highly politicized region, but it has a long tradition of religious amity. The majority of the Malayalis are Hindus, but there are also Jains, Muslims, and Christians, who form more than a third of the population. The Jewish community remains a small, exclusive sect; there is an ancient synagogue at Kochi. It is an educationally advanced state with its own language, Malayalam, and it has the highest rate of literacy among Indian states. Owing to the former matrilineal system, women in Kerala enjoy a high social status. Some of India's most isolated tribal peoples persist in Kerala's wilderness areas.

Kerala is first mentioned (as Keralaputra) in a third-century-CE rock inscription left by the Mauryan emperor Asoka. During the first five centuries AD, the region was a part of Tamilakam and thus was sometimes partially controlled by the eastern Pandya and Cola (Chola) dynasties, as well as by the Ceras (Cheras). In the first century CE Jewish immigrants arrived, and Syrian Orthodox Christians believe that St Thomas the Apostle visited Kerala in the same century. Much of Kerala's history from the sixth to eighth century CE is obscure, but Arab traders introduced Islam later in the period. Under the Kulasekhara dynasty (c.800–1102) Malayalam emerged as a distinct language, and Hinduism became prominent.

The Colas often controlled Kerala during the eleventh and twelfth centuries. By the beginning of the fourteenth century, Ravi Varma Kulasekhara of Venad established a short-lived supremacy over southern India. After his death, Kerala became a conglomeration of warring chieftaincies, among whom the most important were Calicut (now Kozhikode) in the north and Venad in the south.

The era of foreign intervention began in 1498, when Vasco da Gama landed near Calicut. In the sixteenth century the Portuguese superseded the Arab traders and dominated the commerce of Malabar. Their attempt to establish sovereignty was thwarted by the *zamorin* (hereditary ruler) of Calicut. The Dutch ousted the Portuguese in the seventeenth century. Marthanda Varma ascended the Venad throne in 1729 and crushed Dutch expansionist designs at the Battle of Kolachel 12 years later. Marthanda Varma then adopted a European mode of martial discipline and expanded the new southern state of Travancore. His alliance in 1757 with the raja of the central state of Cochin, against the *zamorin*, enabled Cochin to survive. By 1806, however, Cochin and Travancore, as well as Malabar in the north, had become subject states under the British Madras Presidency.

Two years after India's independence, Cochin and Travancore were united as Travancore-Cochin state. The present state of Kerala was constituted on a linguistic basis in 1956 when Malabar and the Kasargod taluka of South Kanara were added to Travancore-Cochin.

Agriculture is the state's main economic activity. Kerala's principal cash yielders are perennial areca nut, cardamom, cashew nut, coconut, coffee, ginger, pepper, rubber, and tea; the major food crops are annual rice, pulses (such as peas and beans), sorghum, and tapioca. Commercial poultry farming is well developed. The forests yield valuable timbers such as ebony, rosewood, and teak, as well as industrial raw materials such as bamboo (used in the paper and rayon industries), wood pulp, charcoal, gums, and resins. Kerala ranks first among Indian states in fish production.

Most of the population is unaffected by industrialization. Unemployment is acute, and low-wage cottage industries, such as the processing of coconut fibre, employ most workers. Food processing is the largest industrial employer. Kerala has well-developed road and railway systems, and three major ports; more than 1,100 miles (1,770 kilometres) of inland waterways form main arteries for carrying bulk freight to and from the ports.

Kerala's cultural heritage contains elements of ancient Hindu culture that have been enriched by centuries of contact with both East and West. The state's impressive array of Hindu temples with copper-clad roofs, later Islamic mosques with "Malabar gables" (triangular projections at the rooftops), and Portuguese colonial Baroque churches attests to this interweaving. Traditional art forms include intricate paintings on wood, thematic murals, and an amazing variety of indoor and outdoor lamps (which has earned Kerala the sobriquet "Land of Lamps").

Literature and learning, in both Tamil and Sanskrit, flourished from the second century CE. The Malayalam language, though an offshoot of Tamil, has absorbed the best in Sanskrit and has a prolific literature. The premier modern Malayali novelist is Thakazhi Sivasankara Pillai. *Kathakali* is the classical martial dance form of Kerala, in which male performers portray both male and female characters. By contrast, the *bharata-natya* style, dating to early Tamil times, is practised exclusively by females.

Kochi (Cochin)

Cochin (now Kochi) was an insignificant fishing village until the backwaters of the Arabian Sea and the streams descending from the Ghats caused the separation of the village from the mainland, turning the landlocked harbour into one of the safest ports on India's south-western coast. The port assumed a new strategic importance and began to experience commercial prosperity.

When the Portuguese reached India's south-western coast, Pedro Álvares Cabral founded the first European settlement on Indian soil at Cochin in 1500. Vasco da Gama, discoverer of the sea route to India, established the first Portuguese factory (trading station) there in 1502, and the Portuguese viceroy Afonso de Albuquerque built the first European fort in India there in 1503. The city remained a Portuguese possession until it was conquered by the Dutch in 1663. Much Portuguese architecture still exists in the city.

Under Dutch rule (1663–1795) Cochin had its greatest prosperity. Through its harbour were shipped pepper, cardamom, and other spices and drugs as well as coir, coconut, and copra. British rule over Cochin lasted from 1795 until 1947. At the beginning of the twentieth century a modern port with dry docks and ship repair yards was constructed, and Willingdon Island (connecting Fort Cochin with Ernakulam and other townships by a rail bridge and road) was built. After India's independence, Cochin became the major training centre for the Indian Navy.

Contemporary Kochi, set among picturesque lagoons and backwaters, attracts a considerable tourist trade. At Fort Cochin is St Francis Church, built by the Portuguese in 1510 and reputedly the first European church on Indian soil. It was for a time the burial place of Vasco da Gama before his remains were taken to Portugal. Other churches as well as Hindu temples, mosques, and the historic synagogue at Mattancheri all stand in the area. The Jewish community in Kochi was the oldest in India, claiming to date from the fourth century CE. Almost all of its several thousand members had emigrated to Israel by the late twentieth century, however.

GOA

Comprising a mainland district on the country's western coast and an offshore island, Goa is located 250 miles (400 kilometres) south of Mumbai (Bombay). It has a coastline of 65 miles (105 kilometres), is hilly and includes a portion of the Western Ghats rising to nearly 4,000 feet (1,219 metres). There are three principal cities: Marmagao (Mormugão), Madgaon (Margao), and Panaji (Nova Goa).

Old Goa is, for the most part, a city of ruins. Panaji, originally a suburb of Old Goa, is built (like the parent city) on the left bank of the Mandavi estuary. Today a modern port, it contains the archbishop's palace and the government house. Marmagao, sheltered by a promontory and with a modern breakwater and quay, is the best port between Mumbai and Kozhikode (Calicut). The population is a mixture of English- and Konkani-speaking Christians and Konkani- and Marathi-speaking Hindus.

The ancient Hindu city of Goa, of which hardly a fragment survives, was built at the southernmost point of the island. It was ruled by the Kadamba dynasty from the second century CE to 1312 and by Muslim invaders of the Deccan from 1312 to 1367. It was then annexed by the Hindu kingdom of Vijaya-nagar and later conquered by the Bahmani dynasty, which founded Old Goa in 1440.

With the subdivision of the Bahmani kingdom after 1482, Goa passed into the power of Yusuf 'Adil Khan, the Muslim king of Bijapur, who was its ruler when the Portuguese first reached India. In 1510 the Portuguese captured the city, massacred all the Muslims, and appointed a Hindu, Timoja, governor of Goa. They left almost untouched the customs and constitutions of the 30 village communities on the island, abolishing only the rite of *suttee*.

Goa became the capital of the whole Portuguese empire in the east, reaching its greatest prosperity between 1575 and 1600. The appearance of the Dutch in Indian waters precipi-tated the decline of Goa. In 1603 and 1639 the city was blockaded by Dutch fleets, in 1635 it was ravaged by an epidemic, and in 1683 and 1739 it was attacked by the Marathas. The seat of the government was moved to Mor-mugão (now Marmagao) and in 1759 to Panjim (now Panaji). Cholera epidemics precipitated a decline in Old Goa, its population dwindling between 1695 and 1775 from 20,000 to 1,600; and in 1835 the city was inhabited by only a few priests, monks, and nuns.

During the nineteenth century, events of importance affect-ing the settlement were its temporary occupation by the British in 1809 as a result of Napoleon's invasion of Portugal; the governorship (1855–64) of Count de Torres Novas, who inaugurated a great number of improvements; and the military revolts of the second half of the century. After Indian claims on Goa in 1948 and 1949, Portugal came under increasing pressure to cede it, with its other possessions in the subconti-nent, to India. In mid-1954, Goan nationalists seized the

Portuguese enclaves of Dadra and Nagar Haveli and established a pro-Indian administration. Tension between India and Portugal came to a head when on December 18 1961, Indian troops supported by naval and air forces invaded and occupied Goa, Daman, and Diu. Portuguese India was, by constitutional amendment, incorporated into the Indian Union in 1962 and attained statehood in 1987.

Today, Goa remains predominantly agricultural. Manufacturers produce fertilizers, sugar, textiles, chemicals, iron pellets, and pharmaceuticals. The tourist industry developed rapidly in the late twentieth century. Economic conditions have caused emigration on a large scale, mainly to the eastern coast of Africa but also to other parts of India.

HAMPI

Hampi is the location of the great ruined city of Vijayanagar (Sanskrit: "City of Victory"), in southern India. The city and its first dynasty were founded in 1336 by five sons of Sangama, of whom Harihara and Bukka became the city's first kings. In time Vijayanagar became the greatest Empire of southern India. By serving as a barrier against invasion by the Muslim sultanates of the north, it fostered the reconstruction of Hindu life and administration after the disorders and disunities of the twelfth and thirteenth centuries. Contact with the Muslims (who were not personally disliked) stimulated new thought and creative productivity. Sanskrit was encouraged as a unifying force, and regional literatures thrived.

The first dynasty (the Sangama) lasted until about 1485, when Narasimha of the Saluva family usurped power. By 1503 the Saluva dynasty had been supplanted by the Tuluva dynasty. The outstanding Tuluva king was Krsna Deva Raya. During his reign (1509–29) the land between the Tungabhadra and Krishna rivers was acquired (1512), the Orissa Hindus were subdued by the capture of Udayagiri (1514) and other towns, and severe defeats were inflicted on the Bijapur sultan (1520). Krsna Deva's successors, however, allowed their enemies to combine against them. In 1565 Rama Raya, the chief minister of Vijayanagar, led the Empire into the fatal battle at Rakasa-Tangadi (also known as Talikota) in which its army was routed by the combined forces of the Muslim states of Bijapur, Ahmadnagar, and Golconda, and the city of Vijayanagar was destroyed. Tirumala, brother of Rama Raya, then seized control of the Empire. Internal dissensions and the intrigues of the sultans of Bijapur and Golconda, however, led to the final collapse of the Empire, and the reduction of the city to ruins, about 1614.

The complex of temples at Hampi, spread over a large area, amid giant boulders and vegetation, has been the source of admiration from travellers since the fourteenth century. The principal monument, Virupaksha Temple, which remains a site of pilgrimage, lies at the western end of Hampi Bazaar. The *gopura* (tower) at its eastern end is 120 feet tall. The sixteenth-century Vittala Temple, with its 56 musical pillars, is approximately 2 miles (3 kilometres) from Hampi, and is at the centre of the temple district, although it is no longer in use as a place of worship. Its columns are decorated with elaborate carvings of animals and figures and an unusual shrine to Vishnu's mount *Garuda* stands guard at the temple's entrance.

INDEX

Note: Where more than one page number is listed against a heading, page numbers in **bold** indicate significant treatment of a subject